Training and Development

Communicating for Success

Second Edition

STEVEN A. BEEBE

Texas State University—San Marcos

TIMOTHY P. MOTTET

Texas State University—San Marcos

K. DAVID ROACH

Texas Tech University

PEARSON

Boston   Columbus   Indianapolis   New York   San Francisco   Upper Saddle River
Amsterdam   Cape Town   Dubai   London   Madrid   Milan   Munich   Paris   Montreal   Toronto
Delhi   Mexico City   São Paulo   Sydney   Hong Kong   Seoul   Singapore   Taipei   Tokyo

Editor-in-Chief, Communication: Karon Bowers
Assistant Editor: Stephanie Chaisson
Editorial Assistant: Megan Sweeney
Marketing Manager: Blair Zoe Tuckman
Director of Development: Eileen Calabro
Project Manager: Anne Ricigliano
Project Coordination, Text Design, and Electronic Page Makeup: Cenveo Publisher Services/
  Nesbitt Graphics, Inc.
Procurement Specialist: Mary Ann Gloriande
Cover Design Manager: Nancy Danahy
Cover Image: © Dave & Les Jacobs / Alamy
Text Permissions: Boston / Jill Dougan
Photo Research: Integra / Melody English
Printer/Binder/Cover Printer: STP Courier

Credits and acknowledgments borrowed from other sources and reproduced, with permission, in this textbook appear on page 310.

Library of Congress Cataloging-in-Publication Data
Beebe, Steven A.
  Training and development : communicating for success / Steven A. Beebe,
Timothy P. Mottet, K. David Roach.—2nd ed.
    p. cm.
  ISBN 978-0-205-00612-0—ISBN 0-205-00612-4
  1. Training. 2. Communication. 3. Leadership. I. Mottet, Timothy P. II. Roach,
K. David. III. Title.
  LB1027.47.B44 2013
  658.3'12404—dc23
                        2011043943

10 9 8 7 6 5 4 3 — CRW —14 13

www.pearsonhighered.com

ISBN 10:   0-205-00612-4
ISBN 13: 978-0-205-00612-0

To Sue, Mark, Matt, and Brittany
S. A. B.

To my loving parents, Carol and Joe Mottet
T. P. M.

To Becky, Lauren, and Lindsey
K. D. R.

BRIEF CONTENTS

DETAILED CONTENTS

PREFACE

Communication competencies are among the most coveted skills on the planet—whether applied in the workplace, social settings, or at home. This book is written to teach people how to develop essential communication and leadership skills. Specifically, this book is written to be the primary text or supporting text for a college course designed to teach people how to be a communication and leadership trainer. This is not just a book *about* training; it is a book that prescribes *how to do training*.

We often tell our students and our clients that if you don't remember anything else about how to develop an effective training program, remember this: *It depends on their needs*. Embodied in that key concept is the essential principle of meeting learners' needs when training them to perform a skill. We believe a needs-centered approach to training is so powerful that during the first class session we tell our students, "If we ever ask you a question related to training and you are unsure of the answer, just say 'It depends on their needs,' and that will, in all probability, be the right answer."

Since the first edition of this book was published, more colleges and universities are offering courses in how to design and deliver training programs—especially communication and leadership skills training. We are gratified that *Training and Development* is a popular choice for these new courses. A surge in training and development courses is occurring not only in communication departments but also in education, business, health care, and many other disciplines.

Many books have been written about training and development. But there are virtually no resources designed for use in a university-level course that are theory based yet help students develop practical skills and methods for designing and presenting *communication and leadership* training programs. This book is written to fill a gap by presenting a comprehensive, needs-centered approach to training that will help both undergraduate and graduate students learn practical principles and the skills for developing a communication training program from start to finish. Although we are all communication professors who emphasize communication skills ("soft" skills training) in the training programs we present, each of us is also a trainer and consultant for a variety of clients. We write this book for instructors in business, education, and other disciplines that teach students how to design and present training programs.

NEW TO THE SECOND EDITION

We are grateful for the many people who found the first edition of our book useful and valuable. Based on the feedback of educators, training professionals, and our own students, we've revised every chapter to make this the most effective learning tool possible for developing professional training skills. Among countless edits, revisions and updates are the following new elements:

New Emphasis on Technology in Training. We've added a new chapter (Chapter 7) devoted to applications of Web-based training, and we've updated our coverage of using technology in training in every chapter.

New Features That Apply Training and Development Content. Each chapter includes the new feature "A Trainer's Toolbox," which presents practical tips and resources to enhance training skills. We've also revised chapter-ending pedagogy and sharpened our focus on the application of training content to real-world situations. Each chapter now ends with new activities for applying training principles and skills.

New Discussion of Careers in Training and Development. We've expanded our coverage of training and development career applications, adding new material in Chapters 1 and 12 that describes contemporary employment opportunities in the training and human resource development field.

Expanded Coverage of Instructional Communication Theory and Principles. Chapter 2 has new material to provide even stronger theoretical support for the practical applications of training and development, including new material on learning styles and adult learning.

New Application of the Training Process as a Communication Process. A new discussion in Chapter 1 more clearly links the study of training and development with the communication discipline.

Applications of the Latest Communication, Training and Development, and Instructional Communication Research. This new edition includes updated research references in every chapter.

Additional Coverage of Key Training and Development Content. **We've added several new sections and revised other material to provide the most contemporary coverage of training and development skills, including new material about how to:**

- differentiate between training goals and training objectives
- make training interactive
- use subject matter experts (SMEs)
- develop and use PowerPoint and other presentation aids
- develop various levels of lesson plan detail
- make applications of the latest instructional communication research to training contexts
- assess training programs
- become a professional training specialist

A NEEDS-CENTERED APPROACH

At the heart of our approach to designing and delivering an effective training program is the philosophy that trainers must meet trainees' needs and that will, in turn, enhance their performance. By its very nature, training has the practical goal of helping trainees learn to perform specific skills. What should be the guiding force in identifying the skills that need to be taught? We believe trainee needs should be that beacon on which a trainer should *always* focus. Training that does not address a need or a specific job junction of a trainee is not effective training.

Training is essentially a communication process of developing objectives, identifying content, selecting methods, and presenting a training message. For over two thousand years, public speaking teachers have stressed the importance of being audience-centered when speaking. Our needs-centered training model is based on that centuries-old wisdom. We didn't invent the needs-centered approach; it has been the key principle that speech and communication instructors have used since Aristotle noted that the audience is central to effective speaking in 333 BCE, when he wrote his classic work *Rhetoric*.

At the core of our needs-centered training model (shown below) is the ongoing process of identifying the needs of the organization, and especially those of the trainees who will be attending the training session. Preparing a training program involves both the rhetorical process of being needs-centered and a series of practical steps. Our needs-centered model captures both the step-by-step sequence of tasks needed to design, deliver, and assess a training program and the continuing process of identifying and meeting trainee needs.

We introduce our needs-centered model of training in Chapter 1 and refer to it in every chapter in which we discuss the nuts and bolts of developing a training program. Viewing the model as a clock, start at twelve with the first step of analyzing the training task, and move clockwise around the model to "develop training

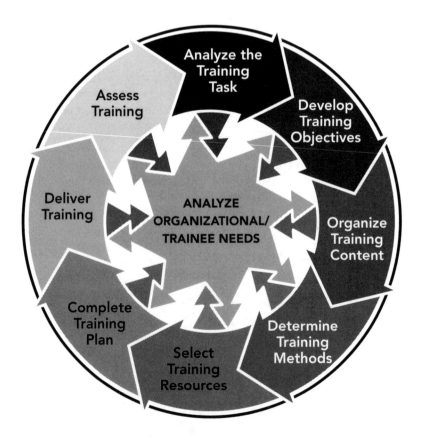

objectives," "organize training content," and so on. At each step of the training process, however, the student is reminded that at the core of the process is the analysis of the needs of the organization and the trainee. Even when conducting the final step of the training process, "assess training," it's important to note how effectively the needs of the organization and the trainees have been met.

THEORY-BASED PRINCIPLES

Our needs-centered approach is anchored in contemporary communication and learning theory. After introducing the needs-centered training model in Chapter 1, we devote Chapter 2 to a discussion of learning theory and principles, with a special emphasis on strategies to enhance communication skill. We discuss general laws of learning and emphasize the importance of considering the needs of adult learners bolstered by the latest research findings about adult learning. Andragogy, the art and science of teaching adults (rather than pedagogy, the art and science of teaching children), informs the training techniques and strategies that we present throughout the book. Because adults need to learn what is relevant to them, and because they are problem-oriented learners, our needs-centered model reflects the importance of addressing the needs of adults.

That adults have different learning styles is yet another reason to focus keenly on the needs of learners. Differences in perceptual learning, learning time, and information processing mean that the effective trainer should be responsive to those learning styles. We do more than just describe learning differences; we identify specific strategies that can enhance adult learning.

Following our discussion of adult learning theory in Chapter 2, the succeeding chapters walk students through the skills that are vital to designing and delivering training programs. Chapter 3 covers assessing trainee needs and analyzing the training task. Developing objectives and the design curriculum are the focus of Chapter 4. How to develop training content, including how to conduct research, is presented in Chapter 5. Chapter 6 reviews the use of training methods and helps students decide which method is best for the type of training objective they seek to achieve. Chapter 7, a completely new chapter, presents principles and strategies for using technological tools in training, with an emphasis on Web-based training. Chapter 8 covers the essential skills for using presentation aids in training. How to design the training lesson plan is covered in Chapter 9. Chapter 10 describes the delivery of effective training presentations and presents applications of the latest research conclusions from the instructional development literature. Chapter 11 identifies specific techniques of assessing training. The final chapter, Chapter 12, identifies trends and career opportunities in training.

GIVE YOUR STUDENTS CHOICES

In addition to the traditional printed text, *Training and Development: Communicating for Success, 2/e* is available in the following format to give you and your students more choices—and more ways to save.

The **CourseSmart eTextbook** offers the same content as the printed text in a convenient online format—with highlighting, online search, and printing capabilities. **www.coursesmart.com**

CourseSmart eTextbook: ISBN: 0205185924

SPECIAL PEDAGOGICAL FEATURES

We do our best to more than talk about how to be an effective trainer; we model training principles and skills with special features throughout the book that help students apply the material in ways that will be useful and memorable.

Learning Objectives. We've revised and polished our learning objectives to make them even more focused and clear. Our objectives model our approach to writing objectives that are observable, attainable, measurable, and specific.

Numerous Examples. Each of us has had considerable experience as a trainer. We have updated our examples and illustrations by drawing on our own experiences of good training practice. We've also learned from our mistakes; what we've learned from our training errors is reflected in the examples we present.

Recap Boxes. Students need to have the key content reinforced. We do that by liberally sprinkling in recap boxes that cogently clinch the learning by highlighting essential principles and skills.

Glossary. Key terms are boldfaced, defined in the text, and presented in the glossary at the back of the book.

Chapter-end Questions. To help students test their knowledge and application of principles, questions for discussion and review appear at the end of each chapter. We want students to do more than recall essential information; we want them to apply what they've learned. To help accomplish this goal we've included questions for application and analysis at the end of each chapter. Many of these questions are like mini case studies that allow students to assess their skill in solving problems related to training.

Chapter-end Activities. Each chapter concludes with one or more individual or collaborative learning activities to help students apply and assess their knowledge of training and development principles and skills.

Useful Support Resources. Accompanying this text is an Instructor's Manual and Text Bank. This supporting material includes detailed chapter outlines; multiple choice, true or false, and essay questions; and activities for use in or out of class. This resource is available for download at www.pearsonhighered .com/irc (access code required).

ACKNOWLEDGMENTS

Writing a book is a team project. In our case, we benefited from working together as a team of authors bouncing ideas off one another, a process that we believe strengthens the book. It's a special joy to work together not only as colleagues but also as good friends. In addition to our own synergy, we've had a support team of editors, reviewers, and colleagues who provided outstanding assistance.

Jeanne Zalesky, Acquisitions Editor during our time preparing this new edition, provided important support and advice. Karon Bowers, Editor-in-Chief of Communication, is a constant source of encouragement and inspiration. Megan Sweeney, Editorial Assistant at Pearson, was exceptionally helpful to us as we managed the myriad of editorial details.

We appreciated the excellent advice and suggestions from our talented reviewers who read the manuscript (some more than once) to help us polish our prose and fine-tune our ideas. Those reviewers are: Paul N. Lakey, Abilene Christian University; Jeff Hudson, Scott County, Minnesota; Jean M. DeWitt, University of Houston; Joseph Chesebro, SUNY Brockport; Jeffrey Schindel, Geneva College; Peter Jorgensen, Western Illinois University; Pamela Kaylor, Ohio University, Lancaster; Susan McMurray, Oral Roberts University; Ryan Loyd, University of Texas at the Permian Basin; and Andrew Rancer, University of Akron.

David thanks his parents, Kenneth and Anita Roach; his fourth grade teacher, Mrs. Hicks; and mentors, Kelly Hamby, Chantry Fritts, Rob Stewart, Ed Townsend, Virginia Richmond, Jim McCroskey, and Steve Beebe for living learner-centered perspectives in their teaching and training. These individuals have been wonderful role models and examples. David also expresses his deep gratitude to Becky Roach, his spouse and best friend, a gifted teacher who has taught him much about teaching. Most of all, David thanks The Great Teacher for modeling perfectly how to meet the real needs of people while showing them a better way.

Timothy expresses his deepest appreciation to his team of trainers, who have invested many hours in developing him: Marilyn and Robert Root, Jane and Chris Brayton, Sue and Steve Beebe, Marian and Steve Houser, Renee and D. C. Cowan, Mary Hoffman, Jim McCroskey, and Virginia Richmond. He is grateful for the mentoring of these role models and hopes that he returns this invaluable gift by mentoring and developing his own students. Timothy would also like to thank his professors at West Virginia University, the impressive list of Ed.D.s who preceded him, and his colleagues and fabulous graduate teaching assistants at Texas State University–San Marcos and the University of Texas–Pan American for giving him a sense of academic community that allows him to grow as a teacher, a researcher, and a higher education leader. Timothy would like to thank his parents, Carol and Joe, for the love and support they continue to give him, and Rick Gonzalez, who brings him a daily dose of joy and merriment.

Steve thanks his three decades of training and development students, both at the University of Miami and at Texas State University, for their feedback, encouragement, and ideas that helped shape the core concepts of this book. Jack Johnson from the University of Wisconsin–Milwaukee is a friend and colleague who was helpful in developing strategies for teaching a course in training and development. Dennis and Laurie Romig, from Side-by-Side Consulting, are good friends as well as skilled trainers and consultants, both of whom have modeled effective training and inspired training paradigms that inform the content in several chapters of this book. Tony Longoria, a former student and a good friend and colleague, collaborated with us in developing material related to technology and Web-based training for Chapter 7. Seth Frei, another good friend and former student, wrote the sample training plan that appears in Chapter 9. Finally, Steve expresses his appreciation to his personal Grammar Queen, musical partner, sometime co-author, all-the-time soul mate, best friend, and spouse, Sue Beebe, for her enduring wisdom, love, and encouragement.

STEVEN A. BEEBE
TIMOTHY P. MOTTET
San Marcos, Texas

K. DAVID ROACH
Lubbock, Texas

The only thing worse than training employees and losing them is not training them and keeping them.

—*Zig Ziglar*

Introducing Communication Training

CHAPTER OUTLINE

CHAPTER OBJECTIVES

After studying this chapter, you should be able to:

- Define training.
- Compare training with the processes of education, development, motivation, and consulting.
- Describe three approaches to consulting.
- Describe the training process as a communication process.

- List skills that are frequently presented in communication, leadership, and management training seminars and workshops.
- Identify and describe the nine steps involved in designing and presenting a training workshop.

It's been estimated that 98 percent of all our problems boil down to "people problems." In the workplace, if the problem involves people, the solution is often improved communication and leadership skills. According to surveys, scholars, and management consultants, as well as corporate chief executive officers, the most important factor for success in today's information-driven marketplace is the ability to communicate and skillfully lead others.[1] Whether it's interacting with customers, clients, or colleagues, the ability to understand and respond to the messages of others is among the most valued strategies in any blueprint for success. Although effective communication and collaborative leadership are practically worshiped by most corporate executives, enhancing the quality of communication, management, and leadership skills can be a challenge.

This book is designed to enhance the effectiveness of organizations—to develop effective communication, leadership, and management skills by training people to improve their interactions with others. There are many strategies and pathways to organizational effectiveness, such as conducting a communication audit, changing the organizational chart to reduce barriers to communication, and redesigning a communication message system. Courses in organizational communication, management, professional communication, and leadership provide the tools, techniques, and theories to enhance communication and achieve organizational effectiveness. But if the goal is to help employees improve their *skills* in speaking, listening, relating, collaborating, solving problems, customer service, and managing conflict, then training people to enhance their communication and leadership abilities is an effective method of developing organizational effectiveness.

In this chapter we'll define training; clarify the differences between training, education, development, and consulting; provide a brief introduction to communication fundamentals, noting how training is a communication process; and point the way ahead by providing an overview of the steps involved in designing and delivering a training seminar or workshop.

TRAINING DEFINED

When you hear the word "training," do you think of lion tamers training beasts to obey the crack of their whip? Or do you picture a drill sergeant training fresh recruits in boot camp? To help you understand what training is, we'll define it, identify the typical tasks professional trainers perform, and describe the benefits of investing in training.

Training is sometimes viewed as a simple panacea for enhancing organizational effectiveness. One of your authors remembers being interrupted at work by a man who brusquely knocked on my office door and announced his name and that he was a "very important person." Unfamiliar with the gentleman's name or accomplishments, I listened politely while he stated his reason for visiting me. He said he knew that I was a communication consultant who had presented communication training seminars for several corporations and organizations and provided one-on-one coaching. After reminding me several times how busy and important he was, he got to his point. He had been told by friends and colleagues that he needed to improve his communication skill. I'll never forget his specific request: He wanted me to *"do something to him"* to make him a better communicator. (I had a momentary vision that he sought a magic potion, incantation, or some kind of laying-on-of-hands ceremony to instill the communication skills he coveted.) He further explained, "I can pay you very well for your services," which led me to believe he knew something about communication because he quickly got my attention. I suggested, however, that enhancing communication skill is not something that can be simply "done to" someone by revealing a few techniques or little-known skills. Developing communication and leadership ability takes effort, time, practice, and a personal commitment to enhancing one's skills and changing one's behavior.

This book does not offer promises of shortcuts or tidy lists of techniques that will enhance organizational communication and leadership effectiveness. What we do offer is a systematic way to enhance communication, management, and leadership skills by teaching you how to develop and present training seminars and workshops to others. Our approach is relatively straightforward. Regardless of your training objective, keep one thing in mind: *Develop and deliver training that meets the needs of the trainees.* We also emphasize that the training process is essentially a communication process. We therefore draw heavily upon communication as well as learning principles to support our strategies.

What Is Training?

Training *is the process of developing skills in order to perform a specific job or task more effectively.* Stated simply, to train is to develop skills.[2] Although training often involves presenting information (cognitive learning), as well as motivating people to work harder or smarter, or to have a positive attitude toward others (affective learning), training focuses primarily on developing specific *actions, skills*, and *behaviors* (the behavioral domain of learning). The goal of training is that a worker will perform his or her job with greater skill and effectiveness.

Communication and leadership training focuses on teaching people how to enhance the skills of relating to others. The short description of these skills is that they are "people skills." How to effectively and appropriately listen, relate, speak, adapt, interpret, interview, lead, manage, and provide feedback are the vital people skills that are the standard elements of communication and leadership training. Communication trainers present virtually all of the same communication skills that are taught in communication classes at colleges and universities. Although the skills are the same, their labels are different. In the corporate world, public speaking skills are called presentation skills; group communication skills are called team skills; interpersonal skills are identified as skills to enhance listening, manage conflict, and interview others.

What Do Trainers Do?

Although we've defined training as teaching specific skills for performing a specific job, you may still wonder exactly what trainers do. The short answer: Trainers teach skills and design and present training programs that enhance individual work performance. Let's take a closer look at precisely what trainers do.

Trainers teach skills. A central focus in our definition of training is the process of developing skills. A **skill** is a desired behavior that can be repeated when needed; it is an ability to *do something* as opposed to knowing something. When you are skilled, you are competent to perform some specific behavior or act. A skilled communicator is one who can effectively and appropriately deliver a presentation, listen empathetically, manage conflict, facilitate a meeting, or conduct a performance appraisal interview. Similarly, a skilled leader is one who can develop a collective vision and help an organization work collaboratively to make the vision a reality. It is true that each of these processes—communication and leadership—involves knowledge (understanding concepts) as well as skill. However, the essential element in making something a skill is proficiency at performing a behavior or task. We're not suggesting that skills are the only or even the ultimate reason for studying communication and leadership strategies; we do suggest that the goal of communication training is the performance of an observable and measurable skill that can be assessed in some way. Although trainers also present such information as teaching workers about policy, rules, and procedures, the primary focus of training is to change behavior through teaching skills.

There are two broad categories of training skills: soft and hard. **Soft skills** are those skills that focus on managing people, information, and ideas such as communication, management, and leadership training. Technical training, such as computer programming or Web page design, is often called **hard skill** training—not because the skills are necessarily hard to learn, but because technical skills typically involve specific right answers or precise procedures to follow. This book focuses on communication and leadership skills, the essential "soft" training skills that are valued in the workplace.

Just what soft skills are most in demand in organizations today? Here's a list of the most popular communication and leadership skills that are the focus of contemporary training programs:

- How to improve listening skills
- How to become more assertive
- How to avoid issues of sexual harassment
- How to use and interpret nonverbal messages of customers
- How to manage conflict
- How to negotiate with others
- How to deal with angry customers
- How to develop a collaborative team
- How to solve problems and make decisions in groups and teams
- How to lead and participate in meetings
- How to deliver a sales presentation
- How to use computer graphics in a business presentation
- How to persuade a customer to purchase a product
- How to manage time and be more productive
- How to present a briefing or report
- How to improve communication among employees
- How to communicate a leadership vision to an organization
- How to communicate with people from a different culture

- How to interpret nonverbal messages more accurately
- How to lead others by being collaborative
- How to develop a cooperative management style
- How to train a trainer to prepare and deliver a successful training program
- How to conduct an employee appraisal interview

Each of these topics involves not just one skill but usually a set of skills or behaviors that will enhance the quality of human relationships and work. Training is teaching people skills. Communication and leadership training teaches people how to enhance their skills in relating and connecting to others.

Trainers design and present training programs. As part of the process of teaching people specific skills, trainers typically perform a host of specific tasks. According to an American Society for Training and Development (ASTD) Competency Study (ASTD is the largest professional training organization in the world) and experienced trainer Elaine Biech, these are common tasks that trainers are called on to do:[3]

- Determine what training is needed
- Design computer-based training
- Facilitate brainstorming team sessions
- Be a training instructor
- Manage training, leadership, and management strategic initiatives
- Design PowerPoint slides and provide instructional technology assistance for training
- Serve as a performance analyst
- Develop specific training objectives
- Develop a training curriculum
- Coach individual performance
- Initiate and facilitate organizational change
- Assist in employee career planning and talent management
- Assess the effectiveness of training
- Serve as chief learning officer
- Serve as employee development specialist
- Train other trainers on specific training programs
- Be a training technology specialist
- Serve as an internal organizational development consultant
- Manage a training and consulting business
- Market or sell training programs to organizations

The primary job of a training specialist, regardless of the specific tasks that he or she may perform, is to ensure that the skills presented will help the organization be successful.

Why Is Training Important?

Corporate training is a multibillion-dollar industry. Why invest in training? Because trained workers are better workers. It not only makes intuitive sense that trained workers are better workers, but several studies have found that training improves both individual and organizational performance.[4] After reviewing numerous studies, training researchers Herman Aguinis and Kurt Kraiger found "considerable support for the many benefits of training for individuals and teams."[5] Workers who have problems communicating with others are less effective, less efficient, and will ultimately cost the organization more money than workers who are better trained. The benefits of well-trained workers include not just enhanced performance, but, according to an impressive amount of research, greater worker satisfaction and increased profits.

Training is big business: Over one million people in the United States make their living in some aspect of training.[6] Communication and leadership skill training make up a large chunk of the training business, and for good reason. The largest part of virtually any organization's budget is for personnel costs. People make organizations function. The number one skill for employees is effective communication, followed closely by the ability to lead and manage others. Regardless of the specific job function or description, what people primarily do on the job is communicate.[7]

During times of economic downturn, companies and organizations may be tempted to trim their training budgets. But the research suggests that when economic times are tough and competition increases, *more* training is needed to enhance both efficiency and effectiveness.[8] Whether it's technical training or communication and leadership training, investment in training enhances individual and corporate effectiveness. Two researchers evaluated the effectiveness of a nine-month communication and leadership training program in a financial services corporation in the United States, Canada, Europe, Latin America, and Asia. At the end of the training there were significant improvements in customer service, a decrease in errors, and an increase in profits.[9] Another training and organizational development training firm documented how the implementation of soft skill training programs helped save millions of dollars because of increased efficiency and organizational effectiveness.[10] For a training specialist, it's important not only to design and present training programs, but also to document how training programs will result in a return on the investment in training. We'll discuss specific strategies for documenting the return on investment (ROI) in training in Chapter 12.

Although we've made important claims about the value of training, training will achieve results only if the training is effective—well designed and well executed. That's what this book is about: How to make communication and leadership training effective.

TRAINING AND RELATED FUNCTIONS

Although it may seem that our definition of training is a straightforward one (teaching people skills to perform a specific job), the concept of training is associated with several related functions in contemporary organizations. Thus the training function may appear on organizational charts under various labels. Sometimes the department is simply labeled *training*; in another organization training may be included in the *human resources department* (which used to be called the *personnel department*). The training function can also be embedded in a department of *human resource development, organizational development,* or *learning and performance.* Because the word *training* is sometimes used to encompass functions that, strictly speaking, aren't training, it is useful to clarify training's relationship to other

▶ A TRAINER'S TOOLBOX

Is Training the Solution to Every Problem?

Although training serves an important function in enhancing the health of an organization, it is not the answer to every worker performance problem. To determine whether training is needed to solve an employee performance problem, consider three questions:[11]

1. Does the person have the necessary skill to perform the job?
2. Does the person want to perform the job?
3. Does the person have permission to perform the job?

Consider the following when reviewing the answers to those three questions:

- If the answer to the first question is no, training may be needed, but there may be other explanations for low performance. The worker may simply need feedback, encouragement, or reassignment to a position that better suits his or her talents.
- If the answer is yes to all questions, then more than training is needed; there could be a problem with equipment, a poor fit between worker and job assignment, or other work problems.
- If the answer is no to the second question, motivation may be the problem, not training. The employee may not sense the importance of the job he or she is performing.

- If the answer is no to the third question, there could be a policy or management problem, or the worker may not understand the work priorities.

Before prescribing training as the solution to a worker performance problem, consider the following questions:

1. Are the appropriate materials available to the worker?
2. Are there appropriate tools or equipment for doing the job?
3. Is there appropriate and clear supervision?
4. Does the worker have the proper basic competencies (hearing, vision, other physical skills) needed to perform the job?
5. Are there appropriate incentives for success, or consequences if the job is not performed well?
6. Is the organizational culture conducive to effective performance?
7. Is there appropriate supervision, management, or coaching to perform the skill?

When a worker lacks the skill to perform a specific task, training is needed, but there may be other explanations for poor work performance. A training specialist needs to recognize when training is called for and when it isn't.

organizational development functions. We'll compare training to four related processes: education, motivation, development, and consulting.

Training and Education

Education is the process of imparting knowledge or information. People can educate themselves by reading, or they can have someone teach them what they want or need to learn. Training, on the other hand, focuses more on skill development and behavior change. John Kline, who is an expert educator and trainer, made several useful distinctions between training and education that clarify how the two processes can be distinguished from one another.[12]

Training emphasizes doing. Education emphasizes knowing. As we have noted, to train is to focus on seeing a behavioral change, while education typically focuses on learning information. Although it's true that information learned may influence behavior or skill, when the primary outcome is learning definitions, concepts, principles, and theories, then that's an education process.

Training emphasizes achieving a certain level of skill attainment. Education often evaluates by comparing one student to another. When you train someone, you want that person to be able to successfully perform a behavior or a set of behaviors. Teaching someone to drive a car is an example of training. Before you hand your car keys to someone, you want to be certain that person has attained a level of driving skill that will permit him or her to navigate the highways successfully. A clearly specified level of skill attainment is required. In many education settings, such as college classrooms, you may be evaluated in comparison to others. You might be graded "on the curve"; your grade won't be determined until all the other tests or papers have been graded. A score of 85 could be an A, a B, or a C, depending on how the grades are curved. Training is less concerned with evaluating you in comparison to others; training emphasizes whether or not you can perform the skill.

Training is a more closed system. Education operates more as an open system. By "closed system," we mean that there are certain right and wrong ways of performing a skill based not on external constraints but on performing the skill properly. Regardless of outside interference, there is a preferred way to achieve a desired result, such as operating a complex computer program or running an electronic personal organizer. When applying principles in education, you may be able to be more creative in solving problems and achieving results. As described by Kline, education occurs when "learning is continuous with no cap or ceiling on how well the graduate may be prepared to handle new responsibilities."[13] In education there is less emphasis on finding the "right answer"; the focus is typically on finding the best answer.

Training emphasizes the requirements for performing a specific job linked to a specific duty. Education is less often linked to a specific job. You might receive training to fry hamburgers so that each hamburger is always cooked the same way. Training, in this example, is linked to performing a specific job with certain specifications. Education emphasizes knowledge with less application to a specific job. When you take a course in history, math, or music, you focus less on applying the information you learn to a specific job description; you learn to use the information in less precisely defined ways. In a public speaking class, you may be taught to give speeches in a variety of situations; in a corporate sales seminar, you may receive skill-development training specifically intended to help you polish closing a sale.

Training is more likely to offer a comprehensive list of the skills required to perform a specific behavior. Education is less likely to provide a summary of all information on a specific subject. When you receive effective training, someone has thought through the various steps involved in performing the task. To be trained in operating a microwave oven is to receive information about how to operate all of the features the oven offers. When being educated, you're less likely to hear your teacher say, "This is everything there is to know on this subject." Scholars and educators are always discovering new knowledge.

Training and Motivation

Have you ever heard a motivational speaker either on TV or in person? If so, you know that the goal of a motivational speaker is to persuade you to take some positive action such as working harder, setting goals, spending more time with your family, or losing weight. Motivational speakers often use strong emotional appeal by presenting personal stories or drawing upon the lives of others to encourage people to improve their lives. Some trainers also work as motivational speakers. **Motivation** is an internal state of readiness to take action or achieve a goal. Motivational speakers attempt to tap that internal state of readiness by encouraging listeners to achieve a worthwhile goal.

Trainers and motivational speakers have some things in common, but they also use significantly different methods to achieve their goals. What do they have in common? Both seek to bring about change in their listeners. They differ in that trainers are more likely to seek individual and organizational change by teaching *skills;* change happens because the listener now has a new repertoire of tools and behaviors that he or she didn't have before. Motivational speakers strive to change people by stimulating emotions and attitudes; their assumption is that if emotions are heightened and attitudes are touched, change will follow. **Emotions** are feeling states that often result in behavior change. **Attitudes** are learned predispositions to respond favorably or unfavorably toward something.

Zig Ziglar, who was one of the best-known motivational speakers in America, started his career as a door-to-door vacuum cleaner salesman. Zig's stories of endurance and commonsense advice told with humor and wit made him a popular motivational speaker. Another well-known motivational speaker, Anthony Robbins, has

---

▶ RECAP

Comparing Training and Education

Training: the process of developing skills for a specific job or task	Education: the process of imparting knowledge or information
Emphasizes doing	Emphasizes knowing
Emphasizes achieving a specific level of skill attainment	Emphasizes achieving often in comparison to the knowledge level of others
Emphasizes a closed system perspective: There are specific right and wrong ways of performing a skill.	Emphasizes an open system perspective: There are often many ways to achieve a goal; creativity and critical thinking are encouraged.
Emphasizes performance levels in order to perform a specific job	Emphasizes knowing information not necessarily linked to a specific job or career.
Emphasizes a comprehensive listing of the skills required to perform a specific behavior; each step in the process is prescribed.	Emphasizes an open-ended approach to achieve a goal; not every step in the process is always prescribed.

provided advice to people in many vocations, including former U.S. presidents. The success of motivating people just by telling stories, using humor, and providing inspirational anecdotes is evidence that motivational speakers have a role in influencing organizational dynamics. There is some question, however, about the staying power of motivational messages. After the emotion has faded, the listener may still need strategies and skills to enact change.

Training and Development

The concept of development is often linked to both training and human resources. You may have seen the phrase "human resource development" or "training and development." The word *development* added to other terms suggests a broadening of the behaviors or strategies to achieve a goal. But what precisely is development?

Development is any behavior, strategy, design, restructuring, skill or skill set, strategic plan, or motivational effort that is designed to produce growth or change over time. Organizations seek *positive* change, not just change for the sake of change. Positive change includes making more money if the organization's goal is to turn a profit for the owners or shareholders. If the organization is a hospital, the desired change is to make people healthy (while not losing money, or even making money if the hospital is a for-profit facility). Educational institutions seek change to enhance student learning. You get the idea; development is a process of helping an organization or individuals in the organization do their jobs more effectively. Development involves a set of strategies that can help an individual or an organization perform more effectively in achieving individual or corporate goals.

How does development differ from training? Development is the broader, more encompassing function. Training is narrower in focus. A variety of organizational or personal intervention strategies may be used to develop an organization; training (teaching people skills to perform a specific job or task) is but one method used to effect change. Education (imparting knowledge) is another strategy that may be used to develop people and organizations. So when the word *development* is linked to the word *training*, it suggests that training is designed to achieve a broader function than just performing a specific skill. Training and development suggest that the goal of the training is to facilitate the transformation of the organization—to bring about positive change not just for one person, but to have a larger impact on the organization.

Figure 1.1 shows the relationship of the functions of training, education, and development. The outer circle, development, encompasses both education and training. Training and education are methods of developing individuals and organizations. Education is a more general function than training, so the "education" circle is larger than the "training" circle. Training is typically a component in a broad-based education program, which is ultimately designed to develop an organization. But don't get the idea that training and education are the only ways to develop an organization. Courses in organizational communication discuss several strategies (such as analyzing and diagnosing communication message flow) that are designed to enhance organizational effectiveness by developing the organization in positive ways.

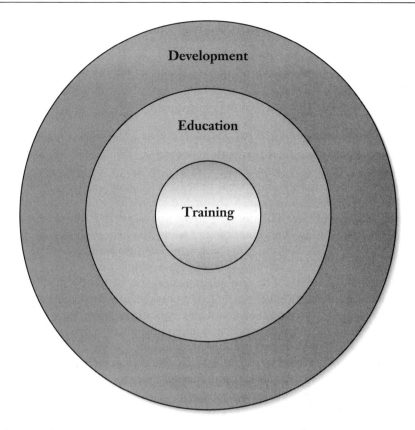

FIGURE 1.1

Comparing Development, Education, and Training

Development—encouraging growth and change—is a more comprehensive process than education and training. Education is broader in scope and purpose than training. Training focuses on enhancing the skills needed to perform a specific job.

Training and Consulting

Another process related to training, education, and development is consulting. Perhaps you have heard of people who do communication or management consulting for an organization in your community. While you may have a vague idea of what consulting is, you may still be uncertain as to precisely what a consultant does. A consultant is often a person brought in from outside an organization, department, or program area to help solve a problem. A consultant offers insight, advice, wisdom, and research- or experience-based intervention strategies that may help an organization more effectively achieve its goals. The goal of consulting is personal and corporate development. A consultant may be external, from outside the organization, or internal, someone who works for the organization. Many organizations have a department, sometimes called "organizational effectiveness," within the human resource development division that specializes in providing internal consultant services.

A communication or management consultant, then, is a person who provides advice about some aspect of communication or leadership in order to enhance organizational effectiveness. A consultant could provide training services or offer an analysis of a communication problem and suggest that training or education could enhance organizational effectiveness. Consultants are problem solvers. They offer skills or services that augment or complement those already resident within a department, program, or organization.

Organizational development specialist Edgar Schein sees three classic approaches to consulting: purchase, doctor-patient, and process.[14] These approaches differ in the amount of involvement the consultant has in determining what problem is being solved. The purchase approach involves the consultant least in diagnosing the problem; the process approach requires the most consulting involvement in determining the problem. The doctor-patient approach is a middle ground that involves both consulting determination and what the client thinks is the problem.

The **purchase approach** to consulting is most often associated with training. A member of an organization has diagnosed a problem and seeks to purchase a solution from a consultant. For example, a manager who has decided that people in her department have difficulty leading and participating in meetings may decide to hire a consultant to train members of the department to improve meetings. As the name implies, the purchase approach maintains when someone decides that a training program should be acquired (either purchased from a consultant outside the organization or implemented from an in-house training department).

The **doctor–patient consulting approach** places greater emphasis on the consultant's diagnosing the problem in the organization. The manager or director may know that something is wrong but is not certain what the problem is or how to manage it. The patient knows he's not feeling well, but he isn't sure what the problem is or what to do about it; the physician, after running a series of tests, figures out what is needed and prescribes a treatment program.

RECAP

Three Approaches to Organizational Consulting

Purchase Approach	Doctor–Patient Approach	Process Approach
Someone in the organization has determined what the organization needs (e.g., training) and seeks a consultant to provide the service to meet the needs of the organization.	A consultant is hired to help diagnose an organizational problem and then prescribe strategies for managing the problem.	A consultant is retained to spend time analyzing the organization and joining with members of the management team to identify problems and obstacles to organizational effectiveness.
There is little consultant involvement in diagnosing the problem.	There is some consultant involvement in diagnosing the problem.	There is considerable consultant involvement in diagnosing the problem.

The **process consulting approach** describes the most direct involvement of the consultant in diagnosing a problem and offering recommendations to solve it. The organization may not yet even be aware that there is a problem. The process consultant uses a variety of measures to assess the overall vitality of the organization and then recommends strategies for improving organizational effectiveness. A communication consultant will focus primarily on the communication processes within an organization, noting how they may help or hinder the organization. Many organizations have a team of process consultants who work for the organization to enhance its wellbeing. Or an external process consultant may be retained to assess an organization's effectiveness. In Chapter 12 we discuss specific career opportunities related to consulting.

TRAINING AND COMMUNICATION

The act of training others, whether in a traditional face-to-face training setting or via computer, involves communicating messages. To explore how training is a communication process, we will review fundamental elements of the communication process, then we'll discuss how training is a vital communication process.

The Communication Process

In the broadest sense, **communication** is the process of acting upon information.[15] Expanding on this definition, we suggest that **human communication** is the process of how we make sense of the world and share that sense with others by using verbal and nonverbal messages to create meaning.[16] Effective communication focuses on the needs of the receiver of a message. Meaning is ultimately created in the mind and heart of the listener (or, in the training context, in the mind and heart of the trainee).

Communication instructors seem to like models. Almost every book about communication includes models to explain the relationships among the variables or components of the communication process. A model is simply a visual or verbal way of representing something else. Just as a model airplane represents an actual airplane, a model of communication shows what the parts of the process look like. Reviewing the key elements of communication as shown in a basic communication model is an effective and efficient way of describing and understanding the complicated process of making sense of our world and sharing that sense with others.

The key elements in most basic communication models are:

Sender: The originator of the message—usually a person, but in today's technological society it could be a machine.

Receiver: The person who decodes or makes sense of the message.

Message: The written, spoken, and unspoken elements of communication to which we assign meaning.

Channel: The pathway through which messages are sent, such as a TV signal, a wireless computer signal, fiber optic cable, or the vibrating air that carries the spoken message of another person in your presence.

Noise: An interfering message that decreases the accuracy of the communication of the message. The noise could be literal (the loud roar of a motorcycle) or psychological (thinking about being on vacation while listening to a trainer lecture).

Feedback: A response to a message.

Most contemporary models of communication view communication as a transactive process in which both the sender and the receiver of a message *simultaneously* express and respond to messages. In the basic communication model in Figure 1.2, the sender of the message is also receiving feedback (responses) from the receiver. *At the same time* the receiver hears or sees a message from the sender, the receiver actively responds to the message. Communication is not as sluggish as batting a tennis ball back and forth; rather, we make sense of messages and respond to them at the same time we hear and see them. Reflecting the transactive nature of communication, the arrow in Figure 1.2 illustrates both the message and the feedback; the source of a message is simultaneously responding to the receiver of the message.

The Training Process: A Communication Process

Reviewing the model of communication in Figure 1.2, you may wonder what it has to do with training. Because a trainer is a communicator who prepares and delivers messages to enhance the skills of trainees, the communication model helps us visualize how trainees understand (or misunderstand) what is taught during training. The goal of a trainer is to eliminate noise—both literal and psychological noise—so that the message presented during a training session is understood and achieves its intended effect.

In the context of communication training, the trainer's job is to help people see how we make sense of what we experience and how we develop the strategies and skills that enable us to accurately and clearly express thoughts, ideas, and emotions. By focusing on the needs of the trainee, the trainer can craft a training lesson that achieves the objectives of the training. A skilled trainer is a skilled communicator.

FIGURE 1.2

Model of Communication As a Transactive Process

The sender of a message and the receiver of the message both express and respond simultaneously.

Communication is inherently a rhetorical process. The classic definition of rhetoric, conceived by the Greek philosopher Aristotle, is *the process of discovering the available means of persuasion*. To train involves not only teaching specific skills for a specific job but also the rhetorical process of *persuading* trainees that the skills being taught are useful and should be integrated into their work behaviors. A more contemporary definition of rhetoric, offered by rhetorician Donald C. Bryant, is "the process of adjusting ideas to people and people to ideas."[17] This perspective suggests that when you train people, you invite them to adjust their ideas of what is effective and appropriate so that they can incorporate the skills you are teaching into their behavior. Specifically, when training people to enhance their communication and leadership skills, you are also providing them with the motivation to integrate the skills you teach into what they do. Thus, training is a rhetorical process: you are implicitly—and sometimes explicitly—persuading trainees to change their behavior as you teach them to enhance their skills.

Communication, management, and leadership training is designed to teach people specific competencies that will enhance the quality of their messages and their relationships. We have found that communication and leadership skills—especially collaborative leadership skills—are often the solution to problems that arise in organizations. When messages are poorly expressed or misinterpreted, the result can be hurt feelings, missed orders, lost customers, colleague conflict, and lost opportunities; lost opportunities result in losing money or failing to achieve the goals of the organization.

Because the training process is a communication process, people don't learn simply because someone teaches, just as a message isn't communicated just because someone has sent it. Both communication and learning happen only when the learners make sense of what they've experienced. Learning also happens best when the focus remains on the needs of the trainees. In most respects, the situation of the trainees determines what should be taught; skilled trainers know how to assess trainee needs and how to meet those needs.

Communication training is not simply a matter of telling people what to do or how to behave and expecting complete understanding. Trainers can't just "do something" and expect learning to occur. As our model of communication shows, the communication process, like the training process, has many components (source, message, channel, receiver, noise, feedback). Just because someone has been to a training session does not mean that skills have been mastered.

Communication is how we make sense of our experiences and share that sense with others. Information in itself is not communication; we are awash in information. Giving people information in this information age does not mean that the information will be useful or acted upon. "Didn't you read the memo?" "Haven't you read the policy?" "Didn't you go to the training session?" Just pronouncing a message does not mean others will "get it." Effective communication must involve the receiver of the message in an active way. This means that training programs need to actively engage the trainee. Confucius put it this way:

What I hear, I forget.
What I see, I remember.
What I do, I understand.

Viewing the training process as a communication process, the trainer should build in strategies that engage the learner. Bob Pike, a well-known trainer of trainers, suggests that at least every eight minutes participants should have an opportunity to internalize what they are learning; a trainer shouldn't just keep piling on more information.[18] Learners need to have experiences to help them make sense of the information and skills presented.

TRAINING STEPS: AN OVERVIEW OF THE TRAINING PROCESS

We've defined training, explained why it's important and how it compares with other methods of developing an organization (educating, developing, motivating, consulting). We've also noted how the training process is a communication process. Now, how do we get about the task of training others? What steps are involved in translating skill and knowledge about human communication to others? The rest of this book answers these questions. In the chapters ahead we offer strategies and suggestions for designing and delivering communication training programs. Here we introduce the major steps in the process. Figure 1.3 presents the **needs-centered model** that anchors our discussion of training. It's a needs-centered model of training because we believe that the primary purpose of any training program is to respond to the learning needs of the trainee. Training that does not address a need or a specific job function of a trainee is not effective training. The major steps of the training process, which we will consider in greater detail throughout the rest of the book, are named and defined in the following paragraphs.

Analyze Organizational and Trainee Needs

At the center of the model in Figure 1.3 is the process of identifying the needs of the organization and especially the specific trainees who will be present in the training session. How do you know what trainees need? You ask them. In Chapter 3, we offer specific strategies for conducting surveys, questionnaires, or interviews and a host of other methods for determining what trainees need. If you've had a course in public speaking, you know that analyzing your audience was an early and essential method of beginning to plan your message. The process of identifying trainer needs is quite similar to analyzing an audience. Analyzing trainee needs is so central to the process of training that it is in the center of the model; every other aspect of designing and delivering a training presentation depends on the needs of the trainees. In addition to analyzing the needs of individuals, it's also important to consider the needs of the organization. To analyze the needs of an organization, consider what the organization needs in order to achieve its mission. Does it need skilled workers? Or does it need competent leaders and managers? After considering the needs of the organization, you'll need to determine how training can address those needs.

FIGURE 1.3
The Needs-Centered Training Model
Focusing on trainee needs drives every step of designing and delivering a training presentation.

Analyze the Training Task

Viewing our model as a clock (after noting that the heart of the model focuses on the needs of the trainee), begin at the top of the clock and work your way around clockwise to explore the steps of designing and delivering a training presentation. After you've figured out what trainees need (skill in listening? skill in conflict management?), an early, critical step in designing a training program is to thoroughly analyze the specific task you want the trainees to perform. You conduct a task analysis: A detailed, step-by-step description of precisely what the trainee should do and know in order to perform that desired skill. If you are going to teach someone how to give a sales presentation, you need to know what those steps are before you can teach them to others. A task analysis provides a comprehensive outline of what you would teach if you had unlimited time. Because you may have only three or four hours to teach a skill, you may have to focus only on the most critical steps.

Developing a task analysis lets you discover the essential elements of the task. Our needs-centered training model is essentially a task analysis of how to train someone. Each piece of the model represents one step in the process. We'll review the details of conducting a task analysis in Chapter 3.

Develop Training Objectives

After you have figured out the steps of the skill you are teaching, it's important to develop objectives or learning outcomes that you want your trainees to accomplish. We emphasize, and we will emphasize again in Chapter 4 when we go into detail about how to write training objectives, that it's vital to specify the precise behavior you want trainees to perform at the end of the training. What do training objectives look like? We begin each chapter in this book with a list of learning objectives. Reviewing those objectives will give you an idea of the format and style for writing training objectives.

Organize Training Content

Once you have your precise training objectives in hand, you can begin work on drafting the information that trainees need to know and describing the behaviors that they will be expected to perform. When teaching people skills, there are specific principles to keep in mind. We'll present those principles in Chapter 5 as we describe strategies to help you conduct research and organize what you will say to trainees.

Determine Training Methods

Training is not synonymous with lecturing. Adult learners do not like to sit and listen to a three- or four-hour speech. That's not good training. You'll need to develop effective methods of presenting information. You may decide that, rather than lecture, it would be better to have trainees participate in a role-playing situation. Or you may have them discuss a case study or brainstorm solutions to a problem that you pose. We will review training methods in Chapter 6 and offer suggestions to help you determine which methods are best, depending on your training objectives and the needs of the trainees. In Chapter 7 we discuss computer-based training methods.

Select Training Resources

Perhaps you've discovered an excellent video that masterfully illustrates a skill you want to teach. Or maybe you've decided to use a small-group method, and you want trainees to respond to discussion questions. Whether you're using a video, discussion questions, or some other resource, you'll need to decide what you have to prepare to present your training presentation. In most training sessions, trainees will expect to see PowerPoint presentation slides illustrating your message. These resources take time to develop. We'll talk about how to develop tangible resources in Chapter 8.

Complete Training Plans

After you've developed your objectives and settled on what you will say, the methods you will use, and the resources you will need, it is important to develop a comprehensive written plan that describes how you will present your session. A training plan—sometimes called a lesson plan in educational settings—is nothing more than a written description of how you will organize and present your training session. These plans have many different formats, which we will present in Chapter 9. Most training module plans include a description of the objectives, methods, training content, and training resources needed, along with an estimate of how much time will be needed to present each part of the lesson.

Deliver Training

Armed with a well-crafted plan, you are ready to bring the training presentation to life. You will not only deliver your training by planned lectures, videos, and activities, but you will also facilitate class discussion by asking good questions. A training presentation should be much more interactive than a speech. The elements of effective speech delivery—eye contact, good posture, effective gestures, varied vocal inflection—are essential when training others, and we will review skills and strategies for asking effective questions in Chapter 10.

Assess the Training Process

When the training session is over, a trainer's job is not finished. Competent trainers will evaluate how effectively their training was received—did trainees like it?—and, even more important did they learn it? The ultimate test of a training session is: Did they use it? Did the training make a difference in how they now communicate with others? We'll talk about how to determine whether your training was successful when we discuss how to assess the effectiveness of training in Chapter 11.

In addition to presenting the nuts and bolts of designing and delivering a training session, we will review principles and assumptions about how people learn, focusing on adult learning theory, in the next chapter. We conclude the book by noting trends and career opportunities in training in Chapter 12.

What do trainers do? Each piece of the needs-centered model of training gives you a glimpse of the essential elements in what a trainer does. Trainers first and foremost focus on the needs of learners and then carefully develop a training program that meets those needs.

SUMMARY AND REVIEW

Training is the process of developing skills in order to perform a specific job. The training function can be compared to other strategies for enhancing the overall effectiveness of an organization.

- *Education* is the process of imparting knowledge or information. Training is more skill focused than education. Training is not always superior to education.
- *Motivation* is the process of tapping an internal state of readiness to take action or achieve a goal.
- *Development* is any behavior, strategy, design, restructuring, skill or skill set, strategic plan, or motivational effort that is designed to produce positive organizational or personal change. All educational, training, and motivational efforts are part of the larger process of development.
- *Consulting* is the process of offering insight, advice, research, or experienced-based intervention strategies to help an organization achieve its goals more effectively. Consultants are problem solvers.

There are three classic approaches to consulting.

- The purchase approach occurs when an organization already knows what it needs and decides to implement a training program or other intervention strategy to solve its problem.
- The doctor–patient approach occurs when a consultant is brought in to help diagnose the problem; the organizational leaders may know the organization needs help but are not sure what help is needed.
- The process consulting approach is used when organizational leaders seek more comprehensive help in assessing the needs of their organization.

Human communication is the process of making sense of the world and sharing that sense by using verbal and nonverbal messages to create meaning. Communication is a transactive process in which messages are sent and received simultaneously. The training process is a communication process.

The needs-centered model of communication training identifies these steps in the training process:

- Analyze organizational and trainee needs
- Analyze the training task
- Develop training objectives
- Organize training content
- Determine training methods
- Select training resources
- Complete training plan
- Deliver training
- Assess the training process

QUESTIONS FOR DISCUSSION AND REVIEW

1. What is training, and how does it differ from education, development, motivation, and consulting?
2. What are three approaches to communication consulting?
3. Why is it important for a communication trainer to understand a basic definition and model of communication?
4. How is the training process like the communication process?
5. What are typical communication training topics for a communication or leadership training seminar?
6. Describe the underlying assumption for the needs-centered model of training on page 19.
7. How does the needs-centered model of training help clarify what trainers do?

QUESTIONS FOR APPLICATION AND ANALYSIS

1. Mark is having difficulty developing training programs that focus on specific training skills. He tends to develop training programs that include too much lecturing, discussions about theory, and conversation about principles rather than emphasizing communication or leadership skill development. Why do you think Mark may be having such difficulty making the transition from education to training? What suggestions would you offer Mark to help him make his training sessions more skill development than information sharing?

2. Wendy is the director of Human Resource Development for a midsized electronics manufacturing company. Based on comments from supervisors in the company, she senses that workers have the technical skill to perform their jobs adequately but that they may need additional skills in collaboration, teamwork, and conflict management. Should Wendy approach someone who has expertise in training or consulting? How might Wendy begin to develop a strategy to diagnose and manage the problems that she senses exist?

3. Alicia has been a high school English teacher for 10 years and has decided to pursue a career in corporate training. She is a skilled writer and would like to make the transition from education to corporate training. She has asked you to tell her some of the differences between teaching and training. What would you tell her? How could you use the needs-centered training model on page 19 to give her an overview of the differences and similarities between teaching and training?

ACTIVITIES FOR APPLYING PRINCIPLES AND SKILLS

1. As you begin your study of communication training, use a 1–10 rating scale to self-assess your current training skill (1 = low skill, 10 = high skill). Then indicate where you'd like to be evaluated when you complete your study of training; perhaps you'd like to be rated 10 in every category. The gap between where you are and where you'd like to be will give you an overview of what you hope to learn.

	Today	Desired
1. I can effectively identify and assess what trainees need to learn using a variety of needs assessment tools and methods.		
2. I can write a well-organized and detailed task analysis of the training skills I teach.		
3. I can write well-written training objectives that are specific, measurable, attainable, and achievable.		
4. I can effectively organize the material into a meaningful training curriculum.		
5. I can use a variety of effective training methods during a training session.		
6. I can use effectively use training technology such as PowerPoint and computer-based learning methods.		
7. I can develop and use high-quality training lesson plans and facilitator guides.		

	Today	Desired
8. I can use effective delivery skills appropriate for adult learners when training.		
9. I can systematically and effectively evaluate the training I conduct.		
10. I can effectively use adult learning principles when designing and delivering training.		

2. Determine whether the following activities are training (skill based), education (knowledge based), or development (overall positive organizational change) by placing a check in the appropriate column for each activity.

Activity	Training	Education	Development
1. Teaching how to manage interpersonal conflict			
2. Developing a new strategic plan			
3. Teaching how to use a new computer system			
4. Teaching strategies for developing a meeting agenda			
5. Teaching employees about their new health benefits			
6. Teaching how to use a new company-wide security system			
7. Teaching how to respond to customer objections			
8. Teaching principles and theories of communication			
9. Conducting an analysis of organizational communication needs			
10. Identifying strategies to enhance organizational communication			
11. Teaching strategies for developing a supportive communication climate during team meetings			
12. Teaching how to use a software program to develop computer-based training.			

13. Teaching trainers how to prepare effective training sessions			
14. Teaching principles of adult learning			
15. Teaching how to accurately interpret nonverbal messages of audience members.			

When you have completed your analysis, indicate for each of the activities that you determined are training activities whether it is a "hard" skill or a "soft" skill.

When the student is ready, the teacher will appear.

—*Chinese Proverb*

Mastering How Adults Learn

CHAPTER OBJECTIVES

After studying this chapter, you should be able to:

- Define and explain learning.
- List and explain the four laws of learning.
- Differentiate andragogy from pedagogy.
- List and explain the five adult learning principles.
- Define learning style.
- Differentiate visual, aural, and kinesthetic learners and explain how trainers can accommodate them.

- Differentiate reflective and impulsive learners and explain how trainers can accommodate them.
- Differentiate whole–part and part–whole learners and explain how trainers can accommodate them.
- Differentiate divergers, assimilators, convergers, and accommodators and explain how trainers can accommodate them.
- Differentiate the matching, bridging, and style-flexing approaches to training.

earning is no longer the mystery it once was. This chapter explores how adults receive and process information so that trainers can be more effective in developing and presenting training programs that produce change. The chapter is divided into three sections. The first section examines four general laws of learning or principles of learning that are directly relevant to the training practitioner. The second section presents a theory of adult learning known as andragogy. The third section examines learning styles. After discussing each of the three sections, we emphasize how you can use and apply this information to your training programs.

To begin, we need a working definition of learning. Here's one that we like: "**Learning** is a change in individuals, due to the interaction of the individuals and their environment, which fills a need and makes them more capable of dealing adequately with their environment."[1] The key words and phrases in this definition are *change, fills a need,* and *makes them more capable of dealing adequately with their environment.* Once trainees have learned something, trainers should be able to recognize change in the trainees' behaviors and attitudes. This change fills a need or takes care of a problem that trainees have been experiencing, which is at the center of the training model introduced in Chapter 1. Trainers don't train for the sake of training; it's too expensive and time consuming. There has to be a need for training. Finally, this change in behavior and attitude allows trainees to manage their environment more effectively. For example, training customer service employees how to handle irate customers makes them more effective on the job, more effective in managing their work environments.

Now that we have a working definition of learning, we can introduce the four general laws of learning that are applicable in the training classroom. They provide the foundation for this chapter on adult learning.

LAWS OF LEARNING

A **law of learning** is a statement that describes the conditions that must be met in order for trainees to learn. Understanding these laws, based on research conducted in the 1920s and 1930s by Edward Thorndike and his colleagues, will give you a foundation for developing a training lesson that will enhance trainee learning.[2] We will review four general laws of learning—the laws of effect, exercise, association, and readiness—and suggest ways that you can use this information in the training classroom to enhance learning.

Law of Effect

The **law of effect** states that people learn best under pleasant and rewarding conditions.[3] We tend to approach situations that are positive and withdraw from situations that are unpleasant. Thus, positive feelings on the part of the learner during the learning process has the potential to increase the likelihood of learning. Here are ways you can use the law of effect to support training programs:

- *Create a pleasant physical environment.* The physical environment is critical to successful learning. Classrooms that are well lighted, temperature-controlled, and clean will promote learning.[4] As a trainer, you may not have complete control over a room's design or décor, but in most instances you will be able to move tables and chairs to facilitate interaction (such as putting the tables in a horseshoe arrangement).

- *Accommodate trainees' work schedules.* Be aware of trainees' schedules and try to give them scheduling options. Providing options for computer-based training using online training modules can give trainees more flexibility in determining when they will receive training. If possible, allow trainees to choose from a list of training times so that they have some control over when they will receive their training.
- *Schedule appropriate breaks.* Trainees can remain attentive only so long before needing a break. Don't make trainees sit too long in any one training program. The general rule of thumb is to take a break at least every 90 minutes. Providing refreshments during breaks is another way to make a training program more pleasant.
- *Make learning fun.* How do you make learning enjoyable? By making it interactive rather than just talking at trainees. Using appropriate activities, exercises, simulations, and games can make learning enjoyable and effective. Interactive training is much better than "Death by PowerPoint," in which trainees simply sit for a lengthy, boring PowerPoint slide presentation with narration.

Law of Frequency

The **law of frequency** suggests that the more often you practice a trained behavior, the more likely you will continue using the desired behavior accurately.[5] Teachers refer to it as "D & P," or drill and practice. It's one of the oldest teaching techniques around, and it till works. Athletes and musicians understand fully the law of frequency. Coaches and directors require their players to practice until they get it right. Practice does make perfect. Here are suggestions for how you can use the law of frequency in your training programs:

- *Make sure trainees are practicing correctly.* In his book *The Talent Code*, researcher Daniel Coyle suggests that one key to learning anything, especially a skill, is using *deep practice*.[6] **Deep practice** is the process of mindfully practicing a skill by chunking it up, repeating it, and then feeling how the skill should be performed. Drawing on neuroscience research, Coyle suggests that to master a skill you need to immerse yourself in using those three procedures.[7]
  - ○ *Chunk it up.* Break a skill into steps and master each step. In addition, it's useful to absorb the entire skill set as a holistic experience—as Coyle says "absorb the whole thing."[8] We are wired to imitate what we see, so as we break something into steps and substeps, it's helpful to observe someone performing the skill in its entirety. To teach someone a complex skill, use the whole-part-whole process of letting the trainee see the entire skill being performed effectively, then slowly practice each substep of the skill before putting it all together in a finished performance.

○ *Repeat it.* After rehearsing a skill, keep rehearsing it. Perform the skill until it becomes a natural and comfortable act. Coyle cites the famed concert pianist Vladimir Horowitz: "If I skip practice for one day, I notice. If I skip practice for two days, my wife notices. If I skip for three days, the world notices."[9] But rather than rehearse mindlessly, practice the skill mindfully aware of what you are doing, refining and polishing as you practice. It's not just repetition that makes practice a truly deep practice. To help learners learn, make sure they are consciously aware of what they are doing as they rehearse.

○ *Learn to feel it.* Coyle says that the most effective practice occurs when you can feel whether or not you are making a mistake in what he calls "the sweet spot"—the spot where it all comes together.[10] Whether it's practicing how to deliver a speech, how to negotiate a sale, or how to manage a conflict, there is an art as well as a science to performing a skill effectively. When you are involved in deep practice, you can tell when you are performing a skill well or not just by sensing how well you are practicing. When training someone to perform a skill, encourage him or her to practice or rehearse sensitively so that he or she has a personal feeling that the skill is being performed well. The goal is to have the learner feel alert, focused, and attentive rather than mindlessly practice a skill over and over. Feel it; sense it; experience it.

- *Make sure trainees are practicing the correct skill.* In other words, practice makes perfect *if* practice is perfect. The law of frequency can do more harm than good if the trainee is practicing the wrong skill. If you've ever learned something incorrectly, you know how hard it is to unlearn it. Relearning an appropriate behavior can be challenging.

- *Use "plus-one" mastery technique.* The **plus-one technique** involves learning a process one step at a time while adding each new step to the preceding steps you've mastered. For example, when training others in how to deliver business presentations, break the presentation down into its smallest parts: introduction, body (first main point, second main point, third main point), and conclusion. Have trainees start by delivering the introduction. Have them repeat the introduction until they've mastered it. Then have them complete the introduction plus one additional step, which would be the first main point in the body of the presentation. Once this is mastered, they add the second main point of the body and so on until all steps are mastered.

- *Have trainees train the trainer.* After you teach a particular skill to a group of trainees, switch roles and have them train you on the same skill, or train each other. Knowing how to do a skill is one thing, but training someone else in how to do a skill is challenging. Trainees believe they know how to do a skill until they are asked to teach others. Then they realize what they don't know. Asking trainees to train others not only emphasizes frequency but also enhances their depth of understanding of the particular concept or skill. Training and organizational development specialist Dan Chairburu found that when coworkers and colleagues are directly involved in the training, learning is enhanced, and there is a greater transfer of skills to the job.[11]

Law of Association

The **law of association** suggests that every new fact, idea, concept, or behavior is best learned if we can relate it to or with something we already know.[12] One of your authors was quite relieved to learn that the Paris subway system was very similar to the system in New York City, his home at the time. Even though he was in a new city where English was not commonly spoken, he felt confident in his ability to navigate the subway system because of his familiarity with New York's subway. Training becomes a simpler process when we help trainees associate new information with something they already know.

Another example would be training people in how to group problem solve after training them in how to manage interpersonal conflict. Many conflict management models are very similar to the group problem solving process. Rather than start over at the very beginning, a trainer would simply ask trainees to recall the interpersonal conflict management model and build on what they already know. Here are suggestions for using the law of association in your training programs:

- *Use analogies.* The late Steve Jobs, who was CEO of Apple Computers, and his associates at Apple computer understood the law of association when they were developing and designing the first desktop computer. They referred to the computer screen as a "desktop." They used terms that trainees were familiar with, such as filing cabinets, folders, trashcans, and "cut and paste." Because trainees were familiar with the language of the office, they learned how to use the computer more easily. Jobs and his associates made the computer more approachable for office workers who were not computer science majors, and ultimately they revolutionized the way we train people in how to use the computer.
- *Compare and contrast with other familiar processes.* As with using analogies, comparing and contrasting familiar processes helps adults learn. When training others how to make presentations, trainers usually begin by teaching the principles of informative presentations. Once trainees understand this process, it's easier for trainers to teach them how to make persuasive presentations. Trainers simply compare and contrast the two types of presentations, pointing out their similarities and differences.

Law of Readiness

The **law of readiness** suggests that learning is more likely to occur when what is being taught is something the learner needs to learn at that time—when the learner is mentally and physically ready to learn. The law of readiness is summarized in the Chinese proverb that opens this chapter: "When the student is ready, the teacher will appear." A trainer can provide the information, but the learner must also be ready to learn.[13] It's important for trainees to understand why what is being taught is something that needs to be learned. Here are the applications of this law:

- *Make it clear why each skill being taught is important to the learner.* When teaching the skill of paraphrasing, for example, cite evidence showing that effective paraphrasing skills can enhance the quality of communication and decrease errors in understanding.

- *Ask the learner to explain why the skill being taught could be of practical value to the learner.* Rather than tell a trainee why learning a particular skill is important, ask the learner to give examples of how using the skill would be of benefit. For example, instead of telling a learner why paraphrasing is important, ask the learner to identify instances in which using this skill effectively would have saved time, money, or frustration.
- *Schedule the training so that the skills being taught will be readily put into practice.* Learners will be ready to learn if they understand that what is being taught will have immediate practical benefits. Training sales persons how to respond to customers who return items will be especially timely right after the Christmas holidays, when customers often return unwanted items.

ANDRAGOGY VERSUS PEDAGOGY

As a student, do you sometimes get upset when a teacher treats you as though you were still in high school? How about a teacher who doesn't give you enough credit for the experiences you bring to the classroom? Some trainers do the same thing. Teaching and training adults is not the same as teaching and training children; adults and children learn differently. This section of the chapter focuses on how

RECAP

General Learning Laws and Putting Laws into Practice

Learning Law	Definition	Putting Laws into Practice
Law of effect	Trainees learn when conditions are pleasant and rewarding.	Create a pleasant physical environment. Accommodate trainees' work schedules. Schedule appropriate breaks.
Law of frequency	Trainees learn when they practice a skill or behavior.	Insure that trainees practice correct skills and behaviors. Use the "plus-one" mastery technique. Have trainees train the trainer.
Law of association	Trainees learn when new facts, ideas, concepts, or behaviors are related to or with something they already know.	Use analogies. Compare and contrast new procedures with familiar processes.
Law of readiness	Trainees will learn when they are ready to learn.	Tell trainees why the skill they are learning is important. Ask trainees to explain how the skill being taught can be useful to them. Schedule the training so that what is being learned will be readily applicable.

adults learn best by examining the principles and practices of andragogy, principles developed by Malcolm Knowles, a leading author in the field of adult education.

Andragogy is the science and art of teaching adults.[14] An andragogical approach to learning is self-directed rather than teacher-directed and is based on the Greek word *aner,* which means "adult." **Pedagogy,** on the other hand, is the science and art of teaching children. It refers to a teacher-directed approach to learning that is based on the Greek words *paid,* which means "child," and *agogus,* which means "guide."

It's important to clarify what we mean by the adult learner.[15] For example, are young adults considered adult learners from the trainer's perspective? It's not so much about chronological age as it is about maturity. **Maturity** is the degree of experience that a trainee brings to the training classroom.[16] Not all young adults are inexperienced or immature, and not all adults are experienced and mature.

Andragogical Training Assumptions

Andragogy, or adult learning, is based on five assumptions that help explain how adults learn best. Understanding these assumptions can help you approach communication and leadership training from the adult learner's perspective.

1. *Adult learners need to know why they're learning something.* Whatever is being taught needs to be meaningful and directly related to the trainees' lives and the problems they experience on a daily basis. Children learn for learning's sake and rarely ask, why something is important. (They might assume it's important because the teacher is asking them to learn it.) Adult learners are more critical of what it is they are asked to learn.

2. *Adult learners bring years of experience to the classroom.* Trainees are not blank slates. They want to use the information they learn in the classroom. When teaching adults, trainers don't often have to start at the beginning of a specific sequence of skills. Rather, trainers can begin with what their trainees already know. Children, on the other hand, have limited life experience; their teachers have to be more thorough and cannot assume what a child might and might not know. Teachers may have to create experiences for the children.

3. *Adults tend to be self-motivated.* Many children learn because they know that getting good grades on a report card will be rewarded. Adults are more internally motivated to learn because learning gives them a sense of personal satisfaction and accomplishment. Adults are less motivated by what others will think of them and more motivated by how they'll personally feel about themselves. Adults understand that their learning is something no one can take from them. Once you learn something, it can be yours for a lifetime. Adults know that learning will enrich their lives and make them more meaningful.

4. *Adults know their own deficiencies, and they know what they need to learn to become successful.* Many adult learners return to the training classroom in order to cope with such life-changing events as starting a new job, getting a promotion, or even losing a job because of downsizing.[17] They know what questions they need answered, and they seek those answers. Most children,

RECAP

Pedagogical and Andragogical Learning Assumptions

Learning Factors	Pedagogy Assumptions	Andragogy Assumptions
Relevance of learning	Learners learn for the sake of acquiring information.	Learners learn to address specific needs.
Role of learners' experience	Experience is minimized and less relevant to learning.	Experience is a rich resource for learning.
Motivation of learners	Learners are motivated by external rewards and punishments.	Learners are motivated by internal incentives and a desire to be effective on the job.
Level of self-direction	Learners are dependent on others for direction.	Learners are self-directed and know what needs to be learned.
Orientation to learning	Subject- or content-centered learning is appropriate.	Problem-oriented learning is required.

on the other hand, have no idea what might hold them back in terms of personal development, and they are dependent on teachers for help.

5. *Adults are problem-centered learners.* This adult learning assumption focuses on the underlying reason for learning. Unlike children, who approach learning subject by subject (math, language arts, science), adults prefer to learn problem by problem.[18] Such problems might include not being as productive as employees they would like to be because they lack particular skills, or not being eligible for promotion because they need additional knowledge and skills in a particular area.

ANDRAGOGICAL TRAINING APPLICATIONS

The five andragogical assumptions we described have practical implications for training. When developing a training presentation, a trainer needs to make training relevant, base training on trainees' experiences, tap trainee motivation, and be learner-centered and problem-oriented.

Make Training Relevant

Relevance is essential for adult learners. Trainees shouldn't leave training programs muttering, "What was that all about?" and "Why do we have to know this stuff?" Employees have busy lives, and they resent having to attend training programs they perceive to be of little relevance to their lives and their work. As training expert Gordon Welty puts it, "Adults have a life-centric orientation to training."[19] When training doesn't seem relevant, trainees will have little motivation to learn.

In order to make training relevant, it's important to conduct a needs assessment, which we will discuss fully in the next chapter. A **needs assessment** is the process of identifying what learners do not yet know or the necessary skills that they can't yet perform. Until a trainer knows what the trainees' needs are, it will be difficult to make the training relevant.

After conducting a needs assessment, keep the following applications in mind to make training relevant:

- *Train for a trainee's "in basket."* Almost every employee has an in basket, whether it's a literal one or a metaphorical one. The in basket, often found on the top of a desk, usually contains items that require immediate attention. Even when there is no actual in basket, there are tasks that have piled up and need to be completed. An employee may have a mental in basket that contains unfinished tasks and projects. Effective and relevant training addresses the real, day-to-day problems and issues that are found in either the literal or the mental in basket. Although many employees can process their in baskets in a short period of time, there are always a few items that remain a challenge. A trainer needs to identify these challenges and help the trainee with the issues, tasks, and problems in their in baskets. The needs-centered training program helps employees process their in baskets.
- *Involve trainees in doing their actual work during the training session.* Rather than use contrived case studies and unrealistic work situations, ask adult learners to bring to the training session actual work—current projects and assignments that need to be completed. If you are presenting a training workshop on how to prepare an informative briefing, ask trainees to bring in an example of a briefing that they recently gave or that they plan to deliver. During the workshop, use the trainees' notes and drafts to develop an effective outline for an informative brief. Similarly, workshops on problem solving could deal with problems that trainees currently face on the job.

Draw on Trainees' Experiences

Unlike children, whose life experiences are limited by virtue of their age, adults bring to the training classroom a rich array of life experiences. Trainers should recognize and use their trainees' experiences to facilitate the learning process. We bring the training content to the classroom, but it's the trainees who must not only learn the content, but also learn how to apply it to their jobs and personal lives.

One general rule of training is that *it's always better to get a message out of someone rather than to put one in.* If you're training a class in how to handle customer complaints or how to process a conflict, ask your trainees how this training content could be applied immediately to their jobs. For example, assume you're training a group of airline customer service employees on how to manage and resolve customer conflict. Ask the ticket agents how they see the training content being applied in the airport. Ask the reservation agents how the content could be applied while talking to a customer over the phone. Ask flight attendants how this training content would work in the cabin of an airplane. By asking trainees these questions, you enable them to learn from each other. Additionally, they learn multiple ways to apply the training content.

There are also potential disadvantages to drawing on trainees' life experiences. Some adult learners have had positive experiences on the job and remain receptive to new communication skills that will improve their effectiveness. Others may have had less-than-positive experiences on the job and will not always be receptive to training. For example, assume you're training flight attendants in how to handle air rage or irate passengers. It would not be uncommon to hear a flight attendant say, "You know this is never going to work, because from my experience . . ."

To what degree do you want trainees to share negative experiences in the classroom? There are times when trainees' negative experiences can help you identify trainees' needs or give you an example that you can turn into a positive example. But it takes skill and the ability to use employee's negative experiences in a positive way. Here are suggestions:

- *Acknowledge their less-than-positive experiences and empathize with trainees, but don't dwell on their negative experiences.* For example, you might say, "I realize you have had some unfortunate experiences, and I'm sorry that you have had to experience them, but this training is designed to help you."
- *Acknowledge that negative experiences are inevitable and that the job of training is to reduce the number of negative experiences.* For example, you might say, "Training is not going to solve all of your problems, but the skills that this training program addresses and develops will hopefully minimize some of the negative experiences."
- *Ask trainees how new training content might address negative experiences.* You might say, "How do you see this training content or these new skills helping you through the negative experiences on the job?"
- *Place the negative experiences in context.* Many times, isolated employees have single experiences that remain negative. But there is a tendency to generalize to all employees and to increase the frequency of negative experiences. You will hear, "It's happening to all of us all the time!" Ask for additional information and help trainees place the experience in a meaningful and more accurate context. You might say, "I realize a group of you had an unfortunate experience, but let me provide you with some additional information that might allow you to see how that unfortunate experience was limited and isolated."

Use the Internal Motivation to Learn

Adult learners tend to be motivated by internal drives such as increased job satisfaction, self-esteem, their sense of accomplishment, and quality-of-life issues. Often they are motivated to learn by life-changing events such as a promotion or the loss of a job. Their drive to improve their own condition in life comes from within. Here are suggestions for how you might use this principle of adult learning:

- *Take advantage of internal motivation.* Find out what the motivations of the trainees are. How? Before a training session begins, engage your trainees in conversation and learn why they are at the training session and what their interests, needs, values, and wants are. Don't assume that trainees are interested only in learning a new skill to make more money or to enhance their career. Appeal to trainees' sense of wanting to do a job right, to enhance their skill sets, and to take personal pride in performing their job effectively.

- *Set realistic expectations.* Trainers must develop reasonable expectations for trainees, given the amount of training time coupled with trainees' abilities and work experiences. Trainees must feel that they can successfully learn. Whether they are learning information or skills, trainees must feel that they can be successful in the training classroom. Provide constant support, praise, encouragement, and constructive feedback.

Teach What Learners Need to Learn

Unlike some less-mature learners who don't know what it is they need to learn, adult learners know and understand their deficiencies. They have a readiness to learn. Many adult learners are at a roadblock in life or their careers and cannot move forward until they obtain additional information or develop new skills. They know where they're deficient, and they need options and alternatives that will allow them to cure those deficiencies. Here are suggestions for applying this principle of adult learning in your training classroom:

- *Make training "needs based" or "learner centered."* Training must be learner centered rather than trainer centered. Training is not about us; it's about our trainees. If our trainees ask, "Why do I have to learn this stuff?" then we have failed them. You will learn how to conduct a needs assessment in the next chapter.
- *Encourage self-directed learning.* Allow adult learners the freedom to work on their own deficiencies. A one-size-fits-all training model doesn't work for must adult learners. Research suggests that adult learners prefer self-directed and self-designed learning projects to group learning projects.[20] It should also be noted that self-directed learning does not mean that adults learn in isolation. Self-directed learning projects involve a variety of individuals who serve as resources for the adult learner, including guides, experts, and encouragers. The flexibility to be self-directed allows adult learners to target their own specific problems and to control start/stop times, which are important when learners must juggle other obligations.
- *Make training timely.* With **just in time** (JIT) training, trainees receive the right amount and type of training exactly when it's needed. Unfortunately, many trainees receive "single shot" training, which is only a one-time training program that includes all the information and skills trainees will need. A single dose of training usually results in information overload: Important information is not retained, and skills are never developed to the proficiency that is needed for trainees to succeed in their jobs.
- *Coach trainees through mistakes.* Trainees have a readiness to learn when they're making mistakes or when they're "stuck." For example, when training others in how to make presentations, many trainees get stuck in the same place each time they practice the presentation; they find a particular part of the presentation difficult to explain. This is where you can coach them

through the difficult part. You provide and demonstrate strategies for how they can make this particular part of the presentation more clear. It's important to note that many adult learners take errors and mistakes personally and are more likely to let mistakes affect their self-esteem.[21] As a trainer, you are encouraged to coach trainees through the process by making the training classroom as safe as possible, by recognizing the trainee's strengths, and by addressing the trainee's performance deficiencies using specific behavioral and descriptive terms rather than general evaluative terms. "I hear you having difficulty explaining your sales figures from last month" is an example of the former, and "Your presentation is not good" is an example of the latter.

Make Learning Problem Oriented

Adults have a problem-centered orientation to learning.[22] Because adult learners bring prior knowledge and experience to the training classroom, they usually know what they need to know. Rather than start from scratch, trainers can often bypass the basic knowledge and jump into how to process and handle specific problems. Here are suggestions to make training more problem oriented:

- *Group your trainees.* Survey your trainees to determine how many years of work experience they have had and to determine the types of problems they have experienced. Based on this information, divide the training class into groups according to years of experience and types of problems experienced. Provide training that is group specific.
- *Ask trainees to forward their specific problems ahead of time to the trainer.* Take time to develop training programs that address these problems, or find ways to address these problems in current training programs.
- *Provide trainees with a bibliography or a set of resources.* Remember, adult learners are self-directed and internally motivated. If you provide them with direction and resources, they'll seek out answers to their problems.
- *Provide trainees with a series of training classes.* Just as in a college curriculum, some students "test out" of the basic classes and are placed in advanced classes. Training curricula should offer similar options to trainees. Some classes should be basic, while other classes should address job-related problems that are more complex.

Now that, we have examined three laws of learning and five principles of adult learning, and how training practitioners can apply these laws and principles to the training classroom, the final section of this chapter will take these laws and principles one step further and examine individual learning styles. Understanding individual learning styles is one more way you can adapt your training to enhance adult learning.

LEARNING STYLES

A **learning style** is the way an individual perceives, organizes, processes, and remembers information. Some people are flexible in how they learn. Others remain more limited and have a preferred learning style or a preferred mode of processing

▶ RECAP

Adult Learning Principles and Training Applications

Adult Learning Principles	Adult Training Applications
Adults need relevant training.	Conduct a needs assessment. Train employees for their in baskets. Involve trainees in productive work during the training session.
Adults bring experience to the classroom.	Ask experienced trainees for their assistance in applying new training content. Give experienced trainees the opportunity to train less experienced trainees. Apply the principle "It's better to get a message out of someone that to put a message in someone" by asking trainees to share examples and their experiences.
Adults are internally motivated to learn.	Keep trainees focused on work-related tasks. Use momentum to pull trainees past the roadblocks and obstacles that adult learners face. Set realistic expectations.
Adults know what they need to know.	Make training needs-based by focusing on the learner. Encourage self-directed learning. Remain timely. Coach trainees through their mistakes by providing constructive and encouraging feedback.
Adult learning is problem-oriented.	Survey trainees and group them by years and types of experience in order to identify relevant problems. Ask trainees beforehand to forward problems they would like training to address. Use real-world examples and case studies rather than contrived and unrealistic situations.

information. Howard Gardner at Harvard University argues that individuals learn differently because they possess different intelligences and that some of these intelligences go beyond the purely cognitive such as processing information. He suggests that learners possess one or more of seven kinds of intelligence:

1. Linguistic intelligence (as in a poet or a novelist);
2. Logical-mathematical intelligence (as in a scientist or a mathematician);
3. Musical intelligence (as in a composer or a performer);
4. Spatial intelligence (as in a sculptor or an airplane pilot);
5. Bodily kinesthetic intelligence (as in an athlete or a dancer);
6. Interpersonal intelligence (as in a salesman or a teacher);
7. Intrapersonal intelligence (exhibited by individuals with accurate views of themselves).[23]

How do you prefer to learn? Read on to learn more about your learning style. We will summarize the research literature by examining perceptual, learning time, information processing, age, and personality differences. Then we will discuss how to apply this information to the training classroom.

Perceptual Learning Differences

Some individuals learn by reading and by observing others; they're referred to as visual learners. Some learn by hearing and speaking; they're the aural or auditory learners. Still others learn by doing and touching; they're the kinesthetic learners. These perceptual learning differences are called modalities. Some learners have a single modality preference, others are comfortable perceiving in two modalities, and yet others remain comfortable learning in all three modalities. Research suggests that the most common modalities are visual and mixed (visual, auditory, kinesthetic), with each accounting for 30 percent of the U.S. population. The research also suggests that about 25 percent of the population prefers learning using the

A TRAINER'S TOOLBOX

How to Transfer Training Skills to the Job

Because adult learners are problem-oriented learners, they will be motivated to learn when they believe that the skills being taught in the training session can solve their on-the-job problems. To ensure that what is taught in a training classroom will be applied back on the job, consider these procedures:

- Have trainees bring actual work-related problems to the training session. Take time during the training session to develop skill-based strategies to address specific work problems.
- Before the training session is over, ask trainees how and when they will apply the skills they have learned after they return to their job.
- Before the training session concludes, invite trainees to write themselves a reminder memo that describes the actions they will take to improve their skill when they return to the job. Collect the memos and send them to the trainees one week after the training has concluded.
- Ask trainees to reinforce new skill attainment in those coworkers who attended the training with

them. One week after the training, ask trainees to write an e-mail message to colleagues whom they see using the skills learned during the training session.

- Tell trainees not to implement all the training skill content presented in the workshop at one time. Ask them to rank the skills they learned and then put into practice the highest priority skill first. When that skill has been mastered, have them implement the second skill. Continue the process until all the skills have been mastered and implemented on the job.
- Give the trainees a checklist or a reminder sheet that they can use when they return to the job. For example, after a training session on "How to Participate Effectively in Team Meeting," provide a checklist that the trainees can use immediately following a team meeting to assess their application of the skills learned in the training session.
- Make sure that the trainees' supervisors are informed about the new skills presented in training so that the supervisors can reinforce effective application of the skills.

auditory modality, and approximately 15 percent prefers the kinesthetic or tactile modality.[24]

Visual Learners.   **Visual learners** learn by reading and viewing. They remain visually oriented and need to see what they're learning. Visual learners want to see how the pieces fit together. Often they will stop what they're doing, look into space, and visualize what it is they're learning. They are easily distracted by visual disorder and movement and become impatient when extensive listening is required. Trainees who are visually oriented learn from reading prepackaged training materials and from trainers who outline content using flip charts, chalkboards, or electronic presentation software (i.e., PowerPoint). They appreciate handouts that contain graphic representations of ideas and concepts along with space to jot down notes and follow-up questions.

Visually oriented trainees also learn by modeling other people's behaviors. With **modeling,** people acquire knowledge, attitudes, beliefs, and values and learn how to perform certain behaviors by observing those who model the behavior. Many parents refer to this type of learning as "monkey see, monkey do." Here's how to motivate the visual learner using modeling:[25]

- *Set realistic expectations for trainees*. They're more motivated to learn when they perceive themselves as being able to imitate the modeled behaviors. Don't set them up for failure. Once trainees experience initial success imitating simple modeled behaviors, then develop more complex behavioral processes with them.
- *Model "real" behaviors*. Trainees are more motivated to learn and perform behaviors they perceive to be "true to life" and "real" than behaviors they perceive to be "artificial." Trainees are more motivated to model behaviors that they know they will have to demonstrate in future situations.
- *Praise models for their behavior*. Trainees are more motivated when they see models (who are often experienced trainers) being rewarded for appropriately demonstrating the behaviors. For example, if you have two models demonstrate how to manage interpersonal conflict by role-playing the appropriate communication behaviors, reward them for their good work in front of the other trainees.
- *Use models who are similar to trainees*. Students appear to be more motivated when they see models who are like them demonstrating the appropriate behaviors. It's not uncommon to hear older trainees say, "I could never do that." However, once they see a model of similar age, they quickly change their minds and become motivated.

Aural Learners.   **Aural learners,** or auditory learners, learn by hearing and speaking. Auditory-oriented learners need opportunities to articulate what they're learning: They clarify their thinking by making the words come out of their mouths. Have you ever tried explaining a concept or an idea to a friend only to realize that once the words left your mouth, you really didn't know what you were talking about? This happens to teachers quite frequently. You think you know something until you try conveying your knowledge to others, and then you realize that you don't know the idea or concept as well as you thought. Aural learners need opportunities to articulate their ideas to others. They also learn from hearing others speak. They prefer processing the spoken word rather than the written word. They do well in traditional lectures or in training contexts where new information is delivered as a series of oral presentations. They learn well from listening to audiocassettes, soundtracks, and peer presentations.

Kinesthetic Learners.   **Kinesthetic learners** learn from touching and doing. Kinesthetically oriented learners are tactile and prefer to be engaged in movement. They are partial to action and have a tendency to express emotion in physically exuberant ways. Kinesthetic learners prefer a hands-on approach to learning. They enjoy involving themselves in the training content and do well by participating in training simulations, case studies, and role play activities. They develop an appreciation and value for training content not by reading or hearing about it but by doing and experiencing it.

Time Learning Differences

Another way to approach learning styles is to examine how a learner uses time during the learning process. Some learners, reflective learners, don't want to be rushed and prefer plenty of time to learn. Other learners are more impulsive and want to learn quickly and efficiently.

Reflective Learners.   **Reflective learners** need time to process information and tend to work with greater care and precision when learning new information. Once they have a persuasive argument prepared for their sales presentation, they go back and review their evidence carefully to ensure its accuracy. When rehearsing their sales presentation, reflective learners take the time to carefully deliver each section,

▶ RECAP

Perceptual Learning Differences and Training Applications

Learning Style	Definition	Training Application
Visual learner	Learns by reading and viewing	Point out appropriate behaviors in others or models. Use prepackaged materials, handouts, flip charts, chalkboard, and electronic presentation software.
Aural learner	Learns by hearing and speaking	Use peer presentations, lectures, audiocassettes, and soundtracks.
Kinesthetic learner	Learns by touching and doing	Use simulations, case studies, role plays, and demonstrations (see Chapter 6).

working out the rough spots, before moving on to the next section. They videotape and review their presentation before presenting it before the actual audience. Reflective learners are often referred to as plodders, meaning that they plod along, slowly but surely. Research suggests that some adult learners tend to compensate for being slow in some behavioral or psychomotor learning tasks by being more accurate and making fewer trial-and-error mistakes.[26]

Impulsive Learners. **Impulsive learners** work quickly and with less determination. Complete accuracy is less important than getting a quick overview of the concept or skill to be learned. When developing, organizing, and rehearsing a sales presentation, they rarely go back to work out the rough spots. In fact, it's rare that they even rehearse their presentations. Impulsive learners might put together a sketchy outline and then wing the rest of the presentation. They're less concerned with how polished a sales presentation is and more concerned with getting the presentation over and out of the way. These individuals are often referred to as sweepers, meaning that they sweep through their work quickly and with less precision.

It's important to consider learning time differences when training others.[27] Our culture often rewards speed more than accuracy. Reflective learners may work from a disadvantage simply because it takes them longer to complete a learning task. Additionally, the accuracy of their work is not always rewarded. Most training programs accommodate the impulsive learner simply because time remains a scarce resource in most organizations. From this author's personal training experience, trainers also approach training programs with instructional objectives that are not realistic. They try to do more than they can accomplish effectively in the allotted time. When developing training curricula, trainers need to remain sensitive to the amount of time it takes learners not only to process the training content, but also to complete all the learning tasks presented.

Information Processing Differences

Another approach to learning styles focuses on differences in information processing. Some trainees grasp abstract concepts easily; others need to see concrete applications. Some trainees learn well step-by-step, while others need to see the big picture before they can make sense of the separate parts. One program of research refers to learners as either whole-part or part-whole learners.[28]

Whole-Part Learners. **Whole-part learners,** also called top-down processors, prefer having the big picture before moving into the details of the concept or idea. For example, if you're training midlevel managers on a model of group problem solving, whole–part learners will want to see the big picture before moving into the details. They want to know what effective group problem solving is going to look and sound like before examining the stages of the group problem solving communication model. When trainers jump into the details before offering the larger concept or model, whole-part learners become a bit anxious.

Whole-part learners need a **schema,** or a way to organize the big ideas, before they're ready to receive detailed information. One way to help trainees develop a schema is to give them a handout or an outline that depicts the model of group

▶ **RECAP**

Learning Time Differences and Training Applications

Learning Style	Definition	Training Application
Reflective learner	Learns by taking time to process information; more concerned with accuracy and precision	Allow ample time for trainees to complete work. Set realistic learning objectives.
Impulsive learner	Learns by quickly processing information and completing tasks; less concerned with accuracy and precision	Discourage impulsive learners by not rewarding quantity over quality. When quantity is more important, encourage this learning style by limiting time.

problem solving with each stage of the model labeled and placed in the appropriate order. Once whole-part learners have the big picture or a schema, they're ready to process the details. Trainers refer to these individuals as lumpers because they have difficulty splitting the parts from the whole.

Part-Whole Learners.   **Part-whole learners,** or bottom-up processors, prefer to examine the big picture in terms of its parts. They don't necessarily need the big picture before examining the parts that comprise it. For example, part-whole learners feel comfortable learning the stages of the group problem solving communication model. They don't need the big picture in order to understand the components of a model. Once they have the pieces, they have the ability to synthesize the stages into a working model of group problem solving communication. Trainers speak of these individuals as splitters because of their ability to analytically examine the big picture in terms of its parts.

▶ **RECAP**

Information Processing Learning Differences and Training Applications

Learning Style	Definition	Training Application
Whole-part learner	Learns the big picture first, then the parts or details that comprise it	Show the trainee what the product will look like when completed, then break down the product into its parts. Use demonstrations and/or other visual representations.
Part-whole learner	Learns the parts or details first, then the big picture	Show the trainee the parts that when put together will make the product. Use demonstrations and/or other visual representations.

Age Differences

Although we make distinctions between adult learners and children and their approaches to learning (andragogy and pedagogy), contemporary research suggests that there may even be differences among generations of adults when it comes to cultural expectations and preferred approaches to learning. Research does not suggest that older workers are necessarily less skilled in learning (although some evidence suggests that older workers may experience a decline in memory and that those over 65 or 70 may have slightly more difficulty with learning and retaining new concepts). However, the generation into which trainees were born may determine to some extent their values and general assumptions about life, and those values and assumptions could affect their preferred approaches to learning.[29]

Generation researchers Neil Howe and William Strauss define a generation as "a society-wide peer group, born over a period roughly the same length as the passage from youth to adulthood, who collectively possess a common persona."[30] *Baby Boomers* is the label for one such generation, those born in the years 1943–1960. *Generation X* is the term used for people born in 1961–1981. Those born in 1982–2002 have been labeled *Millennials* or you are sometimes referred to as *Generation Y.* You are a *Post Millennial,* if you were born after 2002. Researchers Howe and Straus suggest that, as a group, "Millennials are unlike any other youth generation in living memory. They are more numerous, more affluent, better educated, and more ethnically diverse. More importantly, they are beginning to manifest a wide array of positive social habits that older Americans no longer associate with you, including a focus on teamwork, achievement, modesty, and good conduct."[31] The box on p. 46 summarizes the common characteristics and values of four present-day generations.

Generational and age differences may create barriers between a trainer and trainees who are predominately of different generations. For example, a trainer of the Baby Boomer generation may find the examples and illustrations he or she uses don't connect with younger trainees; certain ways of phrasing things or using language may differ as well. Generational differences can also reflect differences between a preference for individual achievement (individualistic cultural values) and a preference for group collaboration (collectivistic cultural values), which can impact learning. One team of researchers who investigated the role of generations in the workforce suggests that Generation X workers are paradoxically both more individualistic (self-reliant and focused on individual accomplishment) and more team-oriented than Boomers are. In addition, Boomers were found to be more likely to have a sense of loyalty to their employers, expect long-term employment, value a pension plan, and experience job burnout from overwork. Generation Xers, on the other hand, seek more of a balance between their work and their personal life, expect to have more than one job or career, value good working conditions over other job factors, and have a greater need to feel appreciated.[32]

What are the implications of generational differences in training workers? Consider the following applications:

■ *Don't assume that because someone is of a certain age that person has the stereotypical values of his or her generation.* Although research has identified generational trends in values and life perspectives, use those findings as hypotheses to be explored rather than conclusions about generational values and assumptions.[33] As we often stress, the needs and characteristics of the individuals whom you train are key elements that effect both training content and methods.

- *There may be generational differences in comfort levels in using and adapting to new technology.* Baby Boomers remember a time before computers, faxes, Facebook, texting, and the other technological tools that have revolutionized the workplace, education, and our personal lives. Millennials and Post Millennials grew up using computers and other technology as a normal aspect of learning. Their different experiences with technology may affect how learners prefer to learn and the tools they use to learn. Understanding the learners' needs, preferences, and comfort levels in using and adapting to new technology can help a trainer customize training to meet the needs and expectations of individual trainees.

- *The greater the generational difference between trainer and trainees, the more sensitivity and mindfulness that may be needed to bridge differences in communication style and approach.* Age differences between trainer and trainee

GENERATIONAL CHARACTERISTICS

Generation	Birth Years	Characteristics
Matures	1925–1942	Work hard
		Have a sense of duty
		Are willing to sacrifice
		Have a sense of what is right
		Work quickly
Baby Boomers	1943–1960	Value personal fulfillment and optimism
		Crusade for causes
		Buy now and pay later
		Support equal rights for all
		Work efficiently
Generation X	1961–1981	Live with uncertainty
		Consider balance important
		Live for today
		Save
		Consider every job as a contract
Millennials or Generation Y	1982–2002	Are close to their parents
		Feel "special"
		Are goal-oriented
		Are team-oriented
		Focus on achievement

Information summarized from N. Howe and W. Strauss, *Millennials Rising: The Next Generation* (New York: Vintage Books, 2000).

should be considered as a cultural difference that calls for greater skill and awareness in communication methods and content. There is ample evidence that people hold stereotypical views of others based only on others' perceived age. In addition, a person's age influences how he or she communicates with others.[34] One study, found that older adults have greater difficulty in accurately interpreting nonverbal messages than younger people do.[35] Older adults don't like to be patronized or talked down to. And younger people value social support, other-oriented and empathic listening, and being mentored more than older people do.[36]

Learning Preference Differences

Some learners have a strong preference for how they like to learn. Kolb's Learning Style Inventory, named after its developer, education researcher David Kolb, is a diagnostic instrument that identifies four major learning preferences. These learning preferences, learning styles, are based on learners' personalities, experiences, and how they like to learn new material.[37] The Kolb Inventory identifies four types of learning preferences: Divergers, Assimilators, Convergers, and Accommodators.

Divergers.   **Divergers** prefer observing a situation rather than taking action. They tend to be innovative, imaginative, and concerned with personal relevance. Divergers have a need to know how new information relates to prior experiences before they learn new information. Here are suggestions for how to work with Divergers.

- *Use buzz groups*. **Buzz groups** are small groups, usually five to ten people, who are given a topic to discuss. Divergers like the interaction with others and the opportunity to add to the ideas of others.
- *Facilitate brainstorming sessions*. During problem solving, the **brainstorming** technique encourages creativity among group members, as does the free flowing of solutions being offered without any group member's evaluating or judging them. Divergent learners like to piggyback on another's ideas to create new solutions.
- *Encourage mentor/mentee relationships*. Because divergent learners enjoy receiving feedback, they find one-on-one conversations a productive learning experience. Consider pairing inexperienced with experienced trainees to form mentor/mentee relationships. These relationships allow inexperienced trainees to shadow more experienced trainees on the job. Through the relationship, Divergers will get answers to their questions "What happened to you? Tell me about your experiences," "Why do you feel that way?" and "Why do you think our attitudes and beliefs are so different?"

Assimilators.   **Assimilators** prefer learning that is efficient, logical, and precise. They value sequential thinking and trust expert opinion. Assimilators enjoy collecting data and organizing it or assimilating it into concise, logical form. Unlike Divergers, Assimilators are less interested in learning from other's experiences and are more interested in learning from the experts who have done the actual work. Here are suggestions for how to work with Assimilators.

- *Give traditional lectures.* A **lecture** presents information efficiently through one-way communication: from teacher to student. Assimilators like learning from lectures because the information is presented in a logical or sequential order. We discuss the lecture training method in Chapter 6.
- *Invite experts to address trainees.* Because Assimilators value expert opinion, they enjoy hearing from people who have considerable experience and expertise. When experts are not available, trainers must become proficient in the training content area and must be perceived as being credible or believable in the content area.
- *Assign individual research projects.* Rather than working in pairs or small groups, Assimilators prefer working on projects individually. Ask trainees to conduct research projects where they collect, process, and present their findings to others.

Convergers. Convergers are always looking for utility in ideas and theories. They approach learning from a problem-solving perspective and enjoy finding practical solutions. Convergers prefer analyzing problems and testing theories to find solutions that can be implemented to achieve results. Here are suggestions for how to work with Convergers.

- *Introduce new problem-solving processes.* Convergers enjoy learning about new approaches or protocols to problem solving. Convergers also like to see how new problem-solving processes work. Through demonstrations, trainees with a converger learning style can see firsthand how these processes work.
- *Use "problem-based" training methods.* After learning and seeing how new problem-solving processes work, Convergers expect a hands-on approach to learning. They prefer training methods such as case studies, simulations, and role-plays, which we discuss in Chapter 6. All of these training methods encourage trainees to apply problem-solving processes to "real" problems.

Accommodators. Accommodators learn primarily from hands-on field experience and by trial and error. They enjoy carrying out plans and involving themselves in challenging experiences. The students who blew up the chemistry sets in your science class in high school were probably Accommodators. Unlike Convergers, who proceed in a logical manner in their analysis of events, problems, objects, and events, Accommodators rely more on gut instinct. And unlike Convergers, who rely more on their own technical analysis when solving a problem, Accommodators are likely to seek out others for their opinions and knowledge. Here are suggestions for how to work with Accommodators.

- *Conduct experiments.* Involve your trainees in experiments in which they test ideas. For example, when training about the expectations people have for other people's nonverbal behavior, ask trainees to violate someone else's nonverbal expectations and report on their findings. (For example, ask trainees to walk into an elevator and stand too close to another person, violating that person's spatial expectations—and then report on the findings.)

- *Place trainees in the field or on job sites.* Accommodators prefer learning on the job or in the field rather than in a training classroom. They also learn best from their own mistakes—by trial and error.
- *Develop internship programs.* Rather than invest money putting Accommodators through formal training programs, place them in internship programs where they will learn on the job with some supervision. Ask them to complete a journal or a log of their experiences. Ask them to identify the skills they need to develop further.

Research by David Kolb and his colleague Simy Joy has found that the cultural background of the learner can affect learning style preferences.[38] Learners from collectivistic cultures, those that value group and team collaboration over individual achievement, tend to prefer more abstract and less precise approaches to learning. They are more comfortable with ambiguity and uncertainty than are learners from more individualistic cultures, such as the United States. People from cultures where assertiveness is more common tend to prefer more reflective approaches to learning. Although the precise applications of Kolb's research have yet to be developed, the research nonetheless suggests that cultural background is an important factor in shaping how people prefer to learn. An informed training specialist should be mindful of how a trainee's culture might influence his or her preferred approach to learning new information and skills.

▶ RECAP

Learning Preference Differences and Training Applications

Learning Preference	Definition	Training Application
Divergent learner	Learns by observing rather than taking action. Learns from others' experiences.	Use buzz groups. Conduct brainstorming sessions. Promote mentor/mentee relationships.
Assimilating learner	Learns by listening to the experts rather than from others' experiences. Learns by ordering information into logical form.	Present traditional lectures. Invite experts to address trainees. Assign individual research projects.
Convergent learner	Learns by doing the work personally. Approaches learning as problem solving. Find solutions by thinking through problems logically.	Introduce problem-solving processes. Demonstrate problem-solving processes. Use problem-based training methods.
Accommodating learner	Learns by doing and by working in the field with others. Solves problems based on gut instinct and discussion rather than through logic.	Conduct experiments. Place trainees in the field. Organize an internship program.

ADAPTING TO DIFFERENT LEARNING STYLES: RECOMMENDATIONS FOR THE TRAINER

We've reviewed a variety of learning styles and suggested ways that training practitioners can use this information. Some learning styles involve learner preferences based on differences in perception, time, and information processing, and Kolb's learning inventory describes other approaches to learning. With so much variation in learning styles, the practical question for new training practitioners is How do I use this information? Consider the following applications:

- *Employ a variety of training techniques and methods appropriate for a variety of learning styles.* Because it's rare that most trainers have the opportunity to survey their trainees ahead of time to find out their learning styles, it's important to develop and be ready to deliver training programs that tap into all learning styles. Review the applications and techniques suggested for each of the learning styles, in addition to training methods (the focus of Chapter 6). Using a variety of techniques and methods will allow you to reach the visual, aural, kinesthetic, impulsive, reflective, whole-part, part-whole, divergent, assimilating, convergent, and accommodating learners.
- *Don't assume that everyone learns like you do.* Trainers sometimes have a tendency to train others in ways that they themselves prefer to learn. If you're a kinesthetic and an impulsive learner, don't assume that all members of your training class learn in this way.
- *Don't always train in the manner in which you were trained.* Trainers sometimes have a tendency to train as they were trained or taught in school. This isn't a problem if you had a good trainer or teacher who used a variety of teaching methods. But you need to be careful not to model or imitate ineffective trainers' behaviors.
- *Be aware of how your training method adapts to trainees' learning styles.* Our final recommendation focuses on how you approach training. You can approach training in a way that will tap directly into trainees' learning styles, or you can approach training in ways that will help trainees broaden how they learn. Three approaches to training that you will want to become familiar with are matching, bridging, and style-flexing. Here's how they work in practice:
  - *Consider using matching.* In a **matching** training approach, trainees are instructed in their own preferred styles. This approach requires some form of large-scale assessment in which all future trainees are surveyed or assessed in order to identify their preferred learning styles. Once those preferences have been identified, trainees are grouped and instruction is presented to match their learning style preferences. The matching approach may require separate training programs all focusing on the same content but tailored in different ways to accommodate learning preferences. Although this approach has been shown to be successful, especially in specialized training environments or special education classes,[39] it has also been criticized for failing to teach trainees how to learn in other ways. Being successful in life requires that one learn how to adapt oneself to one's environment and how to accommodate others.
  - *Consider using bridging.* In a **bridging** training approach, trainers instruct trainees using the trainer's preferred training style; then, when an individual student has difficulty, the trainer accommodates the student's learning

> ### RECAP
>
> **Approaches to Training**
>
> | Training Approach | Description |
> | --- | --- |
> | Matching | Trainee learning styles are accommodated. |
> | Bridging | Trainee learning styles are accommodated only when they have difficulty learning. |
> | Style-flexing | Trainee learning styles are both accommodated and challenged. |

style preference. With this approach, students are not assigned to classes based on learning style preferences. Instead, trainers bridge or find ways to adapt training content so that it makes sense to those trainees who are having difficulty with the content.

■ *Consider using style-flexing.* **Style-flexing** is a process of teaching in a manner that both accommodates and challenges trainees' learning styles. Trainees learn not only the training content but also how to learn in ways that are different from their preferred learning styles. The goal is help trainees become flexible in how they learn and to increase their confidence with learning in a variety of ways. With style-flexing, trainers develop modules where trainees' learning styles are matched at one point and stretched at others. Curriculum developers and training practitioners may find the 4Mat system, designed by B. McCarthy, useful in the training classroom.[40] McCarthy's system is a modification of Kolb's learning style inventory, in which divergers are referred to as innovative learners, assimilators as analytic learners, convergers as commonsense learners, and accommodators as dynamic learners.

SUMMARY AND REVIEW

This chapter examines how adults learn. There are four general laws of learning.

■ The law of effect: People learn best under pleasant and rewarding conditions.
■ The law of frequency: The more often a learner practices a trained behavior, the more likely he or she will continue to use the desired behavior accurately.
■ The law of association: New facts, ideas, concepts, and behaviors are best learned when the learner can relate them to something already known.
■ The law of readiness: Learning is more likely to occur when what is being taught is something that the learner needs to learn at that time—when the learner is mentally and physically ready to learn.

The differences between andragogy and pedagogy are significant.

■ Andragogy is the science and art of teaching adults. Andragogy is student-directed learning.
■ Pedagogy is the science and art of teaching children. Pedagogy is teacher-directed learning.

There are five underlying assumptions of andragogy.

■ Adult learners need to know why they are learning something.
■ Adult learners bring many years of life and work experience to the classroom.
■ Adult learners tend to be self-motivated.

- Adult learners know their own deficiencies and know what they need to learn to become successful.
- Adult learners are problem-centered learners.

Learning styles are the ways individuals perceive, organize, process, and remember information. We identified five classifications of learning styles and identified strategies for adapting to learning style differences.

- Perceptual learning differences: There are individuals who are visual learners, aural listeners, and kinesthetic learners.

- Time learning differences: Some learners are reflective, others are impulsive.
- Information processing learning differences: Some learners are whole-part learners, others are part-whole learners.
- Age learning differences: There are generational differences in approaches to learning.
- Learning preference differences: There are divergent learners, assimilator learners, convergent learners, and accommodator learners.

QUESTIONS FOR DISCUSSION AND REVIEW

1. Define and explain learning.
2. List and explain the four general laws of learning.
3. Differentiate andragogy from pedagogy.
4. List and explain the five principles of andragogy.
5. Define learning style.
6. Differentiate visual, aural, and kinesthetic learners and explain how trainers can accommodate these types of learners.
7. Differentiate reflective and impulsive learners and explain how trainers can accommodate these types of learners.
8. Differentiate whole-part and part-whole learners and explain how trainers can accommodate these types of learners.
9. Differentiate divergers, assimilators, convergers, and accommodators and explain how trainers can accommodate these types of learners.
10. Differentiate the matching, bridging, and style-flexing approaches to training.

QUESTIONS FOR APPLICATION AND ANALYSIS

1. You're a member of a training team who is preparing a training module for new nontraditional students, or students who fall outside the 18-to-22 age range. Rather than going immediately into college from high school, many nontraditional students went into the workforce instead. Using the andragogical assumptions in addition to the andragogical principles and training applications reviewed in this chapter, show how your team would develop a module that trains nontraditional students in how to study and how to manage time. How would your training module differ if you were teaching seventh graders about study skills and time management?
2. Identify your learning style. Are you primarily a visual, aural, or kinesthetic learner? Are you primarily a reflective or an impulsive learner? Are you primarily a part-whole or a whole-part learner? Now, recall a moment when you had difficulty learning. Jot down what you can remember

about this difficult learning moment. What were you trying to learn? What was the concept? How did the teacher teach the concept? Knowing your learning style preferences, what *specific* advice would you offer this teacher that might have eased your learning of this particular concept?

3. You're a member of the same training team referenced in the first question. You're developing a training program for nontraditional college students. You and your team are developing a module that will train nontraditional students in how to study and in how to manage time as a student. Your challenge now is to show how your training module would be modified to fit each of the four Kolb learning styles: divergers, assimilators, convergers, and accommodators. How would you develop and present your training module to ensure that all four of the Kolb cognitive learning styles were accommodated?

ACTIVITIES FOR APPLYING PRINCIPLES AND SKILLS

1. Read each of the following statements once. Mark whether you agree (A) or disagree (D) with each statement. Take a few minutes to do this. After you have marked the statements, form small groups and try to arrive at a consensus about each statement. Try to find reasons for any difference of opinion. If your group cannot reach a consensus, you may change the wording of a statement to promote unanimity.

    1. _____ The student is primarily responsible for the success of learning and training outcomes.

    2. _____ Showing the learner how a skill should be performed is the best training method available.

    3. _____ The more specific the learning objective the better the chances are that learning will be achieved.

    4. _____ All learning needs to be reinforced quickly for learning to be permanent.

    5. _____ A teacher's delivery is more important than the content when it comes to judging teaching effectiveness.

    6. _____ Learners usually overcome ineffective teaching.

    7. _____ Positive feedback is more important than the negative comments in helping learners develop new skills.

    8. _____ Most adult learners do not like negative criticism of their skill attainment.

    9. _____ I think most people need and expect to be entertained when they are in a learning situation.

    10. _____ Most people do not like to be evaluated.

    11. _____ Most people are aware of their own communication problems and needs.

    12. _____ Learning always occurs best when an orderly, systematic process is used to structure the educational experience.

    13. _____ If a student does not learn, it is usually the student's fault.

    14. _____ People will learn what they need to learn.

    15. _____ People learn best by doing.

2. Using the following box and a separate sheet of paper, identify opportunities and pitfalls for training adult learners. Form small groups and share your summary with other group members. If time permits, identify practical applications of the training opportunities and pitfalls that were discussed.[41]

Adult Learners	Opportunities for Training-Learning	Pitfalls for Training-Learning
Adults have longer attention spans than children.		
Adults are more internally motivated than children.		
Adults have a more extensive background and reservoir of life experiences than do children.		
Adults are more problem-oriented learners than children.		

Everybody is ignorant, only on different subjects.

—*Will Rogers*

Conducting a Needs Assessment and a Task Analysis

CHAPTER OUTLINE

CHAPTER OBJECTIVES

After studying this chapter, you should be able to:

- Explain why a needs assessment is crucial to developing a successful training program.
- List, describe, and compare and contrast the affective, cognitive, and psychomotor domains of learning.
- Develop a well-worded needs assessment survey.

- Conduct interviews to assess learner needs.
- Use appropriate observation methods to assess learner needs.
- Describe and use appropriate assessment tests to identify learner needs.
- Write an effective task analysis of a skill appropriate for training.

The two words *needs* and *assessment* are almost self-defining. A need is a deficiency or lack of something. To assess is to evaluate or identify. Hence a **needs assessment** evaluates what is lacking. Conducting a training needs assessment is the process of identifying what learners do not yet know or the necessary skills that they can't yet perform. A needs assessment also seeks to determine what skills and information learners already possess. If you will present a team-building seminar, it will be useful to know beforehand what the learners already know about team building. It would not be productive to spend your time on principles and skills that trainees already know.

Understanding your trainees' needs is at the heart of developing an effective training program. Assessing trainee needs is the primary way to ensure that the skills and information you present will enhance both the individual and the organization.[1] Identifying trainee needs can help solve problems that either individuals or organizations may be experiencing. Most problems boil down to wanting more or wanting less of something. To solve the problem of lagging sales, you assess salespersons' needs to determine whether they lack sales skills. To help manage conflict, you assess workers' abilities to manage conflict, tension, and disagreement. According to master trainer Mel Silberman, assessing trainee needs is the primary way to (1) pinpoint the problem, (2) confirm that a problem really exists, and (3) develop solutions that may involve training to help manage the problem.[2] The research is clear: Conducting a needs assessment is a vital aspect of training. Without a needs assessment, the training is likely to be much less effective.[3]

The needs-centered training model (Figure 3.1) that we introduced in Chapter 1 depicts "Analyze Organizational/Trainee Needs" at its center; this centrality suggests that *every* step or process of designing and presenting a training program revolves around assessing learning needs. From the outset of designing a training program, it's important to consider the overall needs of the organization while also barreling down on the training needs of the people who will be in your training session. We defined training as the process of teaching people skills for a specific job. How can you teach people skills for a specific job when you don't know what they need to perform that job? You can't; you need to know what skills the trainees need to learn.

Closely linked to the process of identifying learning needs is the pivotal process of conducting a task analysis. A **task analysis** is a step-by-step outline that describes the skills you are teaching. The task analysis goes hand-in-hand with the needs assessment; you may need to know the details of a task before you can assess what trainees know or don't know about it. For example, before you can teach someone the steps of problem solving, you need to know what those steps are.

The needs assessment and the task analysis go hand in hand because the difference between what trainees should be able to do (as identified in the task analysis) and what they don't yet know how to do (as determined by the needs assessment) is the precise training that needs to be conducted. The difference between the required performance (the skills needed to perform the job) and the actual performance (the current skill level) determines the specific training need.

Identifying the area between what trainees can and can't do is called a **gap analysis**. The gap between what is expected and what has not yet been mastered is

FIGURE 3.1
The Needs-Centered Training Model
Focusing on trainee needs drives every step of designing and delivering a training presentation.

the gap in skills that needs to be addressed by the training.[4] People don't often know what they don't know; that's what a needs assessment is designed to identify— the gap between current skill level and needed skill level.

The purpose of this chapter is to present the initial steps in the process of designing a training workshop. We'll start by describing how to assess the needs of trainees in the three primary domains of learning—cognitive, affective, and psychomotor. We then present the nuts and bolts of how to conduct a needs assessment and conclude the chapter by helping you conduct a task analysis of the skills you are teaching.

DOMAINS OF LEARNING

An effective training needs assessment is designed to identify the specific skills learners can and can't perform. In addition to skills and behaviors, there are two other general categories or domains of learning. As a prelude to assessing needs, we'll describe each of the three learning domains.

In some college and university classes, such as sociology or psychology, you primarily learn facts, theories, and principles. In a course such as public speaking, voice and diction, or physical education (for example, golf or bowling) you learn to perform certain behaviors. In yet other courses where you also learn facts or skills, you are encouraged to develop a greater appreciation of what you learn. Courses in music and art history have a primary goal of teaching you to value and enjoy great music and art. The different kinds of courses reflect the different domains of learning. Drawing on the work of Benjamin Bloom and his colleagues, we will discuss the three types of learning domains: cognitive, affective, and psychomotor.[5] We introduce these domains of learning here, and we will return to them in Chapter 11 when we discuss how to evaluate or assess the effectiveness of training programs.

Cognitive Domain

The **cognitive domain** of learning emphasizes remembering facts, knowledge, principles, and theories. When you memorize dates in a history class or theoretical principles in a business management course you are focusing on the cognitive domain. In some training sessions there are times when principles are presented, facts are listed, and information is offered. As we learned in Chapter 1, if the primary goal is to present information rather than to develop skills, it's more an education process than a training process. But even while teaching skills, it is typically necessary to present information. It would be difficult, for example, to improve listening skills without describing the listening process or identify some general principles of listening. The essence of cognitive learning is presenting facts, information, principles, and theories. A learning module may be called *training*, but if it focuses on the cognitive domain, it is really more a matter of education. Employee orientation programs, for example, are typically presented by the training department. Yet most "training" orientation programs are information-rich sessions that are liberally sprinkled with rules, regulation, policies, and procedures; they are meant more to educate than to train.

Affective Domain

The **affective domain** of learning focuses on changing attitudes and feelings and enhancing motivation; the affective domain also emphasizes enhancing the value of or an appreciation for something. A speaker who seeks to inspire workers to work more efficiently is promoting affective learning. Teaching employees to value cultural diversity is another training topic that typically falls in the affective domain. Some people may have considerable knowledge and even be able to perform a desired behavior, such as delivering a dazzling PowerPoint presentation, but if they lack the motivation or the desire to perform the skill, they probably won't do it. While all training incorporates some aspect of motivation, many specialists become motivational speakers whose primary goal is to motivate or inspire others. Offering encouragement or empowerment by inspiring listeners to draw on their untapped potential can be an important part of training. Training's goal is to teach people skills, and the affective domain of learning is important to ensure that trainees are motivated to perform the skills you are teaching.

> ## ◤ RECAP
>
> ### Domains of Learning
>
> | Cognitive Domain | Affective Domain | Psychomotor Domain |
> |---|---|---|
> | Focuses on knowledge and factual information | Focuses on attitudes, feelings, and motivation | Focuses on skills and behaviors |

Psychomotor Domain

The **psychomotor domain** of learning focuses on teaching people behaviors or skills. When you teach someone how to do something new or better, you're focusing on the psychomotor domain of learning. The operative word in the last sentence is *do*. The psychomotor domain emphasizes how to perform or put into action the ideas, strategies, and suggestions you present. In communication or management training the goal is often to enhance listening skills, teamwork skills, and speaking skills.

What do the three domains of learning have to do with conducting a needs assessment? When you are assessing learning needs, it's important to know first whether you are assessing the trainees' knowledge (cognitive domain), motivation (affective domain), or skill (psychomotor domain). The essence of conducting a needs assessment is to ask trainees what they need to learn or to find out what they can and can't do in order for you to design the training program that best meets their needs.

HOW TO CONDUCT A NEEDS ASSESSMENT

Assessing Organizational Needs

As emphasized at the center of the Needs-Centered Training Model, it's important to analyze both organizational and trainee needs. For assessing individual trainee needs we'll discuss methods of gathering information from specific members of an organization. But how do you assess organizational needs beyond reviewing an organization's Website? An organization is not a single entity but an amalgam of the people, the structure, the history, and the culture of a workplace. Interviewing individuals within an organization will reveal important information about what is and is not needed in training, but a more holistic approach to looking at an organization may be needed.

Two classic methods of reviewing an organization's overall needs, especially valuable when developing strategic plans or embarking on a comprehensive training program, are PESTLE analysis and SWOTs analysis.[6] The two acronyms abbreviate the multifactored elements of an organization that can help the trainer gain a clearer understanding of the organizational mission and goals as well as the obstacles, needs, and threats that might keep the organization from achieving its objectives.

PESTLE Analysis. PESTLE analysis stands for the assessment of Political, Economic, Social, Technological, Legal, and Environmental factors.[7] These six external factors are likely to have a direct effect of the needs and obstacles that an organization faces. According to organizational development specialist Steve Truelove, assessing these six factors could also help identify the risks that an organization faces when attempting to achieve its goals.

To begin a PESTLE analysis, a facilitator conducts a brainstorming session to identify how the six external factors may impact the goals of the organization. Using a whiteboard, flipchart, chalkboard, sticky notes, or a group electronic meeting system, the facilitator records the results of the brainstorming session for analysis. One term at a time, the facilitator asks the group how each of the six factors may pose a risk or affect the goals and mission of the organization. After the brainstorming session, through discussion and analysis, it may become clearer what individual employee training may be needed to address one or more of the six factors:

- *Political*: What are the current and future political pressures, from local, county, state, or national government agencies, that may affect the organization?
- *Economic*: How does the current and future economic outlook (including such factors as the stock market, inflation, unemployment, interest rates) affect our organization and its mission?
- *Social*: What social factors, such as demographics, life-style changes, cultural and ethnic profiles, could affect the goals and mission of the organization?
- *Technological*: How will current and new technologies have an affect on our organization?
- *Legal*: What local, county, state, and national legislation, including court decisions, could affect our organization?
- *Environmental*: What environmental factors, including the use and misuse of environmental resources, would affect our organizational goals and mission?

As the group shares ideas, risks, and reactions to each of the factors, either the facilitator or a group recorder transcribes the comments being made. Following a review of the discussion, the group may further prioritize the risks and potential needs of the organization. A prioritized list could then be used to identify new skills or refreshed skills that employees may need to address the risks or potential threats that have been identified.

SWOTs Analysis. A second type of organizational analysis, SWOTs, deals with Strengths, Weaknesses, Opportunities, and Threats.[8] Organizational or team members, working either individually or as a group using the brainstorming method (generating ideas without evaluating them), make a list of the strengths, weakness, opportunities and threats of the organization.

Using a template like the one in Figure 3.2, individual members brainstorm ideas to identify the relevant strengths, weaknesses, opportunities, and threats (SWOTs). Note that both strengths and weakness are *internal*, factors that exist within the organization; opportunities and threats are those forces *external* to the organization,

	Strengths	Weaknesses
Internal		
	Opportunities	Threats
External		

FIGURE 3.2
A SWOTs Analysis Template
Use this template to identify internal strengths and weaknesses of an organization and the external opportunities and threats.

either positive factors (opportunities) or factors that may jeopardize a current action.[9] With the SWOTs identified, the next step is to rank the information. What is our greatest strength? What is our greatest weakness? What is our biggest opportunity? What is the most significant threat?

After identifying and ranking each of the four categories, the next step is to consider these questions:

1. How can we build on or maximize our strengths?
2. How can we overcome or reduce our weaknesses?
3. How can we take advantage of the opportunities?
4. How can we address the threats and potential threats?

As a training specialist, your goal would be to review the responses to these questions and consider what additional training may be needed to maximize strengths, minimize weaknesses, build on opportunities, or minimize threats. If, for example, an opportunity is seen in the development of a new upscale shopping mall that is likely to attract foreign visitors who would also stop at a well-established restaurant, then the added workers may need further training in managing cultural and ethnic differences.

Assessing Individual Trainee Needs

We've stressed the importance of meeting individual trainee needs, but precisely how do you conduct individual needs assessments? There are a variety of methods, and all of them have as their goal finding out what learners don't know or can't do that they should know or do to perform their job.

Training expert Karen Lawson sees five steps to conducting an individual needs assessment.[10]

> *Step One*: Identify the general nature of the problem or need (a decrease in sales; a lower production rate; increased customer complaints).
> *Step Two*: Determine what method you will use (surveys, interviews, direct observation, or a more formal assessment center) to gather data to pinpoint the skills that need to be developed.
> *Step Three*: Collect data from individual trainees, supervisors, customers, or clients.
> *Step Four*: Analyze the data to identify what skills are needed.
> *Step Five*: Summarize the findings in a meaningful way that prioritizes the training needs.

We'll discuss four needs assessment methods: Surveys, interviews, observation, and assessment centers. You can earn a graduate degree studying psychometric theory—the scientific study of educational assessment—but our goal in this chapter is just to get you started.

Surveys

The most efficient way to identify learner needs is often by surveying your trainees. A **survey,** also called a **questionnaire,** is a series of written questions or statements for which you seek responses from others to learn about their knowledge, attitudes, or behavior related to your training topic. You've probably responded to dozens of surveys in school, at work, and in other organizations. Surveys and questionnaires are increasingly being distributed electronically via e-mail or the Internet. Electronic surveys have the advantage of speed of return, and software programs can be designed to quickly summarize the data.

Surveys and questionnaires have the advantage of being tailor-made to suit your specific needs assessment purpose. If, for example, you are designing a training program about teamwork, your needs assessment survey would seek to discover how much the trainees know about teamwork. You might also want to ask what some of their current practices are in order to assess their behavior rather than just their knowledge or attitudes. You would use the information from your survey to guide you in deciding what information to emphasize (information they don't have or skills they can't perform) or to deemphasize (when they already know how to perform a skill).

Regardless of the content of the survey, the most important task in designing the survey is to develop clear, unbiased questions. If respondents aren't sure what you're asking, it will be difficult for them to answer your questions and for you to get the information you need. Several formats allow you to gather the information you seek: Likert scale, checklists, yes and no questions, ranking, multiple-choice and open-ended questions, and the 360 survey method.

Likert Scale. A **Likert scale** item first offers a statement and then asks to what degree a respondent agrees, is undecided about, or disagrees with the statement. Here's an example:

> This course in training and development is an excellent course.
>
> Strongly agree   Agree   Undecided   Disagree   Strongly disagree

By noting the intensity of agreement or disagreement with this item, you could assess the attitude a respondent has toward the course. Or, if the respondent had circled "undecided," you'd know that although there was no liking or disliking of the course, the respondent was somewhere in the middle.

Likert scale items can be designed not just to learn attitudes but also to assess the behavior or skill level of respondents. Here's an item that seeks to identify specific behavior:

> I always prepare an agenda for each meeting I chair.
>
> Strongly agree   Agree   Undecided   Disagree   Strongly disagree

If a respondent circles "strongly agree" or "agree," you'll know something about what the respondent does. Even if the respondent isn't sure of his or her behavior or may not know what an agenda is and circles "undecided," you will see that this may be information or skill that the respondent needs. And if "disagree" or "strongly disagree" is circled, you have evidence that the respondent needs to learn this skill or the importance of this skill.

Checklists. Another format for gathering survey data is to provide a list of skills and knowledge and ask respondents to check those items where they may have little need, some need, or a great need to learn information about. As shown on page 64, most checklists should not be too long. In fact, any needs assessment instrument should not be overly long or detailed. You're likely to get more responses to your survey when the assessment instrument can be completed in a short time.

Yes and No Responses. You could be very direct and ask respondents questions in which the only response is yes or no. Although most survey designers suggest that it's better to seek a range of responses to questions, there may be times when you want to have a direct yes and no response. Examples of yes and no questions you may ask include: Have you completed high school? Do you have a college degree? Have you completed a training seminar on the topic of listening?

Rank Order. Yet another method of assessing needs by using a survey is to ask respondents to rank skills or behaviors in their order of importance to them. It's usually best not to ask respondents to rank a list that's too long; ranking six or seven items should be the limit. Note the examples below of how to structure a rating scale or a ranking type of survey question.

◤ "TRAIN THE TRAINER" CHECKLIST

This questionnaire is designed to help the coordinator of an upcoming "Train the Trainer" workshop to determine your needs and interests. All responses are confidential.

Directions: Indicate, by checking the appropriate column, the degree of need you have for gaining additional skill or information.

	Great Need	Some Need	Little Need
How to write training objectives	_____	_____	_____
How to conduct a needs assessment of trainees	_____	_____	_____
How to prepare a lesson plan	_____	_____	_____
How to motivate trainees to listen and respond	_____	_____	_____
How to use audiovisual resources in training	_____	_____	_____
How to deliver a training workshop with skill (e.g., good eye contact, gestures)	_____	_____	_____
How to use a variety of instructional methods in training sessions	_____	_____	_____
How to ask appropriate and stimulating questions	_____	_____	_____
How to make information interesting to trainees	_____	_____	_____
How to facilitate group discussion	_____	_____	_____
How to design an effective training session	_____	_____	_____
How to deal with problem training participants	_____	_____	_____
Other: Please specify	_____	_____	_____

Assessing Your Communication Skills

Rank the following communication skills in order of importance to your job. Place a 1 in front of the most important item, a 2 in front of the second most important item, and so on. Your least important skill will be ranked 7.

_____ listening
_____ note taking
_____ team problem solving
_____ persuasive speaking
_____ informative speaking
_____ participating in meetings
_____ leading meetings

Multiple-Choice Questions. Another format for assessing needs is to ask a question and offer only a limited number of choices for a respondent to select from. In your classes you've undoubtedly taken many multiple-choice tests. The challenge in writing a good multiple-choice question is to write a clear stem, the question or statement to which you want respondents to select a response. The other challenge is to write realistic foils; they are the choices that follow the stem. Here are two examples of multiple-choice items:

1. For every meeting I lead, I usually
   A. develop a clear, written agenda and distribute it before the meeting.
   B. develop a clear, written agenda and distribute it at the meeting.
   C. develop a meeting agenda by asking participants what they want to discuss at the beginning of a meeting.
   D. do not develop or distribute an agenda for meetings.

2. When preparing a persuasive sales presentation, I usually
   A. develop written notes and rehearse my presentation.
   B. rehearse my presentation but do not prepare written notes.
   C. develop written notes and do not rehearse my presentation.
   D. do not develop written notes or rehearse my presentation.

Open-Ended Questions. Sometimes the best way to determine what people's needs are is to ask them an open-ended question. An **open-ended question** is a question in which you provide no structure for the respondent's response. You just ask for information and leave space for the respondent to write his or her answer. Here's an example:

1. What are the most important challenges you experience when you make a sales presentation to a customer?

   Here's another example:

2. What skills would you like to learn in the upcoming training seminar about how to deal with angry customers?

Both questions are designed to solicit responses that could give you relevant information about the issues and needs in designing a customer service training presentation.

Ideally, you should invite all participants who will be attending your seminar to complete and return a survey to you. Sometimes this is not practical or possible. Designing and administering a needs assessment survey takes time and money. Having a representative sample of participants complete a survey would be better than having no survey responses.

360 Survey Method. A survey technique that can be especially effective in conducting a training needs assessment is called the **360 survey method.** The 360 method seeks information not only from the employee but also from the employee's colleagues and those who may be subordinate to the employee, as well as the employee's supervisor. It's called 360 because information is gathered from all perspectives, or at 360 degrees (the circumference of a circle). When comparing responses from the employee and his or her boss, as well as colleagues, a more accurate picture of perceptions of strengths and skill level occurs.

Perhaps you want to assess how an employee manages conflict. Using the 360 survey method, you could design a questionnaire that includes specific Likert-scale items designed to describe how an individual manages his or her emotions, clarifies misunderstandings during conflict, tries to develop collaborative goals, and generates multiple options for resolving conflict. Here's how to structure a 360 survey design:

- First, the employee completes a survey evaluating his or her perception of how well he or she managed the conflict.
- Second, the employee's colleagues complete the same survey, assessing the identical items (not every colleague may be asked to complete the survey—perhaps just five or six coworkers who know the employee fairly well).
- Third, the employee's supervisor evaluates the employee.
- Finally, if the employee works with customers, some of them could be asked to complete the survey.

After the questionnaire has been administered to those who work with the employee, the results are compiled and shared with the employee. Usually charts and graphs are prepared to summarize how others evaluated the employee, compared with the employee's own evaluation. The results of the 360 evaluation can be shared with the trainee during a training session, or they may be shared with the employee a few days before the training.

When using a 360 questionnaire, or any type of needs assessment instrument, it is vital that all responses be kept confidential. Although the employee will see how a supervisor evaluated him or her, the employee should not be able to determine which coworker made specific evaluative comments. A trainer should never reveal the results of a needs assessment with others unless given specific permission to do so by the persons completing the needs assessment instrument. Breeched confidentiality will decrease the likelihood of obtaining honest results from others in the future; it's also unethical. Your own credibility will suffer from any such ethical lapse in judgment.

Interviews

Rather than distribute surveys to trainees before a training session, you may decide it would be best to interview all or some of the participants prior to the workshop. An interview is a form of oral interaction structured to gather information. Interviews often involve two people—the person asking the questions and the person responding—but interviews can involve more than one respondent; it's possible to interview a group of people.

A group interview is usually called a **focus group** interview. One person usually acts as the moderator or facilitator, asks open-ended questions, and then gives group members a chance to share their views on the questions.

Interviews can often yield richer, more detailed information because the interviewer can ask follow-up questions and probe for explanations. Many trainers prefer the interview method of needs assessment to other methods because of the enhanced quality of information that can be gathered. The primary disadvantage to interviews is that they are time consuming to administer. Another problem is that, if the same questions aren't asked of all respondents, it may be difficult to identify consistent themes in the responses. Also, it takes considerable skill to interview. An effective interviewer needs first to establish rapport with the interviewee and

RECAP

Methods of Gathering Information

Likert scale	A statement that asks to what degree a respondent agrees, is undecided, or disagrees with the statement
Checklists	Offer a list of skills or behaviors and ask respondents to check those skills in which they either do or do not need training
Yes and no responses	Ask respondents direct questions that could be answered either yes or no.
Ranking	Trainees indicate which of a list of skills, behaviors, or information is most important, second most important, and so on
Multiple-choice questions	Respondents are asked a question or given a statement and have a fixed number, usually four, options from which to choose an answer
Open-ended questions	Respondents are asked a question with no fixed structure for the answer
360 questionnaires	Respondents are asked to assess their skills; coworkers, supervisors, and, when appropriate, customers and clients also evaluate the trainee to obtain a comprehensive assessment of how the trainee is perceived in comparison to his or her self-perceptions
Interview	A form of oral interaction structured to gather information

then to ask appropriate questions and have good listening skills. Distributing a survey is much more efficient than asking each participant to respond to a set of standard questions.

In an interview you can use the same question formats used in surveys and questionnaires. You may seek basic information such as job description, the amount of time the person has been performing the job, education level, previous training, and other general questions. Interviews are probably best used, however, when you can ask open-ended questions.

Before designing a written survey or questionnaire, you may decide to interview, employees to get a general idea of the issues you want to explore and the questions you need to ask. Sometimes during an interview the interviewee may make candid comments about a superior; in all cases, ensure the interviewee of complete confidentiality.

Like a speech, most interviews have a beginning, middle, and end. During the opening of the interview, put the person at ease; establish rapport by engaging in general conversation rather than immediately firing questions at the interviewee. The middle of the interview consists of getting to the essence of the information you seek. You will probably want to take notes. You may also decide to record the interview, but the presence of a tape- or videorecorder may make the interviewee uncomfortable; you may not yield as much honest information if the respondent knows his or her interview is being recorded. (It is unethical to record an interview without telling the interviewee that the interview is being audio- or videotaped.) Toward the end of the interview you can signal that the interview is over. You may want to give the respondent a chance to provide additional comments about the topic or to ask questions about the process or the training program.

If it's not possible to interview the trainees who will be attending the seminar, you may want to interview their supervisors. Asking for supervisor input about the kinds of skills and information trainees need can often provide important clues about the essential content that you need to present at the training seminar.

Observation Methods

Besides asking trainees to respond to written questions in a survey or by interviewing them, another strategy for determining what trainees need to learn is to watch them work. No, we don't mean that you have to hide behind a potted plant or use hidden cameras to observe workers. You can, however, observe them performing some of the skills you plan to include in your training session. If you will be presenting a seminar about improving meetings, attend a trainees' meeting. Or, for a customer service seminar, watch the trainee working with customers. If you're delivering a seminar on giving sales presentations, watch the trainee interact with a customer; if that's not possible, ask the trainee to videotape his or her sales presentation and share a copy of the tape with you.

An indirect way of observing trainees is to examine reports, sales records, attendance records, job descriptions, or other documents that might give you insight about the skill level of the trainees. Noting the number of customer complaints or congratulatory comments from clients may provide important information about the competence level of trainees. Experienced training expert Garry Mitchell suggests specific behaviors that you could directly observe to assess training needs:[11]

- Absenteeism
- Lateness
- Cleanliness of the workplace
- Number of conflicts and confrontations
- Employee turnover rates
- Number of customer complaints
- Error rates
- Safety violations
- Sales statistics
- Number of service calls
- Number of workers who participate in organization-sponsored community events
- Number of workers who participate in voluntary company programs

Assessment Centers

Many organizations, especially large ones, have formal assessment centers. An **assessment center** is a room or suite of rooms where employees are given performance tests in order to identify proficiencies and weaknesses in their job skills. A person interested in a computer technician position may be given a computer problem to solve. In addition to assessing technical skills, assessment centers may be designed to identify the strengths and weaknesses of someone who seeks a sales or managerial position. A classic assessment center activity for someone seeking a management job is an "in-basket" exercise. To assess how someone handles routine work, an employee or potential employee is given a stack of material that typifies what he or she might find on an average day on the job. The employee is told to sort through the papers and information and organize them from most to least important. This kind of activity assesses an individual's triage skills—the ability to identify what's most important and what's least important in the stack. Assessment centers might also invite people to work on a group or team problem and then observe how effectively the group approaches the problem or how skilled team members are in managing conflict or coming up with a quality solution. Asking individual workers to participate in a role-play situation, where the worker may role play someone handling a customer complaint, is another assessment technique that is often used in assessment centers. Still another approach is to give an employee a case study to analyze to assess the individual's ability to identify problems and recommend specific solutions.[12] Assessment centers can be effective in training needs assessment because of their focus on observable behavior rather than self-reported information.

HOW TO ASSESS NEEDS WITHOUT A COMPREHENSIVE NEEDS ASSESSMENT PROCESS

We have emphasized that conducting a needs assessment is essential to developing an effective training program. But we have to be realistic; conducting a comprehensive needs assessment takes time and costs money. Many training events are scheduled without the benefit of pretraining surveys, interviews, observations, or assessment tests. How can you develop an effective training program if you or your client has not invested in a thorough needs assessment process? Consider the following strategies:[13]

1. Make the first event of your training session a needs assessment activity. Develop a worksheet asking for information and background about the trainee's experiences. For example, let's say you were presenting a workshop on improving listening skills. Consider preparing a worksheet that includes these questions:
   - What are the characteristics of someone who has excellent listening skills?
   - What are the characteristics of someone who has ineffective listening skills?
   - What skills would you like to learn that would enhance your listening skills?
   - Why are good listening skills important?
   After the trainees have responded to the four questions, place the trainees in small groups to discuss their responses. Then have groups report on their results. In just a short time, you will learn quite a bit about what the trainees already know about listening, what they'd like to learn, and why they think listening skills are important.
2. Prior to the workshop, phone or e-mail participants to introduce yourself and ask what they would like to learn in the upcoming workshop.

3. Phone or e-mail the person who invited you to present the workshop. Seek as much detailed information as you can about the needs, skills, interests, and attitudes of the trainees.

4. As participants arrive for the workshop, talk with them about their backgrounds and their interest in the topic. For example, ask if they have had previous training in your topic. Or ask why they have come to the seminar. Even when they tell you "it's required," you've learned something about the attitudes of those you will be training.

5. After introducing yourself, ask participants what they would like to learn and why they are attending the seminar. Write their responses on a flip chart, overhead transparency, or whiteboard. At the end of the seminar, go back to the list that you compiled and note how you attempted to respond to the specific questions they had at the beginning of the workshop.

A TRAINER'S TOOLBOX

How to Learn from a Subject Matter Expert (SME)

If you are developing a training task analysis and *you* are the expert on that training topic, you should be able to develop the task analysis yourself. Otherwise, you'll need to develop expertise before you can prepare the task analysis and design a training program. To develop expertise, you'll need to conduct research and talk with a subject matter expert.

Your first step is to read about performing the skill by consulting books, manuals, and articles. Look for practical, step-by-step instruction that describes how to perform the skill, and rely less on material that reviews theory. Although an understanding of the underlying theory and principles of a skill can be useful (we're not suggesting that a good theory is impractical), be sure to identify information that provides techniques, tips, and suggestions for performing the skill. A task analysis organizes the key behaviors needed to complete the task without describing the underlying theory.

After researching your topic and reading, you may need to consult with a subject matter expert (SME), someone who has had practical experience and a rich knowledge about how to perform the skill. If you are developing a training program for an effective sales person, for example and you have had little sales experience, you may need to interview one or more effective sales persons to identify precisely what they do.

To develop your expertise on a given skill topic, consider asking SMEs these questions:

1. What steps are involved in performing the skill? What do you do first, second, and so on?
2. What advice do you have for someone who is just learning how to perform this skill?
3. What obstacles did you have to overcome when performing the skill?
4. How did you learn to perform this skill?
5. What are your do's and don'ts for this skill?
6. What would you suggest someone read to become more effective in this skill?

In addition to interviewing an SME, if he or she is still performing these skills, consider observing the expert in an on-the-job situation. For example, you might watch an award-winning salesperson interact with a customer. Or, if you are teaching meeting management skills, observe someone who is skilled in leading meetings conduct a team meeting.

6. Develop a presession questionnaire.[14] Before the training begins and as participants are filing into the room, give each participant a brief needs assessment questionnaire that you can review either before the session starts or during the first break. Such a questionnaire could ask for information about the participant's current job, educational background, and previous training as well as the specific objectives that the participant has for the workshop. Of course it would be better if you could distribute the questionnaire and review the results several days or even weeks before the workshop begins. But a short presession questionnaire may at least help you customize your material in ways that you might not have done otherwise.

Each of these techniques will call for you to be flexible in presenting your training content. Based on your impromptu needs assessment, you may need to expand or condense portions of your program. It's always advisable to conduct an extensive needs assessment *before* each training session. But when you can't, some needs assessment is better than no needs assessment. You want to meet trainees' needs, not to present irrelevant information.

HOW TO ANALYZE THE TRAINING TASK

How can you teach someone a skill when you don't know how to perform the skill yourself? You can't. A key component of designing any training program is to identify the specific skills and information that you will teach. To do this you need to prepare a task analysis. As we noted at the beginning of the chapter, a task analysis is a step-by-step outline of the behaviors and knowledge that are needed to perform the desired behavior. Not only do you need to specify what the skills are, but it's important that you organize the skills in the order in which they need to be taught. Think of the task analysis as a blueprint of what trainees should do or know. If, for example, you are teaching someone how to give a persuasive sales presentation, the task analysis would list all the skills and information that the trainee should be able to do to make a sale.

Although we've discussed the mechanics of preparing a needs-assessment survey before we discuss developing a task analysis, it may be useful to prepare the task analysis first so that the list of skills and information can help you design your needs assessment methods. Clearly, the preparation of the task analysis and the needs assessment procedure go hand in hand.

HOW TO PREPARE A TASK ANALYSIS

How do you prepare a task analysis? Here's an overview of how to prepare a task analysis—a task analysis of how to conduct a task analysis.

Step one: Become knowledgeable about the skill or behaviors you are teaching. Because you can't teach what you don't know, you need to become familiar with the skills you are teaching and the job expectations of the trainee. There are three things you can do to learn the steps and procedures for teaching a skill.

First, identify or find the job description for the individuals you are training. What is their job title? What do they do? Whom do they report to? You might find the job description in the human resources or personnel office. Or you may simply ask their supervisor for the job expectations of the persons you will train. As you review job descriptions, be especially aware of what the workers are expected to *do*. Pay close attention to the verbs (action words) in a job description; they will tell you what the employee is expected to do.

Second, to learn more about the specific skills you will be teaching, conduct research. Read. Gather information from the Internet, books, and research summaries. Communication textbooks are especially helpful for analyzing communication and leadership skills because they often describe how to perform a skill in a step-by-step manner supported with research.

A third way to become knowledgeable about specific skills and behaviors is to ask someone who knows how to perform them. You may need to consult a **subject matter expert,** or SME. For some training topics you may be the SME. If you're a communication expert and you are developing your training on communication skills, you are the SME on communication.

Step Two: Identify the sequence of major behaviors needed to perform a skill. After you've read, researched, and consulted with an SME, you will want to lay out the steps in performing the skill you are teaching. It's sometimes easier to develop a task analysis for a technical skill such as operating a piece of machinery or using a computer program than it is for a "soft" skill such as listening, managing conflict, negotiating, or preparing for a meeting. Technical or "hard" skills often have very clear steps and procedures; if the procedures aren't followed, it would be impossible to perform the behavior. The right and wrong ways to perform the skill are clear. For example, when teaching someone to drive a car, it's obvious that you need to show someone how to turn on the engine before you can teach how to shift into the proper gear. There's a clear, right way to sequence the performance of the behaviors.

Our understanding of social skills—communication, management, and leadership skills—is less precise. Inevitably there will be some variation in task analyses of such "soft" skills as giving a sales presentation, developing an appropriate leadership style, and being a supportive, confirming communicator. There is typically more than one agreed upon series of steps for performing communication or leadership skills.

One technique that can help you develop a performance sequence is to brainstorm the components or steps required in performing the skill. Get a sheet of paper or go to your computer and start listing the key steps you identified in your research and in consulting SMEs. Since this is a training program that emphasizes skills, begin each step with a verb; verbs denote action. Because training is doing, not just knowing, pay careful attention to your use of action verbs in identifying the sequence of behaviors to be performed. Of course, trainees do need information as well as skills, so you will include any information trainees need. But even when it's information you provide, use action verbs to describe what trainees will do with the information. If, for example, you were designing a training program about how to give an informative briefing to a supervisor, your list might look like this:

Develop a content outline.
Conduct research.
Analyze the needs of the supervisor for information.

Describe the purposes of an effective briefing introduction.
Gather supporting examples and illustrations.
Determine your purpose and specific objective.
Rehearse the presentation.
Deliver the presentation.
Prepare appropriate presentation aids.

When you've listed the major steps in the process, arrange those steps in the order in which they should be performed. As you will find when you research your topic, there will be differences of opinion in what should be performed first. In the case of how to give an informative briefing, some experts suggest you should first think about your presentation goal, some suggest your should first analyze your listener's need for information, and some suggest you should begin by doing general reading and research.

It's your job to determine the best sequence of events for your trainees. How do you make those decisions? We recommend, as our Needs-Centered Training Model suggests, that the driving force of all decisions you make in designing and presenting a training presentation is a consideration of the needs of your trainees. Your trainees' needs determine what should be presented and the order in which it should be presented. If you consistently consider the needs of your trainees, you'll be on the right track in designing your training presentation.

In our example of designing and presenting an informative briefing to a supervisor, your next step is to return to the steps you've identified and put them in the appropriate order. You may decide that this is the proper sequence:

    I. Assess the needs of your supervisor for information.
   II. Determine your briefing purpose and specific objective.
  III. Conduct research.
  IV. Develop an outline.
   V. Gather supporting examples and illustrations.
  VI. Describe the purposes of an effective briefing introduction.
 VII. Prepare appropriate presentation aids.
VIII. Rehearse the presentation (if time permits).
  IX. Deliver the presentation.

Step three: Add detail to each of the major steps to provide a comprehensive description of how to perform the skills. To add details and spell out precisely how to perform each step in the task analysis, you'll again need to consult your research or follow up with SMEs. You need to add substeps under each major step, and you may need to add additional steps under the substeps. Your task analysis will now look like a traditional outline, with Roman numerals for major ideas, capital letters for substeps below the major ideas, and numbers below the substeps when you need further detail.

It's better to be more detailed than you think you need to be. Research has found that when trainers can perform a detailed task analysis, it's much more likely that the training will be effective.[15] It makes perfect sense: If you don't know the precise skills needed and the sequence of steps (which is what a task analysis reveals), it will be difficult for you to train people to perform the skills. A task analysis can ensure that the skills included in a training session are the skills that will achieve the desired outcome of the training.

If you're finding it difficult to prepare a detailed task analysis, it may be for one or both of two reasons. First, you may be trying to analyze a topic that is not a skill (it may be more information or cognitive based). Make sure that there are verbs (action words) that you can use to describe the task. For example, it would be tricky to perform a task analysis about "intercultural communication." That's a broad topic that is less a matter of performing a skill and more a matter of learning about culture and cultural differences. Yes, there are skills involved in being interculturally competent, but you will need to identify more explicitly the skills to be analyzed, such as how to adapt your behavior to the culture of another person.

Second, you may not have enough knowledge about the skill to describe how to perform it. If, for example, you're doing a task analysis of how to lead a meeting, you'll need to know how to lead a meeting in order to teach how to do it. When you have a general idea but need a more detailed understanding of how to perform a skill, you'll need to do additional research or consult an SME to prepare your task analysis.

We conclude the chapter with a sample of a complete, detailed task analysis.

Task Analysis: How to Present an Informative Briefing to Supervisors

I. Analyze the audience to whom you will be speaking (supervisors).
   A. Conduct a demographic analysis of the supervisors.
      1. Assess culture, ethnicity, and race of the audience.
      2. Design a questionnaire to assess demographic characteristics of the audience.
      3. Administer the questionnaire to assess demographic characteristics of the audience.
         a. Assess the education level of the audience.
         b. Identify to whom the supervisors report.
   B. Conduct an attitudinal analysis of the audience.
      1. Assess attitudes, beliefs, and values audience members have toward your general topic.
      2. Assess attitudes, beliefs, and values audience members may have about you, the speaker.
   C. Conduct an environmental analysis of the speaking situation.
II. Determine the specific objective of your informative briefing.
   A. Write a one-sentence thesis statement for your presentation.
   B. Write a behavioral purpose statement for your presentation.
      1. Write a behavioral purpose statement for your speech that is measurable.
      2. Write a behavioral purpose statement for your speech that is clear.
      3. Write a behavioral purpose statement for your speech that is observable.
      4. Write a behavioral purpose statement for your speech that is attainable.
III. Conduct research that is appropriate for your briefing.
   A. Gather appropriate information from the World Wide Web.
      1. Access the Web using appropriate search engines.

      2. Evaluate Web sources.
         a. Evaluate the accountability of the Web source.
         b. Evaluate the accuracy of the Web source.
         c. Evaluate the objectivity of the Web source.
         d. Evaluate the recency of the Web source.
         e. Evaluate the usability of the Web source.
  B. Select the sources that you need for your research.
  C. Take appropriate written notes.
      a. Make notes legible.
      b. Make notes easy to retrieve.
      c. Organize your notes.
  D. Identify useful visual images or PowerPoint images that you might integrate with your verbal material.

IV. Develop a briefing outline.
  A. Write a preparation outline for your briefing.
      1. Write your preparation outline in complete sentences.
      2. Write your preparation outline using standard outline form.
      3. Write and label your specific purpose at the top of your preparation outline.
      4. Write appropriate signposts and internal summaries in your outline.
  B. Write an appropriate delivery outline for your briefing.
      1. Write your outline in as brief a form as possible.
      2. Write notes summarizing your introduction and conclusion.
      3. Write examples of illustrations.
      4. Write your outline using standard outline form.

V. Gather, when appropriate, supporting examples and illustrations.
  A. Gather appropriate illustrations.
      1. Use illustrations that are directly relevant to the idea or point they are intended to support.
      2. Develop illustrations that are vivid and specific.
      3. Develop illustrations with which your listeners can identify.
      4. Incorporate appropriate personal examples.
  B. Develop appropriate descriptions and explanations for your briefing.
      1. Keep your descriptions and explanations short.
      2. Use specific and concrete language.
      3. Use descriptions and explanations sparingly.
  C. Develop appropriate definitions for your presentation.
      1. Use a definition only when needed.
      2. Use definitions that are clearly worded.
  D. Develop appropriate analogies for your presentation.
      1. Use literal and figurative analogies correctly.
      2. Do not use figurative analogies to prove a point; use them only to illustrate a point.
  E. Use statistics appropriately.
      1. Round off numbers to make them memorable.
      2. Use visual aids to present your statistics.
      3. Interpret statistics accurately.
      4. Make your statistics understandable and memorable.

    F. Use expert testimony and opinions appropriately.
      1. Identify your sources.
      2. Cite unbiased authorities.
      3. Cite opinions that are representative of prevailing opinion.
      4. Quote from your sources accurately.
      5. Use literary quotations sparingly.
  VI. Describe the purposes of an effective introduction.
    A. Develop an introduction that gets the supervisor's attention.
    B. Develop an introduction that introduces the subject.
    C. Develop an introduction that gives the audience a reason to listen.
    D. Develop an introduction that establishes your credibility.
    E. Develop an introduction that previews your main ideas.
 VII. Describe the purposes of an effective conclusion.
    A. Develop a conclusion that summarizes the main ideas.
    B. Develop a conclusion that reemphasizes the main ideas in a memorable way.
    C. Develop a conclusion that provides closure.
VIII. Prepare appropriate visual illustrations for your presentation.
    A. Prepare polished visual aids.
    B. Do not use dangerous or illegal visual aids.
    C. Make visual aids easy to see.
    D. Make your visual aids simple.
    E. Select the appropriate visual aids.
    F. Rehearse with your visual aids.
    G. Establish eye contact with your audience, not with your visual aid.
    H. Explain your visual aid; don't just show it.
    I. Do not pass objects among your audience during your presentation
       unless it is necessary to achieve your presentation objective.
    J. Use handouts effectively.
      1. Don't distribute handouts during the presentation unless your listeners
         need to refer to the information during your presentation.
      2. Keep your listener's attention focused on the appropriate page of the
         handout material.
    K. Time your visuals to control your audience's attention.
    L. Use technology effectively.
      1. Use PowerPoint when appropriate.
        a. Use no more than two font styles.
        b. Do not put too much information on one slide.
        c. Use the same template for the entire presentation.
      2. Bring appropriate hardware, power cords, and other necessary techni-
         cal support materials with you when you present.
  IX. Deliver the briefing.
    A. Use an appropriate extemporaneous delivery style.
      1. Don't memorize the presentation word for word.
      2. Don't read the presentation.
    B. Use appropriate gestures.
      1. Use gestures naturally.
      2. Be definite when gesturing.

3. Use gestures that are consistent with your message.
4. Use a variety of gestures.
5. Don't overuse gestures.
6. Use gestures that are appropriate to your audience.
C. Use effective eye contact.
D. Use effective posture.
E. Use effective vocal delivery.
   1. Speak loudly enough to be heard.
   2. Use correct pronunciation.
   3. Use appropriate articulation.
   4. Use appropriate variations in pitch.
   5. Use appropriate variations in speaking rate.
   6. Use appropriate pauses for emphasis.

What we've presented here is a *detailed* task analysis. You may decide that your task analysis need not be as specific as the example we've provided. Yet an effective task analysis should contain a comprehensive review of the essential tasks to complete the skill. Our task analysis has emphasized the *skills* or *behaviors* that the trainee needs to perform in order to be proficient in the task. You may also find that you need to include knowledge or information that the trainee should learn. Definitions, concepts, and principles could and should be included in a task analysis. However, if the task analysis includes too many elements of the cognitive domain, you're moving into the area of education rather than training. Education rather than skill training may be what the trainee needs. We suggest that you evaluate your task analysis to ensure that you are emphasizing skills if training is what the trainees need.

What if your training workshop will be only two hours long? You certainly could not present all the information we've included in our example of a task analysis in that time period. So how do you determine what to present in the seminar? Answer: *It depends on the needs of the trainees.* You would present those portions of the task that are most relevant to what trainees need to be able to do. How do you know which skills trainees need? You conduct a needs assessment—administer a survey, interview, observe, or use another technique that we've discussed in this chapter. The needs assessment and task analysis are closely related to one another. Before designing your survey or other needs assessment method, you may first prepare your task analysis to help you determine what questions you need to ask when assessing needs.

SUMMARY AND REVIEW

At the heart of an effective training program is meeting the needs of the trainees. This requires conducting a needs assessment as well as a task analysis.

A needs assessment is a method of identifying what trainees need to learn in order to perform their job. There are two dimensions to assessing needs:

- Conduct an organizational analysis to identify the goals, functions, and objectives of the organization. Using the techniques of a PESTLE analysis or SWOTs analysis can help assess organizational needs.
- Assess individual trainee needs using a variety of methods to identify current skill levels of employees.

A task analysis is a detailed, step-by-step description of the skills and behaviors the trainees should perform and the information the trainees should learn in order to perform their job.

As a framework for discussing needs assessment and task analysis, we identified the three domains of learning.

- The cognitive domains focuses on knowledge and information.
- The affective domain emphasizes changing attitudes and feelings and enhancing motivation.
- The psychomotor domain emphasizes skills or behaviors. Effective training will focus on the psychomotor domain but may also emphasize cognitive as well as affective domains of learning.

The most common methods of conducting a needs assessment are surveys, interviews, observation, and assessment tests. The goal of any needs assessment is to identify the skills and knowledge that a trainee does not possess but does need in order to do his or her job effectively.

To conduct a task analysis, it is essential to be personally knowledgeable about the information and skills necessary to perform the task. The process of preparing a task analysis begins with describing in detail the steps or sequence of events needed to perform the task. To analyze the training task, consider two strategies:

- Conduct research by reading and reviewing the techniques of how to perform the skills.
- Interview a subject matter expert (SME) to identify the specific behaviors and techniques needed for performing the skills.

QUESTIONS FOR DISCUSSION AND REVIEW

1. What are the cognitive, affective, and psychomotor domains of learning?
2. What is a needs assessment?
3. What are methods of conducting a needs assessment?
4. What are tips and suggestions for conducting an interview as part of a needs assessment program?
5. What is a task analysis?
6. What are the steps involved in conducting a task analysis for a training task?

QUESTIONS FOR APPLICATION AND ANALYSIS

1. Deonna is scheduled to teach a training session about how to enhance assertive communication skills. She is uncertain what level of knowledge and skill her trainees possess. Which needs assessment method or methods would you suggest Deonna use? Explain your choice.
2. Zach is having difficulty developing a needs assessment questionnaire to assess listening and paraphrasing skills. What should Zach do to help him know which questions to ask to assess listening and paraphrasing skills?
3. Sue works as a training consultant for the Technical Semiconductor Utility (TSU) company. The TSU director of training has asked her to develop a comprehensive needs assessment to determine the need for sexual harassment training. What needs assessment methods should Sue use?
4. Jake is scheduled to present a half-day workshop on the topic of how to manage angry customers. Unfortunately, the organization that hired Jake has not conducted a comprehensive needs assessment to determine the precise content of the workshop. What can Jake do to best ensure that his workshop will meet trainees' needs?

ACTIVITIES FOR APPLYING PRINCIPLES AND SKILLS

1. Using the boxes below, conduct a SWOTs analysis of an organization where you currently work or have worked, or your current or former school, college, or university. After identifying several strengths, weaknesses, opportunities, and threats, identify the implications of the SWOTs analysis on possible training programs that could be developed to enhance strengths, minimize weaknesses, capitalize on opportunities, or decrease threats.

	Strengths	**Weaknesses**
Internal		
	Opportunities	**Threats**
External		

2. To test your ability to prepare a task analysis, select one of the skills below and write a task analysis of it. Follow the guidelines suggested in the chapter for determining the major steps and then subdividing the steps with appropriate levels of detail so that another person could perform the skill. In developing your task analysis, assume that a person has no prior skill in performing the behavior.
   - How to tie a shoe
   - How to set a table for a formal dinner
   - How to drive a car
   - How to ride a bicycle
   - How to prepare spaghetti
   - How to eat a lobster
   - How to make a PowerPoint slide
   - How to iron a shirt
   - How to build a fire
   - How to make a sandwich

Objectives are not fate; they are direction.

—*Peter Drucker*

Developing Objectives and Designing a Curriculum

CHAPTER OUTLINE

CHAPTER OBJECTIVES

After studying this chapter, you should be able to:

- Write training objectives that are observable, measurable, attainable, and specific.

- Organize a training curriculum according to the principle of chronological order.

- Organize a training curriculum according to the principle of teach-ing simple skills before more complex skills.

- Teach a skill by telling, showing, inviting, encouraging, and correcting.

- Perform a set induction for a train-ing session.

- Use examples of stimulus variation.

- Provide closure to a training lesson.

D o you know in what direction north is? Stop reading for a moment and point north. If you're reading this with friends or family nearby, ask them to humor you by pointing to where they think north is. You'll probably get a variety of answers. The point of this odd activity? If you don't know in what direction you're headed, you're not likely to get there. When training others, the way to figure out where you are headed is to prepare clear objectives. Training objectives, based on the needs of the trainees and the task to be performed, provide the direction for the training presentation. In addition to knowing where you're going, you also have to figure out how to get to your destination. Most people achieve their objectives by methodically mapping out the route and then taking one step at a time; this may not be flashy, but if you know where you're going and develop an organized plan for getting there, you will achieve your objective. Determining that objective and mapping out a strategy for achieving it are also important when designing training.

In this chapter we discuss the importance of developing clear training objectives and explain how to write them. Once you have written your objectives, you're ready to start organizing your training content and plotting the overall structure of your training; you will construct your training **curriculum.** The training curriculum consists of your training content and how you organize and arrange the information you present to achieve the training objectives. In this chapter, we'll identify basic strategies to help you organize your curriculum and discuss specific strategies to help you teach a skill. We will present three techniques to ensure that your training will keep your audience attuned to your objectives.

HOW TO WRITE TRAINING OBJECTIVES

A **training objective** is a concise statement that describes what the trainees should be able to do when they complete the training. Because training emphasizes the psychomotor or behavioral domain, we place the emphasis on what trainees should be able to *do* (as opposed to know or feel).

Distinguish Between Training Goals and Training Objectives

Some people use the terms *objective* and *goal* interchangeably, but we make a distinction between them. When we use the term **objective** we mean a more specific, precise training outcome that you are attempting to achieve. A **goal** is a more general statement of what you would like to accomplish.[1] Your goal might be to increase sales or decrease customer complaints; the training objectives for achieving that goal could include how to make a sale to an apathetic customer, how to effectively manage the emotional climate during a sales call, or how to paraphrase the customer's needs. Training people to achieve specific objectives is necessary to attain the overall goal of increasing company sales or decreasing customer complaints. Both goals and objectives state the outcome you'd like to achieve in the training. Objectives, however, are more specific statements of the precise behaviors you would like to see performed.

Identify the Training Skill Outcomes

How do you decide which behaviors should be the objectives for your training program? In order to make that decision you'll need to return to your task analysis (the comprehensive list of specific behaviors for performing the task you are teaching) and your needs assessment (the comprehensive analysis of what trainees currently can and cannot do). As you see in Figure 4.1, everything revolves around the specific needs of the trainee. If the results from your needs assessment suggest that trainees are unable to perform a particular skill, you'll want to develop a training objective for that skill and make it part of your training.

As we noted in Chapter 3, you do a **gap analysis** to learn what skills are necessary and what skills the trainees do not perform adequately. The gap between what is expected and what can actually be performed is the focal point for the

FIGURE 4.1

The Needs-Centered Training Model

Focusing on trainee needs drives every step of designing and delivering a training presentation, including the development of training objectives and the organization of training content.

training objective. For example, assume that your task analysis indicates that most trainees have difficulty managing the emotional climate while responding to a hostile customer complaint. Based on this needs-assessment information, you should develop a training objective somewhat like this:

> At the conclusion of the workshop, trainees should be able to perform three emotion-management skills that would improve the emotional climate during a hostile customer interaction.

If your needs assessment suggests that trainees can't perform the necessary skill, then they need to learn it. You then need to develop a learning objective that reflects the specific behavior the trainee should perform. The list of behaviors that a trainee needs to demonstrate should be found in your detailed task analysis. *If you do not have a detailed task analysis, it will be a challenge to write well-worded, specific training objectives.* In addition, you won't know which of the skill components in the task analysis that you'll need to translate into training objectives until you conduct a needs assessment to learn what trainees can and can't do.

How many training objectives should you develop? To answer that question, you need to know how much time you will have to conduct the training. In most cases you won't have unlimited time; although some training programs last several days or weeks, most training is presented in shorter time periods. A training module is a specified time allotment for a given training topic. Typical time frames for communication training sessions are a half-day (four hours) or a full day (eight hours) of training. Obviously, if you have only a short time period for your training, you will have to be selective in your training objectives.

Increasingly, more training is being conducted in online training modules that trainees may fit into their work schedules. The number of objectives is determined by the amount of training time and *the needs of the trainees*. The shorter the training time, the more important it is that the training focus on the highest priority needs of the trainees.

Develop Observable, Measurable, Attainable, and Specific Objectives

After identifying the specific training outcomes and being mindful of how much time will be devoted to the training, the trainer or curriculum designer prepares a list of the training objectives. A well-worded training objective adheres to four criteria: It is observable, measurable, attainable, and specific.[2]

Objectives Should Be Observable. A well-written training objective should specify some type of behavior that you can observe. For example, you can observe whether a trainee accurately uses the paraphrasing skill in a role play activity. You could not, however, observe whether the trainee *appreciated* learning this skill. Here's an example of a behavior that is observable:

> At the end of the training session, the trainee should be able to accurately paraphrase a one-minute statement by a customer.

Here's an example of an objective that is *not* observable:

> At the end of the training session, the trainee should feel good about understanding what a customer has said.

Although you could observe the nonverbal behavior of the trainee and make inferences about how he or she feels about responding to a customer, it would be difficult to validly and reliably assess the trainee's emotional state. The best training objectives state the desired behavior in a way that someone could verify whether the behavior occurred or did not occur.

Objectives Should Be Measurable.   In addition to being observable, the objective should be measurable. By measurable, we mean that you should be able to assess how accurately or effectively the behavior was performed. If you can't measure how effectively the trainee performed the objective, you will have no way to determine whether the training was successful. You might, for example, observe a trainee deliver the opening three minutes of a persuasive speech. But in order to determine whether the trainee performed the opening three minutes successfully, you need objective ways of measuring the success of the performance. Here's an example:

> At the end of the training session, trainees should be able to write a training objective that includes each of the four criteria of a well-worded objective.

By specifying that each trainee should be able to write an objective using all four criteria, it is then possible to measure whether the trainee did or did not achieve the objective. Here's an example of an objective that is *not* measurable:

> At the end of the training session, trainees should know how important it is to develop training objectives.

The use of the word *know* severely limits the clarity of the objective. How could you measure whether someone knows something? A person could demonstrate whether he or she knows something by being able to define, state, list, describe, and compare and contrast one idea with another idea. A key to writing well-worded objectives is to use an action word that is both observable and measurable. Here are nonobservable words to *avoid* in writing training objectives:

To learn
To appreciate
To use good judgment
To understand

A list of words that are good verbs to use in writing training objectives appears in the box on the following page.

Objectives Should Be Attainable.   Besides being observable and measurable, objectives should be realistic. By realistic, we mean that the objective should be achievable given the trainees' background and ability. If the trainees can't perform what you're asking them to do because it's too difficult or inappropriate for their current job, then you've not written an effective objective. Perhaps you've heard the expression, "Never teach a pig to sing. It wastes your time, it doesn't sound pretty, and it annoys the pig." Don't write unrealistic training objectives. Although it is reasonable to expect someone to use the paraphrasing skill in a training session, it may be unreasonable to expect that person to go back to the office and solve longstanding conflicts just because he or she attended one four-hour training session.

APPROPRIATE VERBS TO USE IN STATING TRAINING OBJECTIVES

administer	correspond	furnish	proceed
adopt	defend	identify	process
advise	define	illustrate	promote
analyze	delegate	implement	propose
answer	deliver	improve	provide
anticipate	demonstrate	indicate	recognize
apply	describe	initiate	recommend
arrange	design	inspect	relate
assemble	determine	instruct	report
assess	develop	interpret	represent
assign	devise	investigate	research
assist	diagnose	issue	respond
authorize	differentiate	itemize	review
calculate	direct	justify	revise
choose	discuss	list	schedule
circulate	dispose	monitor	secure
cite	disseminate	name	select
clarify	distinguish	negotiate	specify
classify	distribute	note	state
collaborate	draft	notify	stimulate
collect	employ	observe	submit
compile	endorse	obtain	suggest
compose	enumerate	operate	summarize
conduct	establish	organize	supervise
confer	estimate	outline	support
consolidate	evaluate	participate	trace
construct	execute	perform	train
consult	exercise	place	transcribe
control	expedite	plan	use
coordinate	explain	practice	verify
correlate	formulate	prepare	

Here's an example of a realistic, attainable training objective:

At the end of the training session, the trainee should be able to list and describe the four characteristics of providing effective feedback to an employee during an appraisal interview.

Here's an example of an unattainable training objective:

At the end of the two-hour training session, the trainee should be able to deliver a 30-minute persuasive sales presentation from memory.

Although this objective is observable and measurable, it is not realistic to expect someone to memorize a half-hour speech in a two-hour training session.

Objectives Should Be Specific.   There are two ways to ensure that your training objectives identify specific rather than vague or general outcomes. First, make sure you have a well-chosen verb (see the box). Verbs such as "know," "feel," "appreciate," and "understand" are not only *not* measurable or observable, they also offer no specific behavior for the trainee to perform. Another way to ensure that your objectives are specific is to identify the precise actions that you expect the trainee to be able to perform. Do you expect the trainee to recall all five elements of a well-presented speech introduction? Or do you expect the trainee to remember only three of the five? Including descriptions of how well trainees should perform the skill is a way to build in specificity. Such specificity will also help you measure how effectively the trainee performed.

You can add specificity to an objective by building in the criteria for successfully mastering a behavior. **Criteria** are standards for an acceptable outcome. Being able to list eight elements from a list of ten is a way to clarify the criteria of the objective.

Here's an example of a specific, criteria-based objective:

At the end of the training session, the trainee should be able to list, describe, and illustrate each of the five steps of providing an assertive communication response.

Note how the objective specifies what the trainee is supposed to be able to do (list, describe, and illustrate) for each of the five steps of providing an assertive communication response. It would be relatively easy to determine whether the behavior was performed properly.

Here's an example of a poorly written, nonspecific objective:

Trainees should understand how conflict can happen in the workplace.

The word *understand* is troublesome because it does not specify precisely what the trainee should be able to do. And no criteria for determining how well the behavior should be performed are stated.

In addition to using a precise, well-chosen verb to make the objective specific, you could identify the specific level of performance that is expected. Suppose, for example, you were teaching trainees to paraphrase the statements a customer makes in a complaint. You may specify in the objective that the trainee should be able to paraphrase customer complaints with 100 percent accuracy. Specifying 100 percent accuracy makes the objective very specific. Of course, you must also decide whether being 100 percent accurate is attainable. Depending on the skill being performed,

> **▶ RECAP**
>
> **Criteria for Well-Worded Training Objectives**
>
> | Criteria | Question to help you assess the criteria |
> |---|---|
> | Objectives should be observable. | Could you actually see the trainee perform the skill? |
> | Objectives should be measurable. | Could you collect data to document whether the skill has been performed? |
> | Objectives should be attainable. | Could the trainees perform the skill, given appropriate practice and feedback, in a reasonable amount of time? |
> | Objectives should be specific. | Does the objective include criteria that provide precise guidelines for describing what the trainee should do? |

80 or 90 percent accuracy may be adequate. How do you determine what level of skill proficiency is needed? Again, *it depends on the needs* dictated by the job, the trainee, and the organizational goal. The following objectives all specify levels of performance:

> At the end of the training session, the trainee should be able to make a sale and achieve a rating of at least 90 percent ("very satisfied") on the customer satisfaction survey.
>
> At the end of the training session, the trainee should be able to type a completed communication focus group summary at fifty words per minute with no more than two errors.
>
> At the end of the training session, the trainee should be able to listen to an oral presentation and score at least 90 percent on a test to measure listener comprehension.

Once you have developed objectives that are observable, measurable, attainable, and specific, you have begun the task of developing your training curriculum. As we noted earlier, the curriculum is the overall content of the training program. Your objectives provide the direction (the "compass") to tell you what to include in the curriculum. But before you can begin to work on the training plans—the detailed description of how to present each segment of the training program—you will need to make some decisions about the overall structure of the curriculum.

HOW TO DESIGN A CURRICULUM

With your well-crafted observable, measurable, attainable, and specific objectives in hand, you know the precise outcomes of your training. But in what order do you arrange the training content? A training **curriculum** is the essential content of a training program—it's the overarching plan for organizing the information and teaching the skills in your training program. To design the training curriculum is to determine the sequence of what a trainer will present to trainees.

Typical questions about curriculum design include: In what order should I address the training objectives? and What content do you teach first, second, last? If you have used your task analysis in developing your training objectives, it may be easier than you think to structure the content of your training session. We'll consider three general principles for organizing a training curriculum: the importance of teaching skills in chronological order, the value of presenting simpler material before teaching more complex skills and concepts, and the appropriateness of implementing a problem-solution curriculum design.

First Things First: Teach Skills in Chronological Order

This principle is a simple one: Teach people how to perform a skill step by step, in chronological order. **Chronological order** organizes information in a time sequence. What a person performs first, teach first. In essence, you will follow the sequence of the task analysis you prepared because the task analysis should be arranged chronologically. In teaching someone to perform a technical task such as how to use a computer or operate a mobile phone, you teach first things first. You wouldn't, for example, teach trainees the function of how to "cut and paste" information in a word processing program before you had taught them to draft new information using the program. Nor would you teach someone how to store names and phone numbers in a mobile phone before learning how to turn the phone on. We said the principle is a simple one, yet surprisingly often it is overlooked when teaching communication, leadership, or management skills. Although the state of research does not permit us to make definitive declarations as to what must be taught first in teaching someone to be a leader, there are nonetheless some ideas, concepts, and skills that should be learned before others. Logically thinking through the order in which material should be learned will help you organize training content. Most skill training will follow chronological order.

Easy Does It: Teach Simple Skills Before Complex Skills

An exception to the "first things first" principle comes when you need to teach elementary skills and concepts before teaching more complex material. For example, it would be helpful to teach the skill of listening before teaching someone how to manage emotional conflict. Or it may be easier to teach trainees the basics of making an informative presentation before teaching them how to design and deliver a persuasive presentation. The rule of teaching material in chronological order does not apply to whether you teach informative speaking or persuasive speaking first. Teach first what is simpler to perform.

Problem and Solution: Teach Problem Identification, Then Problem Solution

A third organizational principle of curriculum design first helps trainees identify problems, issues, and obstacles, then presents skills and competencies that address each of the problems identified. Adult learners appreciate training that is problem-centered and has practical implications for improving work productivity and effectiveness. A problem-solution curricular design is especially valued by trainees who need help identifying work problems and then assistance in implementing specific strategies to address the problems identified.

Using a problem-solution design, you focus early training objectives on how to identify or assess factors that contribute to problems. If, for example, you are conducting a training program with the objective of decreasing customer complaints, you could first include skills of how to identify the potential sources of customer complaints and the typical problems that customers may experience. After helping trainees better diagnose problems, the trainer can present specific skills for resolving the customer problems. Early training skills include how to identify, diagnose, and analyze the problems—how to conduct a problem triage, or the process of identifying which problems are most severe. Then, after trainees have a better understanding of how to assess the cause of a problem, you can provide specific skills for managing or solving the problem.

HOW TO TEACH A SKILL

We have discussed how to establish training objectives and looked at three principles to help you sequence the objectives. Another key element in designing a training curriculum is to organize the appropriate training methods. **Training methods** are the procedures you use to present information and demonstrate the behaviors you want trainees to learn. We'll discuss such training methods as how to organize group participation, structure role plays, and encourage discussion in more detail in the next chapter. Our focus here is on the specific strategy for organizing training content when your goal is to teach a skill. There are five steps in this process. To teach a skill, you should (1) *tell* them, (2) *show* them examples, (3) *invite* them to practice the skill, (4) *encourage* them by pointing out what trainees are doing well, and (5) *correct* errors in their performance.[3] Whether teaching someone how to tie a shoe, drive a car, or learn negotiation skills, these five steps are a way to structure effective skill training.

Tell

The first step, **tell**, is practically self-describing. The first task when teaching a skill is to tell trainees what you want them to do. Most of the time you will tell or describe the skill by giving a short lecture. Other ways to tell trainees what to do are to have them read about the skill or to have an expert describe how to perform the skill. What works best is to describe how to perform the skill either in chronological order from simplest to more complex sequences or to solve a specific problem. In most cases, your task analysis—the detailed step-by-step description of how to perform the skill—will serve as your guide for describing the skill. Most trainers include the tell step when teaching a skill. A problem occurs, however, when trainers tell trainees what to do and then immediately invite them to perform the skill. Trainers need to do more than use words to describe a skill; they need to show trainees how to perform the skill.

Show

The **show** step involves demonstrating how to perform the skill. Learning theorists tell us that behavior modeling (discussed in Chapter 2), which is nothing more than *seeing* a skill performed, is a basic and powerful learning strategy.[4] When growing up, many children naturally emulate their parents. Younger brothers and sisters often look to their older siblings for examples of how to navigate school and other life challenges. Figure 4.2 shows how we learn more when we see how something

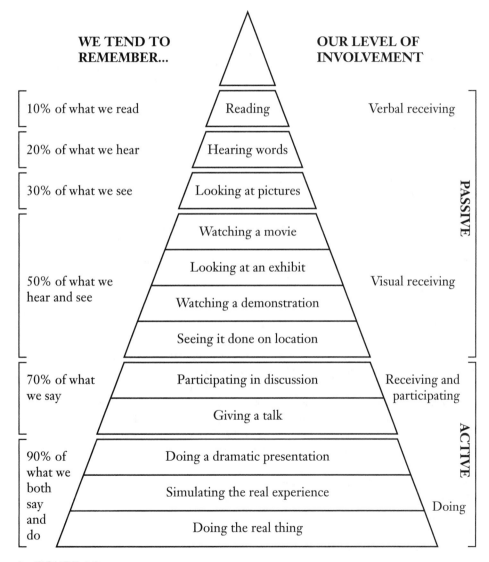

FIGURE 4.2

We are more likely to remember when we are actively involved in the learning rather than when we only read about an idea or hear about how to perform a skill.

"Developing Student's Problem-Solving Skills" by Bruce Hyland. *Journal of College Science Teaching*, 13(2), 1989. Reprinted with permission from the National Science Teachers Association (NSTA).

is done than when we just hear about it. For example, when teaching someone the active listening (paraphrasing) skill, it would be better for the trainer to provide an example of how to listen actively before inviting trainees to perform the skill. The show step need not be lengthy, but it should not be omitted.

Methods of showing trainees how to perform a skill will, of course, depend on the specific skill you are teaching. In teaching the paraphrasing skill, for example, you could ask for a trainee to do a short role play with you in which the trainee tells a short story and you, as the trainer, demonstrate how to accurately and appropriately paraphrase. More complex skills may be more effectively demonstrated by showing a short video clip. For example, if you are teaching how to facilitate a group meeting, you could show a video example of someone performing the skill correctly. You could also, if you think it necessary, show a bad example so that trainees will see how not to perform the skill. Usually, positive skill demonstrations work best.

Invite

After you've told trainees what to do and shown them an example, you're ready to **invite** them to perform the skill. The method you use to invite them to practice the skill will depend on the specific skill, its complexity, and the number of trainees in your class. Usually, the smaller the number of trainees in the class, the easier it is to organize and invite them to perform the skill. With a large class, you'll have more difficulty ensuring that every trainee understands the task and how to perform it.

One of the typical ways to invite trainees to perform a skill is to plan a role play.[5] Provide a brief scenario and ask participants to demonstrate the skill. For example, you could have participants role play a situation that allows them to practice the paraphrasing skill. One person could read a statement or extemporaneously describe a problem, and another person could paraphrase what he or she just heard. Even with a very simple role play or simulation activity, it is a good idea to provide written instructions. Write out step-by-step instructions for participating in the activity, even if you've gone over the instructions orally. While people who learn best by hearing may understand instructions they have just heard, visual learners will appreciate having the instructions written down.

Other methods for inviting trainees to practice a skill include using case studies and simulation, giving the group a problem to solve in which they practice the skills, and asking participants to perform the skill individually. If you were teaching the skill of preparing an agenda for a meeting, you could invite each participant to draft an agenda for his or her next meeting using the skills you taught. Or, if you are teaching the skill of offering nonjudgmental feedback, you could use a structured worksheet containing sample dialogue and ask trainees to select the best nonjudgmental response to the dialogue. Regardless of the method you use, when you're teaching trainees how to perform a skill, it's important to have them practice the skill during the training session. Trainees especially appreciate your inviting them to perform a skill that directly relates to their needs (their in basket); they like working on projects that link to their work, such as having them develop an agenda for their next meeting. Fictional simulations and case studies can be effective, but it is even more effective to have them work on an actual project such as preparing a speech or dealing with a personnel problem. (If you have trainees work on an actual work-related issue, structure the activity so that the identities of workers are protected.) The more realistic the practice, the greater the motivation for the learner and the more likely that the skill training will transfer to the job. We discuss training methods in more detail in Chapter 6.

When inviting trainees to perform a skill, remember our suggestion of moving from the simple to the complex. The first skill you have them practice should be an easy one. After they have gained confidence, you can increase the difficulty of the skill rehearsal. For example, you may first have them practice the conflict management skill on a fictional case study problem and then move to a real conflict situation that they are struggling with.

Encourage

Coach trainees to perform the skill the right way. Most people like and need encouragement. In providing feedback to trainees, first point out what the trainees are doing right, not what they are doing wrong. Especially when trainees are performing a skill where others can see them, such as in a role play situation, find ways to point out what they are doing correctly.[6]

Remember this important training principle from Chapter 2: *It's better to get a message out of people than it is to put a message in them.* Have the trainees tell you what they are doing well. Simply ask, What did you do well when you performed this task? Trainees may avoid this question and tell you what they did wrong. If they list a litany of wrong actions, gently steer them back to what they did right. If they come up blank, you could provide honest feedback about what you observed that was good about the performance. We emphasize that the feedback should be honest. Never patronize trainees with overly positive praise. Unless the trainee is unmotivated or is trying to sabotage the training by purposely performing the skill inaccurately, you can usually find something positive to say about his or her performance. In addition to asking the trainee what he or she did well, you can ask other participants for positive feedback about the skill performance of their colleague. Feedback about what the trainee did well shouldn't be too long; overly verbose praise often leads adult learners to suspect that you're trying to sugar-coat your feedback.

Correct

We learn by our mistakes. The playwright Samuel Beckett put it this way: "Try again. Fail again. Fail better." Although it seems oxymoronic, we learn to succeed by making mistakes and having someone correct our mistakes. As a trainer, after offering praise, you need to follow up with specific suggestions for improving the performance. Again, if time and circumstances permit, ask the trainee for his or her own evaluation of the skill: What would you do differently if you were to perform this skill again? Adult learners want to know what they can do to improve. But when offering suggestions to correct a performance, don't make your list too long. Focus on just a few behaviors. Overwhelming a person with a plethora of suggestions may only confuse him or her and leave the trainee uncertain what to focus on. Sometimes less feedback is more.

If the group is large, it will be difficult for the trainer to provide detailed feedback to each trainee; you may have to be creative to ensure that each trainee receives both encouragement and corrective feedback. One technique to ensure that each trainee receives feedback is to assign one trainee to be an observer while other trainees are performing the training task. For example, when inviting trainees to perform the paraphrasing skill, assign person A to offer a statement (either read or extemporized) to which person B listens and responds with an appropriate paraphrase. Person C could be assigned to observe and provide feedback. Ask person C to first offer encouragement about what person B did well, then to offer feedback that would improve the performance. To help structure the feedback, give C a checklist of behaviors to observe (e.g., Was there appropriate eye contact? Was the paraphrase accurate? Did the nonverbal message support the verbal message?). One way to enhance the quality of the feedback that C provides is to have a brief training session on how to offer appropriate encouraging and corrective feedback before you conduct the activity. You could explain what to do and demonstrate how to provide proper feedback by offering examples of appropriate encouraging and corrective feedback.

Another technique for ensuring that all trainees receive feedback is to ask trainees to write examples of what you are teaching them to do on a chalkboard, flipchart, or sticky notes. Let's again use our example of teaching trainees to provide proper paraphrasing skill. As the trainer, you could read a statement or offer extemporized comments and ask each trainee to write a paraphrase of your message on a sticky note. Then ask trainees to post their notes on the wall. After the notes are posted, trainees could be assigned to review four or five paraphrases and offer written feedback on an additional sticky note; their assignment could be to offer one encouraging or positive comment and one suggestion (if appropriate) for improving the paraphrase. After the paraphrasing comments have been evaluated, the author of the paraphrase could retrieve the note and read the feedback. The bottom line of learning is that each learner receives confirmation that the skill is performed well or suggestions for enhancing the skill performance—and is given another chance to perfect the skill.

◤ RECAP

How to Teach a Skill

Tell	Provide a verbal description of how a skill should be performed.
Show	Demonstrate how the skill should be performed or show a video clip that illustrates how to accomplish the task.
Invite	Ask trainees to practice the skill.
Encourage	Identify what the trainee is doing well.
Correct	Identify how the trainee could improve his or her performance.

In summary, when providing corrective feedback to trainees, keep these suggestions in mind:[7]

1. *Be descriptive:* Identify what you saw the trainee do.
2. *Be specific:* Provide enough detail so that the trainee is aware of what he or she could do to improve.
3. *Be positive.* Even while providing suggestions for improvement, give the trainee hope that he or she can improve.
4. *Be constructive.* Provide honest suggestions that the trainee can put into practice; don't overwhelm the trainee with details that will be a challenge to implement.
5. *Be sensitive.* If you think the trainee may be overly disappointed and dismayed at his or her performance, be considerate. Be gentle with your corrective comments, monitor your tone of voice and your facial expression, and express empathy and concern.
6. *Be realistic.* Provide feedback about areas in which the trainee can improve rather than about behaviors that he or she cannot control.

HOW TO MAKE EVERY LESSON SUCCESSFUL

We've discussed the overall strategy for structuring skill training. Develop clear objectives, consider the overall pattern for organizing the objectives (chronological or from simple to complex), and then map out the general strategy for teaching a skill (tell, show, invite, encourage, correct). We next turn our attention to specific techniques that help you design a specific lesson.

Three techniques, if used effectively, can enhance learner motivation, help you gain and maintain attention, and enhance learner recall of the information and skills you present. The underlying premise of each of the three techniques is this principle: *Learning is more likely to occur when learners are actively involved in material that directly relates to them.* First, we'll describe how to get learners ready to receive your lesson with a technique called set induction. Then we'll describe how to keep a trainee's attention by using stimulus variation strategies. Finally, we'll describe how to enhance retention by using the closure technique.[8]

Use Set Induction: Establish a Readiness to Learn

Set induction is a technique that helps get your trainees ready to learn. Have you been to a track meet and watched what happens when the runners line up for the race? The race manager usually first calls out "On your mark." At this, the runners line up and begin to focus on the task at hand—running the race. But the next pronouncement really gets the runners focused: "Get set." The runners freeze, arch their backs, and are poised to attack the track. They are all ears in anticipation of the starting gun, which will signal them to "Go." A training set induction is the equivalent of telling the learners to "get set." You know you have effectively achieved set induction when the training room becomes quiet and the learners lean forward in their seats, maybe picking up pen or pencil to record what you will tell them. Like the runners, they are poised to conquer the material you're about to share. How to you achieve "set"? Here's how.

A TRAINER'S TOOLBOX

How to Keep Training Interesting

To make training interesting and hold trainees' attention we've emphasized the importance of stimulus variation—periodically changing what trainees are seeing, hearing, reading, and doing. Here are specific tips and techniques for keeping training interesting by building in variety and applying training content.

1. Alternate group activities with individual activities: Switch from a group discussion to having trainees analyze a case study, video, or other presentation individually.
2. Have trainees respond to a video, case study, lecture, or other stimulus using a well-structured individual worksheet.
3. Build in activities that help trainees assess their own skill levels. Trainees like to learn whether they have mastered a skill presented. Trainees also like to note how they have improved during the training session.
4. Make sure that trainees work harder than you do as trainer: Make learning active rather than passive. Ask frequently for trainee responses such as a show of hands in response to an instant poll. Assess trainee attitudes by asking for their reactions to ideas, skills, and other

information using a 1 to 10 "finger scale": Trainees hold up ten fingers to show a completely positive response, five fingers if neutral, no fingers if negative.
5. Plan for more interactive activities, or activities that involve movement after lunch or following a break, to keep and maintain interest.
6. Consider scheduling more breaks in the afternoon, when trainees may tire.
7. Keep trainees involved by asking them to vote for their favorite suggestions or options using sticky notes. Post options on flip charts or chalk or whiteboards; invite trainees to post a sticky note on the option or suggestion they like best. Having them get out of their chairs and move around keeps up their interest and involves them more in the learning process. Kinesthetic learners will like the movement.
8. Use the "think-pair-share" technique during the presentation of lecture material. Periodically stop the lecture, ask the trainees to respond mentally to a question or write an answer on their participants' manual. Then ask the trainees to turn to the person next to them and share their response.

First, determine their needs. Sound familiar? As our needs-centered training model illustrates, virtually every aspect of quality training revolves around meeting the trainee's needs. To induce set, you have to know what will motivate listeners to learn. The runners poised to run the race are motivated by winning; they need no further coaxing; each one is ready to be first out of the starting block. What will induce your trainees to focus on winning their "race"? If, for example, you're teaching a seminar about conflict management, and your needs assessment suggests that most of the trainees have work-related conflicts they'd like to manage, you have powerful information to help you get their attention. Consider the following example of a set induction:

> How many of you currently have or have had a conflict with someone you work with? Do you remember what it's like to have a conflict that saps your mental energy and grinds on you like a dentist's drill? Would you be interested in learning strategies that will help you manage those personal conflicts? Would you like to learn what conflict management research suggests is the *best* technique for dealing with angry coworkers? Stay tuned. That's the focus of today's seminar.

The technique of asking rhetorical questions embedded in this set induction is designed to have the trainees "get set" and focus on the material you're about to cover. The goal of an effective set induction is to have the trainees either verbally or mentally respond, "Yes, I'd like to learn that skill!"

The steps in establishing set are relatively simple: First get the trainee's attention, then say or do something that will motivate them to learn. Remember, the definition of set induction is to establish a readiness to learn. What motivates is a sincere promise that you can and will meet the trainees' needs. Identifying with their needs and pointing them toward a solution that will solve their problems, conflicts, and hassles is at the core of getting them ready to learn.

Among the host of strategies for getting attention and motivating learners to focus on your message are these set induction techniques:

- *Demonstration:* Use a row of dominoes to show that what happens to one person in an organization will affect others.
- *Analogy:* Blow up a balloon and then pop it to show what can happen if change in an organization occurs too quickly.
- *Story:* Tell a story, either true or hypothetical, that describes a problem the trainees may have and illustrates how the problem can be solved.
- *Quotation:* Begin with a well-chosen quotation that dramatizes the issue you will be presenting.
- *Cartoons:* Cartoons from a newspaper or a magazine, enlarged on an overhead, may help you make your point about the importance of the skill you are teaching. (*Caution:* If you plan on reproducing a cartoon in the participants' manual, you'll need permission from the copyright holder of the cartoon.)
- *Statistic:* Use a statistic to show the significance of a problem the trainees may face.
- *Rhetorical question:* Ask trainees a question that focuses their attention on a problem or issue that directly affects them.

So far, it may seem that the only time you will use the set induction technique is at the beginning of a lesson. Yes, we think you should always use a set induction strategy to begin a lesson. But set induction can be used at any time during a lesson when you find attention waning and motivation flagging. You can use a set induction technique when you move from one lesson to the next. Or you could reach for a set induction in the middle of a lesson if you see less eye contact with you, trainees slumping in their seats, or trainees talking to their neighbors. Here's a technique that experienced trainers use: Keep at hand a file of stories, statistics, and cartoons that can be used to help spark attention and motivation when you need it; think of this file as your "emergency set induction kit." Seasoned trainers are always scanning their audience to see whether trainees need a call to "get set."

Use Stimulus Variation: Change Methods
to Maintain Interest

Once you establish attention and a motivated readiness to learn, the challenge will be to keep trainees' attention. You do this by making sure you provide a mix of activities and levels of involvement, monitoring your training delivery style, and being mindful of how long trainees have been subjected to any single activity or method. Active learning is the key. You **vary the stimulus.** As a rule of thumb, we suggest you move to a different activity or learning method at least every 20 minutes. You should be especially sensitive to the length of your lectures (the tell step); training is about teaching people skills, not overly emphasizing information (cognitive learning). The essence of stimulus variation is to make sure you change the mode of your delivery. To do this, consider these strategies:

- *Movement:* Simply changing where you stand can be a visual stimulus for the learner. We're not suggesting that you randomly shuffle around the room, but moving at an appropriate transition or moving closer to learners when you're telling something personal is one way to vary the visual stimulus for learners.
- *Verbal focusing:* Telling your listeners "This next point is one of the most important points of the seminar" can be an effective way to highlight or focus attention on key ideas. Don't overuse this skill. Used appropriately (as with italics or boldfaced words on the printed page), it can emphasize what's important and help maintain attention and motivation.
- *Nonverbal focusing:* Pointing to key words or phrases on your overhead with a laser light pointer or your hand will direct eye contact and help vary what listeners look at during a presentation.
- *Interaction style:* Vary who talks to whom. At times you can talk to the entire group; at other times, you can have trainees talk to each other. Or encourage trainees to interact with you. Seek ways to change the focus and direction of who addresses whom.
- *Pause:* Silence can be an important way to emphasize a point. Pausing before you say something important or after you have said something significant can add emphasis.
- *Reading:* Rather than give a lecture, have trainees read a short passage in their participants' manuals. Or follow up on inviting them to read about a topic (the tell step) by having them write questions over the material that they've read.
- *Visual aids:* We'll discuss the use of visual aids in more detail in Chapter 8, but consider using visual aids as a strategy to vary the visual stimulus of what trainees are looking at.
- *Audio aids:* Using music at appropriate times during training can provide a change of pace and offer variation to the training program. Music before or after a training session can help set or sustain an upbeat mood.

The key to maintaining interest in any lesson is variation. Constantly monitor the nonverbal cues of the trainees (their eye contact, posture, and verbal and nonverbal responsiveness) to determine whether you need to vary the stimulus.

Provide Closure: Tie a Ribbon around the Lesson

To provide **closure** is to conclude one element of a lesson and point the learner to what comes next. Lesson closure involves three steps. First, summarize what has been discussed; state the key points you've covered. Think of it as a brief recap of the lesson. "Today we've learned the four steps of managing conflict. First, manage emotions; second, manage communication; third, manage the goal of the conflict; and finally, manage the number of options you're using to seek agreement" is an example of a brief summary of the major points you've covered. Rather than providing this summary yourself, you could ask the trainees to summarize the key points. Or tell one trainee at the beginning of the session that you'd like her to summarize the key points at the end of the lesson.

Second, provide a psychological conclusion to what has been learned. Help the learner not only to remember what was learned but also to value the new knowledge and show how that new information and skill can be beneficial. Closure is equivalent to tying a ribbon around the lesson. For example, ask a trainee how this new skill or information can help him on the job. If the training is effective, you can involve the

RECAP

How to Make Every Lesson Successful

Technique	Description	Example
Set induction	Establish a readiness to learn by tapping into the learner's needs and desires for success.	Would you like to learn a technique that would help manage the overtalker? "One of the biggest problems in meetings is an ververbalizer. When leading a meeting, have you ever noticed how some people tend to dominate the discussion? In the next few minutes, we will talk about a method of curbing the meeting dominator."
Stimulus variation	Change methods of presenting information; vary the learners' focus.	After a short lecture, show a video and then have trainees read a short story to illustrate a point.
Closure	Tie a ribbon around a lesson by summarizing the training content, describing how the skill can be used, and pointing the trainee toward what's comes next.	"Today, we've discussed the power of paraphrasing, and we've identified the two reasons why paraphrasing is useful: First, it can enhance communication accuracy; second, paraphrasing helps manage emotions during conflict. Armed with this skill, you can dramatically improve your understanding of your colleagues and avoid communication misunderstandings. But you may still have questions about how this skill relates to managing personal conflict and dealing with angry customers. Those are the skills we will discuss right after our break."

trainees in helping you describe how a new skill will be beneficial. Another technique of providing psychological closure is to refer to your set induction. If you began by asking trainees whether they would like to learn how to solve a work-related problem, end by telling them (or better yet, having them tell you) how they can now solve the problem or enhance the quality of their work life.

Finally, the third step of providing lesson closure is to point the trainee to the next phase of the training. Show or describe how the completion of one objective can logically lead to the next one. An effective technique for pointing the way to the next step is to ask a rhetorical question:

> We've not talked about how to manage conflict in typical conflict management situations. But what do you do when you are faced with a particularly rude or disagreeable person? What specific strategies can help you deal with people who have no desire to collaborate with you? Those are the skills we'll talk about next.

Here the trainer provides a link between what has just been learned and what additional skill might be helpful in building on the information presented. Closure can be effective as a transition at any time during a training session when you move from one objective to the next or from one skill or concept to another. Think of it as a technique that can be sprinkled throughout a training session.

SUMMARY AND REVIEW

This chapter discussed how to prepare training objectives and take the first steps in organizing the training curriculum. Training objectives are statements that describe what trainees should be able to do at the end of the training session—they describe the outcome behavior that is the focus of the training content. Well-written training objectives should be

- Observable
- Measurable
- Attainable
- Specific

The first step in designing a curriculum is to identify the sequence in which the training content should be presented. The task analysis provides direction for ordering the steps in presenting training material.

The three guiding principles for organizing a training curriculum are:

- First, consider teaching skills in chronological order, the order in which the behavior's steps should be performed.
- Second, teach simple skills before presenting more complex skills.
- Third, use a problem-solution sequence to help learners see the relevance of the training.

Teaching a skill involves five steps:

- First, tell trainees what they need to know or be able to do.
- Second, show trainees how to perform the skill; model the skill for them.
- Third, invite trainees to practice the skill.
- Fourth, offer encouragement. Provide sincere, meaningful praise for behavior well performed.
- Fifth, correct errors in performance.

A successful curriculum design will include three useful techniques for helping trainees focus on the lesson, maintain their interest, and summarize key information:

■ Set induction establishes a readiness to learn by first catching learners' attention and then motivating them to focus on the lesson.

■ Stimulus variation uses a variety of methods and techniques to present a lesson and maintain interest.

■ Closure, used to end a lesson or to clinch learning at any point in a training session, summarizes key content and notes how the new skill and information can be used on the job.

QUESTIONS FOR DISCUSSION AND REVIEW

1. What are four characteristics of a well-written training objective?
2. What are three principles for designing a curriculum? Illustrate each principle with an example.
3. What are the five steps in teaching a skill? Develop an original example to illustrate each of the five steps.
4. What are various techniques for providing set induction for a training lesson?
5. Describe the rationale behind incorporating stimulus variation in a training lesson.
6. What are the key purposes of the closure training technique?

QUESTIONS FOR APPLICATION AND ANALYSIS

1. Janice is teaching trainees how to develop skills rather than just lecture about her training topic. She knows she needs to organize her session by telling, showing, inviting, encouraging, and correcting, but she is having difficulty differentiating between these five steps of teaching a skill. How should she organize a training session (pick any skill) using these five categories?
2. Phil knows the following training objectives do not meet the criteria of being observable, measurable, attainable, and specific. Rewrite Phil's objectives so that they achieve all four criteria:
   A. After training, the trainees should know how to make an angry customer feel listened to.
   B. All trainees should appreciate the importance and value of using the paraphrasing skill during periods of interpersonal conflict.
   C. At the end of the training session, the trainees should be able to understand what transformational leadership is and its several defining characteristics.
   D. After the training session, trainees should list, describe, memorize, and give an example of the 25 reasoning fallacies that were presented in the training session.
3. Damon is presenting a training session about how to interpret more accurately the nonverbal messages of customers. He's having difficulty thinking of a set induction for his training session. What could Damon do or say to establish set induction for his training session?

ACTIVITIES FOR APPLYING PRINCIPLES AND SKILLS

1. Cross out verbs that won't help you write objectives (those that aren't specific, measurable, observable, or specific):

feel	believe	appreciate
learn	trust	understand
expect	demonstrate	collect
handle	present	select
explain	solve	perform
list	compare	deliver
describe	contrast	draft
state	role play	compose
manage	operate	value
see	build	design
select	eliminate	know

Add two more useful verbs that are appropriate for training objectives:

1. _____

2. _____

2. Select one of the skills listed below and describe how you would design a training presentation using the tell, show, invite, encourage, and correct sequence of teaching that skill. You don't need to provide all of the training content for the training session or a detailed description of the training method. Just describe what a trainer could do to structure a training session to teach the skill.

- How to develop an attention-catching introduction for an informative presentation
- How to write a training objective
- How to develop a meeting agenda
- How to be more assertive
- How to respond appropriately to an angry customer
- How to use brainstorming during a team meeting
- How to use the paraphrasing skill
- How to research a topic using the Internet
- How to structure the problem-solving process to solve a team problem
- How to conduct an employee appraisal interview

3. Draft a sample set induction for establishing a readiness to learn for one or more of the following training skills:

- How to overcome a customer objection
- How to increase interpersonal listening skills
- How to develop a supportive group communication climate in team meetings
- How to lead a team meeting
- How to capture and maintain a listener's attention during a presentation
- How to develop effective visual aids
- How to conduct an employment interview
- How to interpret nonverbal messages more accurately
- How to interact with someone from a culture different from your own
- How to develop a needs assessment for a training program

Never rise to speak till you have something to say;
and when you have said it, cease.

—*John Witherspoon*

Developing Training Content

CHAPTER OUTLINE

CHAPTER OBJECTIVES

After studying this chapter, you should be able to:

- Identify and locate credible sources of training content and materials.
- Identify criteria to evaluate training resource material obtained from the Internet.
- Explain advantages and disadvantages of commercial training content sources.

- List and describe implications for training about copyright laws, cite sources, and obtain permission for information used in training sessions.
- Appropriately apply principles to develop training content.

S everal years ago, one of the authors received an urgent call from a former graduate student who had completed his degree and was employed as a trainer in a major corporation. The call was a request for sources, information, and basic content in a specific area of organizational communication. The trainer in this situation was trying to address a specific organizational problem and was seeking research and materials that could be used in training he was to deliver at several corporate locations. If you are going to train, *you must have something to say.* You must have information and skills to share to meet extant training needs.

After you have conducted a needs assessment and task analysis (as discussed in Chapter 3) and you have determined training goals and specific training objectives (as discussed in Chapter 4), the next step is to develop appropriate and strategic training content. Figure 5.1 illustrates that generating and organizing training content needs to be tied carefully and constantly to the central purpose of addressing organizational and trainee needs.

FIGURE 5.1
The Needs-Centered Training Model
Before developing training content, assess the organizational and trainee needs, complete a task analysis and develop training objectives.

Finding and developing training content can be daunting. You may wonder: What can I say and share that will accomplish my training objectives? and Where do I start looking for information and materials to meet the training needs and goals? This chapter is designed to help you engage in a systematic approach to locating and developing information for your training sessions. Specific attention is directed at identifying and locating training content. Sample content outlines conclude the chapter.

SOURCES OF TRAINING MATERIAL

Experiential Sources

If you are a subject matter expert (SME), your training material can come from what you already know as a trainer—from what you have done, from your experiences, ideas, and knowledge. If, for example, after assessing trainee needs you conclude that workers need to learn how to motivate work teams, you could ask yourself, What do I already know about motivating work teams that would be useful material for a training workshop? and What team motivation have I encountered?

If you've worked as a manager, you will have ideas about the problems, issues, and needs managers face when motivating teams. You have probably tried initiatives that worked and initiatives that didn't. You have encountered effective and ineffective communication behaviors. You have seen other corporate professionals be successful and unsuccessful. Experiential expertise not only serves as a rich source of content, but also provides more confidence and credibility for you as you train.

In a training context, personal experience can serve as a supplement or as the main source for content development. Personal experience is also a useful resource for formulating new ideas, theories, and practices in a given area. It's important to filter your own experience and knowledge for practicality, relevancy, and organizational need. It is also important that experiential materials closely match the training objectives you have established.

After you have considered your own experiences, you may ask: Where can I find good material other than my own experiences? Fortunately, there are many places where you can find high-quality material on training topics. The library, the Internet, subject matter experts (if you're not an SME), and commercially published sources can help you acquire the information you need to develop a quality training program.

Library Sources

A productive place to search for current research and information on training topics is the library. The library traditionally has been a physical place—a building where people go to get information. Today, however, libraries are also virtual places with digitized sources of research and information. The Internet surfing skills you use to access news, weather, sports reports, and social networking can also be used to navigate today's library holdings. You will find full online resources, references to sources, and hard copy holdings archived in libraries. Typically libraries will have the following resources containing information that could be useful in developing your training content.

- Books
- Periodicals
- Full-text databases
- Newspapers
- Reference Resources
- Government Documents

Books. Books are good sources for training content, research, and information, and they can provide rich history and context for training situations. Typically, however, books will not provide the most *current* materials on a given topic. On the other hand, they do provide greater breadth and depth of information than you might find in other sources.

A useful source of information for training can be found in textbooks. Courses in public speaking, interpersonal communication, group and team communication, conflict management, listening, interviewing, business writing, and business and professional communication and leadership typically use textbooks that present research and theory-based techniques, strategies, and principles that focus on the development of specific *skills*. This information can be quite helpful for developing training content.

Periodicals. Magazines and research journals are published *periodically*—ranging from once a month to several times per year. Periodicals are cyclically published works that have more current information when compared to books. Finding the right journal with the information you need is not difficult if you know where to look. Periodical publications that contain communication and training issues, research, and material include:

- *Communication Quarterly*
- *International Journal of Training and Development*
- *Journal of Applied Communication*
- *Management Communication Quarterly*
- *The Academy of Management*
- *Training and Development Journal*
- *Training + Development*
- *Training Directors Journal*

Full-Text Databases. A full-text database is an electronic depository of information found on the Web that provides not only bibliographic data but also full texts of articles that you need. Periodicals are the most common type of resource available in full-text format, but some newspapers and government documents can also be found in this format. Among the most popular full-text databases are *LEXIS-NEXIS, CARL UnCover, ERIC, ABI/Inform,* and *Periodical Abstracts*.

Newspapers. Newspapers may not be the best sources of training content but could be useful in finding current events and examples that would be useful in your training sessions. Reports on world events, training events, and training needs could be quite useful in preparing your training content. Incidents and details found in newspapers could be used to formulate case studies for group training activities.

Reference Resources.   Perhaps you need a statistic, definition, quotation, or other piece of information as an attention-catching set induction for your training. If so, you're likely to find what you need by consulting the references resources available in most libraries. Here's a brief description of the typical reference resources a trainer can find in the library or online.

- *Encyclopedias:* An encyclopedia may be just what you need for a quick description of a term, concept, or process. Most encyclopedias can be found online. Example: Encyclopaedia Britannica is available at www.britannica.com.
- *Dictionaries:* The classic *Oxford English Dictionary* (often simply called the *OED*) is the most comprehensive dictionary of the English language. You'll find it online at www.oed.com. *Webster's Collegiate Dictionary* and *The American Heritage Dictionary* are also popular dictionaries.
- *Books of quotations: The Oxford Dictionary of Quotations* and *Bartlett's Familiar Quotations* are two of the most popular books of quotations. These and other quotation collections can be found online at www.bartleby.com/ quotations.
- *Almanacs and yearbooks:* When you need a statistic or fact to clarify or support an idea, you'll probably find it in one of many almanacs and yearbooks. *The Statistical Abstract of the United States,* for example, is published annually by the Census Bureau and includes statistical profiles of virtually every aspect of American life www.census.gov.

Government Documents.   The federal government publishes information on almost every subject you can think of. Documents published by the government are usually located in a specific area of the library called the government-document section. *The Catalog of U.S. Government Publications* http://catalog.gpo.gov is the most important index of government documents.

Internet Sources

The Internet is a powerful tool that can be used to access a wealth of online information. You can access the library, public and corporate Web sites, training Web sites, commercial Web sites, and government Web sites to discover training materials and ideas. Some materials accessed online will be ready to use. Other materials may need tailoring to your specific training context or can provide ideas for formulating your own training content.

Evaluating Internet Sources.   When using information accessed through the Internet, it is essential to evaluate the information on a specific Web site. Knowing the author of the site, the credentials of the author, the type of site (e.g., .com [commercial], .edu [education], .org [nonprofit organization]), the institution or organization with which the author is associated, and the date of the information on the site are all important considerations for determining the credibility of the information presented.[1] To evaluate Web sites, consider these criteria:

1. *Accountability.* Who "owns" the Web site, and to whom is the Web site accountable? Find out the individual or organization responsible for the Web site. Typically this type of information can be found in the header or footer of the site.
2. *Accuracy.* Is the information on this site credible and true? Know who manages the site and make sure you can trust what is posted. Double checking information with other sources is always a good practice to insure accuracy. Undocumented information should generally be avoided.
3. *Objectivity.* Is the information biased or objective? If the Web site is linked to a product or service (including consulting services), you should be wary of the objectivity of the information presented.
4. *Date.* Is the information recent? A quality Web site will be maintained frequently. At the bottom of many sites you can find a statement that indicates when the site was last maintained. A hyperlink on the Web site may also lead you to the date the site was last updated.
5. *Usability.* Is the information presented in a format that is easy to access? Does the site reference and link to related sites? Does the site have location and author information you can cite clearly?

In addition to these general criteria, many useful Web sites provide information and additional guidelines on how to evaluate Web sites. You may wish to explore the following Web sites to help you evaluate the results of your Web research:

www.lesley.edu/library/guides/research/evaluating_web.html
www.manta.library.colostate.edu/howto/evalweb.html
http://olinuris.library.cornell.edu/ref/research/webeval.html

Professional Training Organizations. Professional organizations are typically non-profit societies composed of professionals in a given career area. These professionals usually meet yearly to discuss issues relevant to their profession. Such organizations provide online information, materials, news, networking, and opportunities for participating members.

Many professional training associations and corporations offer training resources. The **American Society for Training and Development (ASTD)** at www.astd.org is a national association that maintains a comprehensive Web site of useful training resources. ASTD sources particularly relevant and useful to building training content include:

1. Current Books on Training www.astd.org/content/publications/ASTDPress
2. Research Reports www.astd.org/content/research/researchReports
3. Monthly Magazine, *Training + Development*, www.astd.org/TD
4. Digital Training Content, including podcasts, videos, webinars, etc. www.astd.org/digital-content
5. Training Reading Lists www.astd.org/content/research/doYourOwn/ freeReadingList

6. Training Learning Communities www.astd.org/communities/networks
7. Training Materials for Member Purchase and Download
   www.astd.org/content/research/doYourOwn

The International Association of Information Technology Trainers (ITrain) is another nonprofit professional association in the field of training. ITrain focuses on the area of information technology and has a worldwide membership. Similar to ASTD, ITrain maintains a Web site, http://itrain.org, that provides access to research articles, reading lists, white papers, newsletters, and so on.

Subject Matter Experts

In addition to the information available from the library and/or Web sources, another helpful external route to obtaining training content is to access **Subject Matter Experts** (SMEs), those who have much knowledge, experience, and wisdom in a given area. As we have noted, *you* may be an SME. If you want to know more about developing content on corporate team building you might consult some of the following types of individuals at a relevant institution.

- Professors, teachers, and educators
- Researchers
- Corporate trainers
- Human resource professionals
- Corporate managers
- Shift supervisors
- Training consultants
- Communication and leadership specialists

Practitioners and educators who encounter organizational problems on a daily basis can give you cutting-edge knowledge of current training ideas and provide problem-based strategies for formulating specific training content. Strategies to connect with SMEs in a given area include:

1. Contacting CEOs, managers, and supervisors in corporations or nonprofit organizations. Names, positions, and contact information can easily be obtained by visiting corporate Web pages, calling main corporate offices, or visiting corporate headquarters. Attending public corporate meetings or conferences would also be helpful in gaining access to these individuals.
2. Contacting corporate training offices, consultants, or scholars who are hired by corporations to deal with training and development. These people will have great insight into current training topics and materials and corporate training needs.
3. Contacting and/or joining a state, regional, national, or international professional training organization. Membership in these nonprofit organizations can provide valuable access to and networking with knowledgeable professionals and practitioners in a given area of training.

Commercial Sources

Another practical source of training content and materials can be found in marketed training materials. Bookstores and training businesses offer a wealth of listings on a variety of topics that may prove useful to you as you search for training content. Many training or publishing companies have books, packages, workbooks, and video series for purchase on a variety of training topics. Typically these businesses can be accessed with the Internet and their products can be purchased online. Examples of such businesses on the web are many. Three examples are:

- www.trainingindustry.com
- www.thetrainingoasis.com
- www.bizlibrary.com

Note that these types of training materials cannot be used unless they are purchased.

Finding Commercial Training Materials. In addition to bookstore and Web searches, you might also review training advertisements or outlines of commercially prepared training material found in training mail-outs, airplane magazines, and training magazines. Not only could this help you with ideas for training content, it also can provide a good overview of the types of general and specific training topics currently on the market. Typically the most popular training materials and topics advertised will be the ones that corporations most need (and thus are paying for). A review of literature from contemporary business publications can provide not only what is used in training but also what is needed.

Evaluating Commercial Training Materials. When reviewing published training materials, you should make certain that the information and skills presented are based on research and recognized best practices, rather than mere "armchair reflections" of the author. How can you tell if the information and conclusions you're reading are credible and of good quality? Trainers should be wary of published training materials that present lists of skills, techniques, and strategies but include few if any references to support the prescriptions. Footnotes, references to sources and research, and citations of training materials are important ingredients to look for in commercial training materials. As with any external source of information, consider the credibility and accuracy of the information you use.

When you purchase training materials and content, you need to make sure you do not adopt the material as your own for presentation outside the purpose or restrictions of the training package product. This would be unethical and could result in a lawsuit. More considerations of ethical and copyright issues will be found in the copyright section in this chapter.

Advantages and Disadvantages of Using Commercial Training Materials. When a trainer identifies a training topic or need and locates prepackaged commercial training content for purchase, he or she must consider the following advantages and disadvantages of using commercial training materials.

Advantages

- The material is already prepared, sequenced, organized, and ready to use.
- Preparation time for the trainer is shorter.

- Material already has a track record of effectiveness.
- Training sessions can align and match what is being done across the nation (even globally).
- The trainer does not have to worry about copyright issues with purchased materials.

Disadvantages

- Material may not be well suited for the specific needs of the trainees.
- Material may be too general and not closely applicable to corporate needs.
- The trainer does not "own" the material so the delivery is "second person" in nature.
- Cost for the trainees and the corporation may be higher than that of developing the training material.
- The trainer may still have to double check copyright issues with these materials because purchasing the material provides copyright approval for use.

PROCESSING TRAINING MATERIALS

Once you have assembled a large collection of potential training content, the next step is to sort and process it. Material in raw form needs to be refined and assessed. You need to evaluate the quality, credibility, and usability of the material you've gathered.

Evaluating Material

Regardless of the source of your training content, it must achieve your training objectives. Training content must be evaluated through these lenses. The following guidelines will be useful as you evaluate training content you are developing.

Relevance to Objectives.   One of the most important considerations is whether the information you've gathered will help you achieve the training objectives you've developed (see Chapter 4). You may have found interesting information to present, but if it does not help you achieve your training objectives, which are based on the needs of the trainees, don't be tempted to use it simply because it's available. After gathering your training material, take a look at your training objectives and make sure the material clearly and directly helps trainees meet stated objectives.

Credibility of Content.   Training content is credible when it is based on research and proven corporate practice. It is important to identify the sources of the materials. Trainers should also make sure that training content meets the needs of the trainees. Table 5.1 provides a rating scale to help you evaluate training materials found in the library, online, or in a bookstore.

Training Time Constraints.   Deciding what material to use in developing your training content also depends on how much time you will have for your training session. You will typically gather more training material than you can use. Make strategic decisions about what to use and what to cull in view of the following suggestions.

TABLE 5.1					
Evaluating Training Materials					
To what degree:	Low				High
1. Is this material relevant to your training purpose?	1	2	3	4	5
2. Is this material relevant to your trainees' job?	1	2	3	4	5
3. Is this material from a credible source?	1	2	3	4	5
4. Is this material supported by research?	1	2	3	4	5
5. Is this material useful to trainees?	1	2	3	4	5
6. Is this material understandable to your audience?	1	2	3	4	5
7. Is this material in a ready-to-use form?	1	2	3	4	5
8. Is this material relevant to the training objectives?	1	2	3	4	5
9. Is this material relevant to the needs of the trainees?	1	2	3	4	5

- Identify the time slots available for your training session (e.g., one hour, a morning, two days).
- Determine what combinations and sequencing of materials best fit the available time.
- Practice delivering your materials so you can determine the length of time required for accomplishing objectives in different training units.
- Keep time notes from previous training sessions to remind yourself how long it took to go through specific training units. Make adjustments accordingly.

Match for the Cultural Environment. It's important to consider whether the information and skills you plan to present are appropriate for the culture and background of your training group. Management and productivity strategies (such as quality circles) may work well in some contexts (e.g., group-oriented Japanese organizational culture) but not in others (e.g., individualistically oriented U.S. organizational culture). As you do your needs assessment, pay close attention to national, regional, and local corporate cultures and adjust your training content accordingly.

Ready to Apply. In addition to considering the cultural background of the trainees, consider whether information is appropriate for trainee needs. Scholarly research summaries may be too technical or theoretical for a training session. Theory unapplied is not very useful in helping trainees to develop new skills. A mere listing of facts will not seem relevant to trainees. You may need to translate, summarize, or apply information you've gleaned into a form that can immediately be used and applied by trainees. Simply presenting information is not training; training provides skill development for a specific job.

Appropriateness for the Learning Style of the Trainees. Whether purchased or prepared, generated or cited, training content must be matched to the learning styles of your trainees. Purchased products can often be targeted too generally and thus may not work for some specific audiences. Assess whether the trainees are auditory learners, visual learners, or kinesthetic learners and determine whether the training material is designed to address learning styles. Determine perceptions, time, information processing, age, and learning preference norms for your trainee group (see Chapter 2). Make sure your training materials match, and work with trainee learning styles closely.

Citing Material

It is important that you do not use training material that is authored by someone other than yourself *without giving proper credit*. This applies to ideas, drawings, photographs, charts, cartoons, techniques, and so on. "To give credit" means that you footnote or otherwise clearly reference the source of the information. **Plagiarism** is the use of ideas, words, and the work of others as if it were your own. Using someone else's materials as if they are yours is theft. If you are unsure about any materials you want to use, employ the following principles:

1. When in doubt, check it out.
2. When in doubt, cite.
3. Cite, cite, cite.

That you cite sources is critical. *How* you cite your sources is important as well. When training, you must make sure to speak, write, and cite your sources in an audience-centered manner.[2] Trainee audiences are unique audiences, characteristically different from scholarly or academic audiences. In an academic journal, writing is generally heavily sprinkled with names, dates, and page number citations or footnote references. This format is appropriate for an academic audience. Scholars want to know instantly while reading where ideas and concepts originate, and they want to be able to cross-reference and check them quickly.

Trainee mindsets and needs are different from those of academic scholars. Trainees are focused on learning a new skill. They need to be able to digest and apply new concepts quickly in ways that will produce practical outcomes. They are less concerned about citations than scholars are. Citation after citation in training content is likely to frustrate and bore typical trainees. *"Audience-centered" citations for trainees involve making citations available but unobtrusive in training material.* Using footnotes within the text and including a bibliography page at the end of your training materials will be the most audience-friendly way to cite sources for trainees. You may also put bibliographical citations in smaller print at the bottom of a page of material. In summary, when developing training content, always remember to cite the sources of your information. And, as we will discuss in the next section, sometimes you must go further than a citation in developing and presenting your training materials.

Considering Copyright Laws

When developing training content, trainers need to consider whether gathered material is under copyright. If it is, steps need to be taken before it can be used in a training program. Typically, if someone has published an article, book, cartoon, speech, software, music, or poem and a trainer wants to use it in a training session, he or she needs to (1) acknowledge the author and (2) obtain *written permission* from the copyright holder to use the published materials. The copyright holder may charge a fee for use of the information or material if a trainer is using the information in training for which he or she is receiving compensation.

Many examples of court cases regarding copyright issues exist. Recent legal battles have focused on controversies over whether or not stock photos and art work owned by companies like Walt Disney can be posted on personal (e.g., social media) or commercial Web sites.[3] Public K–12 schools are often surprised to find that they cannot show Walt Disney movies to their students in school without proper permission. Copyright issues apply as well when trainers develop training material. Trainers must be very cautious when dealing with copyright. When in doubt, write to the copyright holder for permission. Even if you just use part of someone else's material, you still need to obtain permission. *Generally, if you are using more than 250 words from someone else, you need to obtain permission.*

Teaching Contexts vs. Training Contexts.   Many materials and ideas can be used and shared freely in academic settings such as university classrooms (with appropriate source citation) that cannot be used freely—even with appropriate citation—in professional training contexts where the trainer is being paid. For example, the **Personal Report of Communication Apprehension (PRCA)** instrument[4]— a communication evaluation tool constructed by communication scholars James McCroskey and Virginia Richmond—can be used freely in nonprofit educational settings such as university classrooms. You need only to properly cite the source and give credit to the authors.

If, however, a trainer is being paid to conduct training on communication apprehension and he or she wants to use the PRCA in this training, the trainer should obtain permission from the authors. In "for profit" training contexts, you should:

1. Use only public domain materials (materials that are not copyrighted or materials for which the copyright has expired).
2. Develop original materials yourself.
3. Obtain legal written permission for training content you have located, which may involve paying royalties to the original sources of the material.

Most training corporations that produce commercial material for use in training seminars will require you to purchase a set of their materials for each trainee in your training group.

Obtaining Copyright Permission.   What is the procedure for obtaining permission for materials you wish to use? You need to write to the person or publishing company who holds the copyright to the material. You'll find the name and usually the address of the copyright holder on the title page of the material you are using.

A TRAINER'S TOOLBOX

Dear Permissions Editor:

I am writing to ask your permission to include (all that apply) the following material:
- Reprint
- photocopy
- copy in digital form
- quote from
- incorporate into
  - multimedia courseware
  - online course materials
  - a dissertation/thesis
  - a print publication
  - an electronic publication

Author:

Book Title:

Journal Title: Vol.:   Issue:

Page #(s)   Figure/Image #(s)   Table #(s)
or material located at: [url].

The material will be distributed/published as follows:

Distribution (describe, including medium): Publisher (if applicable): Expected distribution/publication date:
Expected length of work (number of words, pages, images, etc., as appropriate): Target market:
If you do not solely control copyright in the requested materials, I would appreciate any information you can
provide about others to whom I should write, including most recent contact information, if available.

Sincerely,

Rightsholder, please initial any statement that applies below:
- I hereby represent that I have the authority to grant the permission requested herein.
- I am the sole owner/author of the work.

Author Signature   Company Signature

_____   _____

Address: _____   Title: _____

_____   Company: _____

Date: _____   Date: _____

RECAP

How to Process Training Materials

1. Evaluate the quality, credibility, and usability of the material, especially with your audience in mind. Determine the following:

   - What is the source of the material?
   - What is the authority and credibility of the source?
   - Is the source biased?
   - Can this material be applied in the trainee context?

2. Discover who owns materials you want to use in your training sessions and what the use restrictions are for these copyrighted materials.

   - Check the bibliography of the source.
   - If the author cannot be determined from this information, write to the publisher of the materials.
   - Ask the publisher about the restrictions for copyrighted materials.

3. Follow procedures carefully for soliciting and obtaining permission to use copyrighted materials.

   - Contact the publisher and author (by letter, fax, or e-mail).
   - Tell them who you are and what material you would like to use.
   - Tell them why, how, when, and with whom you want to use this material.
   - If the copyright holder agrees to grant permission for you to use the material, ask him or her to sign a release form granting permission and return the form to you (sometimes the publisher has a release form that could be used).
   - Keep your letters and signed release forms on file.

If you do not know the address of the material owner, the following suggestions provide good places to start.

1. Look for contact information on the material. Frequently the contact information will reference the publisher. Many times a telephone number, a Web site listing, or an address will be listed on the materials.
2. Do a Web search for the publisher of the materials.
3. Do a Web search for the author and the copyrighted materials.
4. Enlist the aid of a librarian or a bookstore salesperson to obtain contact information for the publisher and author.

The sample letter in *A Trainer's Toolbox* on page 117 is a guide for writing for permission to use copyrighted material.

SAMPLE TRAINING CONTENT OUTLINES

As you assemble your need-centered training content and activities, it is important to review what already exists in the training market. What skills and content are typically covered in a training session on your topic? In what order are they presented? You'll find that many training programs cover similar concepts but do so from different perspectives and in different ways. Though there are similarities between training programs on a given topic, there will generally be something unique to each program. Typically what makes a training program unique is its adaptation to the special needs of the trainees. After reviewing existing program outlines, identify what is missing or what is not being addressed. Most important: *What skills and content are missing that your trainees need?*

The following brief outlines illustrate typical training content outlines. In many cases, a training content outline resembles the task analysis that we discussed in Chapter 3; it presents an overview of the steps needed to enhance the skill being taught. The difference between the training content outline and the task analysis is that the content outline may not be as detailed as the task analysis. But, like a task analysis, *training content outlines should emphasize skills, not theory.* Because we've stressed the importance of meeting trainees' needs, we recommend that you always customize your training content to your specific training situation. The sample outlines here should be used only as a point of departure for developing training content. The outlines that follow cover the topics of improving listening skills, conflict management skills, and skills for conducting effective meetings.

Improving Listening Skills

People are likely to receive more training about speaking than about listening. Sometimes the results of listening deficiencies or bad habits are merely annoying in a business context. At other times, the results can be disastrous and cost the individual and the company both time and money. The following outline presents content and skills that are typically covered in a training program for listening skill building.

Improving Listening Skills
A. The need for effective listening
B. Why don't we listen well? How to identify barriers to effective listening
   1. How to identify physical barriers
   2. How to identify semantic barriers
   3. How to identify psychological barriers
C. How to overcome bad listening habits
   1. Listen deeply and attentively before formulating a response
   2. Wait until the other person finishes talking before you start
   3. Focus total attention on the conversation (don't multi-task)
   4. Make sure you let the speaker finish his or her thoughts before you speak
   5. Focus on the content of the message rather than on external factors
D. How to improve listening skill
   1. Assess current listening strengths and weaknesses
   2. Promote awareness of strengths and weaknesses
   3. Overcome barriers to effective listening
   4. Focus all attention on the speaker while he or she is speaking
   5. Be objective and open to what the other person is saying
   6. Engage in active listening

E. How to improve empathy skills
   1. Tune out distractions and focus on the other person
   2. Increase awareness of nonverbal cues
   3. Comprehend spoken messages
   4. Imagine what others may be feeling
   5. Check perceptions
F. How to improve feedback skills
   1. Provide responses that are accurate
   2. Provide responses that are timely
   3. Provide responses that are supportive

Conflict Management Skills

One of the most popular and most frequently requested training topics is that of managing conflict. Contemporary perspectives suggest that conflict serves a constructive purpose when managed properly. Without an understanding of conflict, how it operates, where it comes from, and, more important from a training standpoint, how to manage it, problem situations can damage employee morale, slow productivity, cause employee turnover, and effectively slow or halt the achievement of organizational goals. The following outline provides initial ideas for the basic approaches and skills that are covered in conflict management training sessions.

Conflict Management Approaches
   I. Identify conflict components
      A. How to identify causes of conflict
      B. How to identify types of conflict
         1. Intrapersonal conflict
         2. Interpersonal conflict
         3. Role conflict
      C. How to identify conflict stages
         1. Prior conditions
         2. Frustration awareness
         3. Active conflict
         4. Resolution
         5. Follow-up
      D. How to identify effects of conflict to make conflict constructive
         1. Strategies for identifying destructive conflict
         2. Strategies for identifying constructive conflict
      E. How to identify and assess conflict styles
         1. Assessing the nonconfrontational style
         2. Assessing the confrontational style
         3. Assessing the cooperative style
   II. Conflict management skills
      A. How to manage emotions
         1. Managing your own emotions
         2. Managing emotions of others

  B. How to manage goals
1. Identify surface and deep goals for each party
2. Identify parameters for goals
3. Consider goals in the larger corporate context
  C. How to manage communication
1. Establish interaction ground rules
2. Establish a protocol for each voice to be heard
3. Establish rules for questions and challenges
  D. How to manage issues and problems
1. Establish a default procedure when unexpected factors become a part of the conversation
2. Track new situations, issues, or problems back to the communication interaction ground rules
3. Prioritize new issues within the context of the primary issue

Managing Meetings

Most employees have participated in unproductive meetings. Frequently employees will think (and sometimes even say out loud) Why do I have to be at this useless, droning meeting when I could be back at my desk getting some work done? Given all the unproductive meetings most people have attended, participating in a well-conducted meeting is like receiving a cup of cold water in the desert. Good meetings do not happen by accident; they are planned and carefully facilitated. The following outline includes classic content for enhancing the quality of meetings.

Skills for Conducting Effective Meetings
  A. How to identify purposes for holding meetings
1. Disseminate information quickly
2. Brainstorm solutions for group problems
3. Obtain information from group members
4. Assessment and evaluation
  B. How to avoid common problems for meetings
1. Insufficient cause or need
2. Unclear communication of purpose, time, and necessary preparation
3. Physical and psychological distractions in meeting location
4. Bad timing for meeting
5. Starting and ending late
6. No clear meeting agenda
7. Meeting does not accomplish purposes
8. Topics not on agenda take over the meeting
9. Interpersonal problems in the meeting
10. Lack of participation from meeting attendees
  C. How to plan a meeting
1. Make sure there is a definite need for a meeting
2. Pay careful attention to date, time, and place
3. Notify all group members in advance

   4. Notify all group members of information or considerations they need to have in preparation for the meeting
   5. Send reminders for the meeting
D. How to develop the meeting agenda
   1. Determine the meeting goal
   2. Determine the information that needs to be presented to achieve the goal
   3. Develop a sequence of agenda items to achieve the meeting goal
E. How to facilitate an effective meeting
   1. Start on time
   2. Provide an orientation to the agenda
   3. Preview the planned duration of the meeting
   4. Preview the objectives or desired results or goals for the meeting
   5. Get into the "body" of the meeting quickly
   6. Facilitate participation
   7. Keep things moving; don't allow the meeting to stall
   8. Don't allow one person to dominate the discussion
   9. Deal politely but effectively with problem people
   10. Move effectively from section to section
F. How to conclude the meeting
   1. Review the purpose of the meeting
   2. Summarize meeting activities
   3. Review action steps
   4. Preview future action or meetings
   5. Adjourn on time

SUMMARY AND REVIEW

When you develop content for a training program, it is wise to have a strategic and systematic plan.

■ You need to find relevant and current sources of content for your topic. There are many sources of information from your experience, in the library, on the web, from subject matter experts, and from commercial products. All these gathered materials need to be screened and processed. What is relevant? What is useful? How can this material be processed and used in a way that would work in a training program? Make sure that you cover all bases completely when it comes to copyright and

permission. Make sure to give credit where credit is due and gain permission to use materials when they are not your own.

■ Your next task is to assemble your concepts and skill steps into a training content outline that is tailored to your specific training audience.

As a trainer, there are many creative and effective training approaches, materials, and activities that you can create yourself. Once you gather and create all of your materials, you need to consider carefully how to put all your materials together in a fabulous training program, making sure to consider the range of audience and context needs as you do so.

QUESTIONS FOR DISCUSSION AND REVIEW

1. What are four sources of training material? Evaluate their usefulness in developing content for a training program.
2. What are criteria for evaluating web sources?
3. Describe at least three library sources that can help you develop training information. What are the relative strengths of each source?
4. When is it advantageous and useful to use commercial products for developing training material? When is it disadvantageous?
5. When is it necessary to obtain permission to use copyrighted material?

QUESTIONS FOR APPLICATION AND ANALYSIS

1. Daniel has a draft of a training session outline, but the Internet sites he is using to provide content for his session are questionable. Develop a checklist of Internet evaluation criteria to present to Daniel so he can evaluate all his sources and upgrade.
2. Imagine that you are being paid to present training sessions for middle management in a prestigious accounting organization. You want to assess the communication styles of your trainees and have found a useful evaluation instrument that does this nicely. Should you only cite the source of the instrument in the training booklet, or should you obtain author permission to use this instrument in your training? Discuss the steps needed for each approach.
3. Bethany is doing training on nonverbal communication for a large shipping firm. She has found a Web site that provides "research" on how people should dress for work. How does she know whether the research has been conducted scientifically? How should Bethany evaluate this Web site and its information and decide whether or not to use this information in her training session?

ACTIVITIES FOR APPLYING PRINCIPLES AND SKILLS

1. You have been asked to do a training session on improving interviewing skills. Make a list of things you have *experienced* and *know* about good communication in interview situations, from an interviewer and from an interviewee perspective. Share your list with others in your group and formulate a group content outline for a training session.
2. You have been asked to deliver training sessions on How to Conduct Effective Video Conference Sessions. Before the next training session, assign each member in your group to locate potential training content on this topic from one of the following:
   (a) library sources, (b) Internet sources, (c) commercial sources, (d) subject matter expert. Bring this material to the next session and start building a content outline on this topic.
3. Locate coverage of a recent world event in a newspaper and use it to build a case study on the topic Using Effective Stress Management Techniques for Corporate Workers. Formulate application questions and build a role play to exemplify best practice principles.
4. You have been assigned to train managers from a large retail chain of electronics stores to do annual assessments of their sales staff in the area of effective "selling" techniques. Go online and find a commercially produced training package on Conducting Performance Appraisals. Examine the table of contents for this training package using evaluation questions from Table 5.1. Share your observations with the group.
5. Visit the U.S. Copyright Office Web page on the Internet (www.copyright.gov) and select five relevant questions from the Frequently Asked Questions page. Relate these questions to developing training materials. Have trainees discuss these questions in groups and then come up with a joint best practices list.
6. Based on people you know (faculty, friends, colleagues, coworkers), prepare a list of Subject Matter Experts (SMEs) on the topic Corporate Team Building and Motivation. The lists should include contact information for each SME. In groups, discuss and share these lists and then develop questions that you could ask each SME that would assist you in preparing training content.

What I hear, I forget.
What I see, I remember.
What I do, I understand.
— *Confucius*

Using Training Methods

CHAPTER OBJECTIVES

After studying this chapter, you should be able to:

- List and define training methods including lectures, experiential activities, and guided discussions, and compare the advantages and disadvantages of each training method.

- Apply the strategies for developing and presenting an effective, interesting, and interactive lecture through practice.

- Explain the four-step process of managing experiential activities: planning, preparing, presenting, assessing (PPPA).

- Identify types of role plays and case studies a trainer can use and give strategies for using them effectively.

- List and explain the four steps of the EDIT process trainers use to unpack experiential activities.

- Define and explain the importance of facilitated discussion and demonstrate the skills for guiding a discussion.

- Identify and discuss the criteria for selecting the best training method.

125

" **I**cannot believe we have to do this" many trainees mumble under their breath when trainers ask them to participate or get involved in the training content. Some instructors ask their trainees to role-play scenarios or to work through simulations. Others ask their trainees to demonstrate a process or to make formal presentations. What some trainees don't understand is that most trainers have a method to the madness they create in the training classroom.

Most professional trainers do not simply walk into the training classroom and make learning occur. It's not that easy. What trainees don't see is the many hours of preparation that it takes a trainer to remain effective in the training classroom. As a trainee, when you learn something new and the learning was fun and somewhat effortless, you can be assured that your trainer invested *numerous* hours to make it happen. Most of that time was spent in developing a training method, which is the focus of this chapter.

A **training method** is the procedure you use to present the training content (discussed in Chapter 5) in order to demonstrate the behaviors you want trainees to learn. Many trainers use a variety of methods not only to convey their content, but also to involve trainees with the training. Some professional trainers open a training session with a short lecture and then move into an activity where trainees are asked to use the training content. Once this is finished, trainees are then placed in small discussion groups where they're asked to apply the training content to different situations. What most trainees don't see is that all this activity is a carefully orchestrated training method designed to enhance their learning.

Trainers use several types of methods in the training classroom. We're going to discuss three of the more popular categories: lecturing, conducting experiential activities, and facilitating group discussions. This chapter concludes with our recommendations for how to select the best method for your training program.

LECTURING

Lecturing remains one of the most popular training methods among trainers. Being a student, you're quite familiar with the lecture method; many professors lecture in their courses. In a **lecture,** trainers use oral messages to impart large amounts of prepared information to trainees using one-way communication. Trainers are the source of the information, and trainees are the receivers of the information.

How to Develop Lectures

Even though the lecture has a number of strengths, it's usually ranked low in terms of popularity by students, and with good reason. Many trainees complain that the lecture is too trainer-focused and doesn't allow trainees to interact and discuss the content. Although these complaints are valid in many training rooms, it's usually the *lecturer,* not the *method,* that is the problem. A lecture doesn't have to be boring. The modified lecture, or what we call the lecture/discussion, focuses on conveying a lot of new and prepared information to trainees in a short amount of time, but the information is presented in a manner where it is *perceived* as being interactive or as a discussion between trainer and trainees. The important word here is *perceived*. It's not really an interactive discussion because it's next to impossible to have a discussion when you have many trainees and time is limited. But you can modify a lecture so that it focuses more on the needs of the trainee. There are strategies for modifying the traditional lecture to make it more interactive; many of them were introduced in Chapter 2, which examined how adults learn through relevance, organization, schema development, redundancy, engagement, and immediacy.[1]

Create Relevance.   Effective trainers make their lecture content relevant or useful for trainees. Trainees should never want to ask "Why do we have to know this stuff?" or "Why do we have to do this?" Let your trainees know up front why the training content is important to them and their work. Many trainees will resist change until they're convinced that a new procedure or set of behaviors will make their work easier. It's your job to show them *how* the training content will improve their work life. Here are suggestions:

- *Tell a story*. Begin by telling a story that highlights a problem that your participants can identify as occurring on a regular basis. Ask participants to complete the story. What happens when the problem is not managed appropriately? What will happen if the problem is managed appropriately? Share how the training will help participants manage similar problems.
- *Use pictures and videos*. Carefully take pictures or videos of the problem and show the media to the training participants. For example, if you're training in how to manage a meeting, videotape an actual meeting and play it back to your trainees. Ask them to identify problems and explain why they occurred and how to remedy them. If you're training in phone skills, play back conversations from a call center.
- *Pre-assess participants' knowledge and skills*. Give trainees a quiz or ask them to perform a task. Use their quiz scores or their demonstrations to illustrate how their knowledge and skills will be enhanced through the training program you will deliver.

Organize Content.   For North American trainees, effective trainers develop and present lectures that are well organized and chunked. An effective lecture tells a story; it has an introduction, a body, and a conclusion. In the **introduction**, trainers stimulate trainees' interest by leading off with a story, an interesting visual aid, a relevant case study, or a provocative question. Before moving into the body of their lecture, trainers **preview** the lecture, letting trainees know what's ahead. In the **body** of the lecture, trainers organize or chunk their content around three or four main points or ideas. Here's how you can help keep your trainees from getting lost in the lecture:

- *Use signposts*. A **signpost** is a verbal or nonverbal message that tells trainees where they are in a lecture. Signposts might sound like this: "The first point is . . . The second point is . . . The third point is . . . "
- *Use internal reviews and previews*. **Internal review and preview** messages remind trainees where they've been and indicate where they're going in a lecture.

It might sound like this: "Let's recap where we have been. We have discussed. . . . Now it's time to move on. Here's what's in front of us . . ."

- *Use chunking.* Trainees are more likely to remember information when it is carefully chunked, or packaged, in a meaningful way. In Chapter 2 the concept of deep practice was introduced, wherein trainers chunk, repeat, and then get trainees to experience or feel the content to enhance learning. A trainer begins the chunking process while developing the lecture. Some trainers refer to their chunks of information as bumper stickers. In their popular book *Made to Stick*, Chip and Dan Heath synthesize years of communication research into six concise bumper stickers: simple, unexpected, concrete, credible, emotional, and stories.[2] They nicely package and chunk information so that it's easy to understand and use when communicating with others.
- *Use mnemonic devices as memory aids or memory shortcuts.* An acronym is an example of a **mnemonic** device; the "ADDIE" model stands for Analysis, Design, Development, Implementation, and Evaluation.
- *Use a schema.* You will recall from Chapter 2, that a **schema** is an organization system or a category of information. In practice, trainers use advanced organizers to help participants build schema for new information.[3] An advanced organizer is a handout that trainers give trainees to help them organize their note taking. Most participant manuals serve this purpose. These manuals are carefully prepared so that trainees follow the training content while recording notes in designated places in the participant manual.

Be Redundant.   Effective trainers repeat and reiterate information as well as highlight important information. Not all students will understand your message the first time they hear it. Here are suggestions:

- *Repeat information.* **Repeating** occurs when you restate the content in the very same way.
- *Reiterate information.* **Reiterating** occurs when you restate the content, but in different ways. You may use different examples to illustrate the training content. Anticipate where your trainees could become confused and have multiple examples ready to illustrate your concepts and ideas.
- *Highlight information.* **Highlighting** occurs when you emphasize certain content. You point out the importance of a particular piece of information.
- *Use feedforward messages.* **Feedforward messages** are messages that tell the trainee how the information is to be processed: "If you don't understand this stage of the conflict management process, you're not going to be successful in managing conflict" or "What I'm about to tell you is incredibly important."

How to Present Lectures

Developing a lecture that is interactive and discussion-based is only half of the battle. For any trainer, being engaging, personally relevant, and motivating can make the difference between a successful training session and one that is boring and ineffective. Effective delivery includes several verbal and nonverbal strategies that serve to increase trainees' willingness to listen and engage as well as to enhance learning outcomes.

Use Immediacy Behaviors. Effective trainers lecture using an immediate delivery style. **Immediacy,** as we discuss in more detail in Chapter 10, is a perception of physical or psychological closeness; it is created by using certain verbal and nonverbal messages.[4] We are attracted to those who are immediate, and we tend to avoid those who are nonimmediate. Here are examples of effective communication behaviors that have been shown to enhance perceptions of closeness. When these behaviors are conveyed using an appropriate level of enthusiasm, people pay attention.

- *Refer to trainees by name:* Using trainees' names communicates that they are important and that a trainer cares enough about them to know their names.
- *Lean forward:* Forward body posture communicates that the trainer is actively engaged and wants to connect with trainees.
- *Nod head:* Trainers nod to let trainees know that they understand them. A trainer's nodding also encourages trainees to continue engaging in the lecture.
- *Use gestures:* Using appropriate gestures gives the lecture an informal feeling yet emphasizes the content, helps trainees stay on track, and gives your delivery a sense of dynamism.
- *Maintain eye contact*: Looking people in the eye when communicating assures them that you are connecting with them.
- *Self-disclose to your trainees:* Trainers who appropriately self-disclose by telling personal stories and using appropriate humor know that these behaviors personalize the information and enhance the learning process.[5] Effective trainers share with their students how they will use the information and why the information has meaning for them.

Engage Trainees. An **engagement strategy** is any type of communication that encourages trainees to reflect on or to interact with the information they receive. Adult learners want to take an active role in what they learn, and effective trainers find ways to engage their students in the lecture and discussion. Here are suggestions that may keep trainees from losing attention:

- *Use stimulus prompts:* A **stimulus prompt** is a partial statement or a question that requires trainees to complete the statement or answer the question. "Listening is a five stage process that includes _____, _____, _____, _____, and _____" is an example of a stimulus prompt statement. "Will someone review for us the listening process?" is an example of a stimulus prompt question. Using stimulus prompts throughout a lecture keeps trainees engaged and encourages them to interact with the lecture content. They hear each other's voices, and that gives the impression that the lecture is really a discussion.
- *Ask rhetorical questions:* **Rhetorical questions** are questions that don't require answers. Rhetorical questions are usually provocative and sometimes personal; they ask trainees to reflect on their lives and work experiences. A trainer who is conducting a communication workshop for new management trainees might ask, "What do you not like about your current manager's communication style?" The trainer doesn't expect a verbal response to this question, but he or she wants management trainees to think about what in their manager's communication style bugs them. Trainers will then use this

thinking as a springboard to the lecture or a transition to a new idea within the lecture.

■ *Ask trainees to complete a personal thought inventory (PTI):* A PTI is not only an engagement strategy; it also gives trainers feedback on how they are doing in the training classroom. Ask trainees to take a sheet of paper and respond to three questions that relate to a concept just discussed: (1) What is the concept? (2) Why is the concept important? and (3) How do you see yourself using the concept? If time permits, ask volunteers to respond to the questions in class. If not, ask trainees to turn in their PTIs at the end of the lecture. The PTI gets trainees engaged and interacting with the lecture— both its content and its application—and it allows the trainer to get needed feedback from trainees. Trainers can then assess how they're doing and make necessary adjustments for the next time lecture presentation.

■ *Ask trainees to engage in seatmate discussions:* Have trainees discuss their responses to their PTI with a seatmate, or ask trainees to discuss with a seat-mate how they might apply a particular concept to the workplace.

■ *Ask trainees to journal:* Journaling works especially well with training programs that focus on interpersonal communication. One way to remember

RECAP

Developing and Presenting a Lecture

Technique	Definition	Explanation
Create relevance.	Making training content useful.	Show trainees how training content will improve their performance.
Organize content.	Telling a story with your training content.	Use introduction, body, and conclusion. Chunk the body of the training content. Use previews, reviews, and signposts.
Develop a schema.	Constructing an organizational system for trainees to help them receive and process training content.	Give trainees a partial outline or an incomplete diagram that they complete as the training program progresses.
Build in redundancy.	Restating training content.	Use multiple examples to illustrate the same training concept or idea. Repeat your ideas.
Be immediate.	Creating physical and psychological closeness with trainees.	Be nonverbally expressive and animated. Use appropriate self-disclosure and humor; reveal personal anecdotes.
Engage trainees.	Communicating in a way that causes trainees to reflect on or interact with training content.	Use stimulus prompts, rhetorical questions, personal thought inventories, and journaling.

this engagement strategy is by the formula "journal, lecture, diagnose, recommend". Here's how to apply this technique. Before lecturing on conflict management, ask trainees to *journal,* or write about, a conflict they recently experienced. Ask them to describe the conflict and how it was processed, detailing the communication behaviors that were used. Then you give a *lecture* on how to resolve conflict constructively and afterward ask trainees to apply the lecture content to their journal entry and *diagnose* their conflict encounter. What worked, what did not work, and why? They can add to their journal entry, or they can discuss this with their seatmate. Finally, ask trainees to make *recommendations* for their next conflict. What behaviors do they want to continue using? What behaviors do they want to change? This, too, can be done by journaling or through a seatmate discussion.

MANAGING EXPERIENTIAL ACTIVITIES

In an **experiential activity,** trainees develop and practice skills together under the direction of a trainer. Case studies, role plays, and demonstrations are examples of experiential activities; they require trainees to involve themselves physically and/or psychologically in the training content. Managing experiential activities includes four steps: planning, preparing, presenting, and assessing. The box opposite identifies each of these steps and lists ideas to help trainers manage experiential activities.

We'll review two of the more popular types of experiential activities, role plays and case studies. Both activities have been shown to engage trainees in the learning process, build self-confidence, and help trainees transfer their learning from the classroom to the front line.[6]

How to Conduct Role Plays

A **role play** encourages participants to act out unfamiliar roles, attitudes, or behaviors in order to practice skills or to apply what they have learned. Frequently an observer will provide feedback to those who are acting. One way to conducting role plays is to script and stage them. Scripting occurs when you develop in advance the roles and the situations or the content for the role play.[7] Here are options for scripting:

- *Improvisation.* Participants are given a general scenario and asked to fill in the details. This approach to the role play promotes spontaneity and the opportunity to frame an experience from one's own work experience. Actors create a skit without a script. Input and ideas are gleaned from the audience.
- *Prescribed roles.* Trainees are given a well-prepared set of instructions that specify the facts about the role they are portraying and how they are to behave. This approach gives the trainer control over the script, so the dramatic tension you want to create is easily obtained. The weakness is that training participants may not identify with the role and the situation.
- *Semi-prescribed roles.* Trainees are provided with information about the situation and the characters, but they are not told how to handle the situation.

A FOUR-STEP PROCESS FOR MANAGING EXPERIENTIAL ACTIVITIES

Step	Implementation Ideas
Planning	Develop a learning objective for the activity. Identify the importance of the activity. Put the following information on a whiteboard or flipchart paper, inserting the activity or topic in the blank spaces: After this activity, trainees will be able to answer three questions: What is _____? Why is _____ important? How do you do _____?
Preparing	Brainstorm possible experiential activities. Review resource materials to find the correct training activity. Here are three popular resources for you to consider: M. Silberman (2010), *Unforgettable Experiential Activities: An Active Training Resource* (San Francisco: Pfeiffer). E. Biech (2010), *The 2011 Pfeiffer Annual: Training* (San Francisco: Pfeiffer). M. Hughes & A. Miller (2010), *Developing Emotional and Social Intelligence: Exercises for Leaders, Individuals, and Teams* (San Francisco: Pfeiffer). Make a list of all the instructional materials you will need to take to the training classroom: DVDs, preprinted handouts, flipchart paper and markers, whiteboard markers, chalk, tape, colored paper. Write clear instructions for the activity that you will distribute to each participant.
Presenting	Inform your trainees about the activity and the purpose for the activity. Confirm that your instructions are clear and understood. Distribute the necessary materials. Monitor the activity by walking around the room and making yourself available to answer questions. Keep track of the time and provide timing cues when necessary. Provide corrective feedback as needed. Unpack or process the activity using the EDIT process. Refer to the Trainer's Toolbox p.135 for instructions on how to process your activity.
Assessing	Conduct a Personal Thought Inventory (PTI). Ask participants to answer three questions on a piece of paper: What is _____? Why is _____ important? How do you do _____? Give each participant a sticky note and ask him or her to write down the key "take away," or the significant ideas they learned from engaging in the activity.

- *Replay of life.* Trainees can portray themselves and reenact actual situations in which they were involved. This approach to scripting has the advantage of bringing the most realism to the dramatic reenactment.
- *Participant-prepared skits.* Trainees are asked to develop a role play of their own. They create and rehearse the role play before enacting it. Trainees respond well to this option when they are allowed to address real-life problems they face on a daily basis.

HOW TO STAGE ROLE PLAYS

Types of Role Play Staging	Description
Informal role playing	A role play can unfold from a group discussion; because of the spontaneity, most trainees won't have time to become apprehensive.
Stage-front role playing	One pair role plays in front of the training class while others observe and offer feedback. Using a single role play focuses the participants' attention for later discussion and feedback.
Simultaneous role playing	All training participants, in pairs, enact role plays at the same time. Although this reduces stage fright, it makes it more difficult for the trainer to monitor the role plays.
Rotational role playing	Actors can be rotated to give the role play twists and variations. This allows participants to see how a new character introduces a different set of relational dynamics.
Repeated role playing	After receiving initial feedback, trainees reenact the role play. Trainees should see immediate improvement, not only from the feedback but also from the repetition. Role reversal role playing Participants assume the role of a person with whom they interact daily, such as their supervisor.
Revised role playing	Participants assume the role of the person with whom they interact daily, for example their supervisor.

Staging, another form of role play, involves providing only the format and structure to be enacted. The box above describes ways to stage role play activities.

How to Conduct Case Studies

A **case study** is a type of problem-based learning that includes a detailed and contextualized problem that is presented to trainees for solving. A case study is usually a narrative or a short story about a problem and its history, in which the characters involved are described in detail. Case studies can be based on news stories, or they can describe actual problems in an organization. Trainees are expected to put themselves into the case study and solve the problem. Case studies are intended to develop trainees' abilities to solve authentic problems using knowledge, concepts, and skills from the training program.

Selecting Case Studies.   A number of case study books are available in the marketplace. Here are our recommendations:

> J. Keyton & P. Shockley-Zalaback (2009), *Case Studies for Organizational Communication: Understanding Communication Processes* (New York: Oxford University Press).
>
> S. K. May (2006), *Case Studies in Organizational Communication: Ethical Perspectives and Practices* (Thousand Oaks, CA: Sage).
>
> J. R. Taylor & E. J. Van Every (2011), *The Situated Organization: Case Studies in the Pragmatics of Communication Research* (New York: Routledge).

Another source for case studies calls on your trainees to develop their own cases, reflecting the problems they face daily at work. To help them develop quality case studies, you might want to share these tips:

- Change the names of the characters in case studies to ensure confidentiality.
- Provide a context for the case: What history of the organization is relevant? What led to the problem?
- Describe the players in the case study. What are their backgrounds and personalities? What makes them unique?
- Illustrate the problem and make sure it is clearly articulated. Demonstrate the effects of the problem.

Processing Case Studies.   Although there are other ways to process case studies, trainers usually ask participants individually to read and answer prepared questions that tap into training content. Then trainers place participants in groups and ask them to reprocess the case study as a group. It's important that each group member discuss how and why he or she perceives the problem so that other group members can form a perspective. Here are additional suggestions for processing case studies:

- *Describe the problem*. Ask trainees to read the case study and then describe the problem. Compare and contrast their descriptions.
- *Identify symptoms and causes*. Ask participants to diagnose the problem by identifying the symptoms and the causes. Again, compare and contrast the diagnoses.
- *Develop interventions and prescriptions*. Ask trainees to develop solutions to the problem. What interventions and prescriptions do they recommend? Why do they believe these interventions will work?

FACILITATING GROUP DISCUSSIONS

A **facilitated group discussion** occurs when a group of three to ten trainees interact with the assistance of a facilitator who guides the discussion toward specific learning objectives. As a group facilitator, your job is to ask probing questions and to ensure that all group members participate in the discussion. You need to bring out differences of opinion, note areas of agreement and disagreement, and provide internal summaries. Basically, your job is to keep the group on task and to help it make sense of different opinions. Ultimately, you lead trainees to the learning objectives through discussion.

Instructional research shows that one of the most effective ways to create, change, or modify attitudes is to provide a safe and open forum where individuals can voice their opinions.[8] Trainees learn more about their attitudes and beliefs by hearing themselves talk and fielding questions from others. They learn firsthand what opinions are shared and not shared. As a result of an effective facilitated discussion, group members not only learn about their own attitudes and beliefs, they also develop an appreciation for different opinions and viewpoints.

For some learning objectives that focus on the affective dimension of learning, a facilitated group discussion may be the most appropriate training method.

A TRAINER'S TOOLBOX

Unpacking Experiential Activities to Reach a Learning Outcome

One challenge many trainers face is how to process an experiential activity with trainees in a manner that will achieve a learning outcome. We refer to this process as unpacking an experiential activity. One way to unpack an activity is to use the EDIT process.[9] **EDIT** is an easily remembered acronym that represents a natural flow of activity from E, engaging in an experiential activity, to D, describing or talking about it, to I, making generalizations or inferences beyond the activity, and to T, transferring the experience from the training context to the workplace, school, or home.

Experience: Ask trainees to participate in the experiential activity.

Describe: Ask trainees to describe the experience using descriptive rather than evaluative language. Here are a few prompts you can use:

- What did you see, hear, feel, touch, and smell?
- Walk me through the experience step by step as though I was not there.
- When your trainees say, "I saw Tina tensing up. She had a bad attitude," ask them, "What does tensing up look and sound like?" and "What does a bad attitude look and sound like?"
- Rather than tell us what happened, show us what happened.

Infer: Ask trainees what specifically they learned from the experiential activity. Ask participants to go beyond the classroom and predict what would happen if they used their new knowledge and skills in the workplace or at home. Here are prompts to use:

- What have you learned from this experience?
- What do you know now that you did not know 30 minutes ago or before engaging in this experiential activity?
- What would happen if you used this strategy or skill at work or at home?

Transfer: Ask participants how they will use their new knowledge or skills at work or at home. Here are prompts to get you started:

- How do you see yourself using this information?
- What one thing would you like to change immediately in your life or on the job—and how will you make this change?
- How has this experience aided your understanding of what is happening in your life and what changes might need to occur in order to enhance the quality of your life?
- How would you inform others of what you have just learned?

Although the EDIT process may seem lengthy, with practice you can unpack an experiential activity in ten minutes or less. Remember, if the experiential activity is not unpacked, many trainees will question the point of the activity and fail to make the appropriate learning connections.

For example, many of today's corporations invest huge sums of money in sensitizing their employees to cultural and gender diversity issues in the workplace. Many employees do not understand what it means to be a member of a minority in the workplace, and others are insensitive to sexual harassment-related issues. Learning objectives that focus on changing employees' attitudes require training methods, such as the facilitated group discussion, that foster safe environments where communication is free from evaluation.

How to Manage Group Discussions

Like any teaching method, managing a group discussion must begin with a learning objective. Remember, a facilitated group discussion is most effective when the learning objective focuses on creating, changing, or modifying trainees' attitudes and beliefs. One example might be an organization's wanting to sensitize its employees to sexual harassment-related issues; this objective would be considered an appropriate learning objective for group discussion.

Although all facilitated group discussions are different and require different types of preparation, they all require a stimulus, something that is used to provoke a reaction in trainees. Two popular stimuli are media and trigger questions. Media have been particularly effective in provoking discussion; many professional training and development departments have media libraries that contain videos, films, television programs, newspaper and magazines articles, and music (song lyrics), among other materials.

Trigger questions are also useful for stimulating discussion. **Trigger questions,** which usually concern controversial issues, are those that deal with claims of value (What is right and wrong, good and bad?), policy (What *should* be done?), and process (*How* should we do it?). Trigger questions cannot be answered with a simple yes or no answer. And they must ultimately tap into your learning objectives. Your facilitated discussion will be only as good as the questions you ask.

Managing a group discussion is a three-part process comprised of exposing trainees to stimulus, setting ground rules (and making sure they're followed), and asking questions.

Exposing Trainees to Stimulus.   Here are suggestions for using a media stimulus in a guided discussion.

- Present trainees with a set of trigger questions to guide their viewing of the media (a film clip, a video, or the like).
- Review the questions with the trainees to be sure they understand what you are asking them to look for and listen to while viewing the media.
- Ask trainees to view, read, or listen to the stimulus and then reflect on what they experienced.
- Ask trainees to journal their responses to your trigger questions.

Setting Ground Rules.   Trainers create a safe environment before the discussion begins by setting the ground rules:

- Do not interrupt others.
- Respect others' opinions.
- Describe rather than evaluate what it is in others' opinions that you find problematic.
- Disclose how others' comments and opinions make you feel.
- Be nonverbally responsive to others.
- When you disagree, ask questions to achieve understanding.
- Realize that you can understand another's point of view without agreeing with it.
- Monitor defensive behavior such as evaluative language, crossed arms, rolling eyes, and deep sighs.

Asking Questions.   We mentioned that a facilitated group discussion is only as good as the questions a trainer asks. There is an art in asking questions, and good trainers practice this art because it helps reach their learning objectives. Before delving into the types of questions, we'll have a look at Benjamin Bloom's Taxonomy of Cognitive Learning,[10] represented in the box below.

A **taxonomy** is a way to classify information. Bloom's taxonomy is useful in helping trainers formulate questions. Questions that tap into lower-order cognitive learning such as knowledge (identifying information exactly as it was learned), comprehension (identifying information in general terms), and application (relating information or principles to a new context) usually stifle group interaction and conversation. These questions are called **closed questions,** or questions that require the recall of specific information. Because there is a right and a wrong answer to the question "What are the three steps to processing a customer complaint?" it is an example of a closed question. When the trainer asks a closed question, trainees may be reluctant to respond unless they are confident they know the correct answer.

BLOOM'S TAXONOMY OF COGNITIVE LEARNING

Cognitive Level of Learning	Sample Question
Evaluation: Determining the value of something based on learned criteria. Judging whether something is good or bad, useful or unuseful, correct or incorrect, based on a learned set of standards.	What were the strengths and weaknesses of the sales presentation?
Synthesis: Creating something new based on information and principles learned.	Can you create your own model of communication using the following elements and parts? Do you understand how the elements and parts are related?
Analysis: Breaking information learned into separate parts. Identifying interrelationships among components.	Can you identify the elements and parts in the model of communication?
Application: Using information learned to solve a problem or to relate information learned to a new context.	How can you use these communication principles, on the job, to enhance your managerial effectiveness?
Comprehension: Summarizing information in a way other than how it was originally learned to confirm that the information is understood.	In your own words, what does communication mean?
Knowledge: Recalling information as it was learned; recalling facts, dates, names, and definitions.	Can you recall the definition of communication?

Anderson/Krathwohl/Airasian/Cruikshank/Mayer/Pintrich/Raths/Wittrock, *A Taxonomy for Learning, Teaching, and Assessing: A Revision of Bloom's Taxonomy of Educational Objectives, Abridged Edition*, 1st Edition, © 2001. Reprinted by permission of Pearson Education, Inc., Upper Saddle River, NJ.

Questions that tap into higher forms of cognitive learning, such as questions that ask for analysis (breaking a process or event into parts), synthesis (creating something new based on what was learned), or evaluation (assessing whether something is good or bad) often promote group interaction and conversation, especially when the trainer asks open questions. **Open questions** are more ambiguous and usually have no single correct or incorrect response. These questions often call for additional probing and follow-up questions. "Based on your own experiences, what do you consider to be good customer service?" is an open question. Another example: "Would someone break down the process of quality customer service? What steps to quality customer service have you experienced?" Additional probing may take the form of "Why do you think this way?" or "How do you know this?" The box below illustrates the types of closed and open questions that trainers use when facilitating a discussion that taps into the broad spectrum of Bloom's taxonomy.[11]

In addition to asking the appropriate questions, consider these suggestions:

- *Allow ample time for a response to a question.* Good answers require thought. Don't expect immediate responses; be comfortable with silence.
- *Don't answer your own questions.* Many trainers, uncomfortable with waiting for trainees to respond, will answer their own questions. But it's better to get a response out of a trainee than to put one in.

OPEN AND CLOSED QUESTIONS THAT TRAINERS USE

Question Type	Definition or Explanation	Example
Leading	Question suggests the answer.	"Would you agree that training is important?"
Factual	Question seeks facts, data, information.	"What does it cost to process a customer complaint?"
Direct	Question asked of a specific person.	"What are the three Cs of customer service, Gary?"
General	Question asked of a group; anyone can answer.	"What does good customer service mean?"
Controversial	Question has more than one answer.	"Are leaders born or made?"
Provocative	Question incites an answer.	"What do you think of the statement 'Most supervisors drive their employees too hard'?"
Redirected	Question asked of facilitator and returned to group.	Group member: "What is good customer service?" Facilitator: "Let me ask you the same question, what is good customer service to you?"
Yes and no	Question calls for a yes or no response.	"Did you attend the training program?"
Why and how	Question is a follow-up probe of a yes or no response.	"Why was it important that you attend the training program?" "How do you know this?"

- *When appropriate, probe.* Follow up trainees' responses with, Why do you think this is so? How do you know this? Do you agree? Why? Why not?
- *Accept and dignify responses.* When answers are wrong, they need to be recognized as wrong. However, nearly every answer to a question can be used in some way. A wrong response may be due to misunderstanding, unclear instruction, or faulty learning. Dignify the response by tentatively accepting it and examining it to see why it was given. Make sure the trainee knows why the response was not accurate and why the correct response is accurate.

How to Use Facilitation Techniques

Trainers use a variety of facilitation techniques. Three common techniques are interaction management, threaded discussion, and round robin.

Interaction Management. Facilitating a group discussion effectively requires a trainer to use these interaction management strategies:

- *Ask trigger questions.* These are usually the same questions that guided, for example, the trainees' viewing of a video. Other trigger questions might include: Where did you see yourself in this video clip? Do you agree with what just happened in this video clip? Why? Why not?
- *See that all group members contribute to the group discussion in an open manner.* "Remember, all comments are respected and valued."
- *Provide internal summaries whenever and wherever needed.* "Let me review what we've discussed thus far . . ."
- *Probe students' comments and raise additional questions.* "How do you know that? What did you see and hear that led you to that evaluation of your coworker?"
- *Continually redirect conversation in order to meet learning objectives.* "Great discussion! Now, let me turn us back to our learning objective."
- *Monitor nonverbal communication behaviors so you can call on those who appear to disagree with what has been said.* "I can tell you might disagree. We would love to hear from you."
- *Carefully draw out those who are reticent or who do not seem to hold the majority view.* "We have not heard from some of you, and some of you may completely disagree, which is good. Would you care to share?"
- *Tactfully shut down those who are too willing to communicate and would dominate the group discussion.* "Hold that idea just for a moment so we can hear from others. How about the rest of you, we would like to hear from you."
- *Provide a final summary and debriefing that point to your learning objectives.* "Let me review or paraphrase what I have been hearing you say is the problem. Please correct me if my understanding is not accurate."

Threaded Discussion. A **threaded discussion** is one in which you ask a question and then integrate carefully all responses and follow-up questions into a meaningful and coherent conversation. To thread a discussion, ask an open question and wait for someone to respond. When you get a response, turn the response into your next question, redirecting the new question to the same person or to another group member. A threaded discussion might proceed like this:

> TRAINER: What does sexual harassment look and sound like in the workplace?
> SUE: To me, it's someone viewing porn sites on the Internet.
> TRAINER: Why is viewing porn sites on the Internet considered sexual harassment?
> GARY: Because it makes me uncomfortable.
> TRAINER: Why does it make you uncomfortable?
> GARY: Because it's distracting, and I can't get my job done.
> TRAINER: How is it distracting?
> CAROL: I feel pressure to participate.
> TRAINER: Describe the pressure.
> CAROL: They want me to view the sites with them. If I do, I'm going against what I consider to be appropriate workplace behavior. If I don't, they think I'm too rigid, tense, and uptight.

This dialogue shows how a trainer can take responses and thread them back to the group members by reframing them as new questions.

Round Robin. With the **round robin** technique, the facilitator asks a question and then goes around the group, asking each member in turn for his or her response. When a particular group member is not ready, he or she simply passes until all have spoken. This technique is useful when it's important that all group members participate.

RECAP

How to Develop and Facilitate a Group Discussion

Discussion Stage	Example
Present stimulus.	Show a media stimulus.
	Ask trainees to reflect on the stimulus.
	Ask trainees to write out answers to trigger questions.
Set ground rules.	Do not interrupt others.
	Describe rather than evaluate.
	Be responsive to nonverbal activity.
Facilitate group interaction.	Use threaded discussion.
	Shut down those who talk too much and bring out those who talk too little.
	Provide summaries.

SELECTING THE BEST TRAINING METHOD

After reading about the three training methods of lecturing, conducting experiential activities, and facilitating group discussions, you will want to know which training method is best. The answer is, it all depends. It all depends on a lot of variables, including your trainees, your learning objectives, the advantages and disadvantages of each training method, and your level of comfort with the various training methods.

Consider Your Trainees

All decisions we make must begin with our trainees. The needs-centered training model introduced in Chapter 1 reminds us how central our trainees are to our success as a professional trainer. Who are they? What are their experiences? What makes them unlike other groups of trainees? Where do they come from? What are their average age and years of work experience? Answers to these questions will help you gauge better their reactions to your training methods. For example, some experiential activities are fine for college-age men and women, but not for the working professional. If you're working with a group of men and women who have extensive work experience, the group discussion method may be more appropriate because the trainees can learn from each other's work experiences.

Consider Your Learning Objectives

Review your learning objectives. If the learning objective is cognitive ("My students will *understand* interpersonal conflict"), then the lecture training method would be the most appropriate. If the learning objective is behavioral ("My students will know *how* to resolve interpersonal conflict"), then an experiential activity such as a role play may be the most appropriate. If the learning objective is affective ("My students will *value* and *appreciate* interpersonal interaction and how to resolve conflict"), then a facilitated guided discussion may be the most appropriate training method.

Consider Advantages and Disadvantages

Each training method has its advantages and disadvantages. Do the advantages outweigh the disadvantages? Although the experiential activity training method can be artificial, it does give trainees experience in developing the communication skill. For example, training others how to resolve interpersonal conflict using role play may be better than just lecturing to them. At times, however, the lecture may be more appropriate, especially when trainers have minimal training time. It's always important to weigh the advantages and the disadvantages. There's never enough time or money for a trainer to conduct the ideal training program. Trainers must make the best decisions possible given the circumstances.

ADVANTAGES AND DISADVANTAGES OF TRAINING METHODS

Training Method	Advantages	Disadvantages
Lecturing	Lecturing is economical.	Lecturing can be trainer centered.
	Lecturing is controllable.	Lecturing can encourage passive
	Lecturing is flexible.	learning.
		Lecturing can bore trainees.
Conducting experiential activities	Activities can engage all trainees.	Activities may be underdeveloped.
	Activities can increase trainee self-confidence.	Activities can be gimmicky.
		Activities can be artificial.
	Activities can increase trainees' ability to transfer content.	Activities may be perceived as threatening.
Facilitating group discussion	Discussions encourage group members to share and participate.	Discussions can easily lose their focus.
		Discussions can be dominated by one outspoken trainee.
	Discussions encourage group members to learn from each other.	Discussions can become emotional and destructive if they get out of hand.
	Discussions can be a safe environment for sharing honest opinions.	

The box above summarizes the advantages and disadvantages for each of the training methods reviewed in this chapter.

Consider Your Level of Comfort

Although trainers are encouraged to become comfortable with using all training methods and to use a variety of training methods within any training program, not all new trainers will feel comfortable with all training methods. For example, new trainers are often more comfortable lecturing than they are facilitating a group discussion or conducting experiential activities. With the lecture, trainers have a sense of control over the training content. They know where they are, and they know where they need to go. When facilitating a group discussion, trainers never know for sure whether they will be able to summarize or thread the group discussion in a way that will allow them to reach their learning objectives. Similarly, when conducting a new experiential activity, trainers never know whether the activity will work until they have tried it.

SUMMARY AND REVIEW

Trainers can choose from three basic methods when developing a training program: lecturing, activities, and discussions. Lecturing is key to getting main ideas and concepts across. You can keep lectures interactive by following these guidelines:

- Create relevance for the trainees.
- Organize the content to make it easier to learn.
- Develop a schema: attach new knowledge to previous knowledge.
- Build in redundancy—review and repeat to help trainees recall information.
- Be immediate; research has shown that immediacy enhances learning outcomes.
- Engage trainees—getting them involved in their learning will help to solidify their knowledge and understanding and give them practice in skill development.

Experiential activities are important for engaging trainees in behaviors, and they can be effective ice-breakers.

- Before the training session, a trainer's preparation is a four-step process of planning, preparing, presenting, and assessing (PPPA).
- A trainer can use various types of role play.
- Case studies can be very effective in helping learners apply the principles they have learned.
- Because trainees won't always connect an activity with the principle behind it, trainers need to unpack the activity.

- The unpacking process, EDIT, allows learners to Experience, Describe, Infer, and Transfer knowledge from the activity.

Facilitating group discussions can be very useful for the trainer, especially when trainees lack desire or enthusiasm for the program. Discussions can help trainees realize the importance of what they are learning.

- Managing a discussion involves keeping the group involved and talking by providing stimulation, such as a video, a story, or a question.
- Discussions can be regulated by using a facilitation technique such as round robin or threaded discussion.

The process for selecting the best training method for your program is fourfold:

- Consider the trainees. They all bring experiences, expectations, and various skill levels to the classroom.
- Consider learning objectives. Training methods work best when they capture what the trainer wants. Lectures are best for cognitive outcomes; activities are best for behavioral outcomes.
- Consider the advantages and disadvantages. Each method has a positive and negative side.
- Consider your comfort level. At first you may be more comfortable using the methods most familiar to you.

QUESTIONS FOR DISCUSSION AND REVIEW

1. What is a training method? How do each of the methods described in this chapter differ?
2. What steps are involved in developing and presenting an effective lecture?
3. How can an experiential activity benefit a training program? Identify two experiential activities a trainer can use, and describe the four-step process known as PPPA, used for developing activities.
4. What does it mean to unpack an activity? How can a trainer assist the trainees in this process?
5. Describe the skills and techniques used to facilitate a guided discussion.
6. What are the important elements to consider when determining appropriate training methods?

QUESTIONS FOR APPLICATION AND ANALYSIS

1. Think of a topic you know well and could easily give a short lecture on. How would you apply the guidelines provided in this chapter to developing an effective and interactive lecture? Give specific examples.

2. One of your classmates, Mary, has just finished giving a practice lecture in training class. She feels deflated because she believes her presentation was not successful. Mary had a difficult time keeping the trainees focused; they were easily distracted. She never moved away from the podium, and she was unable to answer many of the questions trainees asked. In addition, she never reviewed information she had covered. You had found it difficult to follow her lecture. At the end of the presentation, it appeared that trainees could not recall the material. Considering what you have learned about the effective development and presentation of lectures, what advice would you give Mary to help make her lectures more effective?

3. You are working with a training team on a new leadership ethics training program for a regular client. You have developed training objectives and must decide on the best one to help students practice their new skills. Your team chooses to have the trainees examine and evaluate a case study. How would you go about planning, preparing, presenting, and assessing this activity?

4. After guiding your trainees in the activity in question 3 above, it is important that they understand how to apply what they've learned. How would you go about unpacking this activity? Specifically, what questions would you ask to help the trainee Experience, Describe, Infer, and Transfer (EDIT) learning from the activity.

5. Lucas works in the training department of an organization that recently underwent major changes in management in the production department. The changes have not gone well with employees; peers have suddenly become supervisors, and conflicts have developed among workers. To help employees through the restructuring, Lucas has developed a conflict management workshop for enhancing employee morale. He chooses to begin his program with a guided discussion. Discuss the ways this delicate subject could be handled through facilitating interaction in a discussion.

6. As a member of a three-person training team, you are tasked with selecting training methods for a program in customer service. You know your objectives are primarily affective and behavioral. Your trainees are current employees, and they know their material, but they lack the enthusiasm for developing their skills further. Which training methods would be most suited to this program? Why?

ACTIVITIES FOR APPLYING PRINCIPLES AND SKILLS

1. Working in groups, describe each of the skills discussed in this chapter for an effective lecture and give an example of how you could use each one in preparing a lecture. Compare your answers with other group members.

   a. Create relevance
   b. Organize content
   c. Develop a schema
   d. Build in redundancy
   e. Be immediate
   f. Engage the trainees

2. For each of the following training objectives, identify an appropriate level from Bloom's Taxonomy of cognitive educational objectives. Then discuss how you could go about helping trainees reach each level through a lecture.

   a. Describe the effects of self-esteem on communication competence.
   b. Recall the five steps in the listening process.
   c. Apply a model of conflict management to a real life conflict.
   d. Evaluate a peer's performance of phone etiquette skills.
   e. Examine a needs proposal to determine what training objectives must be met.

3. A trainer can use several types of questions to facilitate a guided discussion. A variety of strategies are used to encourage trainees to open up. For each of the following definitions, identify the question type. Then, working with a partner, write down an example for each. The options are: leading, factual, direct, general, controversial, redirected, why and how.

   a. Directed to facilitator, but turned back to group
   b. The question also suggests the answer
   c. Follow-up probes for further clarification
   d. Directed at a specific person
   e. There are two or more answers or perspectives

4. Many universities and colleges receive student complaints about parking. Imagine you are leading a committee whose task is to evaluate and solve the parking problem on your campus. In groups, take turns practicing leading a short discussion, putting into practice the facilitation techniques learned in this chapter, such as using a threaded discussion or the round robin method.

5. The following list of objectives for various training programs covers an array of skills. For each training objective, which training method would you first recommend?

   a. Appreciate the importance of managing conflict in the workplace.
   b. Understand and explain the five steps to the active listening process.
   c. Develop a budget proposal plan.
   d. Use communication skills to give an effective presentation.
   e. Perform a peer evaluation.
   f. Recall the levels of Bloom's Taxonomy of learning.
   g. Demonstrate the meeting management skill of facilitating interaction.

We need to bring learning to people instead of people to learning.

—*Elliott Masie*

Using Web Training for E-Learning

CHAPTER OUTLINE

CHAPTER OBJECTIVES

After studying this chapter, you should be able to:

- Describe the growing need and usefulness of e-learning training programs.

- Describe the various methods and options for developing Web-based training programs, including rapid e-learning, Web-based delivery, and blended training.

- Recognize the factors involved in determining that the e-learning method is appropriate for a given context, including task ambiguity and media richness.

- Identify the Web-based training tools available to the training professional, including Web 2.0 and rapid e-learning tools.

- Describe and apply appropriate design principles in the development of a Web-based training program.

- Apply the needs-based training model in an e-learning context.

In the past thirty years, Web training, often called e-learning, has become a popular training method for a variety of organizations. For example, both Starbucks and Delta Airlines provide their employees with constant e-learning opportunities that reinforce quality customer service guidelines. The "e" of e-learning refers to the use of computerized training software (or courseware), other custom software applications, CDs, DVDs, and, more recently, the Internet. The "learning" component indicates the cognitive, affective, or behavioral learning objectives. E-learning has led to a changing world for the training and development professional.

As a training and development professional, your understanding of e-learning will make you a more competitive job candidate and enhance your ability to help others make expert-level decisions about the appropriateness of using e-learning. Many organizations rely on the expertise of training and development professionals when faced with training needs. Your job is not only to design and facilitate e-learning, but also to recommend the right type of e-learning and evaluate the effectiveness of Web-based training programs. If you can help an organization meet its goals by making wise decisions about when and when not to utilize e-learning, you will add value to the organization and increase your own value as a training professional.

This chapter has four main sections.[1] The first section explains why e-learning is needed, shows how traditional and rapid e-learning differ, and describes e-learning delivery options. The second section introduces the Web 2.0 and rapid e-learning training tools that training professionals use to develop Web-based training. The third section examines design principles and offers practical tips for developing Web-based training. The final section details how to use the needs-centered training model for e-learning.

UNDERSTANDING E-LEARNING

Because e-learning has now become an important model for training and development in the twenty-first century, it's important to understand why e-learning is needed, how e-learning differs from rapid e-learning, and what e-learning delivery options are available.

The Need for E-Learning

In one study focusing on the need for e-learning, forty-six training managers offered the following reasons for using e-learning in today's organizations.[2]

Minimizes Costs. The key reason for putting training online is that it makes training more cost effective. Online training reduces such expenses as the trainer's fee, the cost of training manuals, and the renting of classrooms. Also, e-learning does not limit the number of trainees to the number of seats in a training classroom. One company's study found that its staff of nine trainers each delivered an average of 4,935 hours of training. Three years later, after the same company had begun using e-learning training programs, it reported that its staff, now only six, each delivered an average of 13,852 hours—an efficiency increase of 321 percent per trainer.[3] These findings confirm a large body of research on some of the economic advantages of e-learning.

Minimizes Down Time.   Some argue that e-learning allows for a seamless integration of work and learning.[4] When the amount of time employees are away from their workstations for training is reduced, employees can maintain a level of productivity or customer service that minimizes the disruption to the workday. Through e-learning, trainees can blend their work duties with their training needs. When extra minutes are available in their workday, employees can quickly complete a Web-based training unit. Some researchers call this type of training **ubiquitous learning**, which is "anywhere and anytime learning."[5] Researchers describe our use of wireless telecommunication as a "calm technology that has receded to the background of our lives."[6] Because of our ease at using wireless technologies, most people are comfortable using these technologies while performing other tasks and duties simultaneously.[7]

Appeals to Contemporary Learners.   Another advantage to e-learning is that it appeals to a younger, more tech-savvy workforce.[8] Since today's workplace sees increasing numbers of Millennials, or Generation Y employees (29 years of age and younger), it is advantageous to tailor training and development programs to the new technologies that this generation are comfortable using.[9]

Rapid E-Learning

One form of e-learning, **rapid e-learning**, is a set of software tools that make it possible for subject matter experts to create and publish interactive e-learning quickly.[10] The evidence is that multihour training programs have become less popular, especially in tough economic times. Delivery times have been squeezed into segments to accommodate busy work schedules. Because of the need for speed, many training professionals are now required to produce training programs in a shorter period of time, and fewer training professionals are being used. With rapid e-learning it's not unusual for one or two training professionals to develop a training program in less than one week. (Traditional e-learning projects usually take a two to six member team four to six months to develop a program.) A number of rapid training tools will be discussed later in the chapter.

Another difference with rapid e-learning is that training departments call on **subject matter experts (SME)** to develop the course. A subject matter expert is a person who has considerable knowledge about the training topic through formal education or professional experience. Rather than have an SME advise an **instructional designer** (someone who develops training objectives, curricula, methods, and assessment instruments), which is usually what happens in e-learning, the SME is contracted to develop the course. In essence, rapid e-learning brings SMEs closer to learners, putting the people with the knowledge in direct contact with the people who need it. This process saves time and puts the rapid in rapid e-learning. Other differences between rapid and traditional e-learning are listed in the box on the following page.

DIFFERENCES BETWEEN RAPID AND TRADITIONAL E-LEARNING TRAINING

Rapid E-Learning	Traditional E-Learning
Content regularly changes or is updated frequently.	Content is fixed or rarely changes.
Content may have a short shelf life or is of a "just-in-time" nature.	Content is generic and will be around for a long time.
Training budget is limited.	Training budget is adequate.
Time to develop is minimal.	Time to develop is appropriate.
Training content can be explained using text.	Training content needs to be conveyed using multimedia and interactive components.

In addition to its speed, trainers may prefer to use rapid e-learning for two reasons that focus on the training content and its objectives. When training content has a short shelf life because the content is constantly changing or being updated, rapid e-learning is more suitable. Also, rapid e-learning is more suitable to training programs with cognitive rather than behavioral training outcomes. Often cognitive learning outcomes can be better reached by using words rather than elaborate visual representations that may require a demonstration. The following training programs are examples of those best suited to rapid e-learning:[11]

- Regulatory or compliance training, such as safety training or training in how a modified public safety regulation will impact operations or how a new employment law will affect hiring practices.
- Customer service support, such as how to trouble-shoot problems and generate solutions to problems.
- New sales or products, such as a line of medicines newly available to pharmaceutical sales reps.
- Software training, such as a step-by-step process on how to operate a new database management system.

E-Learning Delivery Options

The training and development professional needs to select the appropriate delivery option based on a number of considerations. The technology used to deliver the training will affect two important training dynamics: synchronicity of communication and trainer-trainee directedness.[12] **Synchronous communication** occurs in real time and allows trainer and trainee to have a conversation. Although the trainer and the trainee may not be in the same room, they can converse using the communication technology. **Asynchronous communication** does not allow for a real-time conversation; people in different places communicate, but at different times. Training delivery modes can range from fully synchronous delivery to asynchronous delivery.

Trainer-trainee directedness has to do with the relative amount of control the trainer and the trainee have in managing the training content. In trainer-directed programs, trainers are in charge of presenting and pacing the training content. In trainee-directed programs, trainees control the pacing and are more responsible for learning the content on their own.

Figure 7.1 places the four modes of delivery on a continuum from classroom (trainer directed) to online education (self-directed) training.[13]

What delivery modes are most appropriate for a given training program? When you need to answer this question, ask first how ambiguous and complex the training task is. **Ambiguity** indicates there are conflicting interpretations of an idea or an issue. Generally, soft skills such as communication skills (listening, meeting facilitation, presentational speaking, conflict management, employee appraisals) are high in ambiguity. The communication behaviors that one person finds effective may not be those that another person finds effective. Situational factors, or social and emotional cues, may influence how communication behaviors are interpreted. (Whether or not you like a particular person is one such factor.) Because of this ambiguity, there will be more than one way to perform a set of behaviors. Hard skills (operating a computer program, a cash register, or an x-ray machine) are less ambiguous and contain few or no social and emotional cues. Because of the lack of ambiguity, there are right and wrong ways to perform a set of behaviors.

The second consideration in assessing training delivery modes is the richness of the mode. **Media richness** describes the technology's ability to simulate face-to-face communication.[14] Management and marketing researchers Robert Lengel and Richard Daft describe how the channel (face-to-face, video conference, online, distance education) influences how messages are received. For Lengel and Daft, channels are forms of media and different media have different levels of richness, ranging from lean channels to rich channels. The distinguishing characteristic of lean training media is the absence of immediate feedback channels that would allow trainees to ask questions and clarify any confusion. Rich training media are those that offer opportunities for instant feedback, allowing people to interact in real time.

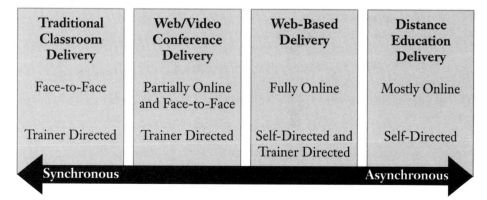

Traditional Classroom Delivery	Web/Video Conference Delivery	Web-Based Delivery	Distance Education Delivery
Face-to-Face	Partially Online and Face-to-Face	Fully Online	Mostly Online
Trainer Directed	Trainer Directed	Self-Directed and Trainer Directed	Self-Directed

Synchronous ◄――――――――――――――――――――――► Asynchronous

FIGURE 7.1
The Training Delivery Continuum

Some Web-based training programs are considered lean because they convey messages using fewer channels (i.e., sight only) and don't allow people to interact in a synchronous manner. Video conferencing is a richer form of training media because it conveys messages using multiple channels (i.e., sight and sound) and allows people to interact in a more synchronous manner.[15] Figure 7.2 illustrates the media richness hierarchy in a training context.

Face-to-Face Classroom Delivery. This mode of delivery is fully synchronous and is usually trainer directed. The traditional training classroom is ideal for training tasks high in ambiguity, such as soft skills, because of its media richness. It allows trainers and trainees to use multiple channels through opportunities for classroom discussion, role playing, and simulations.

Web/Video Conference Delivery. Webinars, Web seminars, or virtual meetings require a Web browser and either traditional phone teleconferencing or a voice over the Internet feature. This training delivery usually permits synchronous communication and tends to be trainer directed. In many Web conference training programs, trainees are shown a slide presentation (i.e., PowerPoint) with trainer narration. Although the technology does a more effective job of exchanging information than does interaction, there are features in the Web conferencing software that allow participation. For example, trainers can ask trainees to respond to polls, post questions, and text chat with the trainer or other trainees. These tools encourage participation and engagement. The Web/video conference is appropriate for training tasks moderately high in ambiguity. Although it allows trainers and trainees to interact in a synchronous manner, trainees and trainers cannot always see each other. Because that means fewer visual cues, the training delivery mode is less media rich.

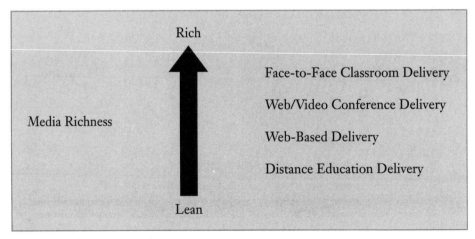

FIGURE 7.2
The Media Richness Hierarchy

Web-Based Delivery. Web-based delivery doesn't usually permit trainees to hear a trainer's voice in real time, and it tends to be both trainer and trainee directed. This category utilizes a Learning Management System (LMS), also known as a Course Management System (CMS) or Virtual Learning Environments (VLE). Popular examples of these types of software systems are Blackboard and WebCT (Current Tools), which are widely used today in business and higher education; they make it efficient for trainees to access course material, including presentations, coursework, and assessments. Trainees can also interact with the trainer through an online portal or intranet Web site. Web-based tools are available to both trainers and trainees. Trainers can facilitate participation, communicate with trainees, collaborate, and evaluate work.[16] In addition, trainees can communicate and interact with other trainees through the Web site. Facilitated transactions software incorporates elements of asynchronous and synchronous communication. One key difference in this category is that the majority of the classroom aids and resources are available online, not as print and CD/DVD materials.[17] The Web-based delivery mode is appropriate for training tasks moderately low in ambiguity. Because it doesn't always allow for synchronous communication with a training professional, it is more suited to hard skills training.

Distance Education Delivery. This e-learning delivery option involves training modules that are offered entirely or partially online, in an asynchronous communication mode. There is typically no online support or real-time communication with the trainer. However, trainees can e-mail their questions or comments to the trainer or facilitator. One major benefit to distance training is that trainees have the flexibility to log in and log out from remote locations, making it easy to stop and restart a training program without losing progress. This form is the most common conception of e-learning, but it is becoming less popular.

Blended Training Models

Regardless of your delivery mode, your e-training will more than likely include a blend of technology. **Blended training** occurs when a trainer mixes and matches training methods, technologies, and delivery systems to meet the needs of trainees and organizations. Three of the most popular models of blended training are the hybrid model, the knowledge/skill rotation model, and the complementary model.[18]

- *Hybrid model.* This model uses a classic mixture of face-to-face and computer-based training. The classroom training is facilitated in between online pre- and post-coursework. For example, trainers assign online pre assessments prior to classroom training, and typically online reading assignments and assessments. Then the trainees participate in the classroom training, and after the classroom training has been completed, trainees return to their workstations and complete an online assessment and/or other learning assignments.
- *Knowledge/skill rotation model.* This model of blended training separates the knowledge content from the behavioral or skill portions of the training plan. Here, trainers can use the online portion of the blended training for meeting

cognitive objectives (knowledge development) while using the face-to-face approach for meeting behavioral objectives (skill development).

■ *Complementary model.* In this model, e-learning is used as a backup for face-to-face training. Trainees can refer back to online course resources while on the job. The online resources are subservient to offline (classroom) training. Many trainers use this model, and it is reported to work well.

TYPES OF TECHNOLOGY TRAINING TOOLS

An abundance of technology training tools is available to the e-learning training designer. One way to review these tools is to divide them into two large tool kits. The first examines Web 2.0 training tools, and the second focuses on rapid e-learning training tools. In practice, most e-learning professionals use tools from both tool kits.

Web 2.0 Training Tools

Web 2.0 denotes the second generation of the Internet. The first generation of the Web, or Web 1.0, was *read-focused:* primarily, agencies, companies, teachers, experts, or vendors posted information online only to be "read" by the general public.[19] Web 2.0 is a *read-write* Web. Today companies actively seek feedback through their Web sites from customers and the general public. For example, Amazon.com regularly asks its customers to complete online surveys following a purchase and to write reviews of the merchandise they purchased. Amazon.com shifted from being a site where customers read and purchased to one where customers read, purchase, and then write comments and reviews.[20]

In addition to the read-write functionality, Web 2.0 offers a variety of applications, including social networking software that allows users to post personal information on the Web at little or no cost. Facebook, LinkedIn, and MySpace are prime examples of this type of social media. The use of social media has increased to the point where, in many instances, it is now a requirement for employment. How do these changes in the Web affect the field of training and development? Let's examine several applications.

Social Networking. Social networking media are software accessed via the Web that offer an interactive, user-submitted network of friends, personal profiles, blogs, groups, photos, music, games, and videos internationally. Social networking media allow users to set up their own personal profiles that can be linked together through networks of friends. Social media can be used in the field of training to enable trainers and trainees to communicate through online chat and messages facilitated through individual profiles. Trainers can even create their own social networks around training content. With online services like *Ning.com*, it is possible to leverage the power and popularity of social networks to create online communities for trainers and trainees.

Wikis. Wikis are collaborative, Web-based sites for sharing text and other resources. The key feature of wikis is their open-editing functionality that allows users to jointly create a resource that can be edited by any and all users. Some trainers develop wikis to complement training programs and allow students to contribute to the knowledge base of the training. Popular Wiki sites are Wikipedia (an encyclopedia), WikiTravel (a travel guide), WikiHow ("how-to" manuals), WikiBooks (textbooks and guides), and WikiSummaries (short summaries of books).

Online Forums.   A forum is a Web site composed of threads (online discussions). Each thread contains a discussion or a conversation in the form of a series of posts written by users. Threads remain saved on the forum host site for indefinite future reading or until they are deleted by the Web administrator. With this technology, trainees can post comments and ask questions related to a training course. This allows other trainees or the trainer the option to respond to a comment or a question, and the history of the discussion can serve to answer similar questions in the future.

RSS Feeds.   Also known as *Really Simple Syndication*, **RSS feeds** are a set of feed formats linked to various Web sites used to publish frequently updated content such as blog and wiki entries, news headlines, or podcasts allowing people to keep up to date on news and other topics. The RSS may contain only a headline, or it may have the full content. This tool enables training professionals to keep trainees updated on training-related issues or news.

Social Bookmarking.   **Social bookmarks** (also known as bookmarking) are Web-based tools that allow users to save a copy of any page they visit on the Web. Social bookmark services like *Delicious.com* allow users to set up free accounts that are accessible by anyone from any computer. Once users have set up an account, they can begin creating a personal archive of Web pages, and this makes it easy to locate a site they want to find again. Social bookmarking is a useful social networking tool for training because of the potential for collaboration through *tagging*. Tagging is adding a Web site to your social bookmarks—in essence, you assign it a tag. Tags are usually single keywords that you create to help you categorize a Web site. You can then quickly find specific Web sites by searching your list of tags and seeing which sites fall under the categories you assigned them. Trainers can use social bookmarking to supplement training materials with a list of tagged Web sites that trainees can view online at their convenience or as part of a training module.

Skype.   Skype is a software application that allows users to make free video and audio calls over the Internet. Typically, Skype communicators use a headset or a webcam and a microphone. *Skype.com* is a popular choice for video conferencing with people all over the world. Many training courses are facilitated through Skype, giving both trainer and trainees a sense of a virtual classroom. Communication involves sending and receiving voice messages via a microphone or via real-time chat with group members.

Podcasts.   Derived from the combination of iPod and broadcast, a **podcast** is a radio broadcast or a similar program made available on the Internet for downloading to an MP3 player, a mobile device, or a personal computer. Podcasts are not limited to the iPod or to Apple brand products. With the increased popularity of mobile devices, podcasting is an effective tool for supplementing classroom and online training. Trainees can review and reuse training lectures at their convenience. **Vodcasts** are the video form of podcasting; trainers can record an entire training session and broadcast it like a podcast. Both podcasts and vodcasts are highly effective training tools.

YouTube. *Youtube.com* is a free social networking site that allows users to upload and share videos. Users can subscribe to other users' video feeds and even leave comments and rate the videos. Many companies utilize YouTube for publishing training recordings and video resource material. With YouTube, trainees can subscribe to the trainer's video account to view training videos and participate in dialogue about the videos. This is an excellent way to facilitate discussion and feedback about training content.

Twitter. *Twitter.com* is a popular, free microblogging service. Users can sign up, create a profile, and send short messages of 140 characters or less, known as *tweets*. Users tweet about whatever they are doing and thinking, and they follow other peoples' tweets. Everybody who is in a user's network may read new tweets unless access is granted only to specific persons. With Twitter, trainers and trainees have the capability to communicate via personal computer or mobile devices. Twitter is now being used in corporate America and in educational institutions with increasing popularity.[21]

Screencasts. A **screencast** is a digital recording of a user's computer screen output that often contains voice narration and presentational material. Screencasts are especially useful in creating software-training demonstrations. Screencasts can be used in combination with PowerPoint slides to create a powerful e-learning tool. Programs such as Snag It and Camtasia Studio allow users to create digital narrations and training videos that can be customized and uploaded into a variety of video output formats. Many trainers and e-learning practitioners use a free Web-based service called *Screenr.com*. Screenr allows users to create bite-sized (five minutes or less) screencasts that are designed for use with Twitter. However, these short screencasts can be viewed on the Internet by a PC or Internet-capable, mobile device.

Screenshots. A screenshot is a snapshot of the user's computer screen; it is useful in creating e-learning tools. Screenshots can be edited and customized to insert in e-learning presentations, to enhance PowerPoint presentations, and to create step-by-step instructions and references. Screencasts make excellent training materials.

Rapid Training Tools

With the growing need to increase the speed at which training programs are developed, training professionals must be versed in how to use rapid training tools. The box below lists a sampling of rapid e-learning tools.

RAPID E-LEARNING SOFTWARE TOOLS

Software Name	Company Name
Keynote	Apple Computer
KnowledgePlanet On-Demand Learning Suite	KnowledgePlanet
Articulate Rapid E-Learning Studio	Articulate
Microsoft Word	Microsoft Corporation
Articulate Engage	Articulate
Articulate Rapid E-Learning Studio	Articulate
Microsoft PowerPoint	Microsoft Corporation
Articulate Presenter	Articulate
StudyMate	Respondus
Adobe Captivate	Adobe Systems, Inc.
Flashform Rapid eLearning Studio	Rapid Intake
Lectora	Trivantis
QMIND Design Collaboration Platform	QMIND, Inc.
Raptivity	Harbinger Knowledge Products
KnowledgePresenter	KnowledgePresenter
Brainshark Presentations	Brainshark, Inc.
Respondus	Respondus
Eilcitus	Harbinger Knowledge Products
WebEx Presentation Studio	WebEx Communications
Vuepoint Content Creator	Vuepoint
Adobe Connect	Adobe Systems, Inc.
Impatica for PowerPoint	Impatica Inc.
KnowledgePlanet Firefly	KnowledgePlanet
Rapidal	Brainvisa
Lectora	Trivantis Corporation
RapidBuilder®	XStream Software
Second Life	Linden Research, Inc.
ReadyGo Web Course Builder	ReadyGo Inc.
Desire2Learn Learning Environment	Desire2Learn Inc.
Corel WordPerfect Office	Corel Corporation
OnDemand Presenter	OnDemand Software
ToolBook Instructor	SumTotal Systems Inc.
Skillsoft Course Customization	Skillsoft
LearnCenter	Learn.com
ToolBook Assistant	SumTotal Systems Inc.
IBM Simulation Producer	IBM
Cornerstone OnDemand Enterprise	Cornerstone OnDemand
Impatica OnCue	Impatica Inc.

Rapid E-Learning Software Features. Although all the software products listed in the box have unique features, these features are common across software products:

- *PowerPoint converter*. Allows you to convert your PowerPoint slides into training programs.
- *Templates*. Allow unlimited flexibility in course layout and provide a consistent look to your training program.
- *Multimedia features*. Allow you to easily integrate Web-viewable graphics, simulations, audios, and videos.
- *Browser compatibility*. Most software is compatible with popular Web browsers such as IE, Mozilla, Chrome, and Safari browsers.
- *Smart phone compatibility*. Some programs allow trainees to participate using smart phones such as Android, Blackberry, and iPhone.
- *Multiple languages*. Many software products allow trainees to select a language; English, Spanish, Japanese, Arabic, French, Italian, and German are among those available.
- *Drill down features*. Allows trainees options for learning more about a particular topic.
- *Interactive activities*. Allows trainees to interact with engagement activities in order to learn from practice.
- *Assessments*. Quizzes reinforce content for trainees.
- *Surveys*. Online surveys provide trainee feedback to the training team.
- *Glossary pages*. Provides trainees with definitions of terms used throughout the training program.

Whatever type of rapid e-learning tool is used, the tool needs to be easy to use. It is important to use authoring tools that can easily import objects, graphics, and clip art from other software programs. This saves considerable time because the trainer won't have to develop a rapid training program from scratch.

Predesigned Templates. A template is a pattern or a model that has already been created that allows for consistency across Web pages. It's a built-in infrastructure where all the designer needs to do is insert the information. PowerPoint is a very popular visual presentation software, in part because it offers users a variety of design templates. Rather than start with a blank page, the designer begins with a pattern that can be carried through the training program.

Off-the-Shelf Training Programs. One popular form of rapid training and development is the complete, off-the-shelf training package. Considering the time and resources required to create original training programs, trainers frequently opt to purchase training packages that can be customized to meet their needs. This allows trainers to focus their time and energy on other areas of training and development. But, while prepackaged training programs can save time and resources, trainers should be aware that one size does not fit all. Essential questions that trainers should ask prior to purchasing an off-the-shelf program are:

- *Do we have the funding to purchase the program?*
- *Do the strengths of the program match the content you must deliver?*
- *Do the delivery processes match your organization's learning environment?*

- *Will this program save enough time to justify the return on investment (ROI)?*
- *Overall, will it provide us with real cost savings?*
- *Will our organizational culture support the program's learning environment?*
- *Will trainees be able to operate the technology required by the program?*
- *Do we have the technology to support and maintain the program under current or future conditions?*
- *Is visible high-level support available for the program and the program's content?*

DEVELOPING WEB TRAINING

It's time to begin developing Web-based training. To enhance your ability to design high-quality Web-based training, this section examines design principles and practical tips for effective Web training design.

Design Principles for Web-Based Training

Because today's trainees have higher expectations for Web design, appropriate design principles are essential for Web-based training programs. Here are the more important design principles for Web training.[22]

Keep It Simple.   One major difference between Google and its competitors is its simple design. This simplicity has made it one of the most popular search engines on the Web. When logging into Google.com, viewers find a very simple home page containing just a window to insert your search terms. (When logging into Yahoo.com, viewers can easily be overwhelmed and distracted; rather than conduct a search, Yahoo! users end up reading the news and checking their horoscope.) Google has reminded people that less is more. A simple user interface is a better design, especially when it is supported by solid technologies that are invisible to the user.

© Google. Used with permission.

Use Three Clicks.   Trainees should be able to find what they're looking for in three clicks. If they can't, the trainer has a design problem. Navigation tools should be easy to see and follow, and they should be in a consistent location throughout the Web site. Advancing to a new chapter, returning to a prior page, taking a quiz, or learning more about a topic or "drilling down," trainees should be able to achieve their intended goal in three or fewer clicks. A flat Web site is one that allows trainees to retrieve information in three or fewer clicks.

Avoid Dead-ends.   In the world of e-learning, Bermuda triangles occur when trainees click into a corner and can find no way out. Trainees continue to click, hoping to escape, and only go deeper into the triangle. The problems arise from poor navigation tools (i.e., faulty forward and back/return buttons), links to other Web sites with no clear way to return, and a lack of visual cues to identify the path that visitors took to get to a location. To avoid these mistakes, make sure a Web site allows users to continue, return, and escape or exit from it, and make sure these options are clearly visible.

Make It Sticky. Because trainees can easily be distracted in a Web-training program (i.e., stopping to check Facebook), trainers need to make the training sticky. Sticky Web sites capture and retain attention; they hook trainees and don't let them go. Trainees won't even think about opening another tab on the browser to multitask. Put simply, they're stuck. Figure 7.3 offers a few suggestions for how trainers might enhance the stickiness of Web-based training.[23]

Simple	Make sure your trainees get the core message. Use minimal words or select images to convey a single idea. If your message is cultivating people and helping them grow professionally, you may want to use an image of a flower garden where all the flowers are in full bloom.
Unexpected	Get trainees' attention by surprising them. Break a pattern. Reveal an idea that is counterintuitive. For example, at Southwest Airlines, customers are not #1, employees are; customers are #2. Showcase this feature throughout your training.
Concrete	Help trainees understand and remember. New trainees need concrete steps. They need language that they can use to Greet a customer, Look for nonverbal cues, Assess needs, Describe products and services, and Close the sale. Develop a mnemonic device (GLAD-C) to help trainees remember the steps to selling.
Credible	Get trainees to believe. Use testimonials from opinion leaders. Oprah Winfrey has strong opinions about the power of communication and the need for communication skill development. Use her personality power to enhance your communication training.
Emotional	Allow trainees to feel the problem—get them to care. Embed appropriate YouTube video clips into your training program. If you're training on how to manage conflict, embed videos that demonstrate effective and ineffective ways to manage conflict.
Stories	Get trainees to act out narratives. For example, Nordstrom's department store is full of stories about how employees go out of their way to meet the needs of customers. When conducting customer service training programs, use stories of employees who provide outstanding customer service.

FIGURE 7.3
How to Engage Trainees in Web-Based Training

Ensure Rapid Downloads.   Most trainees have little patience when working on the Web. If a page does not appear instantly, trainees will become frustrated. When a graphic doesn't materialize within five to ten seconds, you're going to lose your e-learner. Creating content in HTML or EML is probably the simplest and most straightforward method of facilitating rapid accessibility. HTML allows you to create pages that load quickly.

Brand It.   The look and feel of a Web training program should mirror the organization's image. To brand, use the organization's logo, motto, tagline, and corporate colors. An effective method for branding Web pages in a consistent manner is to use cascading style sheets (CSS), which is a Web language or code that allows consistent Web-page design throughout a particular training program.

Chunk It.   Effective Web-based training programs are chunked into courses or chapters of 15–20 Web pages, allowing trainees to spend, on average, one minute per page. Most trainees can concentrate on and complete a 20-minute training program while sitting at their workstations. Another idea is to chunk training into five chapters so that a trainee can complete one 20-minute chapter per day, completing the training course in a week. Trainees have a sense of accomplishment when they can complete a chapter a day and a course a week.

Use Levels to Organize.   Effective Web-based training has an infrastructure that usually remains invisible to trainees. That infrastructure usually includes four levels:

- *Level 1: Previews training program.* This level, the training program's home page, introduces you to the training and provides you with a preview of the entire training program. This is where overall training goals are outlined.
- *Level 2: Previews chapters.* This level, an index, previews all the chapters of the training program. This level provides you with a hyperlink to each chapter where learning objectives are previewed. Level 2 also introduces a service bar, which is a menu of services to help trainees. It typically contains buttons for Help, FAQ, Glossary, Course Map, and access to Wiki or Blog.
- *Level 3: Reviews course content within chapters.* At level 3 you're introduced to the training content. Resembling a book, level 3 showcases course content presented in a clear and engaging manner, with page numbers and navigation tools. Level 3 pages reveal core content, usually highlighted conclusions followed by hyperlinks to more detailed information—which leads to level 4.
- *Level 4: Drills deeper into course content.* Level 4 allows you to drill down into content that you find particularly interesting and relevant to your effectiveness on the job. Because adult learners bring various levels of experience to the training classroom, the drill down feature gives them the opportunity to probe further by linking to a particular downloadable article, a Web resource, an exercise or simulation, a film, or a test.

Practical Tips for Web-Based Training

It is important to remember that e-learning is just another training method and that the Tell, Show, Invite, Encourage, and Correct technique for teaching a skill are still applicable (with some modification). Trainers can apply many of the concepts from Chapter 4 on designing a curriculum to Web-based training in many ways.

Telling. In any training program, the trainer begins by telling, or sharing new information with trainees. Consider these suggestions:

- *Use the four-level organizational structure.* Using slides or Web pages, prepare text where you (1) preview the training program, (2) preview the chapters, (3) review course content within the chapters, and (4) provide drill down opportunities, where trainees can learn more in-depth information about a particular concept, behavior, or idea.
- *Use screencasts.* Screencasts are digital recordings of a trainee's computer screen output that often contain voice narration and presentational material. For a quick review, screencasts can be used in combination with PowerPoint slides to create a powerful e-learning tool. The box on page 157 provides a list of software that you can use in preparing screencasts.
- *Use podcasts.* Convey information by prerecording it in an audio file. Once completed, you can upload it to the Web and trainees can download the podcast using their own computer or mobile device.

Showing. Trainers can demonstrate the communication skills they would like their trainees to develop in a number of ways by using Web-based training. Here are recommended tools and techniques:

- *Use YouTube.* Videos are an excellent way for trainers to show how to perform a set of communication skills. With appropriate permissions and subscriptions, you can easily upload training videos to YouTube.
- *Use Skype.* With a computer and a webcam, trainers can demonstrate communication skills using Skype, which serves as a virtual training classroom.
- *Use digital media products.* Before the training begins, you can prepare a library of DVDs or CD-ROM for shipment to each of your enrolled trainees as part of the media package accompanying the Web-based training.

Inviting. Inviting is engaging trainees in performing the demonstrated communication skills and behaviors. With e-learning, trainees can demonstrate their communication competencies by using Skype or other forms of live video-streaming. They can also video-record their demonstration or performance and upload it to a social networking site. Other ways to invite trainees include:

- *Use simulations.* **Simulations** are interactive, task-driven exercises that allow trainees to experience a concept and develop skills. Most simulations use real-life situations in which individuals or groups must understand their tasks and interact successfully in order to achieve an objective. Games and simulation software can be purchased or even developed in-house if you're fortunate to have instructional technology designers on staff.[24]
- *Use audio files.* Depending on the communication skill you're asking trainees to develop, have them record their voices as a wave (.wav) file or an MP3 file and attach those files to an e-mail or upload them to your Web site.
- *Use quizzes, essays, an online forum, or journals.* If your training objectives are cognitive or affective based, invite trainees to demonstrate their competence by completing an online quiz, essay, or journal.

Encouraging. Encouraging occurs when trainers both motivate and guide trainees through a program. Here are a few recommendations:

- *Make yourself available.* Arrange online office hours or conduct office hours using Skype. Knowing that you're available and accessible is motivating to the e-learner.
- *Encourage trainees to encourage each other.* Create online social spaces, such as a Student Lounge or a Student Café chat room, where you post announcements, encourage casual conversation, and allow students to share best practices for e-learning.
- *Encourage trainees to evaluate information or behaviors.* Encourage them to make judgments about a behavior by assessing it against a standard or criteria. Ask them to compare and contrast a variety of performances or demonstrations.

Correcting. Providing e-learners with feedback is critical if they are to develop a communication skill properly.

- *Give immediate feedback.* Once you view a trainee's performance, provide him or her with specific feedback that showcases strengths and illustrates specific areas for improvement. Do this by using online office hours, creating and forwarding an audio or video file to the trainee, or forwarding an e-mail with an attached evaluation document.
- *Correct by using peer assessments.* Involve other trainees in the correcting process. Assign trainees to a fellow trainee or a team of trainees who will be responsible for providing corrective feedback.
- *Use self-assessment.* Ask trainees to self-assess their own performance by using the same evaluation form you will use to assess their performance.

USING THE NEEDS-CENTERED TRAINING MODEL FOR E-LEARNING

Developing a Web-based training program still requires the eight steps of the needs-centered training model shown in Figure 7.4. As a way to summarize the elements of Web-based training we'll apply the content of this chapter to each of the model's eight steps.

Analyze the Training Task

Two training dynamics that should influence whether e-learning is appropriate for your training task are ambiguity and media richness. If the training task is high in ambiguity, a media-rich e-learning environment will be needed. For example, if you're going to train people to use complex negotiation skills that include reading and interpreting nuanced nonverbal messages, then an e-learning environment that is media rich and allows for synchronous communication is recommended. See Figure 7.2 on page 152 for a review of the media richness of different technologies. Conversely, if the training task is low in ambiguity, then an e-learning environment that is low in media richness will be adequate. For example, if you're training people on etiquette and telephone skills that are highly scripted and routine, then Web-based or distance education delivery is appropriate.

FIGURE 7.4
The Needs-Centered Training Model

Develop Training Objectives

Regardless of the method of e-learning (traditional e-learning, rapid e-learning, blended e-learning), all training requires a set of well-written training objectives that are observable, measurable, attainable, and specific. In the training delivery continuum in Figure 7.5, behavioral training objectives (i.e., skill development) are most suitable for e-learning technologies that allow for synchronous communication. Cognitive training objectives (i.e., knowledge acquisition) can be achieved with e-learning technologies that are more asynchronous. Affective training outcomes (i.e., emotional response) can be met using a variety of delivery methods.

Organize Training Content

We have discussed organizing training content for Web-based instruction using a four-level approach:

- *Level 1: Previews training program.*
- *Level 2: Previews chapters.*
- *Level 3: Reviews course content within chapters.*
- *Level 4: Drills deeper into course content.*

It's also important to build into the organization your set induction, stimulus variation, and closure. Here are suggestions:

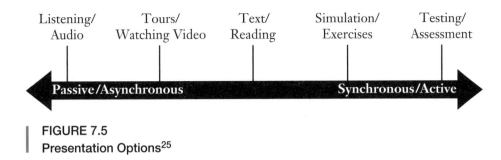

FIGURE 7.5
Presentation Options[25]

Set Induction. For e-learners to be ready to learn, it's important that they see how the training is going to be relevant to them. They need to understand how the training they are about to experience will help them solve a problem. Allow them to see, hear, and feel the problem. Conduct an interview using Skype; have trainees listen to a podcast or view a YouTube video. These activities will help stimulate trainees' readiness to learn.

Stimulus Variation. Retaining trainee attention will always be a challenge in a e-learning environment. When trainers vary the stimulus, they motivate their trainees to remain engaged and focused. In a Web-based training program, trainers have a number of ways to keep trainees engaged. They can use a "level four" drill down technique for the trainee who wants to learn more. They can build in self-assessment quizzes. They can enable trainees to self-pace their own learning with easy-to-use navigation tools.

Closure. Level three organization allows trainers the ability to summarize the content in a particular unit. Many Web-based programs will also include a self-assessment quiz to help trainees summarize their learning.

Determine Training Methods

In the e-learning training context, matching the training method with a particular technology for engaging the trainee is referred to as the presentation option. Effective Web-based training programs provide trainees with a variety of presentation options ranging in degree from passive to active. Figure 7.5 illustrates the options. Passive presentation options are those that require listening and viewing; active options include decision making and problem solving.

Listening/Audio. This option includes embedding an audio file or a podcast in the Web-based training program and navigation tools that allow trainees to stop, rewind, and fast forward in the event they want to take notes.

Tours/Watching Video. For some training content, a tour or a video is most appropriate. If you're trying to develop skills that require a step-by-step approach, such as how to develop a PowerPoint presentation, then the Web designer can prepare a screen-snapshot also known as a tour. A tour is a brief film that shows the mouse moving onscreen to perform the online procedures that the trainee will use to develop a PowerPoint presentation.

Text/Reading. This option offers training content in written form. To aid retention, it is recommended that text be presented as bulleted items. You can be creative by adding text boxes that include tips or interesting facts. Providing drill down opportunities by adding hyperlinks to articles or other Web sites that focus in depth on the training topic can also aid retention.

▶ RESOURCE GUIDE FOR E-LEARNING DEVELOPMENT[26]

Resource Type	Resource Location
Instructor Training Programs	World Wide Learn directory of online courses, online learning and online education http://www.worldwidelearn.com/teaching-online.htm
	How to develop an online course (free tutorial online) http://www.stylusinc.com/online_course/tutorial/process.htm
	Designing Instruction for Web Based Training (Darryl Sink & Associates) http://dsink.com/
	Developing Technology-Based Training (Friesen, Kaye and Associates) http://www.fka.com
Authoring Tools	ReadyGo www.readygo.com/
	Adobe e-learning Products: Adobe Present, Flash, Captivate, Authorware, Dreamweaver, Course Builder, etc. http://www.adobe.com/resources/elearning/
	Articulate Quizmaker and Articulate Engage http://www.articulate.com/
	Flashform http://www.rapidintake.com/flashform_index.htm
	DazzleMax and other e-learning tools http://www.maxit.com/
	Designers' Edge, Manager's Edge, Quest http://www.mentergy.com/
	Toolbook http://www.toolbook.com/
	Outstart Trainer soft http://trainersoft.com/product/OutStart_TrainingEdge.html
	Swish 1.5.1 http://Swishzone.com/
	Hotpotatoes from Halfbakedsoftware (inexpensive) http://web.uvic.ca/hrd/hotpot/
Virtual Classrooms	Citrix GotoMeeting https://www.gotomeeting.com/
	Elluminate http://www.elluminate.com/
	Centra http://www.centra.com/
	WebCt http://www.webct.com/
	WebEx http://webex.com/
	HorizonLive/WIMBA www.horizonwimba.com
	Learnlinc http://www.mentergy.com/
	Blackboard http://www.blackboard.com/
	Astound http://www.astound.com/wc/index2.html
	Asynchronous Voice Tool for online discussions http://www.wimba.com

Simulation/Exercises. In a simulation, as described in Chapter 6, trainees are given a set of circumstances and asked to play or enact roles in order to make a decision or solve a problem. Some very expensive video-based simulations allow trainees to play roles using an **avatar**, which is a computer user's representation of himself or herself in the form of a name, a picture, or another three-dimensional model.

Testing/Assessment. This presentation option asks trainees to assess their learning by answering a series of questions. Trainees are asked to engage in problem solving. In Chapter 11, we explain how to develop a variety of assessment items that can be integrated into Web-based training to allow both the trainee and the trainer to assess training outcomes.

Select Training Resources

The marketplace is full of resources for the new e-learning professional. The box on the opposite page is a select list of references to get you started. In addition to drawing on this list, new e-learning developers are encouraged to review the user-friendly "how to" guides available at local booksellers or through Amazon.com.

Complete Training Plans

Chapter 9, focuses on developing a training plan, a written description of a training session. This document contains training objectives, a summary of training content, a description of methods, and a detailed description of all the presentational aids needed to transform the plan into a high-quality training program.

With e-learning, a training plan is a walk-through of the Web-based training program. Of the many ways to prepare a training plan for Web-based training, the simplest is to develop the two-column plan. The first column details the Web page and the second column details the content and features on the Web page. See Figure 7.6 for a sample of a Web-based training plan.

Deliver Training

As this chapter indicates, there are many delivery options (traditional classroom, Web/video, Web-based, distance education) and tools (Skype, podcasts, screenshots, RSS feeds) to help trainers deliver their training programs. Additionally, blended training programs allow trainers to mix and match training methods, technologies, and delivery systems using one of three models: hybrid, knowledge/skill rotation, and complementary.

Assess Training

A variety of assessment tools (i.e., surveys, quizzes) can be used to assess training outcomes in Web-based training. (assessment techniques and methods will be reviewed extensively in Chapter 11). Although most of these tools are best suited for assessing cognitive and affective training outcomes, with some creativity and adaptation, behavioral training outcomes can be assessed as well.

Assess learning within a chapter. Use test items within a chapter to keep the content interactive and the trainee engaged and focused. This assessment technique gets trainees thinking about the content and helps them remember the most important parts.

Web Page	Content/Features
Program Title	Conducting Meetings: Managing an Agenda and Facilitating Difficult Conversations
Program Preview	This program is designed for the mid-level manager who is responsible for conducting monthly staff meetings. This training program includes 5 chapters.
Chapter 1 Title and Preview	Developing the Agenda In this chapter, you're going to learn how to develop an agenda by (1) identifying discussion, information, and action items, and (2) organizing the items in an appropriate order.
Chapter 1 Content Pages	Provide a Sample Agenda To develop an agenda, first consider all the topics, issues, information, and questions you need to discuss to achieve your meeting goals. As you start to identify the various agenda items, don't worry about what order to place them in; just identify them. Once you have a first draft of your agenda items, you can arrange the topics and issues in a logical structure based on time constraints and other priorities.
Chapter 1 Review	In this chapter, you learned how to develop an agenda by (1) identifying discussion, information, and action items, and (2) organizing the items in an appropriate order.
Chapter 1 Drill Down Pages	To learn more about the different types of agendas and formats, you're encouraged to review the following Web sites for additional information. . . .
Chapter 1 Assessment	To assess your learning, please take a few minutes to complete the following quiz. When you successfully complete this quiz, you will be ready to go to the next unit.

FIGURE 7.6
A Web-Based Training Plan

Assess learning at end-of-chapter. At the end of each chapter, trainers can present a quiz (five to ten items) to ensure that trainees have read and are interpreting the material correctly. To assess a behavioral learning outcome, a trainer may want to upload a YouTube video and ask trainees to identify certain behaviors or upload videos demonstrating the performance of a set of desired behaviors that trainers can assess.

◤ A TRAINER'S TOOLBOX

The Ten Best Practices for E-Learning[27]

Practice	Strategy
1. Help trainees manage control.	Inform trainees of the different decisions they can make about their learning, including the ordering of content, drill-down options, and assessment options.
2. Calibrate expectations.	Inform trainees that they will be expected to manage their time, troubleshoot technology, remain motivated and self-directed, and be expected to participate, interact with others, and assess others' work.
3. More isn't necessarily better.	Don't provide trainees with too many decision points; they're distracting. Rather than focus on the training content, trainees become distracted in making unnecessary decisions.
4. Skipping is better than adding.	Rather than asking trainees to read, view, or interact with additional content, give them the option to skip it. When they already have an understanding, it's important to maintain their motivation by giving them a skip option.
5. Keep it real.	Context control is important. Rather than contextualize the content for trainees, allow them to place the learning in their own context. For example, if you're training on how to provide constructive feedback, allow trainees to put it into the personal or professional context that makes most sense for them.
6. "You are here" tools.	Help trainees remain oriented by providing icons, arrows, or page numbers that remind trainees where they are in the training content. When appropriately engaged in the training content, trainees can quickly lose their sense of direction.
7. Be consistent.	Trainees appreciate consistency in font size, colors, and formats. One goal of e-learning is to reduce the cognitive burden of trainees. If trainees are forced to attend to several things at once, they may be unable to focus their attention appropriately.
8. Create smooth transitions.	It's important to link online training content. Help your trainees see how chapters and content are related to each other by linking segments with a few brief lines of text, such as "for an in-depth description of how to conduct an audience analysis, click here" and "to see a video example of how to manage conflict, click here."
9. Provide feedback.	Inform trainees that they will receive feedback from three sources: self-tests, colleagues, and you.
10. Warm it up.	Share your biographical information with your trainees by posting it to the training Web site or by providing a URL to a personal Web page. Ask trainees to do the same.

Assess learning at end-of-program. At the end of a training program, trainers can assess the impact of the entire program by focusing on all three types of training outcomes: cognitive, behavioral, and affective. A quiz can assess cognitive outcomes. A survey can assess affective outcomes by asking what trainees thought about the trainer and the content. Finally, trainees can upload videos of themselves enacting role plays or other performances to demonstrate their mastery of the behaviors.

SUMMARY AND REVIEW

In our fast-paced society, long on-site training programs don't always provide the best option for people with busy schedules. However, training remains an important part of effective organizational development. This chapter focused on Web-based technologies for developing interactive or fully online training programs. The first part of the chapter introduced e-learning.

- A trainer must first understand the need for and the use of such programs. Web-based training programs can minimize downtime on the job and can be significantly more cost-effective.
- Several training options are available to a trainer, from fully face-to-face training programs to Web-conferencing or blended training options, and to fully online distance-learning programs.
- The appropriate use of these programs depends on the nature of the task and the richness of the selected media channels.

Many tools are available to a trainer to develop, conduct, deliver, and assess Web-based training programs.

- Web 2.0 tools, software programs, and rapid e-learning tools all provide trainers with the technology to assist in the development of Web-based training programs.

- Because Web-based training occurs in a different environment from traditional, face-to-face training programs, trainers should make use of design principles and tips to enhance effective Web-training design.

Next, we discussed design principles and practical tips for developing Web training.

- Design principles are: keep it simple, use three clicks, avoid dead-ends, make it sticky, ensure rapid downloads, brand it, chunk it, and use levels to organize.
- Practical tips for Web-based training include how to apply the tell, show, invite, encourage, and correct model of teaching skills in an online environment.

While e-learning programs are increasing in popularity, it is important to remember that the needs-centered model of communication training still applies to an online or interactive training course.

- While developing an e-learning program, a trainer must make consistent use of the needs-centered training model introduced in Chapter 1.
- To get the most out of an e-learning program, it is vital to evaluate the effectiveness of the training for both the trainee and the organization's needs and objectives.

QUESTIONS FOR DISCUSSION AND REVIEW

1. Why are e-learning and Web-based training programs becoming more important and more popular? What benefits do they provide to the workforce?
2. Explain the variables that need to be considered when deciding on a model or a method for developing an e-learning program.
3. How can you begin developing skills at using Web 2.0 and rapid training tools while you're in school?
4. What design principles should you use when developing a Web-based training program?
5. What would you advise a client on how to apply the needs-centered training model to Web-based training?

QUESTIONS FOR APPLICATION AND ANALYSIS

1. Joel has recently been contracted to develop a Web-based training program for a new customer service call center. The program needs to focus on enhancing agents' communication skills on the telephone, with particular attention paid to appropriate handling of angry or irate customers. Considering the ambiguity of the task and the various categories of media richness, which Web-based delivery option or method would you recommend that Joel use? Why?

2. Rebekah's training and consulting firm has had much success in her region. The training program they provide on enhancing leadership communication effectiveness is one of their most popular programs. Recently, Rebekah has noticed that attendance is down at her training seminars, and people's busy lives have kept them from spending time in a training classroom. She'd like to modify a five-hour training program into an e-learning program. What recommendations do you have for her?

3. Jose, looking over the trainees' assessments of his Web-based middle-management training program, has noticed several concerns. Many people found his program confusing; they couldn't tell where to click to move forward. Some pages took time to download because of their large graphics and images. In addition, while trainees were developing skills involving communicating with subordinates, they had no opportunity to practice these skills in real time in order to assess their effectiveness. In what ways could Jose work to make his Web-based training more effective? How can he overcome these concerns?

ACTIVITIES FOR APPLYING PRINCIPLES AND SKILLS

1. Using a training program you are developing, or taking one that has already been developed, make the appropriate adjustments and redevelop this training program for an interactive, Web-based environment. Make sure to apply each step of the needs-centered training model as you do this, including analyzing trainee needs as well as the task, developing training objectives, organizing content, determining the training methods and resources, developing a plan, and delivering and assessing the training.

2. You've just been hired as the new Web-based training program developer at a popular training and consulting firm. This firm conducts training programs in customer service skills training, media software training for new companies, effective leadership training, conflict management, and team building seminars. Your job will be to analyze these training programs and select those that would be best suited to a Web-based environment. Which of the programs and skills might work well in an e-learning environment? Why? Select the models and options that would work best as a Web-based format for each skill set. To do this, consider the ambiguity of the task and the richness of various media channels.

3. This chapter ends with a list of the ten most effective practices for Web-based e-learning training programs. Take some time to analyze a popular training program according to this list of research-supported suggestions. Where are its strengths? Where are its weaknesses? What improvements would you recommend?

A room hung with pictures is a room hung with thoughts.

—*Sir Joshua Reynolds*

Using Presentation Aids in Training

CHAPTER OUTLINE

Purposes of Presentation Aids

Promote Interest
Clarify
Demonstrate
Enhance Retention
Enhance Training Transfer

Strategies for Using Presentation Aids

Keep Presentation Aids Simple
Communicate with Trainees, Not to Your
    Presentation Aids
Make Presentation Aids Large Enough to Be Seen
Be Ready to Present Without Presentation Aids
Practice Using Your Presentation Aids

Types of Presentation Aids

Participant Guides and Handouts
Dry-Erase Boards
Document Cameras
Video
Internet
PowerPoint

Summary and Review

Questions for Discussion and Review

Questions for Application and Analysis

Activities for Applying Principles and Skills

CHAPTER OBJECTIVES

After studying this chapter, you should be able to:

- List and explain four purposes for using presentation aids.

- Discuss and implement five strategies for using presentation aids.

- List and describe two advantages and two disadvantages each for using handouts, dry-erase boards,

  document cameras, video, and the Internet.

- Discuss two advantages and two disadvantages of using the Internet in presentation aids.

- Describe three strategies for designing and delivering PowerPoint slides.

John Godfrey Saxe's (1816–1887) famous poem "Blind Men and the Elephant,"[1] based on an ancient tale from India, relates how six men proclaimed very different descriptions of "elephant" based on the part of the elephant each one touched. One can get a very different understanding of "elephant" based on whether one touches a side, a tusk, the trunk, a leg, an ear, or the tail. A person's *involvement* with "elephant" is critical to one's *understanding* of "elephant." Imagine how much deeper and broader one's understanding of "elephant" could be if one could also see elephant, hear elephant, smell elephant, feed elephant, and ride elephant. In the training context, "elephant" can be more fully understood by trainees when the trainer does more than just tell them about "elephant." Wise is the trainer who can use presentation aids to deliver training content from multiple sensory modalities to involve and engage trainees. Effective use of presentation aids in the delivery of training can enhance trainee learning, recall, performance, and achievement. Poor use of poor presentation aids can have a negative effect even on good training material.

This chapter takes an in-depth look at using presentation aids in training. We focus first on the purposes of presentation aids, then, we discuss strategies for the effective use of presentation aids. The third section of the chapter examines types of presentation aids and discusses the best practices for using them well in training. The last portion of the chapter addresses the use of technology in generating and presenting presentation aids.

PURPOSES OF PRESENTATION AIDS

Before discussing the types of presentation aids or how to use them effectively in training, it's important for trainers to ask themselves, Why use presentation aids in the first place? Presentation aids are just that—aids. Presentation aids are *not* the presentation or the training content. Presentation aids can trigger training success or ruin a training session. Using them requires extra thought and work.

A trainer should have specific reasons for using any presentation aid. If a good reason for using an aid cannot be identified, the trainer should not use it. As a trainer prepares training material, he or she must continually ask these questions: Why am I using this? How does this engage and involve the trainees? In what way will this aid help trainee retention? How does this help accomplish training goals? Presentation aids fulfill several purposes that involve the trainee in the presentation.

Promote Interest

Presentation aids promote interest and capture trainee attention. A training topic such as how to prevent sexual harassment in the workplace could become boring if a trainer drones on for hours just talking. But presentation aids with current statistics, legal cases in related corporations, listings of top infraction trends, and short video clips of role play situations can do much to involve trainees in the training. A presentation aid can link the content to trainees by showing how the training is relevant to them. On the topic of sexual harassment, for instance, a trainer could display PowerPoint slides depicting statistics and federal laws regarding harassment.

The trainer could provide a pie chart showing harassment frequency trends in cases in the trainee's organization. A trainer could use video dramatizations of typical harassment scenarios in the workplace.

Incorporating training aids enhances trainee interest in any topic. Trainee interest, in turn, promotes trainee involvement and engagement in the session and the training content. Increased interest and involvement can translate into appropriate workplace behaviors as a result of the training.

Clarify

A presentation aid can help explain complex concepts or ideas to trainees. An organizational chart quickly can show the relationships between levels and reporting lines of management in a corporation. Leadership models can demonstrate the components, attributes, and approaches of various leadership styles. Video dramatizations of various approaches to corporate team building can allow trainees to see inclusion strategies being used. Current research indicates improvements in accuracy of understanding of numerical concepts regarding health risk information when "icon arrays and bar graphs are added to numerical information."[2] Other studies "confirm the supportive function of the illustrations used in . . . learning programs on factual knowledge when compared with text-only information."[3] Researchers point to the importance of using visual aids in a medical context to facilitate better patient understanding, compliance, and adherence to treatment regimes.[4] Whether in medical training contexts or in corporate training contexts, research on presentation aid use indicates the value of presentation aids in promoting both comprehension and clarity.

Demonstrate

One of the most effective ways to help trainees understand a skill or a behavior is to *show it*—to demonstrate a key step and offer a prescription for how to teach a skill. In a **demonstration**, the trainer or a model performs the desired behavior or shows others enacting it. Demonstrations are particularly useful with hard or soft skill training. Trainees can be shown how to set up a ledger sheet with a computer software program. Trainees can be shown a video of effective strategies that can be used to deal with difficult customers. Interactive Web sites can be accessed during a session to display effective communication in employee exit interview situations.

Enhance Retention

Retention is the amount of material a trainee remembers when the training session is over. If trainees cannot remember training content the day after a session, you have failed as a trainer. Memories stimulated by our five senses (individually or in tandem) start sooner, go deeper, and last longer than those we gain simply from hearing language. Seeing, hearing, and doing are more likely to create a vivid memory for trainees, which in turn tends to promote the memory of training content.

One can find examples of this in both hard and soft skill training applications. In a recent study involving the use of visual aids in chemical safety training, researchers found that visual aids improve retention of safety knowledge and enhance safe work practices.[5] Interestingly, in large lecture settings, researchers have found that using two screens with related but different material improves student retention.[6] Presentation aids that integrate both visual and auditory stimulation are engaging because they require us to use multiple senses to process information. Engagement and multisensory processing promotes retention.

Enhance Training Transfer

Another challenge for trainers is to get trainees to use new behaviors and skills on the job. It's one thing to read and discuss material from a training manual in a training session, and it is quite another to be able to apply and enact the material in a particular work-related context. Presentation aids may help in this transfer process. Technology and media allow trainers to turn training sessions into simulated work environments that more closely resemble what trainees encounter on a daily basis.

Some training programs, for example, feature video clips that portray workplace situations and ask trainees to respond in discussion to these situations. Internet simulations may allow trainees to role play in corporate situations. In both approaches, trainees can work through situations cognitively and enact simulated behavioral responses in various communication situations. Once trainees have responded to training simulations like these, they can be more prepared and skilled when encountering the real thing in a corporate setting. Presentation aids that show and place training skills in the real world can motivate trainees to incorporate and use new behaviors. Simulations used as presentation aids can provide practice and behavior response sets for on-the-job communication situations.

► RECAP

Purposes for Using Presentation Aids in Training

Purpose	Description
Promote interest	Stimulates attention and involvement with your training content
	Draws your trainees to want to know more about the training concept
	Motivates trainees to attend to, look at, and involve themselves in training concepts
Clarify	Provides a visual or auditory example of how the training concept works
	Shows a model of how something works conceptually
	Makes important explanations about the training content
Demonstrate	Shows how a training concept can be or should be used (for example, how to handle a hostile customer)
	Takes the concept and puts it into an observable and concrete form for the trainees
Enhance retention	Complements training material in such a way that trainees can remember it longer
	Provides cognitive triggers to stimulate recall at a later time
Enhance training transfer	Shows how the training concept fits in the world of the trainee
	Portrays a setting where a specific concept or approach could be used

STRATEGIES FOR USING PRESENTATION AIDS

Our experiences reveal that trainers sometimes have a difficult time using presentation aids well. This section reviews fundamental principles that apply to all presentation aids; later in the chapter we offer specific advice for using particular types of presentation aids.

Keep Presentation Aids Simple

Resist the temptation to put too much material in a presentation aid. It results in information overload and confusion. Trainees don't know where to direct their attention. Here are several ways to keep your presentation aids simple:

- *Narrow and focus the purpose of the aid.* Each presentation aid should serve a single purpose that is specifically related to a training objective and that ultimately meets the needs of your trainees. If the presentation aid is not related to a training objective, it is probably not needed.
- *Use key words or short phrases.* Rather than using long sentences, use **bullet points**, short phrases, key words, or short quotes. Avoid paragraphs of text. Avoid data dump presentation aids that feature more numbers than people can digest in a session (see Figure 8.1).
- *Use appropriate fonts.* **A font** is the design and size of the printing type. A font can be serif or sans serif. **Serif** means "*stroke or line* . . . and refers to the little extra stroke at the edge of letters."[7] This "stroke" tends to be decorative and stylized. "**Sans serif**" means "without stroke or line." You must consider which font to use when preparing presentation aids. *When using printed material,* the following fonts are recommended:

  Times New Roman
  Book Antiqua
  Bookman Old Style
  Calisto
  Garamond

FIGURE 8.1
Sample presentation aid:
PowerPoint Slide

- *When using electronic materials,* the following fonts are recommended:

  Arial
  Century Gothic
  Eras
  Franklin Gothic
  Helvetica
  Lucida Sans
  Tahoma
  Verdana.[8]

Notice that the fonts recommended for print materials tend to be serif fonts and the fonts recommended for electronic materials (like PowerPoint slides) tend to be sans serif fonts.

- *Pictures vs. Words.* Images often convey material more accurately and deeply than words can. Research suggests that a picture may be effective in promoting understanding and retention.

Communicate with Trainees, Not to Your Presentation Aids

Some trainers have a bad habit of facing their white boards and PowerPoint screens rather than talking with their trainees. Looking at your presentation aid instead of your trainees reduces eye contact and interpersonal connection with the trainees. Consider these tips:

- *Know your content.* Being familiar with the training content will keep a trainer from having to read the presentation aid to remember what needs to be said. Remember, the presentation and content comes *from the trainer—not from the presentation aid.* The basic communication connection must be between the trainer and the trainees, not between the presentation aid and the trainees.
- *Know your presentation aid sequence.* As a trainer personalizes content from one training session to another, he or she can lose track of which PowerPoint slide comes next. This can be embarrassing, lead to verbal stumbles, and cause the trainer to spend too much time looking at the presentation aid. When this happens, trainers lose trainee attention and break interpersonal links with them. Trainers should make sure all aids are in the appropriate place and should know that order.
- *Get to know your trainees before the session and before you use presentation aids.* The link between trainer and trainees needs to be established before and during the training. Especially when using extensive multimedia presentation aids, it is good practice to make personal contact and establish rapport with trainees before launching into your multimedia presentation.[9] When trainers fail to make contact first, trainees may perceive the training to be a bit impersonal and may see the trainer as superfluous.

Make Presentation Aids Large Enough to Be Seen

It seems obvious, but it is the most neglected skill in using presentation aids. Many trainers use presentation aids that are too small for trainees to see clearly. How large is large enough? Make presentation aids large enough so trainees in the last row can see them. When in doubt, make it larger than it needs to be. Here are additional suggestions:

- *Determine the size and shape of your training room.* Is the training room large or small, long and narrow, or short and wide? The shape of the room will influence the size of your presentation aid. The presentation aid you use for a long and narrow training classroom should not be the same size as the one you use for a short and wide training classroom.

- *Determine the size of the projection screen image.* Is the screen small, or is it large enough to be seen by all? Is the projector far enough away from the screen to make the image sufficiently big?
- *Is the trainer's handwriting on a white board big enough?* Trainers must write larger than normal when using a white board. Writing must be large enough and legible for the back row of trainees to see. As trainees get older and vision is challenged, this issue becomes even more critical.
- *Have handouts ready to distribute as an option.* Regardless of the number of trainees you have or the shape of the training classroom, it is helpful to have handouts of presentation aids available for distribution.

Be Ready to Present Without Presentation Aids

Murphy's Law, the notion that what *can* go wrong *will* go wrong, is often in full force with presentation aids, especially technology-based presentation aids. Expect and anticipate the worst when it comes to using your presentation aids! It's not uncommon for presentation aids to be lost or damaged in shipment. It's not uncommon for the technology you requested, confirmed, and verified for the training program to be inoperable or unavailable at the last minute. It's also not uncommon for computer systems to be incompatible or for the Internet to go down.

Here are suggestions for overcoming Murphy's Law:

- *Carry an extra electronic copy of the presentation aid with you.* Even if your presentation aids fail to make it to the training location, you should have an original copy with you that you can have reproduced at any office supply store, or professional business center. Flash drives are conveniently small and quite useful for this. Many businesses that support professional trainers operate 24/7 and can make emergency hard copies of handouts quickly and with professional quality.
- *Put presentation aid materials online (on a Web site or in an e-mail) as a backup.* If presentation aids are not delivered, if your luggage containing handouts is lost by the airlines, if local equipment goes down, you can use your own laptop to access presentation aid materials on the Internet.

Practice Using Your Presentation Aids

Knowing your material inside and out and using presentation aids well is important. To use your presentation aids effectively, we recommend the following general strategies.

1. *Rehearse with your presentation aid in the training room.* A short early "room visit" will let you determine the best placement for the aid and where you should stand while presenting and using the aid. Practicing beforehand allows you to discover blind spots in the room, glare on the screen, air vents that blow materials off the desk or wall, potential distractions, and other problems. Locate electrical plugs, light switches, window blind controls, and podium controls *before* the training session.
2. *Practice to ensure ease of using equipment.* Make sure you know how to use *this* model of document cam. Rehearse advancing your slides smoothly with a hand-held clicker. Know how to connect your flash drive or laptop to the

Internet connections and to the projector. Be familiar with how to hook up and control sound with your PowerPoint presentation.

3. *Practice to ensure seamless transitions.* Spend time working through your transitions so that you can transition *to*, *between*, and *from* presentation aids in a smooth and meaningful manner. Rehearse switching between PowerPoint slides and video clips. Practice display and hide techniques with your presentation aids so you can direct trainee attention strategically. You want the training presentation and the use of presentation aids to appear seamless.

TYPES OF PRESENTATION AIDS

A number of presentation aids are available to help trainers enhance the content, delivery, and retention of training content. In this section, we discuss strategies for using such aids as handouts, posters and flipcharts, dry-erase boards, document cameras, and video. Computer generated and Internet based presentation aids are becoming more and more common in training contexts, so we will explore these two presentation aids in detail.

RECAP

Presentation Aid Strategies and Prescriptions

Presentation Aid Strategies	Recommended Prescriptions
Keep presentation aids simple.	Don't use ornate fonts or formats. Make points short and concise. Use bullets to itemize lists. Keep the focus on the main ideas rather than on the presentation aid "decorations."
Communicate with trainees, not with the presentation aids.	Interact with people, not inanimate presentation aids. Establish and maintain eye contact with trainees.
Make presentation aids large enough to see.	Don't copy text from a training manual; scan and enlarge it so it can be projected on a screen. Make sure projections are large enough for trainees to see clearly.
Be ready to present without presentation aids.	Don't rely totally on your presentation aids. If something goes wrong with the presentation aids, keep moving forward—without them if necessary. Ensure that problems with presentation aids will not cause you to cancel a presentation.
Practice using presentation aids.	Make sure you have used the presentation aids before you present. Rehearse with presentation aids and relevant equipment.

Participant Guides and Handouts

The most basic presentation aid is the handout or participant's guide. **Handouts** are typically hard copy documents that you design and distribute to your trainees. Trainers often assemble individual handouts into a packaged form in a notebook or workbook. This collection of materials is referred to as a **participant's guide**. In Chapter 9 we discuss how participant's guides should be constructed. Handouts and participant's guides can also be distributed to trainees on computer disks or flash drives.

Handouts and participant's guides have both advantages and disadvantages. Handouts can be quite useful; they can also be a waste of paper, costly, and difficult to transport. Electronic handouts are a bit more efficient and easier to manage, but they don't have the immediate tactile benefit of hard copy documents. Consider your purposes and then use handouts and participant's guides to the greatest advantage.

Some handouts are helpful *during* the training. PowerPoint slides allow trainers to print handouts that are coordinated with the slides. One advantage of preparing handouts for your training presentation occurs in the event there is a technological problem and you're unable to use the computer to present the slide program. Another advantage with handouts is that they help trainees to follow along and to take notes (see Figure 8.2). Rather than jotting down all the information being presented, they can focus on taking notes to help them understand and remember the training content.

Some handouts or guides will be useful as reference materials *after* the training to aid in trainee review and recall. Materials trainees can take away from the session allow them to reference and review the training content as needed.

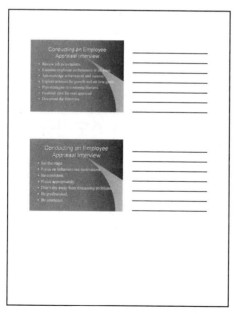

FIGURE 8.2
Sample presentation aid: PowerPoint handout

Using handouts or guides during a training session requires a degree of trainer finesse. Here are suggestions for *using* these materials well *during* your training sessions.

1. *Practice to make sure handouts are error free.* You would be surprised at the number of handouts that contain typographical or statistical errors. Handouts are a reflection of you and your work, and they need to be professional in quality (see Chapter 9).

2. *Do not distribute handouts while you are speaking.* This diverts trainee attention from you to what is being distributed. Try to distribute your handouts before the training session starts, during session breaks, or when the session is over.

3. *Let trainees know when to reference handouts.* As the training session starts, and during the session, make sure you share how and when the handouts will be used—so the trainees do not have to guess. Make sure to **signpost** during the session to review where you are on the handout. These strategies allow you to manage your trainees' attention patterns and keep them on the same page with you. Chapter 9 provides more suggestions for participant guide use.

Dry-Erase Boards

Dry-erase boards, or **whiteboards**, are white, laminated panels that allow trainers to use markers rather than chalk and to erase with ease. They can be an immediate presentation aid and, with various markers, they can be quite colorful. If the training room does not have one mounted on the wall, a dry-erase board can be quickly set up on a tripod and used effectively.

The advantages of using whiteboards as a presentation aid include ease of use, generative and fresh idea building, immediate display of dynamic trainee comments, and impromptu picture or graphic possibilities. Dry-erase boards can be used as screens for projected pictures as well.

Disadvantages for whiteboard use include difficulty of transport (when it is portable) and limited ability to prepare graphics beforehand. Poor trainer handwriting can be a problem; marker stains or residual marks from previous presentations can also be a problem.

If you want to use whiteboards in your presentation, do it smoothly and professionally. Here are suggestions for using dry-erase boards well:

1. *Use appropriate markers for the whiteboard.* Many a whiteboard has been ruined because someone used permanent markers on it rather than dry-erase markers. Make sure your markers are dry-erase markers.

2. *Bring your own dry-erase markers.* Don't depend on the training facility to provide you with dry-erase markers. Bring a backup marker with you if you intend to use a whiteboard as an aid. You'll want to use fresh markers with enough ink to get you through the day and with an assortment of color options for highlighting training content.

3. *Use dry-erase markers correctly.* Most markers must be held at a down angle (*with*, not *against* gravity) when writing on the board, or the ink flow will fade and the marker will stop working in the middle of your training presentation. This is a very common problem that you can avoid by mastering the correct procedure.

Document Cameras

A document camera is a mounted video camera connected to a video projector and projected on a large screen. This presentation aid can be very useful for displaying unscanned pictures, documents, and often-used material. Anytime you want to display an actual document in real time and enlarged on a screen, the document camera is a handy tool. The document camera also allows the building of lists and ideas in response to trainee comments during the training session. Training rooms are often equipped with a document camera, but there are also portable models that you can take with you to training sites.

Document cameras work quite well for some purposes and content and quite poorly for other purposes and content. When you want to show, for example, an organizational chart or a company vision statement, document cameras can be very useful. If you want to write down trainee comments as the session progresses and project them for all to see, document cameras can be quite useful.

One disadvantage for document cameras can be the size of the print. Typically, paper documents are made to be read at a distance of 1 to 1.5 feet. Font sizes for most documents are not appropriate for big screen projection and will often be too small for trainees to read. Another problem occurs when the document camera blocks the view of the screen for certain areas of the training room.

Make sure you have a specific purpose for using a document camera. Otherwise, use other presentation aids and devices. Note the following "best practice" suggestions for using document cameras well.

1. *Locate the document camera in an appropriate place.* Typically, document cameras are set on a technology cabinet at the front of the training room. They can be portable as well, however, so the trainer needs to locate the document camera strategically so that he or she can use it while facing the trainee group.

2. *Turn the document camera off when not in use.* The trainer should take care to turn the camera off when no image is being shown. Alternatively, the trainer can cover up the document with a folder or sheet of paper. During display, the trainer can strategically cover parts of the document with a sheet of paper and move it down as he or she covers new points. This technique of "cover and reveal" works quite well.

3. *Attend to the size of the document content.* A typical 8.5 × 11 inch document in 12-point text is fine for holding in one's hand and reading from 20 inches away, but it is not appropriate for projecting on a screen for a room full of trainees. Don't fall into the trap of using the document camera to project content that is not large enough for an audience to see clearly.

Video

Video clips are powerful presentation aids that trainers can use with a degree of ease and effectiveness in the training context. Videos allow trainees to view a variety of animated (versus static) representations of the content set in a normal, realistic context.

The advantages of using videos in training are clear: People love videos. Videos provide rich images *and* appeal to our senses. Videos, because of their movement and sound, capture our attention unlike any other presentation aid. Videos can provide visual narratives, and trainees are naturally drawn to a story.

Yet videos can be used poorly. Some trainers may allow the video to *be* the training session, with little input from the trainer. Trainees in these situations are expected just to watch and learn. Another disadvantage for videos can occur when trainees view the video for entertainment purposes rather than for training purposes. Make sure your video is targeted at specific training goals and that you reach these goals.

Make sure you use videos appropriately, in purpose, duration, and form. Here are suggestions for the effective use of videos in training sessions.

1. *Determine your relationship as a trainer with the video.* Before the training session you have to determine who is doing the training—you or the video. Is the video a support device for you, or are you the support device for the training video? If you are the trainer and the video is a presentation aid intended to illustrate aspects of the training content, then use the video accordingly. It may be that your primary role is to facilitate discussion of the training video or the hands-on application of it after it is completed. If the *total* of the training is in the video, however, you can find a nontrainer to start and stop the video. If the video *is the training* and you are not really needed, send the video to the trainees on DVD or in a link to a training Web site.

2. *Use brief clips.* Rather than present a lengthy video, it's best to use brief clips or excerpts. Because video can be seductive, many trainees get caught up in the video and forget to view it critically to determine which parts will enhance specific training objectives. The video should be used to supplement what you do to accomplish your training goals.

3. *Provide an introduction or context.* Rather than start a video cold, take a few moments to introduce the video. Warm your trainees up to the video. Who are the characters? Where are they? What has been happening? What do you want the trainees to watch for in the video? This briefing will help trainees interpret the video and extract the appropriate meaning for your training objective.

4. *Cue up your clip.* Take time to cue up your video before the training session starts. Before you begin, review the video and know where you're going to start and stop. It's a waste of time to hop from place to place through a video during a training program, looking for the appropriate spot. If you do this, you'll lose your training momentum and the attention of the trainees. You want a video presentation to be a smooth, seamless extension of your oral presentation.

5. *Apply and discuss the video clip.* Make sure that you move quickly into a discussion of the clip immediately after it is shown. This is a ripe time for trainee analysis, application, and assimilation.

Internet

Corporate training rooms are commonly set up with Internet connections, and this can be a great asset to the training session. Many Web sites can be explored and projected on a screen for the entire training group. Trainers can show photos, other images, and illustrations (static and dynamic) from all over the world. Short online video clips and excerpts can be accessed and used via the Internet. The Internet can be used in the training session to access real world data, such as current stock market trends, in real time.

Another use for the Internet in training sessions is to allow trainees to have hands-on time with an Internet-based presentation aid. It is one thing to show trainees visuals and audios that involve them in your training content; it is a more positive application to allow the trainee to interact with the presentation aid. Various Web sites have interactive and dynamic programs that trainees can manipulate and test to illustrate training content you are presenting. The Internet can be used to engage trainees in joint interactive training activities that require them to work together. A variety of simulations, threaded discussions, or group interactions could be used to provide trainees with hands-on experience using the content derived in the training sessions.

A trainer can use the Internet to make a live, real-time connection with a recognized subject matter expert for comments and a question and answer time for the trainees. The Internet can be used to coordinate trainee interactions and comments for simultaneous training sessions in different locations. But make sure that you can still facilitate the training session even if the Internet goes down!

PowerPoint

Trainers today have access to powerful, user-friendly software programs that enable them to develop and present training programs using computer-generated images. Presentation software programs allow trainers who have some experience to design color slides using a variety of audio and visual options including text, bulleted points, pictures, graphs, sounds, and even video clips. In this section, we review principles and suggestions for designing and delivering computer-generated presentation aids.

▶ RECAP

Advantages and Disadvantages of Presentation Aids

Presentation Aid	Advantages	Disadvantages
Participants Guides and Handouts	Relatively inexpensive Provide much information Provide trainees something to take back to the office with them Do not require technology to use Easy to transport	Hard to control trainee attention once they are distributed Can be a distraction Use large amounts of paper
Dry-erase boards (Whiteboards)	Easy to use Can double as a projection screen	Hard to transport; needs to be already in the room Must make sure you have fresh markers Must know how to use markers properly Must have legible handwriting
Document Camera	Easy to use, versatile Can be used spontaneously or with prepared documents	Documents can be too small even when projected Equipment can be a barrier between trainer and trainee—visually and perceptually
Video	Attention-catching visual possibilities, static or moving Captures the audience's attention Gives great images of concepts in action	Equipment failure always a possibility May compete with trainer for attention Audio capabilities sometimes a problem, especially in large rooms
Internet	Can provide up-to-date information in real time Can facilitate access to Web materials	Connections and connection rate can be unpredictable and can go down during session Information from the Web needs to be screened for accuracy and credibility
PowerPoint Slides	Can produce professional and useful visuals quickly Easy to transport; can produce handouts for trainees from slides Can bring in videos, sounds, demonstrations	Slides can become the focal point of the training Can be distracting and overshadow the content and the trainer Can be overused to the point of boring trainees

Principles for Using PowerPoint. The most common computer program used in generating and delivering presentations is PowerPoint. In his article *"Death by PowerPoint,"* David Taylor provides a clever and insightful critique of presentation aids—PowerPoint specifically—and "bad" presentations.[10] Some of his observations reflect keen insights into the dangers of poor presentations and poor presentation aids:

1. Use of PowerPoint sometimes requires dimmed lights. Depending on the room, this often makes it difficult for the audience to see the presenter or for the presenter to see the audience. This hampers communication, connection, and responsive adjustment during the presentation.
2. Unthinking presenters often subject audiences to a PowerPoint barrage of visual and auditory data at rates faster and quantities greater than the human mind can process and absorb.
3. PowerPoint audiences are required to match what they read on the slides with what they hear the presenter say. Many possible contrasts might exist in this situation.
4. Expert presenters use PowerPoint to "illustrate what they are saying rather than to replace their lecture."[11]

Some might argue that using many presentation aids makes trainees lazy and can reduce retention. In a recent study, researchers found that "in spatial tasks, visual guidance can impair training effectiveness because it encourages shallow performance strategies and little exploration."[12] Explanations for this suggest that visuals can be a drawback in that "they can act as shortcuts in achieving the performance standards without having the trainees actually being engaged in elaborate processing about the relationship between task elements, or exploring the spatial environment."[13]

On the other hand, many research studies point to positive outcomes from presentation aid use. Despite the disadvantages of PowerPoint and the usage transgressions of many presenters (trainers and otherwise), the program can be quite useful for generating and presenting presentation aids in a variety of presentation settings. Research indicates that college "students prefer PowerPoint and respond favorably to classes when it is used."[14] Students prefer "pictures and graphs when accompanied by text explanations.[15] Overall, presentation aids, when constructed strategically and used well, have positive effects in training contexts.

Designing PowerPoint Slides. We encourage you to consider a few basic design principles when preparing your slide presentation:

1. *Keep slides simple and concise.* Don't crowd too much information into one slide; the audience cannot absorb it all. With visual design, *less is more.* Notice Figures 8.3 and 8.4.
2. *Balance images.* Make sure your images have symmetry and balance. You don't want all of the text at the top of the slide or off to one side. Graphic experts Joyce Kupsch and Pat Graves encourage slide designers to strive for balance, symmetry, and placement on each slide to avoid slides that are lopsided.[16]

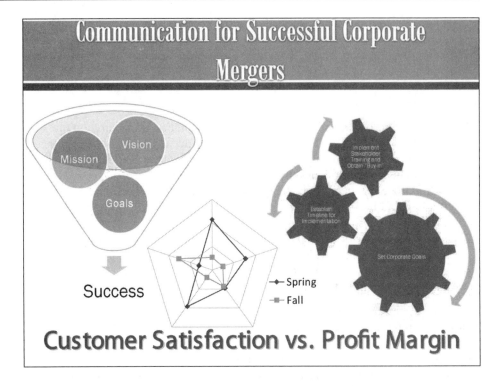

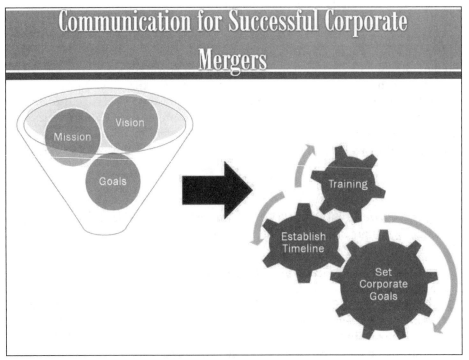

FIGURE 8.3
Complicated versus Simple: PowerPoint Slides

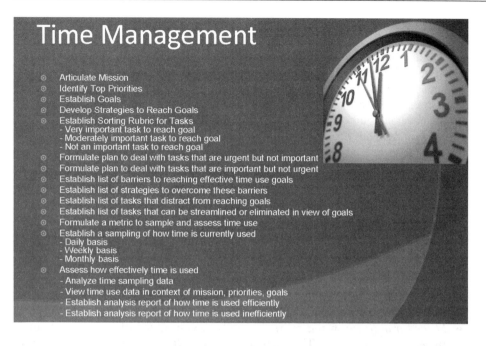

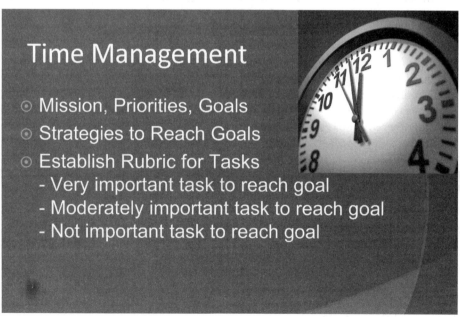

FIGURE 8.4
Appropriate Size: Too Small versus Large Enough to Be Seen Clearly

3. *Don't use animation.* One business professional noted: Comments from business professionals tend to say this: "I'd abolish 99 percent of all transition and animation effects. There is almost nothing as annoying as sitting through 23 text slides with *every bullet* flying in one at a time."[17] If you want to use slide builds, you should do so strategically, without being obnoxious.

4. *Use sound effects sparingly.* Slide sounds (applause, drum roll, explosion, etc.) are novel but quickly become annoying. It is generally suggested that you don't use sounds at all. If used, sound effects should be kept to a minimum and used only for specific emphasis. Be aware that research indicates audience preference for sounds that match or relate to "pictures or graphics on slides."[18]

5. *Use appropriate colors.* Students prefer color PowerPoint slides,[19] but shocking your audience with garish colors, poor contrast, or limited visibility detracts from slide content. Cool blues, greens, and purples are best suited for backgrounds, whereas hot colors such as reds, oranges, and yellows draw attention and are best suited for foreground items.[20] The color blue is the "background color of choice in over 90 percent of business presentations."[21] Typically, warm colors project and foster "excitement and interest," while cool colors project and foster "calm" and peace.[22] Notice the shading and legibility problems in Figure 8.5.

6. *Strive for uniformity and consistency.* Carry your design theme throughout the entire presentation. This includes layout, bullets, colors, spacings, fonts, and images.[23] Your design theme will not only provide a common thread throughout the presentation but will give your trainees a pattern that will make it easier for them to assimilate the information.

7. *Regulate and coordinate the number of visuals.* Trainers should match the number of images with the amount of time allotted for the presentation. Making 50 images meaningful to your trainees in a 15-minute presentation is unrealistic and a drawback to comprehension and retention. One or two slides per minute is a good rule of thumb.[24]

A TRAINER'S TOOLBOX

How to Use PowerPoint Effectively

PowerPoint experts Jennifer Rotondo and Mike Rotondo offer the following checklist for designing PowerPoint slides:

- Use only one point or major concept per visual.
- Leave out information that the presenter can say.
- Use phrases, not sentences.
- Use parallel structure (all phrases start with verb or noun and worded in the same form).
- Use 24-point font size.
- Avoid cartoon clip art.
- Spell check!
- Use the 8 × 8 rule: No more than eight words per line and eight lines per slide.
- Put in a graphic or a chart every three to five slides.[25]

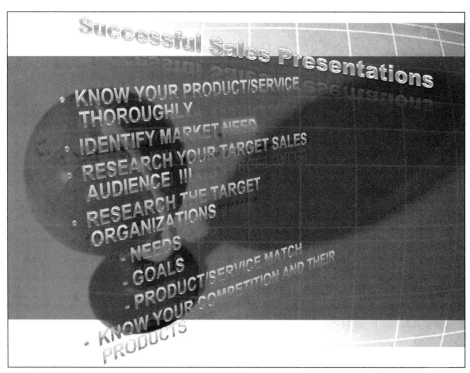

FIGURE 8.5
Too Complex and Detailed; Inappropriate Contrasts

Delivering Computer-Generated Presentation Aids. After you've designed your images, consider the following suggestions for polishing your presentation:

- *Set up and test the presentation.* When the training session starts, you should be seeing your projected PowerPoint slides for the second or third time—not the first time.[26] Trainers should arrive early to the training room to locate all necessary electrical outlets, start all necessary equipment, check out sightlines for the trainees, and do a test run through the PowerPoint to make sure it works well. Any equipment or compatibility problems should be quickly identified and addressed.
- *Control the lighting in the training classroom.* Even though projector bulbs are bright, some manipulation of the room or background lighting may be necessary. Too much ambient room or window light will cause eyestrain and frustration for you and your trainees. Many training rooms allow trainers to dim or turn off the lights that are nearest the screen while leaving enough lighting so that trainees can take notes. Make sure that the trainees can see you, the trainer, while the PowerPoint projector is on.
- *Display and hide slides effectively.* At times, it is strategic to have trainees attend to or look at the PowerPoint slide on the screen. At other times, it is strategic to have trainees focused on the trainer or something else in the training session. If the trainer hits *the* "B" key on the computer during a Power-Point session, the screen will go to black. Hitting the "B" key again will bring

RECAP

Design Principles and Prescriptions for PowerPoint Presentations

Design Principle	Design Prescription
Use simple and concise information.	Keep fonts consistent.
	Concentrate on including only main ideas or images. Leave off extra details.
	Don't crowd pictures.
	Less is more.
Balance visuals.	Make sure there is symmetry to your visuals.
	Place text in logical places in symmetrical formats.
	Balance your pictures.
	Pay close attention to constructing a professional-looking layout.
Use minimal animation.	Use sparingly if at all.
	Remember that too many animations, especially moving cartoons, are distracting.
	Use only animations that are central to your main ideas.
Use sound effects strategically.	Text constantly zipping in to the sound of bouncing balls or ringing bells will becomes irritating.
	Avoid using sound effects. Use them only with specific purposes and specific points.
	Use sounds primarily with pictures or video clips.
Use appropriate color schemes and design formats.	Computer programs are carefully programmed with balanced formats and coordinated colors.
	Default templates generally have visually appealing symmetry and visibility.
	Standard schemes and formats are the safest route.
Avoid design shock.	Use caution when changing standard color schemes.
	Be cautious of using colors that clash, irritate the trainees, or are hard to see.
Strive for conformity and consistency.	Avoid having new colors or designs for each slide.
	Stick with a standard template and use it for all slides.
	Use the same fonts and font sizes throughout a presentation.
Regulate and coordinate the number of images.	Though a picture speaks a thousand words, one can have too many pictures or slides.
	You don't need a picture on every slide.
	Limit the number of slides to fit within your allotted presentation time.

the slides back on the screen. Many hand-held clickers that advance the slides can also blank the projector screen. Practice these techniques of display and hide—at the beginning, during, and at the close of the training session—so you can direct trainee attention appropriately.

■ *Prepare a **contingency plan**.* With PowerPoint, the Internet, or any other electronic media, you should have a *backup plan* in the event you're unable to use the computer to present your training program. A trainer needs to be prepared to use other presentation aids, such as a dry-erase board. Experienced and prepared trainers always have contingency plans that allow them to effectively facilitate the content *without any presentation aids if necessary.*

RECAP

Principles and Prescriptions for PowerPoint Slide Presentations

Delivery Principle	Delivery Prescription
Plan, set up, and test PowerPoint presentation.	Set up the room early.
	Set up your presentation aids strategically.
	Make sure your slides are working and are in the proper order. Make sure all trainees can see the screen.
	Check to ensure all equipment cords and links are working. Check for boot-up time.
Control lighting in the training classroom.	Check to ensure that your projected images can be seen and are not faded by overhead or window light.
	Determine whether you must dim or turn out room lights for trainees to be able to see your projected images.
	If the room does not have ambient light, bring a small flashlight so you can see when the lights are out.
Prepare handouts and participant guides.	Make sure the handouts are grammatical, neat, and purposeful.
	If trainees are inappropriately looking at your handouts and not at you, redirect their attention where you want it to be.
Have a contingency plan.	Be ready in case a bulb goes out, the electricity goes off, the computer crashes, your handouts are lost with your luggage at the airport.
	If one thing breaks, plan to use the equipment that still works.

SUMMARY AND REVIEW

Before using presentation aids, the trainer should have a good understanding of the basic purposes for presentation aid use. What do presentation aids do? How can they enhance a presentation? Why use them with this content—or at all? Awareness of fundamental principles of presentation aids must be constant as trainers prepare training content and presentation materials.

Keeping these questions in mind, trainers need to consider basic presentation aid strategies as they are preparing their presentation aids. Presentation aids used poorly tend to hamper the effectiveness of training presentations. Presentation aids used strategically will make training presentations more effective.

In this chapter we have explored five presentation aid purposes:

- Promote Interest
- Clarify
- Demonstrate
- Enhance Retention
- Enhance Training Transfer

Strategies for presentation aid use include:

- Keep presentation aids simple
- Communicate with trainees, not "with" your presentation Aids
- Make presentation aids large enough to be seen
- Be ready to present without presentation aids
- Practice using your presentation aids

Finally, we discussed several different presentation aids, including:

- Participant's guides and handouts
- Dry-erase boards
- Document cameras
- Video
- Internet
- PowerPoint.

Presentation aids can do much to enhance the training session by engaging and involving trainees in the content. In the poem "Blind Men and the Elephant" the characters' perceptions of what an elephant is were dictated by their engagement and experience with the elephant.

Each person in the story perceived the elephant based on the part of the elephant he touched. Presentation aids allow trainees to "touch" training content in a variety of ways. Presentation aids allow trainees to remember "elephant" more vividly and to apply "elephant" communication concepts in career settings. Multimodal training content exposure, provided by trainer use of presentation aids, promotes more understanding and retention of the training content. Presentation aids aid trainers and trainees in delivering and assimilating training content.

QUESTIONS FOR DISCUSSION AND REVIEW

1. Explain how and why presentation aids enhance trainee retention of the material presented.
2. Discuss what will happen if you are not prepared to give your training session without your presentation aids. Why is it important to be prepared?
3. Why is it so easy to get caught up in talking to your presentation aids rather than keeping your focus and face on the trainees? Why is talking "to" the presentation aids a problem?
4. What could happen if you fail to practice with your presentation aids?
5. Compare the advantages and disadvantages of using computer-delivered PowerPoint slides.

QUESTIONS FOR APPLICATION AND ANALYSIS

1. Emily is apprehensive about training groups of people. She tends to write most of her data and content points on the dry-erase board as she trains, and she spends most of her time talking to the board rather than to the trainees. What suggestions could you make to Emily on how to improve her training presentation?
2. Analyze the advantages and disadvantages of distributing copies of PowerPoint slides for trainee reference *during* the session. Using presentation aid principles of attention focus, explain how you will address the disadvantages of this technique.
3. What significant issues and challenges in developing and using presentation aids do trainers face when using distance delivery systems such as the Internet for training? Explain and demonstrate how you would deal with two specific Internet challenges.
4. You have a video clip showing "customer centered" communication and "customer hostile" communication. How can you set the stage for this video so your trainees can achieve the highest level of recall for the positive behaviors shown in the video? How can you debrief trainees after the video to further enhance recall?

ACTIVITIES FOR APPLYING PRINCIPLES AND SKILLS

1. Using PowerPoint slides from a training module you have developed or obtained, answer the following questions:

   A. Based on pages 174–176, what are the specific purposes of the PowerPoint slides?
   B. Based on pages 185–193, how would you evaluate the overall effectiveness of the PowerPoint slides?
   C. How could you conduct this training presentation if you had technological problems and were not able to use the PowerPoint slides?

2. Design 3 PowerPoint slides for training content on enhancing listening skills using basic PowerPoint design principles listed in this chapter. Using the same content, design an alternate set of 3 PowerPoint slides using the same chapter principles. Compare and contrast the two slide sets, choose one for presentation, and explain why this one is the better set.

Planning is bringing the future into the present so that you can do something about it now.

—*Alan Lakein*

Developing Training Plans

CHAPTER OUTLINE

CHAPTER OBJECTIVES

After studying this chapter, you should be able to:

- Describe the key purposes of a training plan.
- Identify and perform the key steps in writing a training plan.
- Develop and use three types of training plan formats.
- Write a training plan using four practical training planning tips.
- Identify, describe, and implement three methods of testing the quality of a training plan.

T raining plans are to training what an orchestral score is to a conductor; a training plan is like musical notation that becomes glorious sound in the hands of a skilled maestro. In many respects, being a trainer is like being a conductor. The conductor does not make the music; rather, he or she facilitates it into being. Similarly, the trainer does not make learning happen but is a resource to assist the learner to learn. And just as composers learn how to write musical notation that can be reproduced by others, so a trainer should develop the skill of preparing a training plan.

This chapter discusses how to prepare the training plan. A **training plan** is a written description of a training session; it contains (1) the objectives, (2) a summary of the training content, (3) a description of the training methods, and (4) a detailed description of all presentation aids and resources (e.g. handouts) that are needed to transform the plan into a training session. Training plans can range from a simple narrative description that a trainer will develop and personally use to a detailed minute-by-minute plan that is written to be used by other trainers.

Why is it necessary to learn how to prepare a training plan? Can't a trainer just make a few notes or jot down a few ideas? No, it's vital that a training plan ensure that each of the elements that make training instruction effective has been incorporated. Just having a general idea of what you'll do during a training session, even a short training session, is not adequate. A professional trainer prepares a written plan to capture all the necessary information that should be incorporated into a comprehensive training plan. And some trainers are employed to prepare training plans for others; designing a curriculum for another trainer is sometimes an important training function that may be a job in and of itself. One bit of encouragement we offer is that as you gain experience and additional knowledge about both your subject matter and how to prepare training plans, the task will get easier.[1]

In previous chapters, we've discussed the parts of a training plan: objectives, methods, audiovisual resources. We've also discussed strategies for sequencing instruction (tell, show, invite, encourage, and correct). In this chapter we explain how to put everything together in a written format that describes how to bring the training to life.

THE PURPOSE OF TRAINING PLANS

Training plans have two specific purposes. First, training plans connect what the trainee needs to learn (needs assessment) with training objectives. Second, a training plan connects the training objectives with the methods the trainer uses to help trainees master the objectives. If the training objectives aren't clearly linked to what trainees need to do in order to successfully perform their job, the training will have little value. The training plan describes the step-by-step behaviors that the trainer performs in presenting the training; the plan provides the sequence and a detailed overview of what you will present. Without reviewing the trainee needs, objectives, and methods, the training plan sequence may not achieve your intended results.

Connect Training Needs with Objectives

As we have emphasized throughout our description of how to design and deliver communication training, the process of planning a training session begins with a focus on what a trainer needs to learn. As shown in Figure 9.1, the development of the training plan occurs after the trainer has made several decisions about key elements of training design. Driving the entire process is an ever-present focus on the needs of the trainee. We will discuss several types of training plan designs in this chapter. Regardless of the specific training plan format you select, each training session should focus on a clearly worded training objective that is based on what the trainee needs to learn. If a training plan fails to make the link between needs and objectives, the training plan will be ineffectual.

How do you ensure that a training plan is built on the strong foundation of addressing trainee needs? As you begin to assemble the pieces of the training plan (lecture content, activities, presentation aids) to organize them into a coherent whole, review the results of the trainee needs assessment you conducted. If you or the organization for which you're preparing the training session has not conducted a formal needs assessment, marshal what information you do have about your trainees. What skills do they need? What is your best guess as to their current levels of competency? At a minimum, talk with supervisors or human resource personnel to ensure that your objectives appropriately address trainee needs. In essence, we suggest that you reflect on the alignment between the perceived trainee deficiencies and the training objectives.

FIGURE 9.1
The Needs-Centered Training Model
The trainer is ready to develop and complete the training plan after decisions have been made about training content, methods, and resources.

Connect Training Objectives with Methods

Once you are reasonably certain that the training objectives are appropriate, the next critical function of a training plan is to align the training methods you've selected with the training objectives. In Chapter 6, we reviewed classic training methods and described their primary functions. Before developing your training plan, reflect on the primary methods you've selected to confirm that what you *do* during the training is the best strategy for accomplishing what you want trainees to be able to perform. If, for example, the objectives call for the development of specific communication or leadership skills and you are primarily lecturing to the trainees, there is a disconnect between what you're trying to accomplish (skill development) with the method of achieving your objective (in this case, lecturing). Skill development occurs when trainees have ample opportunity to practice the skill you are teaching. Training plan objectives that contain verbs such as *demonstrate, perform,* and *present* should include training methods that give trainees an opportunity to enact the skill being taught.

The primary functions of a training plan are to document that the planned training meets trainee needs and that the training methods will appropriately address the planned objectives. Building in success starts by ensuring that the critical training functions are aligned; the trainee needs, training objectives, and training methods should be clearly and logically connected. Without an alignment of these critical functions, the training plan will be flawed.

PREPARING TO WRITE A TRAINING PLAN

If you've been following the action steps described in the needs-centered training model, you've got most of the information you need to start drafting your plan. After developing your objectives, you assemble the information and methods you need to accomplish your goal. The typical action steps include (1) conducting research, (2) developing training content, (3) determining training time frames, (4) selecting training methods, and (5) selecting training materials. Let's review each critical step.

Conduct Research

You're a human resource trainer because you already know something about communication, leadership, managing change, organizational development, or other human resources skills. But whether you have a Ph.D. in communication or only a limited academic background in "people skills," you will not be able to draft training plan content off the top of your head. You will need to read, review, and research to find the most up-to-date information for your training presentation. Make use of the World Wide Web and library sources, as well as interviews. Review our strategies for conducting research, presented in Chapter 5.

Develop Training Content

Training content is the information, definitions, descriptions, concepts, and skills that you present to trainees, whether in spoken or written form. The training content is the heart of the training session. How do you transform your research efforts into material that you can use in a training session? The short answer is: *Focus on trainee needs.* It is possible to feel overwhelmed with all the information that you could present in a training session; one reason a trainer may spend too much training time lecturing and not enough time developing skills may be that the trainer has not been a good editor. Just because you have information to present does not mean the information is useful. Edit, sift, evaluate, and cut training content that does not relate to your training objectives. Review Chapter 5 for some tips on developing training content.

One strategy for developing training content is to identify key action steps or skills that trainees need to master; consult your task analysis. As you surf the Internet and read books and journals, keep your training objectives handy. Consider organizing your notes so that you have each training objective on a separate sheet of paper or in a separate computer file. As you find information that relates to an objective, summarize the information using the objective as the heading. Your training objectives will help you focus your research and develop training content that is aligned with trainee needs. In the early stages of drafting training content, don't worry about capturing all the details of a training resource that you uncover. Make your notes brief, jotting down references to page numbers so you can go back and find more detailed content if you need the information. When sketching out training content, many trainers like to begin with a general outline of key points rather than developing a detailed script of the training content. (We don't recommend that you develop a word-for-word transcript of your training presentation.) Focus first on general ideas and skills, and come back later and fill in the details as needed. Expanding on the music analogy that began this chapter, first develop the general melody before working out the details of the harmony, rhythm, and instrumentation.

Each trainer may use a slightly different method of drafting training content. Some trainers grab a pad of paper and find a place where they won't be disturbed and begin jotting down ideas. Do you think better at a keyboard? If so, you may want to reflect on your research and the notes you've taken and begin tapping out your ideas into your computer. At this point in drafting training content, the goal is to generate more ideas than you'll use. The brainstorming technique involves generating as many ideas as you can without evaluating them. Once you've assembled a draft of your ideas, then go back and edit and revise. Many people can be more creative if they give themselves permission to capture all ideas before self-censoring them. When you have a list of key topics, you can begin to whittle the list. One key criterion for determining what eventually will remain in your training session is the amount of time you have to present your training.

Determine Training Time Frames

As you begin making decisions about training content, you should simultaneously being making preliminary decisions about time constraints. In the corporate world, the cliché "time is money" remains true. Managers and supervisors want training to be presented in as short a time as possible so as to minimize trainees' time away from their jobs. As we've noted, training is expensive is not only for the cost of designing and delivering the training but also for the work time lost when trainees are in a training session rather than performing their duties. Multiply the hourly wage of a worker (plus benefits) times the number of trainees in the training session, and you can quickly identify the true cost of training. Thus, there is pressure to make training as efficient as possible.

Although training could be presented in any number of time blocks, standard time formats for a training period are typically two-hour sessions, half-day sessions, six-hour sessions, and the full eight-hour day of training. A skill such as listening could be introduced in a two-hour training session, but it may take a full day or longer to incorporate ample practice to master the skill. There is often tension between the need for additional time to adequately present training skills and the drive for trainees to "get in and get out" of the training session. The complexity and importance of the skill, coupled with the training budget, are factors that determine the amount of time devoted to a particular training session.

The more time allotted for a training session, the more likely you will be able to incorporate appropriate skill practice time (the invite, encourage, and correct steps). A shorter time often means trainers must rely only on the less effective lecture (tell) approach. In addition to the amount of training time, the number of participants plays a role in how "skill oriented" the training session will be. With more than twenty or twenty-five trainees, it is difficult to provide feedback (encourage and correct) to help trainees master the skills being taught.

A training session longer than one or two hours is constructed around a sequence of training modules. A **training module** is a specific block of training focused on a particular skill or concept without a break. Most training modules run from a minimum of 30 minutes to no longer than two hours. It would be ideal if each training module could focus on one or more training objectives centered on a cogent, discrete skill or set of skills. Sometimes, however, breaks may be needed to accommodate the needs of trainees before a module can be concluded.

Determine Training Methods

With a knowledge of the essential training content and a general understanding of the time constraints, the trainer can make informed choices as to what precise methods will be used to deliver the training. If time is short, you'll need to select a method that is efficient as well as effective. As we discussed in Chapter 6, the lecture method is often the most efficient way to present training content, but it's typically not the most effective. In Chapter 2 we noted how adult learners prefer to be actively involved in solving problems rather than listen passively to someone present information. Work sheets, structured discussions, videos, and reading material are alternatives to lectures when you need to present information in a short period of time.

Another factor that will influence your choice of training methods is the size of the audience you're training. It's easier to make a training session interactive when your training group is small (20 or fewer); inviting trainees to practice listening and feedback skills and to participate in role plays are examples of interactive experiential methods. With a very large group of people, it is more difficult to monitor the trainees' behavior and gauge whether they are appropriately performing the skill or activity. There are, nonetheless, ways of maintaining the attention and active involvement of trainees, even in a large group. Using structured worksheets and dyadic activities that can be performed while people are seated are two strategies for making even a large group session interactive.

As you're making decisions about which training method to use, you may need to revise your decisions in the light of time constraints and the size of the audience. When developing your training plan, remain flexible as you consider training method alternatives. When you write a research paper you rarely use your first draft; so it is when you prepare a draft of your training plan.

Select and Develop Training Materials

Although our needs-centered training model in Figure 9.1 shows the elements of training in a seemingly step-by-step sequence, you will make several decisions about training design simultaneously. As you are making decisions about training methods, you are also making decisions about the materials that you will need to implement your training. Some decisions will be easy. If, for example, you plan to show a video, you will obviously need the appropriate equipment. If you plan to use a case study, you will need printed copies of it for participants to read. Other decisions are less obvious. When, for example, you are presenting lecture material, you'll need to decide whether to display some information on a PowerPoint slide.

Your training plan should refer to all materials that you will need to conduct the training. Audiovisual equipment, PowerPoint slides, activities, case studies, and role play instructions should all be clearly described in your plan. To make it simple, you may want to reference the page number in the training plan from the participant's guide so that you can quickly direct trainees' attention to the information or case study when needed. The **participant's guide** is the workbook that each trainee will have during the training; it contains all handouts and any other information needed. The participant's guide is analogous to the textbook you have for a class; it includes all essential content that you'd like the trainee to remember. In most cases, it should eliminate the need to pass out paper during your training session. We offer tips on preparing the participant's guide later in the chapter.

RECAP

Preparing a Training Plan

What to Do	How to Do It
Develop training content.	Identify key training topics.
	Be guided by training objectives.
	Brainstorm training content based on research.
Determine training time frames.	Determine or conform to training time limits.
	Make decisions about the length of each training module.
Determine training methods.	Use a variety of training methods to achieve the training objective.
	Use active rather than passive training methods.
Select training materials.	Develop the participant's guide.
	Identify and describe all training tools, such as PowerPoint visuals, flip charts, and markers, that you will need.

TRAINING PLAN FORMATS

When you've researched your topic, decided on the essential content of your training, and made decisions about the time frame, methods, and materials, you're ready to draft the training plan. What does a training plan look like? If you are working as a trainer in a large organization, the department in which you work may provide a specific format for you. Regardless of the look of the training plan, five elements should be included in any written plan:

1. *Objectives:* A complete statement of all training objectives.
2. *Training content:* A summary of the information you will present either in lecture, lecture/discussion, video, or key information from the participant's guide.
3. *Time:* An estimate of the amount of time needed for each lecture, activity, video, or other component of the training.
4. *Method:* A clear description of the methods to be used.
5. *Materials:* A brief description of all materials to be used in the training session.

If you have the option of developing your own approach, we offer three formats for including these five elements. The format you select will be based on your own preferences or the preferences of the client if you're preparing a training plan that others will use. The three primary training plan formats are:

- **Descriptive format:** The least structured approach, the descriptive format consists of a narrative summary that describes the training content and methods, using subheadings and paragraphs to describe each training element.
- **Outline format:** As its name implies, the essential elements of the outline format are organized in the manner of an outline. The training content is listed and the methods and materials needed in the training are integrated in the list.
- **Multicolumn format:** The most structured plan, the multicolumn format organizes the information in four columns that support each training objective. The four columns include information about time, content, methods, and materials.

What's the best training plan format? If you need detailed instruction for presenting a training plan, the descriptive format may be best. The outline format's structure allows you to easily find information and lecture notes. The multicolumn format is preferred by many trainers for the ease of finding information and noting time cues for each activity or change of activity.

Descriptive Format

The descriptive format presents the five essential elements of a training plan in much the same way as a textbook would. Using selective subheadings, this format presents information in a narrative, expository style. Figure 9.2 illustrates a training plan in the descriptive format.

The objective, an estimate of the training time, and the list of materials needed are presented at the beginning of the training plan. What follows is a narrative that integrates the content of the training (a virtual transcript of what the trainer will say) with the methods the trainer will use.

Session I: Introduction to Listening

Objective: At the end of this session, the participants should be able to describe three reasons why listening skills are important to their job.

Time: 9:00 AM–9:30 AM

Materials needed: Flipchart and markers
Participant's Guide, page 1
Overhead Transparency # 1

Training Content and Methods

Introduction:

Introduce yourself and describe the logistics for the workshop (e.g., where the refreshments are, ground rules for attendance, restroom location). Establish set induction with the following question: Do you know a good listener? [Ask for a show of hands.] Ask: Do you know a bad listener? [Ask for a show of hands.] Ask participants to write brief responses to the following questions, which are listed on page 1 of the participant's guide:

1. Describe the characteristics of a good listener.
2. Describe the characteristics of a bad listener.
3. What would you like to learn about listening skills today?
4. Why are listening skills important?

[Give the participants five minutes to write responses to these four questions. After they have made written responses, place them in groups of four or five and ask them to share their responses. After about seven minutes of discussion, debrief the activity by asking participants how they responded to the first question. Record their responses on a flipchart. Ask them how they responded to the second question. Record their responses on a flipchart.] Tell them that they have just given themselves the short version of the seminar: Do what they said good listeners do and don't do what they indicated bad listeners do. Then ask them: If you already know this information, why should we have this seminar? Summarize their responses orally. They will probably talk about how it is one thing to know what to do and another thing to put what they know into practice.

Ask them what they would like to learn. [Record their answers on the flipchart or on a pad of paper that you can use to guide you through the activities. In essence, you are conducting a brief needs assessment to check your understanding of what skills they need.]

Importance of Listening Skills: Lecture/Discussion

Ask them to share their responses to the fourth question. [Invite them to tell you why today's workshop is useful (e.g., get the message out of them rather than putting a message in them)] After they have shared their reasons, present a short lecture in which you describe why listening skills are important. Include the following information:

(continues)

FIGURE 9.2
Descriptive Training Plan Format

1. Some research suggests that listening comprehension of a message drops 50 percent 24 hours after it was heard.
2. Additional research indicates that listening comprehension is reduced to 25 percent comprehension 48 hours after the message was heard.
3. Younger children are attentive listeners, but their attention span is short: 90 percent of first graders could repeat what the teacher was saying in the class; 80 percent of second graders could repeat what a teacher had just said; 44 percent of junior high students could repeat the teacher's message; and 28 percent of high school students could repeat their teacher's lecture content. There is evidence that as we get older we become less attentive.
4. We spend more of our communication time listening than any other activity, but we spend relatively little time receiving listening skill training.

Conclude this section of the training by providing a preview of the specific listening skills that will be presented in the seminar.

FIGURE 9.2
Descriptive Training Plan Format (*continued*)

The advantage of this format is that it provides a comprehensive summary of what the trainer will do and say. Beginning trainers may find comfort in having a script to follow that provides a detailed blueprint of the training. The disadvantage of this format is that it may be more difficult to quickly and easily separate the training content from the training methods. More structured training formats may permit a trainer to more readily identify the training methods and content.

Outline Format

The outline format provides more structure to the training plan content than a narrative format. The same five key elements of objectives, time, methods, content, and materials should be included in the plan. The difference here is that the training content is presented as an annotated outline in the traditional style (Roman numerals, capital letters, Arabic numbers, lowercase letters). Annotations to the lecture content written as bracketed notes, can indicate how long each part of the training should last. Methods are labeled, and enough information is presented so the trainer can follow the outline and annotations to present the training. Figure 9.3 shows an example of the outline training plan format.

Many trainers like the structure of the outline format because it makes it easier to find information at a glance. Because the outline format does not provide a word-for-word narrative, this format also has the advantage of permitting the trainer to adapt to immediate trainer needs rather than follow a transcript. And trainers can more easily add their own notes and annotations to the outline.

Multicolumn Format

Trainers who want even more structure in their training plan may prefer the multicolumn format, wherein each element is still more prominent. The most structured

Module 3: How to Prepare a Meeting Agenda

Objectives: At the end of this session, trainees should be able to write an agenda for a team meeting using the four principles of an effective meeting agenda.

Lecture/Discussion [15 minutes]

   I. Determine meeting goals [Overhead # 1]
      A. Information items include what the team needs to know.
      B. Discussion items give the team an opportunity to share information.
      C. Action items are those in which the team needs to make a decision or do something.
  II. Identify items that need to be included on the agenda [Overhead # 2]
      A. Brainstorm for meeting agenda items.
      B. Eliminate agenda items that do not relate to meeting goals.
 III. Organize the agenda items to achieve the meeting goals [Overhead # 3]
      A. The first item on the agenda should be to ask for other items.
      B. Consider high-priority items early in the meeting.
      C. Place items early where you think there may be consensus.
      D. If the information is not needed in the meeting, place information items last.
 IV. Test and evaluate the agenda before the meeting [Overhead # 4]
      A. Before the meeting, ask for feedback about the agenda.
      B. At the beginning of the meeting, ask if everyone can agree on a meeting ending time.
      C. List major topics for discussion using a flipchart, overhead projector, or PowerPoint slide.
      D. At the end of the meeting, evaluate the effectiveness of the meeting and meeting agenda.

Demonstration [2 minutes]: Show participants examples of well-constructed meeting agendas.

Individual Activity [10 minutes]: Ask participants to individually draft a meeting agenda for the next meeting using the principles and strategies for drafting an agenda.

Group Activity [15 minutes]: Place participants in groups of four or five to share their agendas and ask group members for feedback.

Instructor Feedback [10 minutes]: Following the group activity, the instructor can point out examples of effective agenda design and offer suggestions for improving participant's agendas.

FIGURE 9.3
Outline Training Plan Format

training plan format presents the essential training plan elements in four columns of information that support one or more training objectives. The specific training objective should be written at the top of the page; the information in the four columns (time, content, method, materials) supports the objective or objectives. Some trainers write the training objective at the top of the long side of the page (horizontal format) to allow more room for information in the four columns. Each column describes crucial information the trainer needs. Another way to enhance the clarity of the multicolumn format is to incorporate icons in the training plan to represent the methods or materials needed. Figure 9.4 presents a sample half-day training program using the multi-column format and incorporates icons that indicate the materials and methods to facilitate ease of use.[2]

Time. The first column gives the time frame for each training event or activity. When drafting the time elements, start by estimating how much time you will need for lecture, videos, activities, and feedback. As you continue to develop the plan, you may need to revise the time estimates. You need not make time estimates to the exact minute; rounding off estimates to five minutes may be sufficient.

Content. The second column describes the key training content. The information in this column may include information from the participant's guide that summarizes essential training content. Or it may include information presented in Power-Point slides or other visuals that you may use. Although a word-for-word transcript of the content may not be needed, provide enough detail so that you or another trainer could present the training if only the training plan notes were available.

Method. The third column describes the training methods. It is helpful if each method is clearly labeled (lecture, case study, role play) so that the trainer can easily identify the method being used. It may also be useful to indicate which function of the training process (tell, show, invite, encourage, correct) is used. By labeling the training function you can easily keep a training lesson in its proper sequence. You can ensure, for example, that you're not inviting trainees to perform a skill unless you've first told them how to perform it and shown them examples of how to perform it. You can also ensure that you have provided enough time to appropriately encourage and correct the skill attainment. Without feedback (both encouraging and corrective), trainees will not have ample evidence that they have mastered the skill.

Materials. The final column describes the materials you will use to present the training. You could identify specific pages from the participant's guide that trainees should be reviewing, and you can indicate which PowerPoint slide should be visible at a given time.

The multicolumn format has the advantage of permitting the trainer to see very quickly the overall structure of the training session. It's also easy to check whether the proper time has been allotted to each training element and whether the proper sequence of tell, show, invite, encourage, and correct is in place. A disadvantage of the multicolumn format is that it may be more challenging to draft because of the constraints of organizing material in each column. Consider using the table function on your word processing program to create the columns.

The box on page 216 summarizes the key training methods, noting the primary function of each method (Tell, Show, Invite, Encourage, Correct) and reviewing the key advantages and disadvantages of the method.

FIGURE 9.4 Multicolumn Training Plan Format

Module 1.1

Learning Objective: At the end of this session, trainees will be able to demonstrate the three active listening skills of orienting their body toward the customer, psychologically attending to the customer, and limiting stereotyping to notice details in a dialogue.

Time	Content	Methods	Resources
9:00 AM		**INTRODUCTION OF TRAINER BY CONFERENCE HOST**	1. "Introduction of Trainer" Sheet (Page 103)
9:02 AM		**SET INTRODUCTION** Think about the last time you had to deal with a furious customer. - Maybe they were angry because of something you did. - Maybe they were angry because of a company policy. - How did that situation end? - Now, just thinking about that may cause some frustration, so let's throw those memories away and start over by learning the best way to deal with those customers.	
9:05 AM	Working with customers is an unpredictable experience. By learning how to listen with the active listening skills, you can show the customers that you care about what they're saying. The active listening skills are: 1. Orient your body toward the customer. - Lean in to customer.	**LECTURE (TELL)**	1. PowerPoint Slides 1 and 2 2. Participant's Guide: Page 1-2

(continues)

FIGURE 9.4 Multicolumn Training Plan Format *(continued)*

Time	Content	Methods	Resources
	- Keep open posture. - Look the customer in the eye. 2. Psychologically attend to the customer. - Remove psychological noise. - Mentally think about what the customer is saying. - Listen only to the customer. 3. How to limit stereotyping. - Avoid putting customer into pre-established groups. - Look for originality in what the customer is saying.		
9:10 AM		**"DIALOGUE ACTIVITY" DEMONSTRATION (SHOW)** 1. Ask trainees to turn to page 3 in the participant's guide. 2. Give them time to read the story and understand the situation. 3. Ask for a volunteer to come to the front of the room and help you with the dialogue. 4. The trainee will play the role of the customer, and the trainer will be the store worker. 5. Instruct the group that whenever the trainer is not using the active listening skills (Orienting body, Psychologically attending, Limiting Stereotyping), the volunteer or	1. Participant's Guide: Page 4 – Example Story 2. Volunteer

FIGURE 9.4 Multicolumn Training Plan Format

Time	Content	Methods	Resources
		trainer will say PAUSE and we will correct the listening skill. 6. Begin the interaction with the customer.	
9:15 AM		**"Dialogue Activity" (Invite)** Have each member of the training session think back to a point where they dealt with a customer. It does not need to be a time where the customer was angry, just an interaction where they had to listen. Have the participants write down a few notes about the experience in the participant's guide. The story should take them about 3–4 minutes to tell.	1. Participant's Guide: Page 4
9:20 AM		Ask members to pair up into dyads where they will share their story. As they are sharing their story, remember that each person should be looking for active listening traits in the other person. If they notice that they are not following active listening, have them say PAUSE and address what should be changed. Remind them that there should be a lot of PAUSES as we want to help make sure everyone knows what active listening is.	1. Participant's Guide: Page 4
9:25 AM		**"Dialogue Activity" Feedback (Encourage/Correct)** While each group is sharing their stories, go around the room and	1. Participant's Guide: Page 4 – with their notes that they just took.

(continues)

FIGURE 9.4 Multicolumn Training Plan Format (*continued*)

Time	Content	Methods	Resources
9:35 AM		encourage them in what they are doing correctly as far as active listening. If they are not doing something correctly, politely say PAUSE and let them know how they can fix their active listening skills. **DEBRIEF "DIALOGUE ACTIVITY"** Pull the group back together as a whole. Ask them: 1. What were the hardest active listening skills to demonstrate? 2. Did you feel better understood as the customer when your partner used active listening skills? 3. Describe how the customer will feel if you use these same behaviors.	

FIGURE 9.4 Multicolumn Training Plan Format

Module 2.1

Learning Objective: At the end of this session, trainees will be able to demonstrate as least 3 minimal encouragers in a conversation with another person in the training session.

Time	Content	Methods	Resources
10:00 AM		**SET INDUCTION** Have you ever been in a conversation where it felt like you were talking to a brick wall? Who here has been in a conversation that had an awkward silence where you had no idea what to say? What if I were able to show you how to avoid those situations by knowing how to keep a conversation flowing and using silence effectively in a conversation? Would you be interested in learning that skill?	
10:01 AM	1. Minimal encouragers help to keep a conversation going. 2. Examples of minimal encouragers are: Yes, Mmmhmm, Sounds good, And?, Then?, Ok, Go on, etc. 3. There is a point where you can use too many of these. 4. In the end, when you use minimal encouragers, it tells the speaker that they can continue. Minimal encouragers can be integrated very well with paraphrasing to follow in a conversation.	**LECTURE (TELL)**	1. PowerPoint Slides 5 and 6 2. Participant's Guide: Page 7

(continues)

FIGURE 9.4 Multicolumn Training Plan Format *(continued)*

Time	Content	Methods	Resources
10:05 AM		**"TELL ME A STORY" DEMONSTRATION (SHOW)** In a moment, each person is going to have the chance to create a story with the following parameters: 1. It must be fictional. 2. 3–4 Minutes Long 3. Impromptu, made up on the spot 4. It contains 1 fire-breathing dragon 5. It contains a bicycle 6. It contains a blue rock, and the reason that the rock turned blue. A volunteer will give you a short example of a speech from a prewritten story. GIVE EXAMPLE While they read the example, I will demonstrate how to use minimal encouragers in a conversation.	1. Participant's Guide: Page 8 2. Volunteer from the audience 3. Example Speech
10:15 AM		**"TELL ME A STORY" ACTIVITY (INVITE)** 1. Now I would like everyone to partner up with the same person you did the last activity with. 2. If you forgot the parameters of the story, you can take a look at page 8 of the participant's guide. 3. Take turns with the first person telling the story and the other person using minimal enouragers.	1. Participant's Guide: Page 8

FIGURE 9.4 Multicolumn Training Plan Format

Time	Content	Methods	Resources
10:20 AM		4. Be aware of how many minimal encouragers are used by the listener and write the number down at the end.	1. Participant's Guide: Page 8
10:24 AM		Switch partners and have the other person share a story. **DEBRIEF (ENCOURAGE/CORRECT)** Walk around during this activity, but do not interrupt because it may influence the amount of minimal encouragers being used. Instead, wait until everyone is done sharing and bring the group back together as a whole to ask the following questions: 1. How many times did you use minimal encouragers? 2. How can you use minimal encouragers in conversation? 3. How does being aware of minimal encouragers help in conversations? Discuss the ways that people used minimal encouragers well. Ask the trainees if there is a way to improve their use of minimal encouragers. Comment on the high or low number of encouragers if applicable.	
10:30 AM		**SHORT BREAK**	

SUMMARY AND EVALUATION OF TRAINING METHODS[3]

Method	Function	Advantage	Disadvantage
Lecture	Tell	Efficient; can present a lot of information in a short amount of time. Lecture can be customized to adapt to trainee needs.	Trainees are not involved in training and may become bored. Trainers may not spend enough time showing, inviting, encouraging, or correcting trainees.
Video	Tell Show	Can be used to present information in interesting ways. Can show demonstrations of how to effectively perform a skill.	A video may not directly relate to the specific objective. The video may be too long. The video may be out of date. Special equipment is needed.
Role Playing	Show Invite	Effective for modeling skills. Effective for giving trainees an opportunity to practice skills.	Some adult learners do not like to participate in role plays. Requires planning and skill to implement and debrief.
Games and Simulations	Show Invite	Actively involves learners. Maintains interest.	May take considerable time. Trainer may lose control of training session.
Worksheets and Checklists	Invite Encourage Correct	Can be tailor-made to fit learning objectives. Involves everyone in the training. Effective for having trainees evaluate their mastery of a skill	Takes time. Some trainees do not like to write. Needs a skilled trainer to debrief and process.
Observation and Feedback	Encourage Correct	Promotes interaction and trainee interest. Helps trainees assess their skill attainment.	Trainees may not have mastered the skill to observe effectively. Trainees may not have skill to provide appropriate feedback.

DEVELOPING THE PARTICIPANT'S GUIDE

As we noted in Chapter 8, at the beginning of most training sessions, each participant is given a **participant's guide**—a collection of handouts or a workbook that contains all the information, worksheets, activities, and activity instructions to be presented in the workshop.

The Importance of the Participant's Guide

Adult learners like to have a comprehensive summary of all information that will be shared during the workshop. Because the participant's guide is often the first thing a trainee sees at the training session—it is usually handed out before the training starts or is already in place in front of the trainee—the appearance of the participant's guide is important. Your credibility as a trainer is often indicated by the quality and appearance of the participant's guide.

Many participant's guides are assembled in three-ring binders; some are simply handouts that have been stapled together. For seminars attended by a large number of people, the participant's guide may be professionally published.

Some participant's guides consist of nothing more than all the PowerPoint vis-uals to be presented during the workshop. One visual may be printed per page, or three slides may appear on the left hand side of the page with room for participants to make notes on the righthand side. Although the duplicate PowerPoint approach will work, it's not very creative. Also, the PowerPoint slides may not contain all the information and experiential activities presented in the workshop. The availability of computers and desktop publishing software leads most participants to expect to be given an attractive and polished set of materials.

How To Prepare the Participant's Guide

Key decisions you'll need to make in preparing the participant's guide concern the information to be included and the level of detail to follow when summarizing for the trainee. Consider these suggestions for developing the participant's guide:

Use the training objectives to determine the content that will appear in the participant's guide. A principal way of preparing the participant's guide is to use your learning objectives as the overall outline of the seminar and to draft training content that relates to each learning objective. You don't have to include the learn-ing objectives in the participant's guide (some trainers do, many do not), but the learning objectives can help you frame the content of the workshop.

Include all activities and instructions in the participant's guide. In addition to the key content, the participant's guide should contain directions for participating in the activities and exercises you will present. Place the activities in the participant's guide in the order in which you plan to use them. It is helpful if *every* activity, even very simple ones, have written directions. There will always be a participant who isn't listening and who will need to have directions he or she can read. One final note: You may not want to include an activity or a case study in the participant's guide if you plan to distribute the activity or case study during the training and you don't want trainees see it in advance. If you do notice that trainees are skipping ahead, just remind them gently which page of the participant's guide you'd like them to focus on. You could say, "I see that some of you are interested in the activ-ity on page 27; we'll get to that activity later in the day. We're now on page 14."

Use the lesson plan to organize the participant's guide. Organize the partici-pant's guide just as you organize the workshop. Each training module could be given a title to help participants understand the overall structure of the training. A table of contents at the beginning of the participant's guide will help participants quickly locate information.

Determine the participant's guide format. Some trainers like to put only a few words or phrases on each page of the manual. This helps you control the attention of the participants. When, for example, a page lists only four or five principles, you can keep participants focused on that list of principles rather than let them read informa-tion that does not support your spoken comments. Other trainers like to economize by making the participant's guide as short as possible, in which case each page is packed with information. We suggest, however, that information be organized in a way that lets you control the focus and attention of your trainees. Therefore, we think less is more. A brief list of information or skill steps is best because then your participants won't be tempted to read detailed information you're presenting while you're presenting it. If you want to provide more extensive information on a topic than you'll be discussing in the workshop, consider putting that information in an appendix at the back of your participant's guide. Then participants will have the information, but they won't be distracted by it while you're talking. Examples of pages from a participant's guide appear in Figure 9.5 on pages 219–220.

Number all pages. Be sure to number clearly *each* page of the participant's guide. You'll want to be able to tell participants where to find information.

Obtain copyrights and provide source information for all borrowed material. If the material you are presenting is not original material, you will need to reference the sources of the information in the participant's guide. You can provide a bibliographical citation at the bottom of the page, or you can provide a citation in a complete bibliography at the end of the guide. If you're adapting material from another work, you'll need to indicate that the material is adapted. And you will need to ask for permission to include more than 250 words of material from a source if the material is to be published. When in doubt, write for copyright permission if you are using any extensive material that has been published. And never fail to give the author of adapted material credit in the participant's guide.

Consider using a customized participant's guide as you training guide. Rather than use one of the training plan formats presented in this chapter, some trainers simply annotate their participant's guide with notes, examples, and other material that they plan to present during the workshop. An experienced trainer may find this training plan format the most useful. For beginning trainers, developing a comprehensive training plan helps the trainer think through the entire presentation.

PRACTICAL TRAINING PLAN TIPS

Most experienced trainers have learned useful tips that serve them well when constructing training plans. The following suggestions may help you coordinate the complex task of planning a training workshop.

Determine the Amount of Detail Needed

The amount of detail needed in the training plan depends on how the plan will be used. If you are both designing the training plan (you are the subject matter expert) and the only person using the plan, you may not need overly detailed descriptions of the training content or methods. But when you are developing the training plan for someone else, your plan may need to be quite detailed. Consider three general levels of detail:

Level One: Highly Detailed Plan.   The level one plan is a plan you prepare for someone else to use. The training content may be written to serve almost as a transcript of what the trainer may say. Although we don't recommend that any trainer read training content to trainees, the detailed plan provides a script that a skilled trainer can customize. Description of the training methods is so detailed that a trainer whom you may never meet will be able to follow the directions to implement the training.

Level Two: Moderately Detailed Plan.   The level two plan is one that you may draft for yourself but that you may not use immediately. You will want enough detail to capture the key information and description of the methods, but you need not provide a full script. You'll want a general outline of the content, but the

What Do You Want to Learn?

1. What are the characteristics of an *effective* speaker?

2. What are the characteristics of an *ineffective* speaker?

3. Why is it important to learn effective presentation skills?

4. What do you want to learn today in this seminar?

1

Speaking Skill Assessment

Rate your current level of skill attainment (10 = High; 1 = Low) on the following skills:

	Rating Today	Rating Desired
1. I analyze my audience well before I speak to a group.	_____	_____
2. My speech objective is clear and well thought out before I give a presentation.	_____	_____
3. I present clear and easy-to-identify major ideas when I give a speech.	_____	_____
4. I organize my ideas effectively for a speech.	_____	_____
5. I use interesting examples and other forms of support when I speak.	_____	_____
6. During the opening moments of my talk, I effectively capture the attention of my listeners.	_____	_____
7. During the conclusion of my talk, I effectively summarize the two or three major ideas I presented.	_____	_____
8. I prepare an outline before I give a presentation.	_____	_____
9. I have effective eye contact when I give a presentation.	_____	_____
10. I use gestures effectively during speeches.	_____	_____
11. I speak with a lively, varied vocal tone during speeches.	_____	_____
12. I am aware of audience feedback during my presentation.	_____	_____
13. My overall rating of my speaking ability is	_____	_____

2

FIGURE 9.5 Sample Pages from a Training Participant's Guide

Presentation Worksheet:
Your Speech, Purpose, Your Speech Central Idea

Speech Purpose Example: At the end of my speech, the listener should be able to describe three benefits of our new insurance program.

Your Speech Purpose: At the end of my speech, the listener should be able to _____ (list, describe, identify, restate, perform, buy)

Central Idea Example: Our new insurance program will cost the employee less, provide better coverage, and reduce office paperwork.

Your Central Idea: A one-sentenced summary of your speech:

_____

_____

_____

_____

3

Verbal Transitions

DESCRIPTION	EXAMPLE
Repeating a key word, or using a synonym or pronoun that refers to a key word	"***These problems*** cannot be allowed to continue."
Showing the relationship of a new idea to a previous one	"***In addition to*** the facts that I've mentioned, we need to consider one additional problem."
Enumerating (signposts)	"***Second,*** there has been a sudden increase in the number of accidents reported."
Using internal summaries and previews	"***Now that we have discussed the problems caused by illiteracy, let's look at possible solutions.***"
Asking a rhetorical question	"***Now that we have talked about the problem, you may want to know the answer to their question: How do we solve the problem?*** That leads me to my next point."

4

FIGURE 9.5 (*continued*)

Adapted from Beebe, Steven. "Audience-Centered Business Presentations." Unpublished Training Material. © 2011. Used by Permission.

detailed content will appear in the participant's guide and on the PowerPoint slides. Imagine that you're designing a plan to use in a training program several weeks or months from now. You'll need enough detail to be able to present the training with the notes that you've prepared.

Level Three: Nondetailed Plan. If you're designing a training plan for yourself to use and you are the subject matter expert on the topic, you may need only brief notes summarizing the training content and methods. Or if the key content appears on your PowerPoint slides or in the participant's guide, your lesson plan may be only a brief outline of the topics, with time cues to signal elements of the presentation. When you're presenting a training program that you have already given several times and you merely need to customize it, your training plan may be brief. The level of detail in the plan is always determined by who will use the plan and the degree of specificity the trainer needs in order to implement the plan.

Draft the Participant's Guide First

Because the key information that you want trainees to learn is contained in the participant's guide, consider drafting the participant's guide first. Once you have assembled the handouts and lecture summary and thought about when you may need activities, simulations, case studies, or other more interactive methods, you're really preparing the training plan itself. Even if you don't incorporate all the activities and methods that you'll use in the workshop, preparing the participant's guide may help you distill the key content you're presenting. A fine-tuned focus on the content can help you fine-tune the decisions you'll make in constructing the overall structure of the trainings you present.

Remember the 20-Minute Rule

Every 20 minutes, you should strive for a change in method or activity. The exception to this rule is that, if the activity involves considerable interaction on the part of the trainee, then the activity can be sustained for longer than 20 minutes. After you've drafted your training plan, review the length of each activity. If you planned on lecturing for more than 20 minutes, consider an interactive training strategy that can be more engaging (andragogical) than passively sitting and listening. You can do the math: If you have a one-hour training session, you should have at least three types of training activities or methods within that hour. If it's a 90-minute block of time, then you'll need four to five different types of activity. Although you could have two 20-minute blocks of lecture because of a change in training method, it's best to sprinkle lecture or lecture/discussion sessions evenly throughout the day rather than concentrate a heavy dose of lecture in one segment of the training session. Once you've drafted your training plan, it should be easy to see if you've violated the 20-minute rule; if you have, develop creative options to keep the training interesting and trainees involved (stimulus variation).

Build In the Skill Training Sequence

One way to ensure that you have a variety of training methods is to review your training plan to determine whether you have used the five-step sequence for teaching a skill we introduced in Chapter 4: Tell, Show, Invite, Encourage, Correct. The "tell" step is usually the easiest but least novel method to incorporate in training; the challenge will be to ensure that you're not overdoing the "tell" step. After you present a lecture about your training topic, do you have a "show" step? Have you demonstrated either in person, with a simulation or using a video example, how the skill you are teaching should be incorporated? Check to make sure that you appropriately demonstrate how to perform the skill you're teaching. If you're truly teaching a skill, the next activity should invite participants to perform the skill. If you're not teaching a skill, this step will be hard to incorporate. Invite the participants to practice the skill you've taught. After they perform the skill, find ways to provide feedback so that they have positive messages to encourage their accurate performance. But also make sure you've provided appropriate correction. If trainees perform a skill but are not

▶ A TRAINER'S TOOLBOX

How to Speed Up or Slow Down Training

Although you carefully developed a training plan and estimated the time needed for various activities, there will undoubtedly be instances when you fall behind schedule and need to speed up, or an activity takes less time than you thought it needed and you have extra time to use. Here are practical techniques for accelerating or deaccelerating a training session.

How To Speed Up a Training Session

- If you had planned a group activity, put people in dyads instead. The smaller the group, the less time it will take to have a discussion. If time is very short, cut the group activity and ask individual trainees to respond to your questions, a case study, or some other activity in writing.
- Consider cutting the amount of time for an activity by providing some of the analysis yourself rather than have trainees reach conclusions on their own.
- Decide what the greatest need of the trainees is and eliminate less important objectives. As always, what you present during a training session *depends on their needs*.
- Rather than have a group provide an oral summary of their discussion, ask each group to record their ideas on a flipchart as they identify

them. Then invite participants in other groups to walk around the room and review the written summaries.
- Rather than have a group summarize *all* their points or ideas, ask them to share their best idea, top two ideas, or an idea that no other group has yet mentioned.

How to Add More Time to a Training Session

- Keep a collection of stories, poems, and anecdotes that you can read or present when you have extra time.
- To increase the time an activity takes, add more members to each group. More group members will take more time for each member to present his or her ideas to the group.
- As you present a short lecture, periodically ask trainees to turn to the person next to them and share a personal example that illustrates a point you have made. Or ask trainees to identify ways that the material you are presenting could be applied on the job.
- If you have budgeted more time than you need for training, don't prolong the training session. Exceed trainees' expectations and end a session early if the work has been accomplished.

given corrective feedback to improve their performance, they may leave the session thinking they have mastered the skill when they haven't.[4]

Plan for Contingencies

Although we've stressed the importance of careful planning in this chapter, we realize that rarely does a trainer follow the exact time frame that was planned. For example, if your session starts a few minutes late, you'll have to shorten a lecture or an activity. If participants take longer than expected with a group activity or need more time to complete an assessment inventory or to respond to an activity in which they write their responses, you'll need to find ways to save time. In some instances you can move through material more quickly than you planned. If your trainees can master the objectives in less time than needed, there is no need to prolong a session unless they can't return to work or you cannot dismiss them early.

Revise, Revamp, Reconstruct

Before the age of word processing, it was more difficult to revise and edit a training plan that the trainer may have thought was complete. Today, however, words are malleable. There's really no excuse not to revise training plans before training. If at all possible, complete a draft of the training plan far in advance of the training date so you will have time to let your ideas incubate.

TESTING THE TRAINING PLAN

The plan has been prepared, and you're ready to put it into action—or almost ready. When you have the time, consider several strategies for testing the effectiveness of your plan and avoiding problems with a new training plan.

Conduct a Focus Group

A **focus group** is a few people selected to discuss a particular topic so that others can better gauge how people will respond to it. Advertisers often use a focus group for market research. The objective of most focus groups is to analyze or evaluate information, ideas, or products. A focus group could be asked to review a draft of a training plan and to offer feedback about the objectives, content, methods, and materials proposed. Or the group could hear an oral description of the training program. The focus group leader would then ask questions and probe for a detailed response to the plan. The reactions of focus group members can be used to improve the training session.

Conduct a Pilot Test

To **pilot test** something is to perform a trial run on it before officially releasing it for wider presentation; the goal is to determine how effective the program is or to identify what needs to be changed. Instead of having a focus group read about the training or react to verbal descriptions of a training session, the training could be presented for a small group of people; following the training session, they could be asked for suggestions to enhance the training and comments on its virtues. A pilot test is especially useful if the training is going to be presented to many groups of people. The pilot test can be used to make changes and adjustments to the training and to the participant's guide before the training is rolled out. A pilot test is to training what a beta test is to assessing new software: The bugs can be identified and fixed before the product is made available.

Invite an Expert to Review the Materials

Besides focus groups or a pilot test, the training could be given to experts in the subject matter area for review and refinement. If, for example, you have designed a training program that focuses on cultural diversity, it would be wise to have one or more experts review the training design and content to ensure that the information is accurate. Before you print dozens, hundreds, or even thousands of participant's guides, an expert may be able to spot errors in the applications of research conclusions. It's also useful to have another set of eyes review the training material just to check the grammar, spelling, and punctuation of the text. After working with a manuscript or training material for some time, you become oblivious to errors that will be readily apparent to someone else. Most publishing houses have expert copyeditors review final manuscripts before a book is published. You may not be able to secure the services of a professional, but it is a good idea to have someone other than the author to read through all material before presenting it to others.

SUMMARY AND REVIEW

This chapter focused on the practical process of developing training plans. The purpose of a training plan is to provide a written description of the five elements included in every training lesson:

- Training objective
- Training time estimates
- Training content
- Instructional methods
- Materials

The functions of training plans are:

- To connect trainee needs with the training objectives.
- To provide a connection between the objectives and the training methods.
- To specify training objectives and methods that are aligned with the trainee needs.

Five steps are involved in preparing a training plan.

- Conduct research: Gather the appropriate material needed to develop training content based on the training objectives.
- Develop training content. The content for the training is developed from reading, research,

and consulting with subject matter experts; training content forms the essence of what will be presented in lectures and in the participant's manual.

- Determine training time frames: The amount of time for the training will dictate the amount of information to be presented and the methods used.
- Select training methods: The shorter the time frame, the more efficient the training methods should be—while also providing opportunities for trainees to be actively involved in the learning. Final decisions about the training method are made after the objectives and the content have been developed.
- Select training materials: Audiovisual materials, technology resources, the participant's guide, and other tangible materials are determined and described in the training plan.

There are three types of training plans:

- The descriptive plan is prepared in a narrative format and includes information about the objective, content, methods, time, and materials.

- The outline format presents a more structured approach by using an outline pattern to organize the training content.
- The multicolumn format may be the most preferred because of its ease of use: trainers can readily identify the content, methods, and materials at given times throughout the training session.

   Practical planning tips include:

- Draft the participant's guide first
- Remember the 20-minute rule
- Build in the tell, show, invite, encourage, and correct training sequence, and plan for contingencies

- Constantly revise and edit the training plan

   The chapter concluded with three strategies for testing a training plan before it is presented to trainees.

- Ask a focus group for feedback based on your written or verbal description of the training.
- Conduct a pilot test (trial run) for a small group and ask for feedback; this is especially effective in determining whether there are problems with the training content or sequence.
- Ask an expert to review the training plan and to evaluate both the content of the training and the strategies for presenting it.

QUESTIONS FOR DISCUSSION AND REVIEW

1. What are the primary purposes of developing training plans?
2. What steps are involved in preparing a training plan?
3. What are the three formats for developing a training plan? Describe the advantages and disadvantages of each format.
4. What are five practical tips for developing training plans?
5. How can you test a training plan to ensure that it will achieve your training goals?

QUESTIONS FOR APPLICATION AND ANALYSIS

1. Tiffiny is having a hard time getting started in developing a training plan on the topic of how to give an effective performance appraisal interview. She's having difficulty because she's not sure how to go about presenting an effective performance appraisal interview. What advice would you give her to help her get started?
2. Travis has completed his training plan, but he'd feel more comfortable if someone else reviewed it before he presents it at a training session. He's asked you to do this. What criteria could you use to evaluate his plan?
3. Mandee is not sure which training plan format to use—descriptive, outline, or multicolumn. She is presenting a half-day workshop on the topic of how to be interviewed by a member of the media. She's not very knowledgeable about this topic and will need to be able to present her training session without appearing to spend considerable time reading from her training plan. Which training plan format would you recommend that she use? Explain your choice.

ACTIVITIES FOR APPLYING PRINCIPLES AND SKILLS

1. Revise the training plan presented in the outline training plan format shown on page 207 by using the multicolumn format instead. Identify the advantages and disadvantages of the outline format compared to the multicolumn format.
2. Imagine that you have been asked to teach new trainers on how to develop training plans. Based on the information in this chapter, develop the five elements of a training plan.

   - Write the objective or objectives for the training plan.
   - Present a brief outline of the training content.
   - Estimate the amount of time it will take to achieve the training objectives.
   - Describe the training methods as you incorporate the Tell, Show, Invite, Encourage, and Correct skill sequence.
   - Describe the materials you would need to present the lesson.

Eloquence is the essential thing . . . not information.

—*Mark Twain*

Delivering the Training Session

CHAPTER OUTLINE

CHAPTER OBJECTIVES

After studying this chapter, you should be able to:

- Deliver a training session that considers the physical and psychological needs of the trainees.
- Identify, analyze, and appropriately use environmental factors to enhance the training session.
- Describe and use techniques that promote nonverbal immediacy during a training session.

- Describe and make language choices that promote verbal immediacy during a training session.
- Explain and use conflict management techniques that address training problems during delivery.

Imagine that a CEO has commissioned a new orchestral work for a benefit concert for the local hospital; the performance is one month away. The composer, working frantically, has written the music in less than twenty-five days. The composer has also selected musicians from the best orchestras available. But although the music is now written and the orchestra members are skilled professionals, the players have not had time to rehearse. Having the completed score on the music stand does not mean the orchestra is ready to perform. Similarly, having a well-prepared training plan neatly placed on the lectern does not mean that you're ready to deliver your training session. This chapter looks at delivery from a practical perspective. Specifically, we explore how to plan and deliver a training presentation in a way that enhances trainer credibility and facilitates learning. We'll discuss ideas to help you plan your delivery and offer strategies to help you deliver a well-polished presentation. We'll give specific attention to planning, connecting with an audience, and dealing with potential conflict in training sessions.

PLANNING YOUR TRAINING DELIVERY

Planning your training delivery involves the careful consideration of and integration with training methods, content, and objectives. Specifically, when preparing to deliver your training session, it's important to consider (1) your audience (the trainees) and (2) the training environment.

Consider Your Trainees' Needs

True to our emphasis on need-centered training, one of the first considerations when preparing your training delivery is the needs of your trainees. What physical needs do they have? How long can trainees be attentive to a training presentation? What delivery method will best reach this group of trainees?

Basic Needs. No matter how mesmerizing a trainer's delivery, listeners need periodic breaks. **Maslow's Hierarchy of Needs** lists five basic need categories, the most basic level of which is **physiological needs**.[1] Classic training advice is: Don't keep adults sitting for more than two hours at a time. You'll find that as you approach the 90-minute mark in a training session, most trainees are ready for a break. Even though you are energized and ready to plow through your training material, you need to plan stretch breaks for others.

In addition to *physiological* needs, Maslow posits that individuals have needs for *safety*, *love and belonging*, *esteem*, and *self-actualization*.[2] Although some hard skills training (such as operating a forklift) might involve some physical danger, most soft skills training poses no safety risks. The environment where the training takes place must be a secure one. Trainees are part of a team of professionals, and trainers should treat them as professionals in training sessions. Trainers should focus on content and delivery that will increase trainee effectiveness, efficiency, and self-actualization.

Attention Span.   Another aspect of audience consideration is **attention span**—the amount of time people can focus on a given event or activity. Some speculate that adolescents have attention span limits of about eight minutes, corresponding roughly to the length of television programming between commercial breaks. Adults, too, have attention span limits. Long, drawn-out lecture sessions are likely to lose trainees' attention even when the information and delivery are effective. A motivated, interested audience can focus on any one task for only a certain amount of time— roughly, twenty minutes. The successful trainer will keep this in mind when considering curriculum design, content development, training methods, and the use of presentation aids.

Delivery Style.   In addition to being mindful of the length of training sessions and using a variety of methods of presentation (see Chapter 6), consider the overall tone you want to establish. A training style should connect with people rather than merely emphasize information. Communication occurs when listeners understand and respond to the content presented. Successful presentations are interactive dialogues between trainer and trainee.

The best way to create a sense of dialogue during a lecture is to adopt a *conversational delivery style*. Asking strategic questions during a lecture and throughout the session will stimulate dialogue and interaction. Chapter 6 provides further ideas on training methods that will actively engage trainees.

Trainers should take care not to come across as being pompous, and they should never speak over the heads of trainees. Trainers who use an extended vocabulary, exaggerated verbal cleverness, and page-long sentences will not be warmly received. The best approach is to be authentic, sincere, and natural. Talk to trainees conversationally, just as you would talk to a colleague or a friend.

The four classic methods of training delivery are:

Manuscript delivery
Memorized delivery
Impromptu delivery
Extemporaneous delivery

A conversational delivery style is most readily achieved through *extemporaneous* delivery. When trainers speak extemporaneously, they use notes or an outline but they do not read from a manuscript, speak from memory, or speak in an impromptu style. Extemporaneous presentation allows a trainer the flexibility to adapt and respond to trainee comments and reactions. Trainers can stop, ask questions, and discuss the content. Using a memorized message or reading from a script doesn't leave room for trainee needs and spontaneous questions. Your delivery will be a monologue, not a dialogue.

When preparing to deliver a training session, remember not to talk too long; training is not public speaking. Extemporaneous delivery allows trainers to engage trainees more readily in discussion, small group activities, and experiential exercises. Vary your training methods so that the focus is on trainee needs. And remember to speak extemporaneously and conversationally; don't plan on writing out your material to read or to deliver from memory.

Consider Your Training Environment

A second major consideration for a trainer is the training environment. Two relevant environments to consider are the *physical* and the *psychological*. On the physical level, issues to consider include the location, smoking policies, restroom availability, and other logistics. On the psychological level, trainers must be sensitive to the mindset of the trainees within the context of the larger organization. Knowing what predicated the need for training sessions; what the mission, vision, and goals of the organization are; and what the relationship is between management and workers will be important to the success of the training.

Physical Environment. In the training room, many environmental issues could influence the delivery of the training. Room temperature and lighting are frequently an issue. Often it's an advantage when the trainer has no or limited control over the temperature of the room because trainee preferences will vary, and trying to accommodate everyone is impossible. Yet a room that is too cold or too warm will detract from the delivery and the overall success of the session. Room lighting is another important factor. Making sure the PowerPoint screen is sufficiently bright and that trainees can see their handout materials are important matters for trainers.

Especially important is the seating arrangement, which often determines the amount and type of interaction during a training session. In the rare instances when short lectures are appropriate, the traditional row and column arrangement of chairs is generally best (see Figure 10.1). More commonly, when you want

Traditional Seating

Delivery goal:
  Lecture
Purpose:
  Information dispensing

Horseshoe Seating

Delivery goal:
  Facilitated discussion
Purpose:
  Application, participation

Modular Seating

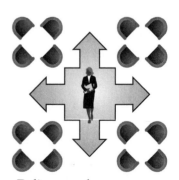

Delivery goal:
  Facilitated small group
Interaction purpose:
  Brainstorming, group
  discussion, teamwork

FIGURE 10.1
Seating Arrangements by Trainer Goals

to promote interaction and discussion among trainees, the horseshoe or circle arrangement is best. If you want to foster team brainstorming activities, the modular arrangement will work best. The strategic choice of seating format can help the overall success of training sessions.

Another consideration regarding the physical environment is potential sources of *distractions,* both visual and auditory. Cell phones have a great potential to disrupt a training session. Imagine the irritation of hearing someone's cell phone go off in a movie theater or at the symphony. Libraries, courtrooms, airplanes, and university classrooms have firm restrictions regarding cell phone use, and people are directed to turn their cell phones off. Cell phones ringing (or playing a tune) during a training session are a serious distraction. The wise trainer will remember to ask cordially that cell phones be turned off at the beginning of a session.

Other potentials for distraction are hall traffic, renovation or construction noise, music in the hall, fire drills, slamming doors, lunchroom smells, and sputtering intercom systems. A visit to the training site the day before can give the trainer time to manage or alleviate potential distractions and to find out what corporate activities may be scheduled next door.

Psychological Environment. One psychological characteristic of an environment that may have an effect on training delivery is the organizational culture. **Organizational culture** refers to the norms, rules, policies, customs, practices, values, history, and characteristics of an organization. Trainers need to be familiar with an organization's "heroes" and "villains." Most organizations have myths, legends, and logics that are important for trainers to know. Some corporations value innovation, and it is part of the employee mindset. Other corporations have a tall structural hierarchy with poor communication between levels, which can lead to an atmosphere of distrust, apathy, and "do what you are told even if it does not make sense." The relevant psychological environment can even go beyond corporate walls to include recent world, state, and community events.

Thus the trainer needs to consider the likely attitude of the trainees. Are they compelled to be at this training? Will they find the training topic controversial? Trainees may view the training as valuable, a necessary evil, or a waste of time. Though trainee mindset is arguably an audience factor, individually and collectively it shapes and frames the training landscape, and thus it must be considered in the environment category as well. The better a trainer can answer questions about the organizational culture and the trainees' thinking, the better he or she will be able to customize delivery and address issues of interest.

A sensitive trainer is aware of the environmental factors, both physical and psychological, surrounding the training session. But awareness is just the first step; the trainer must plan and shape the delivery to maximize results. Different environments will call for different delivery formats, sequences, and styles, and the trainer should be ready to adapt delivery in view of trainee needs and environmental constraints.

RECAP

Planning Your Delivery

What to Do	How to Do It
Consider your trainees.	Meet the needs of your listeners.
	Arrange for breaks.
	Pace your delivery.
	Be interesting by presenting content that will be seen immediately as useful.
	Be relevant by researching, planning, and delivering your content to apply to current needs.
Consider the training environment.	Make sure that environmental conditions are favorable for training delivery.
	Identify potential visual, auditory, thermal, and psychological disruptions and work beforehand to alleviate or dampen their effects.
	Ask that cell phones be turned off.
	Consider where you will stand during the training.
	Plan for the seating arrangement that will best suit your training purposes.

HOW TO CONNECT WITH TRAINEES

At its essence, training delivery is effective when it connects with the trainees and facilitates learning and retention. Quality delivery invites participation, engages trainees, and fosters retention and the assimilation of content. Conversely, poor training delivery is one that hampers or detracts from achieving the training objectives. Typically, successful delivery involves good eye contact, appropriate vocal volume and variation, professional posture, and illustrative gestures. Effective delivery should not call attention to itself; it should enhance the achievement of the training objectives without trainees thinking "What great gestures" or "What neat vocal cues."

In addition to using these strategies, however, connecting with trainees requires a positive interpersonal relationship between trainer and trainee. Riley suggests that the traditional three Rs of education (*reading, writing, arithmetic*) should be reconceptualized into a new model: *relationship* from the teacher's viewpoint, *relationship* from the student's viewpoint, and an emphasis on the instructional *relationship* from educational leadership.[3] A trainer can connect with trainees communicatively and interpersonally through immediacy and affinity seeking in the delivery of training content.

Trainer Immediacy

Trainers should deliver a session that ultimately enhances trainees' desire to approach the material, not avoid it. Audience approach–avoidance feelings are highly influenced by trainee delivery. Effective delivery helps trainees to listen and pay attention; ineffective delivery triggers inattentiveness. Psychologist Albert Mehrabian framed a concept known as **immediacy**, defined as "the degree of physical or psychological closeness between people."[4] **Immediacy behaviors** are those that communicate and foster liking and feelings of pleasure. Certain verbal and nonverbal behaviors are perceived as immediate and thus foster a general level of immediacy (liking) between trainer and trainees. A trainer fosters immediacy when he or she establishes eye contact with trainees, avoids distracting movement and gestures, has a pleasant and varied voice, and conveys interest and enthusiasm.

Communication research on immediacy has documented significant correlations between immediacy and perceived, affective, and cognitive learning.[5] Studies show that when teachers are perceived as immediate, student learning,[6] motivation,[7] and ratings of instructional quality are enhanced.[8] Furthermore, research indicates a linked causal relationship between instructor immediacy and student learning:[9]

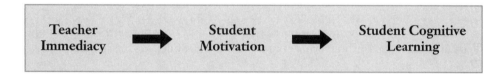

One research study found that higher levels of teacher nonverbal and verbal immediacy used together produce higher levels of student recall.[10] Another study found that high teacher immediacy and high teacher credibility foster higher levels of student motivation and affective learning.[11] Instructor immediacy can even have an impact on student anxiety. Further research found that "instructor immediacy has been found to be related to a reduction in graduate students' statistics anxiety."[12]

These research studies have much relevance in training contexts. Primary objectives of training include recall and skill development. If, as research indicates, higher immediacy is significantly correlated with recall, trainers should strive to be immediate. Successful training involves being able to motivate trainees, so research cited above suggests again that trainers should strive to be immediate. Interestingly, positive effects of trainer immediacy are found in training research. Specifically, studies show that "effective trainers use more nonverbal immediacy," and this produces higher affective learning.[13] Immediacy also affects trainees' perceptions of your skills as a trainer. When you deliver your training content, it is important to be perceived as immediate.

Nonverbal Immediacy. *Nonverbal immediacy* is the unspoken aspect of how you present yourself. Eye contact, posture, and movement all influence how you are perceived by others. (We'll discuss *verbal immediacy,* the way you use language to convey a sense of interest and involvement with others, later.)

Nonverbal immediacy is communicated and fostered by unspoken, nonverbal behaviors and communication. **Nonverbal communication** is behavior other than written or spoken language that creates meaning for someone. A trainer, for example, does not have to hear a trainee say "I am bored with this session" to know the trainee is bored. The trainer can *see* trainees' bored facial expressions, drumming fingers, wiggling legs, or slouching posture. A trainer might also *hear* the exasperation in a trainee's voice when responding to a question.

Nonverbal communication tends to be more influential and believable than verbal communication.[14] If there is a discrepancy between what a trainer says and what he or she expresses nonverbally, trainees will almost always believe the nonverbal message.[15] A trainer who begins a training session by stating how happy he is to be here today but speaks in a monotone, frowns, and makes no eye contact is not likely to be believed. Nonverbal communication is the primary way people communicate their emotions and attitudes.

Because nonverbal messages are important in communicating feelings and emotions, a trainer's delivery style plays a crucial role in how trainees evaluate the entire training experience. Many post-training evaluations tap trainees' affective response to the training (e.g., did they like the trainer and the training?). Because affective responses are often related to how a message is delivered, it is important that a trainer focus wisely on a training style that communicates immediacy; the evaluations of the trainer's work are highly correlated with the quality of training delivery.

Channels are the avenues or paths that carry and transport message meaning. Typically, channels for nonverbal communication include:

Vocals
Eye contact
Gestures
Space
Touch

Through these channels, nonverbal messages can convey interest, openness, friendliness, helpfulness, relationship, willingness to communicate, and emotional mood. The messages can also convey disinterest, unfriendliness, apathy, and cold, distant emotions. Each of these messages, positive or negative, has a significant influence on perceptions of immediacy. In view of this, it is important that a trainer be aware of effective nonverbal communication and behaviors in each nonverbal channel. It is important to examine nonverbal channels of appearance, facial and eye behaviors, kinesics, proxemics, and vocal cues, and to look specifically at how a trainer can promote immediacy through each channel.

Appearance. Appearance is generally the first nonverbal message we receive from another person. If you're training in a large corporate environment, a "business look" is often expected in a training setting. One rule of thumb for trainers is to dress slightly better than the trainees. Trainers need to observe carefully the trends and norms among business people and adjust their appearance accordingly, taking care that their clothing, grooming, artifacts, and formality match that of the trainees.

An important appearance category is clothing. Research suggests that student perceptions of instructor dress (formal and professional) are significantly associated with learning and ratings of instruction.[16] Similarly, research indicates that "formally-dressed instructors are perceived as more credible than casually-dressed instructors."[17] Other studies have shown that, though more casually dressed female instructors are seen as more approachable and flexible, they are also given ratings of least respect.[18] Based on these studies in classroom settings, it is reasonable

▶ RECAP

Guidelines for Trainer Appearance

1. Strive for a professional but approachable look.
2. Keep jewelry to a minimum—small not large, tasteful not gaudy; view jewelry as an accessory rather than being the focal point of your appearance.
3. Dress at the same level or slightly more formally than your trainees.
4. Your grooming and attire should be crisp, clean, and professional.
5. The attire differential should not be too large between you and the trainees.

to conclude that in the corporate context, trainers should dress appropriately to achieve a positive image.

What should trainers wear? It depends on the expectations (and needs) of your trainees. The classic business look for men includes a pressed white shirt, polished shoes, and an appropriate tie. For women, business suits are commonly expected. Experts suggest that closed-toe pumps, neutral-colored hosiery, and matched pant-suits or skirts with a jacket create a business image for women.[19] For both men and women, dark grays, charcoals, and navy blue are typical colors in corporate contexts.

Although we can't prescribe more precisely what you should wear as a trainer, we do suggest that you pay careful attention to your professional appearance. Remember that appearance influences immediacy and immediacy can influence the success of your training. If you were training assembly line workers in a factory, you would want to dress nicely but a bit casually; if you are training middle management employees in business suits, you should wear a business suit as well to produce a higher perception of connection and immediacy.

Facial Expressions. The face is the primary source of emotional expression.[20] We look naturally to someone's face to determine his or her mood, intentions, and connotative meanings for what is said. When a training session starts, it is a new and uncertain journey for the trainees. Often they won't know what to expect and will look to the trainer for preview, assurance, and motivation. The trainer may have many of the same uncertainties and reservations, but he or she also has the responsibility for setting the stage, establishing bridges to the trainees, initiating relationships, and building trust. Much of this starts facially.

A simple, genuine smile from the trainer at the beginning of a training session has a tendency to relax an audience and open lines of communication. Consider this general principle: Positive, concerned, and sincere facial expressions generally produce better results than do negative, sarcastic, and faked facial expressions. Positive facials tend to foster immediacy; neutral, negative, or no facials tend to be perceived as nonimmediate.

It is also important for trainers to have good "response face," "attentive face," and "listen face" when trainees make comments or ask questions. Part of this entails looking at the faces of trainees when they are talking. Even more, you must be *nonverbally responsive* while looking and listening. Smiles, facial reactions, head nods—even grimaces—all serve to let the trainee know that she or he is being heard.

Eye Contact. The eyes have been referred to poetically as the "windows of the soul."[21] Much information can be sent and received via eye behaviors. In North America, direct eye contact is expected in a business context as a sign of respect, openness, and attentiveness.[22] In public speaking situations, increased speaker eye contact enhances speaker credibility.[23] Functionally, trainer eye contact does much to influence how trainees will respond to the training. Even in a large group, each trainee needs to feel that the trainer is frequently making specific and personal eye contact with him or her. This is called **eye depth**—how deeply or personally you see your audience.

Eye scope is the range of eye contact—making sure that all trainees receive eye contact from the trainer. Even the best of trainers will tend to look most frequently toward certain sections of the room. Sometimes "look" zones are predominately focused in the V pattern (see Figure 10.2). When this happens, trainees sitting outside the V are not visually engaged by the trainer. "Overlook" happens when the trainer looks beyond the first few rows of people, toward those in the middle and back of the room. The "*no look*" happens when the trainer looks above the heads of all trainees and never gets "radar lock" with their faces. Sometimes, as we noted in Chapter 8, trainers make little or no eye contact with an audience because they are spending too much time looking at their presentation aids. Trainers should always remember that the conversation is between the trainer and the trainees, not between the trainer and the PowerPoint slides.

Two methods to use in achieving good eye contact, and thus immediacy,[24] are:

- A **scan**. An eye scan generally starts at one side of the room and sweeps systematically to the other side of the room. If done carefully and naturally, this technique will ensure trainer eye contact with all trainees on a continuous basis.
- A **spot grid**. Here the trainer looks systematically at specific zones in the room. If the spots are spread strategically across the room, the trainer will be able to make visual contact with clusters of people continuously.

In using either of these eye contact techniques, the trainer needs to remember to garner *depth* of eye contact. There is a difference between making eye contact with a trainee and simply gazing in the general direction of his or her face. You must make

The V

The Overlook

No Look

FIGURE 10.2
Poor Trainer Eye Contact
Avoid looking only at the center of the room, looking over trainees' heads, or avoiding eye contact with trainees.

personal visual contact with the trainee, especially when the trainee asks a question. This lets trainees know that the trainer is giving them careful and personal attention and that the trainer values and respects the comments being made. The trainer should not shuffle papers, check notes, look at notes for the answer, check the time, or look at presentational aids during trainee questions.

In most training contexts, trainer eye contact will typically correlate with trainee perceptions of trainer immediacy. The more eye contact a trainer has, and the deeper the eye contact, the more he or she will be perceived as immediate.[25] Conversely, less trainer eye contact will be associated with less immediacy. A trainer must be cognizant of cultural norms for appropriate eye contact and must flex accordingly.

Kinesics. Kinesics is the study of human movement and gestures and how these phenomena create meaning. Trainees tend to pay more attention to trainers who use appropriate gestures in their presentation. In contrast, it is difficult to pay attention to a trainer who remains stiff and still for long periods of time. Here are our suggestions for the effective use of gestures:

- Gestures should be natural, like those used in informal conversation, and should serve to illustrate and emphasize the material.
- A trainer should not use too few or too many gestures.
- A trainer should not put his or her hands in his or her pockets. If a trainer rests her or his hands on the lectern or puts them in her or his pockets for the entire presentation, immediacy will be diminished.
- Trainer gestures should be moderate. If the trainer's hand and arm motions are wild, exaggerated, and overdone with every word spoken, they will only be distracting, and they will diminish immediacy.

Vocal Cues. It's not what you say, but how you say it that makes the difference in how a message is interpreted. The term **vocal cues** refers to the volume, articulation, dialect, pitch, inflection, rate, and use of pauses as you speak. In keeping with the principle that nonverbal messages are more believable than verbal messages, if vocal cues conflict with verbal messages, the audience will typically put more weight on the vocal messages. Vocal messages provide much information about the speaker's emotions and interest in a topic. Given the power of vocal messages to communicate enthusiasm and interest, one of the worst errors a trainer can make is to speak in a monotone.[26] A **monotone** delivery is one with a droning, one-pitch tone; it is boring, and trainees typically tune out the message.

If a trainer speaks in a monotone, the trainees will perceive him or her as being low in immediacy.[27] Trainees are likely to decide that the trainer is bored with the material and with them and conclude that he or she does not want to be there. Admittedly, there may be trainers who really are excited about their material and simply have monotone voices. But most people have lively voices when conversing with friends, so most people expect and prefer a natural, varied speaking voice.

Other vocal characteristics that need careful attention are volume and projection. Speak with appropriate intensity—the proper combination of volume and pitch variation. Trainers need to vary the loudness and softness of their voices to match the content and momentum of the delivery. When speaking softly, trainers need to ensure that they are projecting enough to be heard clearly.

Verbal Immediacy. Verbal immediacy is the psychological closeness that is promoted by words and word choice. The specific language or words you use as a trainer promotes or discourages immediacy. A verbally immediate message communicates liking and inclusion.

One of the best ways to be verbally immediate is to use personal pronouns and other words that reference you and the trainee as a team. The words *we, us,* and *our* communicate that you and the trainees are joint participants working for common goals. Trainer talk should connect you and your trainees. Using *we* implies that we are a team and we are going to do something together; it shows that trainees can approach you with their questions, comments, and ideas.

Nonimmediate verbal messages divide people. They put the trainer on one side, the trainees on the other side, and frame the trainer as an impartial observer. The key is to use words and phrases that align you with your trainees. The following statements pair inclusive immediate and noninclusive, nonimmediate statements on the same subjects.

Verbally Nonimmediate Statements	Verbally Immediate Statements
(1) *Your* goal is to formulate a better plan than that of your competition.	(1) As *we* consider this problem *together, we* need to generate a plan that is better than that of *our* competition.
(2) You can't smoke in the building; it violates company policy.	(2) When we go on break, we need to not smoke inside the building.
(3) So what are *you* going to do about this *mess* you've caused? Why won't *you* listen when *your* manager is telling *you* about necessary cost reductions? *Your* supervisor says *you* don't work well in teams. This has to stop.	(3) So how are *we* going to address this *problem?* What causes *us* difficulty in listening to opposing viewpoints in a conflict? *Our* goal is to work together better in teams.

In addition to using inclusive language, verbally immediate trainers attempt to involve trainees actively in discussion rather than treat trainees as passive listeners. Interacting with trainees before and after the formal training session also increases verbal immediacy; it suggests that you're interested in the trainees as people beyond their taking part in your training class. Additional verbal immediacy behaviors include:

- Using personal examples or talking about your personal experiences outside class.
- Asking questions to encourage trainees to talk.
- Addressing trainees by their first names.
- Providing feedback on individual trainee work by offering specific, relevant comments.
- Asking trainees how they feel about requests and assignments given by the trainer.

Being verbally immediate requires you to "think immediately"—to be immediate by including your trainees in conversation. Don't talk at them; talk with them. And don't write down specific verbal immediacy phrases that you can then periodically insert in your conversation. Scripted verbal immediacy is likely to be ineffective; most listeners can spot a phony. Work to develop inclusive, immediate ways of talking with trainees by encouraging interaction and dialogue. If you condition yourself to "think immediate" with your trainees, being verbally immediate will come more naturally.

Trainer Gestures and Proxemics

Trainers who typically do not use gestures but would like to incorporate them in their delivery are often uncertain about when or how to gesture. Nonverbal behaviors can add support and emphasis to training content delivery in six ways.[28]

1. *Repeating:* Gestures can repeat what you've said to a training group. You can say, "I have three major points to talk about today," and then hold up three fingers.
2. *Contradicting:* Because more trainees will believe what you communicate nonverbally than verbally, be careful that your gestures do not contradict what you say. Saying "Have a nice day" with a frown on your face would be contradictory. On the other hand, there are times when strategic nonverbal contradicting can be purposeful and functional (e.g. with humor).
3. *Substituting:* Without saying a word, you can hold up the palm of your hand to calm noisy trainees or put your index finger to your lips to signal that you would like the training session to be quiet.
4. *Complementing:* You can underscore the importance of a point with a sweeping motion of your hand. In this way, a gesture can flesh out—develop more fully—what you are saying.
5. *Emphasizing:* By shaking a fist, making a slicing gesture, or pounding your fist on the lectern you can emphasize or underscore a point.
6. *Regulating:* Gestures can regulate the interaction between you and your trainees. When you want your training group to respond to a question, extend both palms to invite a response. During a question-and-answer session, your gestures can indicate when you want to talk and when you want others to talk.

Another aspect of movement that requires careful trainer consideration is that of adaptive behaviors. **Adaptors** are nonverbal behaviors that satisfy some physical or psychological need. A wise trainer will take note when an audience fidgets to indicate that they need a stretch break or that they are no longer engaged. Trainees also have psychological needs that may show up in adaptive behaviors. Those who are nervous or bored will often reveal it by consciously or unconsciously bouncing a leg, drumming fingers, fidgeting, twirling hair, twitching a pencil, looking around the room, or doodling on note paper.

Trainers may also enact adaptors, consciously or unconsciously, that could have a negative influence on a training session. Trainers who are nervous will often demonstrate idiosyncratic behaviors that have no apparent function, such as twitching, rubbing their nose repeatedly, head scratching, twirling hair with their fingers, cracking their knuckles, pacing, or jingling keys in their pockets. These adaptive behaviors can lower the perceived immediacy of the trainer. Consequently, trainers need to be aware of and to control and eliminate as many of their own adaptive behaviors as possible.

Proxemics.   *Proxemics* is the study of space and how the use of space communicates. Every individual has an invisible bubble of space that surrounds him or her. You have a need for specific spaces in front of you, in back of you, and at your sides. This applies to the physical distance between a trainer and the trainees: If you violate someone's space by getting too close to him or her, perceptions of immediacy will go down. And, up to a point, the further you are from people, the less immediate they will perceive you.

Anthropologist Edward Hall presents a classification system of interaction proxemics and the types of behaviors that typically occur in each classification zone.[29]

- The **intimate zone** has the proxemic characteristics of touching to 18 inches. Typically, this zone is reserved for intimate or very close friends. Generally, trainers would want to stay out of this zone with their trainees.
- The **personal zone** is generally 18 inches to about 4 feet. This zone is reserved for family and close friends. Again, trainers would probably not want to enter this zone with their trainees.
- The **social zone** measures 4 to 12 feet and is populated by casual friends and acquaintances. This is the zone in which most business encounters occur, and it is the optimum proxemic zone for a trainer. Most training sessions and even breaktime visits with trainees will occur in this zone.
- The **public zone** measures 12 feet and beyond and is generally the zone used for public speaking and presentations. A trainer presenting a PowerPoint presentation at the front of the training room is likely to be operating in this zone. (A training session in a small conference room would probably function in the social zone.)

A trainer who remains far away from the trainees or hides behind the lectern will not be perceived as immediate. In fact, trainees may perceive her or him as cold and distant. Conversely, the trainer who constantly violates norms by entering the personal or intimate zones of trainees will also be perceived negatively. There is a time and a place for each proxemic behavior. Before training sessions, at breaktime, and after sessions, it is appropriate for the trainer to interact with trainees in the social zone and perhaps, in a limited way, on the fringes of the personal zone. During training sessions, it is most appropriate for trainers to use the social and public zones. Careful balance and attention to proxemic norms and expectations will promote good levels of trainer immediacy with trainees.

◣ RECAP

Classification of Spatial Zones

Zone	Distance	Activity
Intimate zone	0 to 18 inches	Communicating personal information
Personal zone	18 inches to 4 feet	Personal conversation with friends
Social zone	4 feet to 12 feet	Working in teams and small groups
Public zone	12 feet and beyond	Public lectures and presentations

RECAP

Guidelines for Nonverbal Immediacy

1. *Appearance:* Take your cue from the appearance of your trainees; dress slightly better than trainees, but don't overdo it.
2. *Facial expressions:* Trainers should openly express interest and positive feeling through their face and eyes. Smile sincerely and appear genuinely friendly.
3. *Eye contact:* Eye contact—have it in abundance! Remember scope and depth.
4. *Movement:* Involve your body with the message. Move appropriately with the material.
5. *Space:* Vary the space between you and your trainees depending on the training activity. When lecturing you can be farther away (12 feet or more) than when working with trainees in small groups or teams.
6. *Vocal cues:* If you are bored with the material, trainees will hear it in your voice. Speak so that all trainees can hear you clearly and distinctly.

Trainer Affinity Seeking

In addition to immediacy, trainers need to use affinity-seeking strategies effectively. **Affinity** is a positive attitude that one person has for another, and affinity seeking is the process by which individuals attempt to get others to like and feel positive about them.[30]

Research indicates that we are more willing to do what others ask us to do, and less willing to resist others, when we like them.[31] Think about an instructor you recently had whom you liked and another whom you disliked. Assume that both have given you very demanding assignments that will require extensive research. Studies suggest that you would consider the liked instructor's request reasonable and appropriate, and you would probably work hard to please that instructor.[32] You wouldn't want to let that instructor down.

Research also suggests that your level of cooperation with the disliked instructor would be quite different. First, you might consider the assignment unreasonable; second, you would probably resist completing the assignment in a meaningful manner. If you decided to complete the "unreasonable" assignment, you would probably resent the instructor and complete it just to obtain the reward or to avoid the punishment.[33] One can quickly see the value of affinity seeking in training contexts.

Some trainers will have no problem getting other people to like them. Others will find it a bit more difficult. Communication researchers have identified communication strategies people use to get others to like them.[34] Specific research in this area yielded a list of twenty-five affinity-seeking strategies. Seven of the more powerful or more effective strategies, along with communication examples, are listed in the box on page 242.[35] You're encouraged to give these seven affinity-seeking strategies a try in training contexts and specifically with your training delivery. We believe you will see a difference in how your trainees behave toward you and respond to the training content.

AFFINITY-SEEKING STRATEGIES AND EXAMPLE BEHAVIORS

Assume equality: The trainer attempting to get a trainee to like him or her presents himself or herself as an equal of the other person. For example, he or she avoids appearing superior or snobbish and does not play one-upmanship games.

Comfortable self: The trainer attempting to get a trainee to like him or her acts comfortable in the setting, comfortable with himself or herself, and comfortable with the trainee. He or she is relaxed, at ease, casual, and content. Distractions and disturbances are ignored. The trainer tries to look as if he or she is having a good time, even if he or she is not. The trainer gives the impression that nothing bothers him or her.

Conversational rule-keeping: The trainer attempting to get a trainee to like him or her follows closely the culture's rules for how people socialize by demonstrating cooperation, friendliness, and politeness. The trainer works hard at giving relevant answers to questions, saying the right thing, acting interested and involved in conversation, and adapting his or her message to the particular trainee or situation. He or she avoids changing the topic too soon, interrupting the trainee, dominating classroom discussions, and making excessive self-references. The trainer using this strategy tries to avoid topics that are of no interest to trainees.

Dynamism: The trainer attempting to get a trainee to like him or her presents himself or herself as a dynamic, active, and enthusiastic person. For example, he or she acts physically animated and very lively while talking with the trainee, varies intonation and other vocal characteristics, and is outgoing and extroverted with the trainees.

Elicit other's disclosure: The trainer attempting to get a trainee to like him or her encourages the trainee to talk by asking questions and reinforcing the trainee for talking. For example, the trainer inquires about the trainee's interests, feelings, opinion, and views. He or she responds as if these are important and interesting and continues to ask more questions of the trainee.

Facilitate enjoyment: The trainer attempting to get a trainee to like him or her seeks to make the situations in which the two are involved enjoyable experiences. The trainer does things the trainees will enjoy, is entertaining, tells jokes and interesting stories, talks about interesting topics, says funny things, and tries to make the classroom conducive to enjoyment. The trainer attempting to get a trainee to like him or her includes the trainee in his or her social activities and groups of friends. He or she introduces the trainee to his or her friends and makes the trainee feel like one of the group.

Optimism: The trainer attempting to get a trainee to like her or him presents herself or himself as a positive person—an optimist—so that he or she will appear to be a person who is pleasant to be around. He or she acts in a happy-go-lucky manner, is cheerful, and looks on the positive side of things. He or she avoids complaining about things, talking about depressing topics, and being critical of himself or herself and others.

HOW TO MANAGE POTENTIAL CONFLICT IN TRAINING SITUATIONS

Because training involves working with people, trainers—even with the best planning—may encounter unexpected conflict stemming from personalities, communication, or behavior of the trainees. **Conflict** is typically defined as the disharmony between individuals as a result of differing goals, objectives, values, beliefs, and attitudes. In this chapter we discuss **interpersonal conflict,** conflict that occurs between two people and is the result of one person's blocking the achievement of the goals of at least one other person. Trainers must be able to deal with conflict effectively *while the training is in session.* The secret of dealing with conflict effectively is to anticipate the types of problem trainees, to use strategies targeted to a type, and to engage general conflict management techniques.

Problem Trainee Types

Every individual—every conflict—is unique, yet experienced trainers encounter general "types" or genres of problem trainees. Recognizing the types of challenging trainees and targeting specific communication strategies at resolving conflicts with these individuals can keep training sessions from being derailed or halted. The box below identifies four types of problem trainees and lists strategies for coping with them.

Using Conflict Management Skills

Conflict management skills are communication skills that enable a trainer to deal in a professional manner with a problem trainee. Our training experiences have

PROBLEM TRAINEES AND HOW TO MANAGE THEM

Source of Conflict	Communication Strategies
Dominant trainees	Don't encourage them to keep talking.
	Acknowledge their contributions graciously and note that others may have differing but equally valid perceptions.
	Graciously interrupt and refocus if certain trainees are dominating talk time.
	Make sure other trainees get the floor to share their views.
Negative trainees	Make sure training sessions are relevant to specific skills they need.
	Try to give them some control and choice in the training process.
	Empathize and then redirect to the positive.
	Show how your training is intended to make things better.
Aggressive trainees	Establish rapport by learning names before the session and by affirming positive contributions during the session.
	Let them know that you do not condone nor will you allow them to be verbally aggressive to others during the session.
	Focus them on supporting and helping other trainees.
Quiet trainees	Avoid putting them on the spot.
	Avoid assigning seats to them.
	Don't evaluate or assess them based on how much they talk.
	Make discussions safe for them to express their feelings and opinions by being supportive.
	Preview session activities so there are no surprises.
	Praise their contributions.

shown that trainees who are performing well want to see a problem trainee's behaviors addressed and refocused. When a trainer avoids a conflict, trainees become more resentful of the trainer than the problem trainee. When a trainer manages the problem trainee well, trainer credibility increases and ultimately makes the training more successful.

Manage Emotions. Many conflict encounters are emotionally charged situations. If you're not aware of your own emotions, they can get in the way and exacerbate a conflict, in effect adding fuel to the fire. In conflict situations, emotions need to be managed and brought under control. Here are pointers to help you manage emotions:

■ *Take time to cool off.* Rather than jump into a conflict situation with a problem trainee, take a few minutes to calm down and collect your thoughts. Take slow, deep breaths. You might even need to take a break and leave the training classroom to give yourself the time and space to find perspective and to analyze the situation. If the trainee becomes emotional, offer a time-out so that both of you can collect your thoughts.
■ *Select an appropriate time and place to address the conflict.* Another way to manage emotions is not to address the problem in front of other trainees. Addressing the conflict before others may make the problem trainee feel humiliated and resentful. And the other trainees will be uncomfortable and may find your approach to managing conflict inappropriate. But when the problem trainee's behaviors are severe, the problem must be addressed immediately. Give the group a break, and ask the problem trainee to remain behind. Then close the door and begin your discussion.
■ *Remain nonverbally responsive.* In conflict situations, our natural tendency is to close up nonverbally. We fold our arms, we decrease eye contact, we lean backward, and we distance ourselves from others. These nonverbal messages make us unapproachable.[36] Our suggestion is to resist this natural tendency to back away and instead use forward body leans and head nods and make eye contact. These nonverbal messages make us approachable and help reduce defensiveness.[37]
■ *Plan the conversation.* Unlike many superior–subordinate relationships, where the two may see each other on a daily basis, the trainer–trainee relationship is temporary. If time permits, write out your goal for the conversation. Outline how you see the discussion unfolding. Describe the behaviors you consider problematic. When addressing the conflict with the problem trainee, stick to your plan.

Describe Behaviors. With your emotions in check, you're ready to address the conflict with the problem trainee. We recommend a two-step process. The *first step* is to describe the behaviors you consider problematic, not to evaluate the person. The *second step* is to explain how you feel in the situation. Consider two suggestions for separating the behaviors from the person:

■ *Identify and describe the problematic behaviors.* Take the time to identify the behaviors that you see as the problem. Often it will be the trainee's communication style. What exactly is bothersome about it? What do problematic communication behaviors look and sound like? Be prepared to describe the offending behaviors. Does a trainee interrupt others? Does a trainee dominate the discussion by not letting others talk or by controlling the conversation with nonverbal behaviors? Does the trainee call other trainees names and use profanity?

- *Use "I" messages rather than "you" messages.* Statements that begin with "you" often have an edge or an accusativeness to them. "You have an attitude problem," "you're a know-it-all," "you're rude." These messages are more likely to create an emotional backlash instead of helping to describe the problem; they may result only in an escalation of anger and frustration. A more effective approach is to make the first word of your sentence "I." This makes your message more a description of how you feel than an accusation. Rather than say "You're a know-it-all," say "I see and hear you responding to every question I ask. I see you dominating the discussion not only with your talk, but also with your nonverbal hand gestures that shut others down. I feel annoyed when I see you doing this." Rather than say "You're rude," say "I see and hear you attacking others by calling them names rather than addressing training-related issues. I see and hear you interrupting others. I see and hear you using profanity. I feel frustrated when I see and hear you treating others in this manner."

Paraphrase Content and Emotions. To ensure an accurate understanding of each other's messages, it's always important to paraphrase. Paraphrasing is restating in your own words what you heard another person say. Paraphrasing is not the same as parroting; parroting is when someone repeats back to you what she or he heard you say, using your exact words. After you have described the problem trainee's behaviors and disclosed your own feelings, it's a good idea to ask the trainee to paraphrase what he or she heard from you. At times, you'll be amazed at what you hear: The message received is not the message you sent. This process allows you to clarify misunderstandings.

Here are suggestions for improving how well your problem trainee understands you:

- *Ask the problem trainee to paraphrase the content of the conflict conversation:* You can do this by asking the trainee to complete one of these statements:
  - "So, here is what seemed to happen . . ."
  - "This is what I hear you telling me . . ."
  - "You seem to be saying . . ."
  - "Are you saying . . ."
- *Ask the problem trainee to paraphrase the emotional content of the conflict conversation:* You can do this by asking the trainee to complete one of these statements:
  - "So you feel . . ."
  - "Emotionally, you are feeling . . ."

Use Immediacy and Affinity Seeking. Nonverbal immediacy, verbal immediacy, and affinity seeking have positive effects not only in training delivery but also in conflict situations. It is relatively easy to be immediate and to use affinity-promoting strategies when trainees are positive or even neutral. When there is a conflict, however, it is more difficult because then individuals do not feel physically or psychologically close to one another. In conflict situations it is even *more critical* that the trainer remain immediate and open. The trainer needs to be professional and firm and at the same time nonverbally and verbally approachable. The trainer needs to avoid any impulse to withdraw from the trainee and to continue to use communication techniques that promote relationship and interaction. As you consider conflict situations, refer to the delivery sections above that deal with immediacy and affinity seeking. Take the same principles and apply them to resolving conflict with problem trainees.

Use Prosocial Behavioral Alteration Techniques. Another set of strategies, one that may prevent conflict from occurring in the first place, involves compliance-gaining, or what some classroom researchers refer to as **behavior alteration techniques** (BATs).[38] Behavior alteration techniques are communication strategies that are intended to control and direct student behavior. They are ways for getting other people to do what you want them to do (see boxes on next page).

There are basically two types of behavior alteration techniques: prosocial and antisocial. **Prosocial behavior alteration techniques** are positive strategies that are grounded in constructive trainer–trainee relationships. For example, "From my experience and from what I have learned, it's a good idea. I encourage you to do it." The prosocial power that trainers possess comes from the quality relationships they have with their trainees. **Antisocial behavior alteration techniques** are negative strategies that are grounded in destructive trainer–trainee relationships (for example, "I'm the trainer, do it or else."). The antisocial power that trainers possess comes from their "trainer" titles and their ability to punish and reward trainees.

The techniques that trainers use will ultimately influence their relational development with trainees. In an organizational context, J. J. Teven found that "supervisor prosocial power use and nonverbal immediacy were positively and significantly related to subordinates' self-reported satisfaction, liking for the supervisor, and work enjoyment."[39] If trainers use prosocial behavioral alteration techniques, they will be more successful in establishing, developing, and nurturing constructive trainer–trainee relationships, which in turn will reduce trainee conflict in the classroom and increase trainees' willingness to engage in session activities designed to accomplish training objectives. Conversely, if trainers use antisocial behavioral alteration techniques, they will be less successful in developing relationships. Your trainees will resent you, and ultimately they will resist your training attempts. You will encounter conflict more often. One thing we know: when you are managing conflict, you are not moving toward your learning objectives, which is what you're getting paid to do as a trainer.

The two boxes on the next page list prosocial and antisocial behavioral alteration techniques and give examples of **behavior alteration messages** (BAMs). We encourage you to review this list of communication strategies for several reasons:

1. Trainers can reduce conflict by using prosocial rather than antisocial behavioral alteration techniques.
2. The awareness and use of multiple strategy and message options increases trainer effectiveness in resolving potential conflict situations.

PROSOCIAL BEHAVIORAL ALTERATION TECHNIQUES AND SAMPLE MESSAGES

Immediate reward from behavior: You will enjoy it. It will make you happy. Because it is fun. You will find it rewarding or interesting. It is a good experience.

Deferred reward from behavior: It will help you later on in life. It will prepare you for getting a job.

Reward from others: Others will respect you if you do. Others will be proud of you. Your friends will like you. Your supervisor will be pleased.

Self-esteem: You will feel good about yourself if you do. You are the best person to do it. You are good at it. You always do such a good job. Because you're capable!

Responsibility to others: Your group needs it done. The group depends on you. Your friends are counting on you. Don't let your group down. You'll ruin it for the rest of the group.

Normative rules: The majority rules. All of your friends are doing it. Everyone else has to do it. The rest of the group is doing it. It's part of growing up.

Altruism: If you do this, it will help others. Others will benefit if you do. It will make others happy. I'm not asking you to do it for yourself; do it for the good of the group.

Peer modeling: Your friends do it. Peers you respect do it. The friends you admire do it. Other trainees you like do it. All your friends and colleagues are doing it.

Positive trainer–trainee relationship: I will like you better if you do it. I will respect you. I will think more highly of you. I will appreciate you more if you do. I will be proud of you and supportive of you.

Trainer modeling: This is the way I always do it. When I was your age, I did it. People who are like me do it. I had to do this when I was in business. Trainers you respect do it.

Expert trainer: From my experience, it is a good idea. From what I have learned, it is what you should do. This has always worked for me. Trust me—I know what I'm doing. Research indicates this is best.

Trainer feedback: Because I need to know how well you understand this. To see how well I've trained you. To see how well you can do it. It will help me know your problem areas.

3. It is helpful to diagnose your own communication patterns in compliance-gaining situations; you may be coming across negatively and not realize it.

Research, experience, and trainee-centered communication all point to the importance of trainer use of prosocial BAT and BAM in conflict situations.

HOW TO EVALUATE AND IMPROVE YOUR DELIVERY

Each trainer has unique personality and communication characteristics that will influence his or her delivery of the training material. As you prepare for your training sessions, reflect on your strengths and weaknesses.

- *Time management in training sessions*: Do you have a tendency to hurry through your material and finish early?

ANTISOCIAL BEHAVIOR ALTERATION TECHNIQUES AND SAMPLE MESSAGES

Punishment from trainer: I will punish you if you don't. I will make it miserable for you.

Punishment from others: No one will like you. Your friends will make fun of you. Your supervisors will punish you if you don't. Your peers will reject you.

Guilt: If you don't, others will be hurt. You'll make others unhappy. Others will be punished if you don't.

Negative trainer–trainee relationship: I will dislike you if you don't. I will lose respect for you. I will think less of you if you don't. I won't be proud of you. I'll be disappointed in you.

Legitimate higher authority: Do it, I'm just telling you what I was told. It is the rule. Others have to do it, and so do you. It's policy.

Legitimate trainer authority: Because I told you to. You don't have a choice. You're here to work! I'm the trainer; you're the trainee. I'm in charge, not you. Don't ask, just do it.

Debt: You owe me one. Pay your debt. You promised to do it. I did it the last time. You said you'd try this time.

- *Talk time versus trainee talk time*: Do you find yourself dominating the talk time in a session, or are you good at drawing the trainee comments?
- *Use of presentation aids (including equipment)*: Do you tend to stand in front of your visual aids?
- *Use of humor in training sessions*: Are you good at planning or spontaneously using humor in your presentations?
- *Immediacy with trainees*: Do the trainees perceive you as approachable?
- *Credibility and message organization*: Do you come across as competent and professional?
- *Ability to respond to trainee questions*: Do you handle spontaneous inquiries well?

All trainers have delivery techniques that are effective and work well. Yet many trainers may have delivery characteristics that detract from their message and make the sessions less effective. Being aware of how to improve your training delivery is the first step in improving your delivery style.

One way to examine and enhance your training delivery skills begins with discovering trainee perceptions of your nonverbal and verbal immediacy. The evaluation forms on pages 249–250, with rating scales adapted from communication research, can be used for doing this.[40] Knowing how you come across to trainees can be helpful, and evaluation scales such as these can reveal trainee impressions of your immediacy and identify specific areas that may need improvement. You can then take steps to improve your immediacy in the areas identified by the scales.

Other effective delivery assessment strategies include reviewing videos of your delivery, asking a colleague to sit in on your training session and provide feedback, and conducting a careful review of the training evaluation feedback forms from trainees and the organization.

EVALUATION OF NONVERBAL IMMEDIACY BEHAVIORS

Instructions: Below is a series of descriptions of things some trainers have been observed doing in training sessions. Please respond to the items *in terms of the training class you are taking now.* For each item, please indicate on a scale of 0–4 how often your trainer engages in those behaviors.

Use this scale: never = 0, rarely = 1, occasionally = 2, often = 3, and very often = 4.

_____ 1. Gestures while talking to the group.

_____ 2. Looks at the group while talking.

_____ 3. Smiles at the group while talking.

_____ 4. Touches trainees in the training session.

_____ 5. Moves around the room while training.

_____ 6. Has a very relaxed body position while talking to the group.

_____ 7. Smiles at individual trainees in the training session.

_____ 8. Uses a variety of vocal expressions when talking to the group.

EVALUATION OF VERBAL IMMEDIACY BEHAVIORS

Instructions: Below is a series of descriptions of things some trainers have been observed saying in training classes. Please respond to the items *in terms of the training class you are taking now.* For each item, indicate how often your trainer responds this way when teaching.

Use this scale: never = 0, rarely = 1, occasionally = 2, often = 3, and very often = 4.

_____ 1. Uses personal examples or talks about experiences she or he has had away from training.

_____ 2. Asks questions or encourages trainees to talk.

_____ 3. Gets into discussions based on something a trainee brings up even when this doesn't seem to be part of his or her lecture plan.

_____ 4. Uses humor in the training session.

_____ 5. Addresses trainees by name.

_____ 6. Addresses me by name.

_____ 7. Gets into conversations with individual trainees before or after the session.

_____ 8. Has initiated conversations with me before, after, or outside the session.

_____ 9. Refers to class as "our" training group or what "we" are doing.

_____ 10. Provides feedback on my individual work through comments on papers, oral discussions, and the like.

_____ 11. Asks how trainees feel about an assignment, a due date, or a discussion topic.

_____ 12. Invites trainees to telephone or meet with him or her outside class if they have questions or want to discuss something.

_____ 13. Asks questions that solicit viewpoints or opinions.

_____ 14. Praises trainees' work, actions, or comments.

_____ 15. Will have discussion about things unrelated to class with individual trainees or with the class as a whole.

_____ 16. Is addressed by his or her first name by the trainees.

EVALUATION OF TRAINER DELIVERY

Instructions: Please rate your trainer's delivery skills, using the following items and scale.

	Poor	Fair	Average	Good	Excellent
1. Vocal projection	1	2	3	4	5
2. Eye contact	1	2	3	4	5
3. Credibility	1	2	3	4	5
4. Use of natural gestures	1	2	3	4	5
5. Conversational style	1	2	3	4	5
6. Connection with audience	1	2	3	4	5
7. Confidence	1	2	3	4	5
8. Responsiveness to audience	1	2	3	4	5
9. Facial expression	1	2	3	4	5
10. Vocal variety	1	2	3	4	5
11. Time use	1	2	3	4	5
12. Pacing of presentation and material	1	2	3	4	5
13. Use of presentation aids	1	2	3	4	5
14. Ability to hold audience attention and interest	1	2	3	4	5

No training presentation is perfect; no trainer reaches a point where his or her training delivery is flawless. But by using the approaches listed above, trainers can hone and enhance their delivery continuously. Professional trainers constantly assess and adjust their delivery for maximum effectiveness. The evaluation checklist below is designed to be used by trainees, by yourself, or by a colleague rating your delivery.

A TRAINER'S TOOLBOX

How to Eliminate Trainer Misbehaviors

Research has found that college teachers sometimes misbehave in the classroom (by doing something that is unacceptable to students and detracts from learning). It's likely trainers may also be guilty of doing things trainees don't like.[41]

How do you make sure *you're* not misbehaving? You need to be aware of what trainees find objectionable and to monitor your behavior so that you're not misbehaving in the training room.

What are the most common instructional misbehaviors? In a study focusing on students' perceptions of college teachers, researchers identified 28 instructional misbehaviors. The following list reflects all of the cited misbehaviors, ranked by frequency; we've also suggested strategies for avoiding each misbehavior.[42]

Ranked Instructor Misbehaviors by Frequency and How to Avoid Them

Instructor Misbehavior	How to Avoid the Misbehavior
1. Boring lectures	1. Make sure lectures are audience centered and focused on trainee needs; remember to use stimulus variation.
2. Stray from subject	2. Keep close to your planned, announced agenda.
3. Unfair testing	3. Make sure assessment practices are perceived as clear and valid.
4. Confusing or unclear lectures	4. Follow sequential outlines and delivery.
5. Late in returning work	5. Set and keep due dates for returning promised material to trainees.
6. Information overload	6. Consider audience when apportioning material; lecture no longer than 20 minutes at a time.
7. Deviating from syllabus	7. Stay on the announced training schedule.
8. Tardiness	8. Always be on time. Treat time from a displaced point perspective.
9. Keep trainees overtime	9. Keep to your schedule and be considerate.
10. Early dismissal	10. Make sure you have ample training content to fit the time.
11. Unfair grading	11. Assess trainees by objective and be equitable to all.
12. Negative personality	12. Monitor how others are perceiving you. Use immediacy and affinity-seeking behaviors.
13. Foreign or regional accents	13. Bolster interpersonal relationships with trainees.
14. Information underload	14. Prepare plenty of material and emphasize application.
15. Sarcasm and putdowns	15. Correct without making negative personal comment.
16. Bad grammar or spelling	16. Prepare and proofread visual material in advance.
17. Absent	17. Don't miss your own sessions. Be there!
18. Apathy towards trainees	18. Develop a positive relationship with students.
19. Inappropriate volume	19. View a videotape of yourself. Ask trainees.
20. Shows favoritism or prejudice	20. Be professional and equitable.
21. Unreasonable or arbitrary rules	21. Have specific and obvious objectives for rules.
22. Unresponsive to students	22. Practice active listening.
23. Negative physical appearance	23. Dress professionally.
24. Inaccessible to students	24. Make it clear when you are available for questions or for e-mail or online assistance.
25. Unprepared or disorganized	25. Marinate in the training schedule before you teach.
26. Verbally abusive	26. Be assertive but don't denigrate the person.
27. Does not know subject matter	27. Be familiar with the training content and methods.
28. Sexual harassment	28. Always model effective and appropriate behavior.

SUMMARY AND REVIEW

Effective delivery starts in the planning stage. When planning your delivery, consider both the needs of your trainees and the physical and psychological training environment. When considering your trainees' needs, remember not to talk too long without varying your methods or without taking a break. Be guided by the organizational culture when you fine-tune your delivery approach, content, and style.

As you deliver your training material, monitor your appearance, facial expressions, eye contact, movement, space use, and vocal cues, using them in such a way that the trainees are drawn to you and to your material. Establish nonverbal immediacy between you and the trainees. Immediacy cues communicate liking and closeness between you and others; they include having an appropriately professional appearance, making eye contact with your trainees, and appropriately reinforcing your movement and gestures to support your message. In addition, use space appropriately and speak with interest, appropriate volume, and enthusiasm. Use verbal immediacy; speak *with* rather than *at* trainees. Use effective affinity-seeking strategies to establish good interpersonal relationships with trainees.

Improving your delivery skills is an ongoing process. After you present a training presentation, watch videos of your training to assess your nonverbal behavior. Cope with unexpected conflict situations. Take note of comments from trainees on evaluation forms that address delivery issues. Then, adjust and deliver!

QUESTIONS FOR DISCUSSION AND REVIEW

1. Why is it important to plan for an effective delivery? What are the prime considerations when planning to deliver a training session?
2. What is effective training delivery?
3. What is the difference between verbal and nonverbal immediacy? How does each of them influence your training delivery?
4. What principles should guide a trainer's selection of clothing and appearance?

QUESTIONS FOR APPLICATION AND ANALYSIS

1. Josh's cultural background and personality predispose him to stand quite close to people, sometimes as close as 12 to 24 inches, when he is delivering a training session or talking with trainees at breaktime. This has made several trainees uncomfortable. Josh is not aware that he violates other people's space. He believes that he is being appropriately immediate. Explain how Josh is violating Edward Hall's interaction zones.
2. Florence wants to facilitate small group interaction during her training session. Describe three seating arrangements that she might use in her training, and discuss the relative advantages and disadvantages of each for promoting interaction. Which seating arrangement would maximize interaction?
3. Adrienne has been receiving poor evaluations following her training presentations. Several trainees in Adrienne's sessions have made general comments about her overall ineffective delivery and the low level of enthusiasm she exhibits, but they have not offered specific comments for improving her training. What should Adrienne do to improve her training delivery? What kinds of delivery cues would increase her perception as an immediate trainer? How can she increase her credibility?

ACTIVITIES FOR APPLYING PRINCIPLES AND SKILLS

1. Complete the nonverbal immediacy scale in the evaluation form on page 249, as it applies to yourself. What is your overall level of nonverbal immediacy? What can you do to be more immediate?

2. Based on our discussion of behavior alteration techniques (BATs) and behavioral alteration messages (BAMs), identify the correct BAT category for each of the following groups of prosocial BAM phrases.

   _____ Others will respect you if you do. Others will be proud of you. Your friends will like you. Your supervisor will be pleased.

   _____ Your group needs it done. The group depends on you. All your friends are counting on you. Don't let your group down. You'll ruin it for the rest of the group.

   _____ If you do this, it will help others. Others will benefit if you do. It will make others happy. I'm not asking you to do it for yourself; do it for the good of the group.

   _____ You will enjoy it. It will make you happy. Because it is fun. You will find it rewarding or interesting. It is a good experience.

   _____ From my experience, it is a good idea. From what I have learned, it is what you should do. This has always worked for me. Trust me—I know what I'm doing. Research indicates this is best.

3. Before the training session begins, it's a useful idea to analyze the audience by casually visiting with trainees to establish an affinity toward you. List three questions you could use when you are visiting with trainees to encourage them to disclose and open up to you.

   a. _____

   b. _____

   c. _____

4. Using the evaluation form on page 250, rate your own delivery skills. What are your top three areas of strength? What are your top three areas of challenge? What three things are you going to do to improve your top three areas of challenge?

All assessment is a perpetual work in progress.
—*Linda Suske*

Assessing Learning Outcomes

CHAPTER OBJECTIVES

After studying this chapter, you should be able to:

- Define assessment and list and explain two reasons why assessment is important to trainers.

- Differentiate between Bloom's taxonomy of learning and Kirkpatrick's levels of assessment.

- Develop an instrument to measure affective learning.

- Develop an instrument to measure the domains of cognitive learning.

- Develop an instrument to measure behavioral learning at the atomistic, analytic, and holistic levels.

- Describe how to interpret assessment data to ensure that learning objectives were met.

- Prepare an assessment report including a cost/benefit ratio to document a training program's return on investment.

There is always a sense of accomplishment and relief for the trainer at the end of a long day of training or at the end of an extensive training program. Many trainers call it a day by packing their bags and moving on to the next training assignment. But for others, the process remains incomplete until the training program has been fully assessed to determine its overall effectiveness. These trainers want to know if they're getting a return on their investment. They invest considerable resources—time, money, and energy—planning and developing their programs. These training professionals meticulously walk through the training strategies outlined in Chapters 3 through 10, and they want to know whether their training is making a difference.

One way to see if your hard work is making a difference is to assess your training program, which is the final step of the needs-centered training model illustrated in Figure 11.1. **Training assessment** is the systematic process of evaluating training programs to ensure that they meet the needs of the trainees and the organization. In Chapter 3 we introduced needs assessment, which occurs at the front end of the training model in the "analyze the training task" step. You will recall that a needs assessment is the process of identifying what learners do not yet know or the skills and behaviors they cannot yet perform. Now we're ready to conduct another

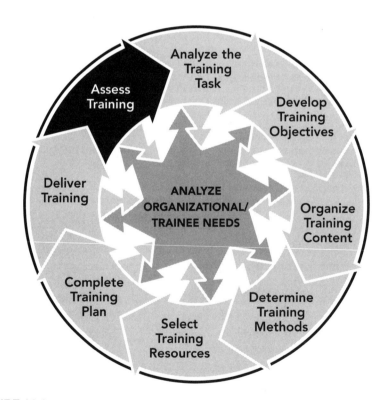

FIGURE 11.1

The Needs-Centered Training Model

Assessing whether the training program addressed the needs of the trainees is the last step in the needs-centered training model.

assessment, this time at the end of the training model. We want to know whether the trainees learned anything from the training program. These two assessment processes work like bookends: The needs assessment identifies what trainees *need to learn*, and the final assessment identifies *whether trainees learned* what they were supposed to learn.

In the first of this chapter's five sections we introduce you to a model of assessment and explain why the assessment process is important to quality training and development. In the next three sections, we provide practical tips on how to assess affective, cognitive, and behavioral learning outcomes. Finally, we describe how to interpret assessment data and how to analyze, use, and report that data.

UNDERSTANDING ASSESSMENT

Knowing how to assess learning outcomes is important to anyone who teaches and trains. Before describing the skills involved, we present a model of assessment, explain why training professionals value assessment skills, and discuss how Donald Kirkpatrick's levels of assessment have influenced training assessment.

Model of Assessment

Assessment is a systematic process that ultimately recycles itself. The model, reflected in Figure 11.2, has three stages. In the first stage, a trainer develops learning objectives, as we discussed in Chapter 4. Assessing learning outcomes is not possible without learning objectives. Learning objectives describe the outcomes trainers look for

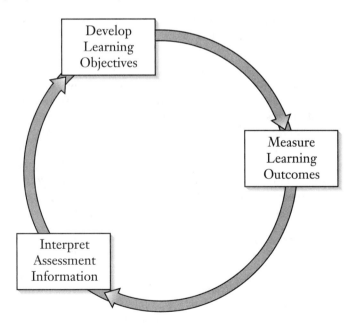

FIGURE 11.2
A Three-Stage Model of Training Assessment

at the end of the training program, such as trainees' being able to recall specific information, express certain attitudes, or perform a set of skills. In the second stage, learning outcomes are measured by collecting data from trainees, using many of the same methods reviewed in Chapter 3, such as surveys and interviews. In the third stage, the assessment data are interpreted. When trainees have completed the surveys and other assessment measures, it's time to make sense of the information. What does it mean, and what does one do with it? The information obtained through the assessment process is important to improving your training program. Before beginning the next training program, you may find reasons to modify the learning objectives, to refine the training curriculum, or to use other methods that more accurately measure the learning outcomes. Feedback from the assessment process is invaluable information for improving your effectiveness as a trainer.

Need for Assessment

Assessment is important to trainers for at least two reasons. First, it ensures the survival of the fittest in an organizational climate concerned with downsizing or doing more with less. Second, it ensures that quality remains consistent with contemporary management philosophies, where work processes must be reexamined constantly for their efficiency and effectiveness.

Assessment Ensures the Survival of the Fittest. Assessing training effectiveness has become a priority in many training organizations throughout the country. As the marketplace becomes more competitive, organizations keep looking for ways to trim operating costs and increase profit margins. Many organizations decide to accomplish this by reducing the number of employees or by eliminating departments.

Until recently, trainers haven't had to document their value to an organization with such precision; it was assumed that they were invaluable. In today's marketplace, trainers who cannot show their value to an organization don't last long in the organization. The trainers who survive downsizing are those who are able to demonstrate that they make a difference in terms of increased income and reduced expenses.

Executives make decisions based on the return on investment (ROI) ratio.[1] **Return on investment** is a phrase that suggests that an investment should yield or produce a return that is greater than its initial amount. For example, an advertising department that invests huge sums of money in developing ineffective advertising will not long survive. But a department of training and development that invests thousands of dollars in a communication training program for front-line managers that reduces employee grievances and sicktime and increases employee morale, motivation, productivity, and commitment to the organization will survive and flourish.

Assessment Ensures Quality Training. Assessing learning outcomes is consistent with many organizational cultures that subscribe to total quality management (TQM). **Total quality management** is a philosophy that advocates that doing a job right is more important than doing a job quickly. W. Edwards Deming, the person primarily responsible for this shift in management philosophy, believed that in order to improve quality while using fewer resources and fewer employees, organizations must remove all barriers that would prevent employees from doing their best work.[2] According to Deming, employees should be trained in how to do their jobs right the first time, not the second or third time.

Total quality management is partially responsible for the assessment culture that exists in many of today's organizations. Training from a total quality management perspective means that trainers use feedback from trainees to ensure that they're meeting the learning objectives that are the purpose of the training program.

Although assessment may seem intuitive and obviously useful, trainees have been systematically assessing learning outcomes in the training classroom only for the last 25 to 30 years. Today, when we learn that our trainees are not learning, we make immediate changes in the training program to ensure that it remains needs-centered and effective. If we find that our trainees are learning, we will still continue to refine the training program, making it even better.

Kirkpatrick's Levels of Assessment

Donald Kirkpatrick is best known for creating a highly influential model for training evaluation that consists of four levels.[3] The four levels, described in the box below, parallel Bloom's taxonomies of learning.[4] Although there are many similarities between Bloom's taxonomies (Affective, Cognitive, Behavior) and Kirkpatrick's four levels of assessment, we use Bloom's work to guide our assessment practices simply because we write from an instructional design perspective rather than an assessment theory perspective. But it's important that new trainers, who will want to become certified (see Chapter 12), understand Kirkpatrick's contribution to training assessment because his work is included on the certification exam of the American Association of Training and Development.

Kirkpatrick's first level assesses reaction, or the trainees' satisfaction with the training program, which is similar to affective learning. The second level assesses

COMPARING KIRKPATRICK'S LEVELS OF ASSESSMENT WITH BLOOM'S TAXONOMIES OF LEARNING

Kirkpatrick's Levels of Assessment	Description	Bloom's Learning Taxonomies	Description
Level 4: Results	To what degree targeted outcomes occur as a result of the training event and subsequent reinforcement.		
Level 3: Behavior	To what degree participants apply what they learned during training when they are back on the job.	Behavioral Learning	Focuses on developing skills and changing behaviors.
Level 2: Learning	To what degree participants acquire intended knowledge, skills, attitudes, confidence, and commitment based on their participation in the training event.	Cognitive Learning	Focuses on acquiring knowledge and factual information.
Level 1: Reaction	To what degree participants react favorably to the training.	Affective Learning	Focuses on changing attitudes and enhancing motivation.

the extent to which trainees acquired new knowledge, which is similar to cognitive learning. The third level assesses behavior, or how well participants apply what they learned in training when they return to the job, which is similar to behavioral learning. The fourth and final level raises practical questions: What were the tangible results of the program in terms of reduced costs, improved quality, and improved quantity? Very simply, your mission is to see if the trainees liked it (affective), learned it (cognitive), and can do it (behavioral).[5] Once these questions have been answered, you should be able to measure the tangible and practical benefits of the training program. We address the practical benefits of a training program in the final section of this chapter.

To begin assessing learning outcomes, a trainer needs three sets of measuring instruments, one for each domain of learning.

ASSESSING AFFECTIVE LEARNING: DID THEY LIKE IT?

Affective learning focuses on whether your trainees liked the training program and found it valuable. **Affect** is the degree of liking, appreciation, respect, or value that one has for something. In the training context, affect would be the amount of liking trainees have for their trainers and how valuable they considered their training. We want to know whether the training program made a change in trainees' attitudes and motivation levels.

Domains of Affective Learning

You want your trainees not only to like you but also to like and respect your training content. Training is more than just conveying content and developing skills; it's also teaching trainees how to value and respect what they learn. Four domains of affective learning are important to the training professional.

Assess If Trainees Liked and Valued the Training Content. Trainees do not always come to a training program valuing the training content. Showing trainees how the new information will enhance their ability to make better decisions and solve problems is one way to enhance trainees' affect for the training content.

Assess If Trainees Liked and Valued the New Behaviors. Trainees need to know why certain behaviors and skills are important. People who work in hospital admissions need to know why it is important to talk with new patients in a soft voice and in a semi-private area and what questions they can ask that do not violate patient privacy. If they understand the Health Insurance Portability and Accountability Act of 1996 (HIPPA) and its Privacy and Security Laws, they will value the communication behaviors that protect patient privacy.

Assess If Trainees Liked and Valued the Trainer. Trainees are more likely to comply with your request to develop new behaviors and skills when they like and respect you. Research suggests that if trainees like or have affect for you and your training content, they will be more motivated to learn the training content and use their new skills on the job.[6]

Assess If Trainees are Likely to Use New Content and Skills. Most trainers consider this the most important domain of affective learning. They want to know how likely it is that their trainees will apply and use the new information and skills on the job. In the training research literature, this is referred to as training transfer.[7]

Tools for Assessing Affective Learning

Both formal and informal tools are used for assessing affective learning. Formal tools (surveys and questionnaires) may be more appropriate at the end of a training program; informal tools may be more appropriate to conclude each day of a multiday program.

Surveys and Questionnaires. The most common method of assessing affective learning is to develop a survey or questionnaire. Your survey or questionnaire should include scale items that assess trainees' reactions to the four domains of affective learning. Two scales that can help you measure trainees' affective learning are the Likert scale (introduced in Chapter 3) and the semantic differential scale. With a Likert-type scale, trainees are usually presented with a statement and asked to indicate whether they "strongly agree," "agree," "disagree," or "strongly disagree" with it or are "undecided" about it. The survey illustrated in Figure 11.3 contains Likert-type scale items that measure trainees' affect for a training program just completed.

Directions: For each item, circle the number that reflects your level of agreement.

I considered the content of this training program to be valuable.

Strongly Disagree	Disagree	Undecided	Agree	Strongly Agree
1	2	3	4	5

The skills we developed in this training program are important to me.

Strongly Disagree	Disagree	Undecided	Agree	Strongly Agree
1	2	3	4	5

The trainer was effective in helping me develop the skills I need to do my job well.

Strongly Disagree	Disagree	Undecided	Agree	Strongly Agree
1	2	3	4	5

I will use what I learned in this training program.

Strongly Disagree	Disagree	Undecided	Agree	Strongly Agree
1	2	3	4	5

FIGURE 11.3
Measuring Affective Learning Using Likert-Type Scale Items

The **semantic differential** scale measures attitudes by asking people to choose between opposite positions, for example, good and bad or liked and disliked. An incomplete statement may be followed by pairs of opposite or bipolar terms separated by a number sequence. Trainees would be asked to circle the number that most accurately reflects the degree or strength of their attitude (belief, value, or feeling) for each word pair.

The survey form shown in Figure 11.4 is an affective learning measure developed by communication researcher James C. McCroskey and his colleagues (primarily Jan Andersen) at West Virginia University.[8] This affective learning measure assesses trainees'

Instructions: Using the following scales (there are four scales for each item), evaluate the training class you just completed. Circle the number for *each scale* that best represents your feelings.

The behaviors recommended in this training program were:

Bad	1	2	3	4	5	6	7	Good
Worthless	1	2	3	4	5	6	7	Valuable
Unfair	1	2	3	4	5	6	7	Fair
Negative	1	2	3	4	5	6	7	Positive

The content or subject matter of this training program was:

Bad	1	2	3	4	5	6	7	Good
Worthless	1	2	3	4	5	6	7	Valuable
Unfair	1	2	3	4	5	6	7	Fair
Negative	1	2	3	4	5	6	7	Positive

The trainer was:

Bad	1	2	3	4	5	6	7	Good
Worthless	1	2	3	4	5	6	7	Valuable
Unfair	1	2	3	4	5	6	7	Fair
Negative	1	2	3	4	5	6	7	Positive

In real-life situations and on the job, your likelihood of actually attempting to use the behaviors developed in this training program is:

Unlikely	1	2	3	4	5	6	7	Likely
Impossible	1	2	3	4	5	6	7	Possible
Improbable	1	2	3	4	5	6	7	Probable
Would Not	1	2	3	4	5	6	7	Would

Your likelihood of wanting to take another training program related to this topic is:

Unlikely	1	2	3	4	5	6	7	Likely
Impossible	1	2	3	4	5	6	7	Possible
Improbable	1	2	3	4	5	6	7	Probable
Would Not	1	2	3	4	5	6	7	Would

FIGURE 11.4

Measuring Affective Learning Using Semantic Differential Scale Items

attitudes toward the content and behaviors taught, trainees' attitudes toward their trainer, and their anticipated behavioral choices. Remember, if a training program increases trainees' affect, trainees will be more likely to engage in the behaviors taught in the training program, which is ultimately your learning outcome.[9] You might also want to complement your assessment of affective learning outcomes with a more traditional evaluation form, such as the one illustrated in Figure 11.5.[10]

Other Tips and Tools.   If you don't have a formal instrument for assessing affective learning, there are informal ways to assess trainees' reactions to your training. These tools also work well when your training program lasts more than one day.

Directions: For each item, circle the number that reflects your level of agreement.

Training Content

Learning objectives were clear.

Strongly Disagree	Disagree	Undecided	Agree	Strongly Agree
1	2	3	4	5

Training content was interesting.

Strongly Disagree	Disagree	Undecided	Agree	Strongly Agree
1	2	3	4	5

Training content was relevant to my job.

Strongly Disagree	Disagree	Undecided	Agree	Strongly Agree
1	2	3	4	5

Training Resources and Methods

Participant guide was organized well.

Strongly Disagree	Disagree	Undecided	Agree	Strongly Agree
1	2	3	4	5

Experiential learning activities were appropriate.

Strongly Disagree	Disagree	Undecided	Agree	Strongly Agree
1	2	3	4	5

There was adequate balance among lecture, experiential activities, and group discussion.

Strongly Disagree	Disagree	Undecided	Agree	Strongly Agree
1	2	3	4	5

FIGURE 11.5
Training Program Evaluation Form   *(continues)*

Trainer's Presentational Skills

Trainer was organized.

Strongly Disagree	Disagree	Undecided	Agree	Strongly Agree
1	2	3	4	5

Trainer was clear and articulate.

Strongly Disagree	Disagree	Undecided	Agree	Strongly Agree
1	2	3	4	5

Trainer was expressive and energetic.

Strongly Disagree	Disagree	Undecided	Agree	Strongly Agree
1	2	3	4	5

Trainer answered our questions satisfactorily.

Strongly Disagree	Disagree	Undecided	Agree	Strongly Agree
1	2	3	4	5

Trainer integrated our life experiences into training program.

Strongly Disagree	Disagree	Undecided	Agree	Strongly Agree
1	2	3	4	5

Overall Assessment

I would recommend this training program to my colleagues.

Strongly Disagree	Disagree	Undecided	Agree	Strongly Agree
1	2	3	4	5

I would recommend this trainer to my colleagues.

Strongly Disagree	Disagree	Undecided	Agree	Strongly Agree
1	2	3	4	5

FIGURE 11.5 (*continued*)

At the end of each day, you can get immediate feedback and adjust your delivery to ensure that trainees like and value the content, the behaviors, and you.

- *Use two flipchart pages.* At the top of one, write "Likes"; on the other, "Changes." Ask participants to list their likes and dislikes and to make suggestions for enhancing the training.
- *Use sticky notes.* Ask participants to indicate likes and changes on sticky notes. Ask them, when leaving the training, to stick their likes on one wall, their changes on another.
- *Pass out index cards.* Ask participants to rate the day on a 1 to 7 scale, with 1 being low and 7 being high. Ask participants to add one comment to support their assessment.
- *Use text messages.* Ask each trainee to send you a text message indicating what's working well and changes he or she would like to see.

ASSESSING COGNITIVE LEARNING: DID THEY LEARN IT?

Cognitive learning focuses on whether trainees learned the training content. Did the trainees understand the material? You will recall from Chapter 3 that the cognitive domain of learning emphasizes the ability to understand knowledge and facts. When we conducted our needs assessment at the start of the training program, we were interested in understanding how much our trainees knew about the ideas and behaviors we were considering including in our training program. We wanted to make sure that our training was appropriate to the needs of the trainees.

Domains of Cognitive Learning

At the end of your training, you want participants to leave with new knowledge that will help them solve problems and make better decisions. Three domains of cognitive learning are important to the training professional.

Assess If Trainees Understand Training Content.   At a minimum, you want participants to be able to understand the new ideas discussed during training. If you're training managers on how to prepare and conduct a performance appraisal interview with a new employee, you want them to be able to answer these questions:

- How does a performance interview differ from a job interview?
- What is the difference between supportive and corrective feedback?
- What is a gaps analysis?

Assess If Trainees Can Analyze and Synthesize Training Content.   This domain of cognitive learning assesses how well trainees can analyze and synthesize information. When trainees can break down a process into its parts, they have the ability to analyze. When they can pull together ideas and information, they have the ability to synthesize. By asking training participants to describe the aspects of a performance appraisal interview, you are assessing their ability to analyze a complex process. Asking trainees to develop a script for a performance appraisal interview is a synthesizing activity because they will need to show how they would open, process, and close the interview.

Assess If Trainees Can Evaluate Training Content.   This domain of cognitive learning assesses whether trainees can apply a set of criteria to a situation in order to determine its quality. For example, asking trainees to evaluate a performance interview video by applying a set criteria (1 = very poor, 2 = poor, 3 = good, 4 = very good) is one way to assess their ability to evaluate. The assessment might include these questions:

- How well did the interviewer provide constructive feedback?
- How well did the interviewer describe the problem behavior?
- How well did the interviewer describe the changes needed to enhance employee performance?

Tools for Assessing Cognitive Learning

When assessing the three domains of cognitive learning at the end of the training program, you will use many of the same assessment methods discussed in Chapter 3.

We begin by constructing a survey or an exam. An **exam** is a specially designed survey, or pencil-and-paper test, that assesses whether trainees learned the training content. Exams take a variety of forms; the most popular are multiple choice, matching, essay, and fill-in-the-blank.[11]

Multiple-Choice Exam Items. **Multiple-choice** is a type of exam item that challenges trainees to choose among three to five answers to a question. See Figure 11.6 for an example of a multiple-choice item. This type of exam item contains two parts, a stem and a set of foils. A **stem** is the question or incomplete statement that you want your trainees to answer or complete. In Figure 11.6 the stem is. "Which of the following reflects the appropriate order of the listening process?" For each stem, there is a set of foils. **Foils** are the alternative choices that follow the stem, one of which will correctly answer or complete the stem. In Figure 11.6 the foils are the lists of verbs following the question. The foil that contains the correct answer is called the **keyed response**. The incorrect foils are called **distractors**.

The advantages of using multiple-choice exams as post-training assessment measures are:

- They're inexpensive compared to other assessment instruments.
- They require minimal time to administer and score.
- They're flexible. They can be easily adapted and revised to assess specific cognitive learning outcomes.

The disadvantages of using multiple-choice exams that are poorly written are:

- Trainees can find the correct answer through a process of elimination.
- The exam may assess trainees' test-taking abilities rather than cognitive learning outcomes.
- The exam may allow trainees to rely on memorization to answer the item rather than have them apply the training content.

To avoid the pitfalls when writing and using multiple-choice exam items, consider these suggestions:

- Avoid making the correct answer too obvious. Incorrect responses should be plausible. Administer the items to a colleague and have him or her check for item difficulty.

Which of the following reflects the appropriate order of the listening process?

A. attending, selecting, responding, understanding, retaining
B. selecting, attending, understanding, remembering, responding
C. selecting, attending, understanding, remembering, retaining
D. responding, selecting, attending, understanding, retaining

---

FIGURE 11.6
Multiple-Choice Exam Item

- Avoid making the correct and incorrect responses look different. All foils should appear similar in length, parallel in construction, and equally precise in expression. Notice in Figure 11.6 that all foils contain five words and are the same length.
- Avoid making the "C" foil the correct response too often. Keyed responses should be evenly distributed among the letters throughout the exam.
- Avoid negatively worded or double-negative stems and/or foils. This becomes an assessment in logic rather than of training content. An example: "Which of the following responses is *not* an *in*effective sequence of how the discussion should unfold with the customer?"
- Avoid writing grammatical cues that give the correct answer away. For example: "When listening to a customer on the telephone, make sure you use a _____. (a) affect displays, (b) back channel cue, (c) adaptors, (d) emotional cues." The keyed response, (b), is obvious because only the singular noun would be appropriate and the article *a* must be followed by a noun that begins with a consonant.
- Avoid using "all" or "none of the above" foils. This is usually the sign of a lazy or uncreative writer. Develop four to five complete foils for each stem.

Matching Exam Items. A **matching** exam item asks trainees to connect or attach two words or phrases together. These exam items contain a set of stimuli and a set of possible responses. See Figure 11.7 for an example of a matching exam item. Stimuli are usually presented as a set of terms, statements, phrases, definitions, or incomplete statements. With most exams, the set of stimuli is presented on the left side of the exam, the list of possible responses on the right. Responses are possible answers that can be matched to stimuli on a *specified* basis.

Matching exam items are useful especially when there is a lot of content to assess, and they require a minimum of space on the exam. Like multiple-choice exam items, matching items, if written poorly, can allow students to find correct

---

Directions: Match the definitions on the right with the terms on the left.

Set of Stimuli	Set of Possible Responses
1. ____ Selecting	A. Focusing on a particular sound.
2. ____ Attending	B. Physiological process of decoding sounds.
3. ____ Understanding	C. Arousal of the senses.
4. ____ Remembering	D. Information that interferes with reception.
	E. Confirming your understanding of a message.
	F. Recalling information.
	G. Sorting through competing sounds.
	H. Assigning meaning to messages.

FIGURE 11.7
Matching Exam Item

answers through a process of elimination. Additionally, matching items do not always allow a trainer to assess higher forms of cognitive learning, such as how trainees might apply or evaluate training content.

To avoid the pitfalls when writing and using matching exam items, consider these suggestions:

- Make sure that the two sets (stimuli and responses) remain similar in terms of the content. If you're assessing the five listening activities (selecting, attending, understanding, remembering, responding), make sure all the items in your two sets are related to the listening process. It would not be appropriate to include items related to the process of resolving conflict.
- The list of stimuli should be no longer than eight items, and the list of responses should be 50 percent longer than the list of stimuli to prevent trainees from selecting the correct response by a process of elimination.
- The list of possible responses should contain plausible answers. Incorrect responses should include common misinformation. For example, if you were assessing listening, you would want to include responses that assessed hearing, because listening and hearing are often confused.

Essay Exam Items. With **essay** items (and fill-in-the-blank items), trainees are not given a list of possible responses but are asked to generate the correct response. They must recall, explain, and organize information in a manner that addresses the exam item. Like the other two types of exam items (multiple-choice and matching), essay exam items have advantages and disadvantages. Two advantages are:

- Essay items eliminate the possibility of guessing and focusing only on memorization. Trainees have the ability to discuss, in their own words, what they have learned and what it means to them.
- Essay items allow trainees to apply information directly to their personal and professional lives.

Two disadvantages of using essay exam items are:

- Essay items require more time to read and evaluate; they're not as efficient as multiple-choice or matching exam items. A trainer must carefully read each essay, evaluating the discussion and application of key concepts and ideas.
- The quality of a trainee's answer is often only as good as the quality of the trainer's question. If you write an ambiguous and poorly focused essay question, you will get an ambiguous and poorly focused answer.

To avoid the pitfalls in writing and using essay exam items, consider these suggestions:

- *Define the task presented in the essay question.* The trainer's intent must be obvious to the trainee taking the exam. For example, if you want the trainee to compare and contrast the informative and persuasive speech making processes, make sure your essay question includes the terms "compare and contrast."
- *Focus the essay question.* If essay questions are not properly defined and limited, trainees will be frustrated in deciding how much to write, how many aspects of the problem to address, and where to put the emphasis. Essay questions are meant to assess trainees' cognitive learning, not their ability

to assess the trainer's intent. Here's how you might focus an essay question using the example above: "In a 250-word essay, compare and contrast the informative and persuasive speech making processes, paying particular attention to audience analysis and adaptation."

- *Write clear and specific directions.* Directions should be thorough and specific. Trainees need to know how much time they have, how important each essay question is, and what factors will affect the grading of the exam.
- *Allow ample time for trainees to answer all essay questions.* Essay exams require more time for a trainee to complete; therefore, it's important to develop an exam with an appropriate number of essays given the time allotted for completing the exam.

ASSESSING BEHAVIORAL LEARNING: CAN THEY DO IT?

Behavioral learning focuses on whether trainees can do what they have been trained to do. Because the primary purpose of training is skill development, the behavioral domain is the most important domain to assess. Numerous research studies have suggested that when individuals develop an appreciation for a set of skills and behaviors (affective learning) and develop an understanding about why the skills are important and relevant (cognitive learning), they are more likely to develop and perform the new behaviors (behavioral learning).[12]

Domains of Behavioral Learning

The three domains or levels of behavioral learning assessment are atomistic, analytic, and holistic.[13] Understanding these domains is important because the tools you choose to assess behavioral learning will depend on the domain or level you want to assess.

Atomistic Assessment.   The lowest level of behavioral assessment is called **atomistic assessment,** the identification of small, observable behaviors. When you assess on this level, you're interested only in determining whether the behaviors were performed. For example, imagine that you're assessing a sales presentation. Did the presentation include an introduction? At the atomistic level, you're not interested in how well the introduction was performed, just that the sales presentation included an introduction. This level of assessment may also include some quantification: How many times was the trained behavior performed or not performed? Because a part of your training included eye contact, an atomistic level assessor might count the number of times you looked at your audience.

In many management-training programs, managers are trained in how to inform employees of performance deficiencies. Such dialogues are referred to as coachings. For a coaching dialogue to be constructive and effective, it's important that managers successfully walk through a series of steps in the appropriate order. If you were to assess at the atomistic level, you would be assessing whether the behaviors occurred and, if they occurred, whether they were performed in the correct sequence.

Analytic Assessment.   The midlevel of behavioral assessment is **analytic assessment,** or assessing how *well* each individual behavior was performed. For a coaching dialogue to be constructive and effective, it's important that managers not only walk through the steps in the appropriate order but that each step is performed well. If one step is performed poorly, employees are more likely to perceive the coaching dialogue as punitive. For example, a manager may have begun a coaching dialogue successfully, but, when describing the employee's performance deficiency, she was accusatory, and that led to defensiveness on the part of the employee. An assessor at the analytic level judges not only that the behavior was performed but also how *well* was it performed.

Holistic Assessment. The highest level of behavioral assessment is **holistic assessment,** where the assessor determines the overall quality of the employee's performance. Here assessors are less interested in the process than they are in the product. The process consists of the individual behaviors performed well and in the correct sequence; the product is the individual's new ability to perform the behaviors well and in the correct sequence. If you were assessing a manager's ability to conduct an employee coaching, you would pose and answer these questions: Did the employee leave the dialogue realizing that there was a performance deficiency? Did the employee learn how to modify his or her behavior to remedy the problem? And did the employee perceive the coaching session as constructive or punitive?

Tools for Assessing Behavioral Learning

Because effective training programs are designed to meet the specific needs of a particular group, it's difficult to find prepackaged instruments for assessing the skills you helped your trainees develop. So you will probably need to develop your own behavioral learning assessment instrument—which is fairly easy to do. You will work with three kinds of tools to develop an assessment instrument.

Behavioral Items. The behaviors developed in the training program are referred to as **behavioral items.** Figure 11.8 is an example of a behavioral assessment instrument

---

Please check if you observed behavior.

_____ Manager greeted employee.

_____ Manager described employee's inappropriate behaviors by using "I" statements.

_____ Manager was able to get employee to agree that a problem exists by paraphrasing.

_____ Manager and employee discussed and analyzed solutions to performance problem.

_____ Manager and employee agreed on a solution.

_____ Manager received verbal commitment from employee on solution.

_____ Manager reviewed with employee consequences for not meeting commitment.

_____ Manager offered encouragement and support.

_____ Manager thanked employee for his or her time.

FIGURE 11.8
Coaching Behavioral Items for an Evaluation

that contains items developed as part of a communication training program. If you were assessing behavioral learning at the atomistic level with this instrument, you would check whether the behaviors occurred and in the appropriate sequence. If the assessment were to occur at the analytic level, you would need skill ratings.

Skill Ratings. The series of numbers or a scale that indicates the level or quality of performance is referred to as **skill ratings**. Many behavioral instruments include five skill ratings: 1 = very poor, 2 = poor, 3 = fair, 4 = good, and 5 = very good. Figure 11.9 is a behavioral instrument that assesses an informative speech presentation.[14] This instrument contains clusters of behavioral items along with skill ratings. Like many such instruments, this one assesses informative speech-making skills at both the atomistic and the analytic levels. The instrument asks you to check off those behaviors you observed, which is the atomistic level of assessment, and to place a skill rating next to each behavioral skill cluster (Introduction, etc.), which is the analytic level of assessment.

Skill Criteria. In addition to skill ratings, assessors need **skill criteria**, that describe in behavioral terms what each skill rating reflects. What does a skill rating of 1 look and sound like? How does a skill rating of 1 differ from a skill rating of 2? Before assessors can study behavioral learning, they must have a clear standard for the behavior(s) that will receive a particular skill rating. At the analytical level, assessors discriminate between levels of performance. The descriptive statements in Figure 11.10 describe the skill criteria for the coaching behavioral items listed in Figure 11.8. Notice how all the evaluative terms in the criteria are described in behavioral terms.

INTERPRETING ASSESSMENT INFORMATION

Figure 11.2, which introduced this chapter, depicts the assessment cycle. You'll recall that the first stage in the assessment process is to develop learning objectives, the focus of Chapter 4. The second stage examines how to measure learning outcomes, the focus of this chapter. We're ready now for the third and final stage of the assessment process, which is interpreting or making sense of assessment information. Kirkpatrick referred to this level of assessment as results.[15] What do you do with the data once you have them? In this section of the chapter, we review how to analyze and interpret assessment data, how to use assessment data as feedback, and how to report assessment data.

Analyzing Assessment Data

To analyze assessment data, it will be necessary to use the learning objectives developed in the first stage of the assessment process as benchmarks or starting points. Assume that the following behavioral learning objective was developed after an extensive needs assessment:

> *Behavioral learning objective:* At the end of the training session, front-line customer service employees will be able to reduce customer complaints by 25 percent over a six-month period.

Instructions: Place a check mark next to each behavior that you see and then rate the skill cluster with an overall skill rating.

____ Introduction (1 = Very Poor, 2 = Poor, 3 = Fair, 4 = Good, 5 = Very Good)
     ____ Introduction gained attention.
     ____ Introduction was effective in establishing credibility of speaker.
     ____ Introduction included thesis.

____ Content (1 = Very Poor, 2 = Poor, 3 = Fair, 4 = Good, 5 = Very Good)
     ____ Speaker maintained audience interest.
     ____ Speaker showed relevance of information.
     ____ Speaker used information that was intellectually stimulating.
     ____ Speaker explained information appropriately.
     ____ Speaker used the following to aid audience understanding and retention:
         ____ Repetition   ____ Humor   ____ Associations
         ____ Transitions   ____ Visual aids

____ Organization (1 = Very Poor, 2 = Poor, 3 = Fair, 4 = Good, 5 = Very Good)
     ____ Speech contained three to four clear main points.
     ____ Speech followed
         ____ Time order.
         ____ Space order.
         ____ Topic order.
         ____ Causal order.
     ____ Speech organization was appropriate for topic.
     ____ Speech contained appropriate summaries and previews.

____ Language (1 = Very Poor, 2 = Poor, 3 = Fair, 4 = Good, 5 = Very Good)
     ____ Language was clear.
     ____ Language was vivid.
     ____ Language was expressive.
     ____ Language was appropriate.

____ Delivery (1 = Very Poor, 2 = Poor, 3 = Fair, 4 = Good, 5 = Very Good)
     ____ Speech was delivered enthusiastically.
     ____ Speech was delivered with appropriate eye contact.
     ____ Speech was delivered spontaneously.
     ____ Speech was delivered using appropriate vocal variety and emphasis.
     ____ Speech was delivered using appropriate pronunciation and articulation.
     ____ Speech was delivered using appropriate bodily action.

____ Conclusion (1 = Very Poor, 2 = Poor, 3 = Fair, 4 = Good, 5 = Very Good)
     ____ Conclusion tied speech together.
     ____ Conclusion brought closure to speech.

FIGURE 11.9
Informative Speech Assessment Instrument

A TRAINER'S TOOLBOX

Assessing Communication Skills Using Instruments Endorsed by the National Communication Association.[16]

Instrument	Description	Source
The Competent Speaker Speech Evaluation Form	This instrument is designed to assess presentational speaking skills. The instrument assesses 8 competencies: Chooses and Narrows Topic, Communicates Thesis, Provides Appropriate Supporting Material, Uses Appropriate Organizational Pattern, Uses Appropriate Language, Uses Vocal Variety, Proper Pronunciation, Uses Appropriate Physical Behaviors.	S. P. Morreale, M. R. Moore, K. P. Taylor, D. Surges-Tatus, & R. Hulbert-Johnson, (eds.) (2007), *The Competent Speaker Speech Evaluation Form.* (Washington, DC: National Communication Association).
Competent Group Communicator	This is an assessment tool designed to evaluate the performance of individual members who participate in task-oriented small group discussions. The assessment instrument is used to help group members determine whether their group is communicating effectively. The instrument assesses 4 competencies: Problem Oriented, Solution Oriented, Discussion Management, Relational Competencies.	S. A. Beebe, & J. K. Barge (2003), "Evaluating Group Discussion," in R. Y. Hirokawa, R. S. Cathcart, L. A. Samovar, & L. D. Henman (eds.), *Small Group Communication: Theory and Practice* (Los Angeles: Roxbury), pp. 275–288.
Conversational Skills Rating Scale (CSRS)	This tool is used to asses conversational competence in interpersonal settings. The CSRS consists of 25 molecular skill items (e.g., speaking rate, articulation, posture, questions) and 5 molar items (e.g., inappropriate interactant–appropriate). The behavioral items can be divided into 4 skill clusters: attentiveness (i.e., attention to, interest in, and concern for conversational partner), composure (i.e., confidence, assertiveness, and relaxation), expressiveness (i.e., animation and variation in verbal and nonverbal forms of expression), and coordination (i.e., the nondisruptive negotiation of speaking turns, conversational initiation, and conversational closings).	B. H. Spitzberg, (1995), *The Conversational Skills Rating Scale: An Instructional Assessment of Interpersonal Competence* (Washington, DC: National Communication Association).

(continues)

(continued)

Assessing Communication Skills Using Instruments Endorsed by the National Communication Association.

Instrument	Description	Source
The Listening Styles Profile	This 16-item instrument is useful as a quick self-report measure of typical listening behavior. It often useful for educational or organizational training sessions where instruction will be assessed at the beginning and end of a training program.	K. W. Watson, L. L. Barker, & J. B. Weaver, (1995), "The Listening Styles Profile: Development and Validation of an Instrument to Assess Four Listening Styles," *International Journal of Listening, 9*, 1–13.

This objective, which is observable, measurable, attainable, and specific, serves as a benchmark to determine the training program was effective. Without a training objective, there is no way to assess training effectiveness. One way to analyze this objective would be to compare two groups. One group gets the training (training group) and the other group doesn't (control group). To show that training was effective, the training group would have to have had a 25 percent decrease in customer complaints while the control group would have to have had little or no change in the number of customer complaints.

1 = *Very Poor:* Manager failed to demonstrate behaviors, and/or behaviors were demonstrated without proficiency. Without proficiency = language does not have clarity, language remains evaluative rather than descriptive, nonverbal messages remain incongruent with verbal messages, nonverbal cues are not appropriately expressive for coaching conversation.

2 = *Poor:* Manager demonstrated few behaviors, and most of them were demonstrated without proficiency. Without proficiency = language does not have clarity, language remains evaluative rather than descriptive, nonverbal messages remain incongruent with verbal messages, nonverbal cues are not appropriately expressive for coaching conversation.

3 = *Adequate:* Manager demonstrated some behaviors, and all demonstrated behaviors were moderately proficient. Moderately proficient = not all language has clarity, not all language remains descriptive, not all nonverbal messages remain congruent with verbal messages, not all nonverbal cues are appropriately expressive for coaching conversation.

4 = *Good:* Manager demonstrated all behaviors, but not all behaviors were proficient. Proficiency = language has clarity, language remains descriptive, nonverbal cues remain congruent with verbal messages, nonverbal cues are appropriately expressive for coaching conversation.

5 = *Very Good:* Manager demonstrated all behaviors, and all behaviors were demonstrated with proficiency. Proficiency = language has clarity, language remains descriptive, nonverbal cues remain congruent with verbal messages, nonverbal cues are appropriately expressive for coaching conversation.

FIGURE 11.10
Skill Criteria for Behavioral Items

Using Assessment Data

After analyzing the assessment data, you should be able to determine which learning objectives were met and which were not. For many assessment experts, the assessment process ends here because of a lack of time and resources. But it is important that you act on this information because assessment data are important feedback that can be used to make poor training programs better and good training programs excellent. Similar to feedback in the communication process, feedback from trainees allows trainers to refine their training messages.

If you met your learning objectives, you'll want to refine the training program with the assessment data you've collected and administer it again. This time, however, you'll want to see even more improvement in cognitive, affective, and behavioral learning objectives. Never settle for the same level of learning outcomes; continue to raise the benchmark on your training effectiveness and make yourself and your training team indispensable to the organization.

If your data analysis reflects that you did not meet your learning objectives, you'll need to diagnose the problem(s). Where is the training deficiency? Is it with the cognitive, affective, or behavioral learning objectives? Having three sets of objectives and assessment instruments allows trainers and assessors to diagnose more accurately the weaknesses and limitations of a training program.

If you augmented your quantitative assessment data with qualitative data, you'll also want to look for themes in the qualitative assessment data. What are your trainees trying to tell you? The data are incredibly important because they capture and describe nuances that quantitative data sometimes fail to detect.

Reporting Assessment Data

We've reviewed how to analyze assessment data to determine whether learning objectives were met, and we've stressed the importance of using feedback to improve training program quality. Now we return to an idea that we used to introduce this chapter. One of the main reasons assessment is conducted today is to show decision makers and senior executives that training makes a difference in the organization. In our corporate culture, training and development departments that cannot show their effectiveness will be vulnerable to being downsized if not eliminated entirely. Departments that remain immune from personnel cuts and funding are usually those that remain profit centers for the organization or can show their effectiveness in terms of improving the organization's bottom-line performance and profitability.

Ultimately, executives look for a return on their training investment. When organizational dollars are invested, most executives expect a return that shows that their investment was a wise one. One way to show this is by preparing a report that documents the cost/benefit ratio (CBR).[17] The **cost/benefit ratio**, (depicted in Figure 11.11) examines the training program's benefits to the organization in relation to how much the training program cost. When there are more benefits than costs, decision makers are more likely to reinvest in the training department's efforts. However, if the program's costs are greater than the program's benefits, decision makers will be less likely to reinvest in training.

$$CBR = \frac{\text{Program Benefits}}{\text{Program Costs}}$$

FIGURE 11.11
Cost/Benefit Ratio for Determining Return on Investment

When reporting assessment results, you need to find ways of showing the benefits of your training to the organization's bottom line. Using the behavioral learning objective in which front-line customer service employees will be able to reduce customer complaints by 25 percent over a six-month period is one place to start. Assume that we met this objective; how much does a 25 percent reduction in customer complaints save or benefit the organization?

Although benefits are sometimes difficult to compute, we believe most organizations can estimate how much a single customer complaint costs the organization. If not, you need to find out. To start, determine how much it costs the organization to process the complaint. How long does it take a customer service employee to resolve the complaint? How much are these employees paid? Most complainants also request for compensation. Let's assume that it takes $25 of an employee's time, on average, to process a customer complaint and it takes $150 compensation, on average, to make the customer happy. Therefore it costs the organization $175, on average, to process a single customer service complaint.

Using the same scenario, we believe that our communication training has reduced customer complaints by 25 percent, and let's assume that this equals 100 fewer complaints. In order to calculate the benefit, we take the average cost per complaint, which is $175, times 100 fewer complaints, which equals $17,500. The benefit to the organization is that it is spending $17,500 less over a six-month period than it has in the past. We now know the benefit to the organization.

To calculate how much the training program costs the organization, you would need to review the training budget. (We review this important part of your training proposal in the next chapter.) Let's assume that the communication training program, which was used to train employees on how to resolve customer complaints, cost the organization $6,000. To calculate the CBR, or the organization's return on investment, you would divide the benefits by the costs, as shown in Figure 11.12.

$$CBR = \frac{\$17,500}{\$6,000}$$

FIGURE 11.12
Return on Investment Calculated

Although the training professional cannot say with certainty that it was his or her training program that reduced the number of customer complaints by 25 percent, it's safe to assume that the training program played a role in saving the organization $17,500 with an initial investment of only $6,000. This type of reporting will resonate with organizational decision makers and will ensure that trainers continue to thrive in an era of downsizing.

SUMMARY AND REVIEW

Assessment is an important part of the ongoing training and development process. Consistent and appropriate assessment is the key to keeping training programs effective and relevant. The first part of the chapter focused on understanding assessment and its value in the learning process.

- The model of assessment involves first developing learning objectives, then measuring whether those objectives were met at the end of the training program, and finally, interpreting those results to adapt the program to trainees' needs.
- Assessment is necessary for effective training and development programs because it ensures that the training is high quality and produces a good return on investment.
- Both Bloom's Taxonomy of Learning and Kirkpatrick's Levels of Assessment add to our understanding of domains of learning and measurement.

Selecting assessment methods depends on the domain of learning of the objective. We discussed the domains of affective learning, and ways to assess the outcomes.

- Did the trainee value the training content?
- Did the trainee appreciate and plan to use the new behavior?
- Did the trainee like the trainer(s)?
- To assess these outcomes, have learners answer surveys and questionnaires or write responses in a journal or even on a sticky note.

The cognitive domain of learning is the acquisition of new knowledge through compre-

hension. We focused on three levels of cognitive learning and discussed ways to measure cognitive outcomes.

- Trainers may want to assess what learners understand.
- Trainers can measure trainees' ability to analyze and synthesize material.
- Trainers can measure whether participants are capable of evaluating ideas or the performance of desired behaviors.
- Most often, cognitive outcomes are measured through the use of a quiz or an exam consisting of multiple-choice, essay, matching, or fill-in-the-blank items.

We covered behavioral objectives and the methods for measuring performance outcomes. There are three domains of behavioral learning assessment.

- Atomistic assessment involves checking a box to signify that a desired behavior was performed. This identifies simply the behavior itself, not the skill level.
- Analytic assessment involves measuring the skill level shown during the performance. This identifies not only whether the behavior was performed, but whether it was performed well.
- Holistic assessment is the evaluation of a performance, based not on observable behaviors but on an overall impression.
- Tools for assessing behavioral outcomes involve developing a set of behavioral items, skill ratings for those items, and skill criteria for each skill rating.

After assessing each domain of learning, it is important that you interpret the data effectively to ensure that your training program was beneficial to the trainees and the organization.

■ Analyzing assessment data is the first step in evaluating the overall value of a training program.
■ Use assessment data for maximum value, noting what needs to be changed to make training more

effective and efficient. The data also allow you to measure which training objectives were met, and give valuable input to help you adapt the program.
■ Prepare a report of the assessment data that determines the return on investment ratio. This number will provide information on whether the training was of utmost value.

QUESTIONS FOR DISCUSSION AND REVIEW

1. Why is assessment a crucial part of a training program? How is assessment included in the ongoing development process of effective training?
2. Describe the cognitive domain of learning. What methods can you use to effectively measure cognitive learning?
3. Define and discuss the dimensions of affective learning. How can you measure affective learning in a training context?

4. Describe the behavioral domain of learning. What is the difference between atomistic, analytic, and holistic behavioral assessment?
5. How do you interpret and use assessment data to improve your training program and determine whether it was cost effective?

QUESTIONS FOR APPLICATION AND ANALYSIS

1. Devin is a manager of a local restaurant. He just completed a two-hour customer service training program with his wait staff. Now he would like to see if his training made a difference in how his servers perform their jobs. He has never had any type of training and development course and doesn't know anything about assessment. He would like you to develop a behavioral assessment instrument. Before you can develop this instrument, you have a series of questions that you will need to ask Devin. For example: What was your behavioral learning objective? What level of behavioral assessment would you like me to assess—atomistic, analytic, or holistic? What are the other questions you would need answered before you can develop this behavioral instrument? Why are these questions important to your being able to assess Devin's training?

2. Jodi trains sales representatives for a national pharmaceutical company. She trains representatives in all five regions of the country. She just completed a new training program with her reps in the Southwest. She wants to know if her training is making a difference. She wants a rigorous assessment design. Which assessment design would you recommend she use and why?
3. Clay just completed a four-hour training program with 150 student leaders at his college. This training program focused on issues related to college life, including date rape, diversity, sexual harassment, and binge drinking. How would you advise Clay to calculate his cost/benefits ratio? What would be some of his costs? How could he go about assessing the benefits of the training program? How would you advise him to report his findings to the Dean of Student Life at his college?

ACTIVITIES FOR APPLYING PRINCIPLES AND SKILLS

1. Using the following guide, identify the appropriate learning domain for each training objective. Then select the best assessment tool for that objective.

Objective *At the end of this training program, the trainees will:*	Learning Domain	Assessment Tool
Be able to demonstrate effective customer service phone skills.		
Describe the five steps of the active listening process.		
Appreciate the value of servant leadership, or leading by example.		
Be able to apply the model of conflict management to a real life conflict.		
Be able to demonstrate the five steps of the small group problem solving process.		
Understand the importance of balancing the two dimensions that comprise all meetings.		
Identify and describe the five cultural values.		
Explain the five functions of a presentation introduction.		
Demonstrate two methods for analyzing an audience.		

2. Develop several learning objectives for a potential training program. They should include affective, cognitive and behavioral objectives. Then develop an assessment instrument to measure each of the objectives. This instrument should include Likert-type and semantic differential scales, multiple-choice, matching, and essay items as well as behavioral items, skill ratings, and skill criteria.

3. Working in groups or individually, conduct a short training program using the objectives from activity 2. Next, assess the trainees' learning using the instrument you created to determine whether learning objectives were met. Interpret this data.

4. Develop a cost/benefit ratio of the training to determine whether the training was cost effective and brought a return on your investment. Determine how you could adjust your training objectives or your program to meet the needs of trainees more effectively.

There is nothing training cannot do. Nothing is above its reach.
It can turn bad morals to good; it can destroy bad principles
and recreate good ones; it can lift men to angelship.

— *Mark Twain*

Becoming a Training Professional

CHAPTER OBJECTIVES

After studying this chapter, you should be able to:

- List and describe the types of training jobs available for beginning professional trainers.

- Describe strategies for obtaining a job in training.

- Compare and contrast the options of working full-time or part-time as a trainer.

- Identify and explain the two types of training needed today:

fundamental soft skills and project management training.

- Differentiate between training generalists and training specialists, and explain why each is important today.

- Develop skills in writing and presenting needs assessment proposals.

- Develop skills in writing and presenting training proposals

W hat is the future of training and development? More specifically, what is *your* future in communication training and development? Each year the American Society for Training and Development (ASTD), the professional organization for training professionals, publishes a State of the Industry report on the training and development profession. ASTD monitors training trends and practices, and it tracks how much money organizations are investing in developing human capital. Here are a few of their most recent findings.[1]

- U.S. organizations invested $134 billion in training and development in 2008. On average, organizations invested $1,068 per employee.
- Because of the struggling economy, training and development professionals were asked to train more employees with fewer resources, forcing training organizations to be more efficient in their practices. In 2008, each trainer was responsible for training an average of 253 trainees, up from 227 in 2007.
- The average cost per training hour fell from $56 in 2007 to $52 in 2008, which indicates that learning professionals were operating efficiently and managing their training and development costs.

Although organizations constantly seek ways to operate more efficiently, especially during poor economic times, the training function in most organizations has not been reduced significantly as a result of a lagging economy. The data in the ASTD State of the Industry report reinforces the importance that U.S. organizations place on training and developing human capital. Yet this report suggests that training and development professionals, like most other professionals, will have to continue to provide services using fewer resources. Training professionals must work smart. The purpose of this chapter is to help you develop and launch your training career while making sure that you're versed in current training needs and trends. Your ability to convince a potential employer that you can develop, deliver, and assess high quality training in an efficient and cost effective manner will enhance your ability to land that training job.

This chapter focuses on three topics: (1) how to get a job in training, (2) how to identify training needs, and (3) how to write and present training proposals that will help you get a job in training.

HOW TO GET A TRAINING JOB

There are a number of ways to land your first training job. You might conduct a strategic search to find the perfect training job, or if you have the ability to easily develop relationships with others and can describe complex processes in understandable terms, it may only be a matter of time before a training job finds you. To begin your search, it's important to know the types of positions that are available, the strategies for getting a training job, the benefits of doing training on a part-time basis, and the process for becoming a certified trainer.

Types of Training Jobs

A trainer may be asked to do a variety of jobs, depending on the type of organization. There is a training job for almost every step of the Needs-Centered Training

Model we introduced in Chapter 1. Here are nine jobs, tasks, or roles you might be asked to complete or fill.[2]

1. The **needs analyst** is responsible for conducting the needs assessment, which was reviewed in Chapter 3. The needs analyst identifies what learners do not yet know or the important or necessary skills that they can't yet perform.
2. The **task analyst,** like the needs analyst, was described in Chapter 3. The task analyst's primary job is to take the important skills identified by the needs analyst and break them down into a step-by-step outline. Trainers will use this outline to teach how to perform the skill.
3. The **program designer** translates needs into learning objectives (Chapter 4), develops training curricula (Chapter 5), selects appropriate training methods (Chapter 6), and develops lesson plans (Chapter 9).
4. The **media specialist** works closely with the program designer in selecting and/or designing audio and visual media to complement and support the training program. Some of these ideas were discussed in Chapter 8. Today's media specialists are also advising and coaching teletrainers, who use interactive television to broadcast their training in addition to developing and designing sophisticated multimedia software programs that allow trainees to complete programs at their own pace using their personal computer.
5. The **presenter,** or trainer, delivers the training program, which was the focus of Chapter 10. Presenters work closely with program designers and media specialists to make sure that training programs are delivered in an effective manner. They present information and direct structured learning activities.
6. The **assessment specialist** is responsible for measuring the outcomes of the training program, which was the focus of Chapter 11. Was the training program effective? Did the trainees reach the intended learning objectives? Did the training fill the need identified by the needs analyst?
7. The **training and development manager** is responsible for planning, organizing, staffing, and controlling training and development operations, and for bridging the operations of the department with other units within an organization to ensure that the organization's needs are met.
8. The **training and development administrator** works closely with the manager and ensures that the facilities, equipment, materials, participants, and other components of a learning event are in place and that training programs run smoothly.
9. The final job we will discuss is that of the **Web-based training specialist.** In the coming years, more and more training is going to be designed, developed, and delivered using the personal computer and the Internet. One reviewer for this textbook, a training practitioner, attended a national training conference in Atlanta where over 75 percent of the panels at the conference focused on Web-based training and technology's impact on the training industry. Knowing this, we encourage new trainers to remain abreast of the multimedia technologies and Web-authoring tools that are used to create Web pages and Web-based training programs. Although we don't have room to explore this topic at length, we do want to give a sampling of what Web-based training specialists know and do. We also provided a list of resources at the end of the chapter that should be useful.

Strategies for Getting a Training Job

There are a number of ways to gain entry into the communication training and development profession. Here are our recommendations:

- *Obtain a college education.* Most training positions require a college degree. While just having a degree is sometimes more important than the field of study it is in, we recommend you take courses that focus on training. Many training courses are offered in departments of communication and business. Look for courses titled Training and Development, Human Resource Development, Employee Relations, Instructional Communication, Communication Assessment, Organizational Communication, and Small Group Communication. We also recommend that you take courses in research methods and social science statistics; They will be useful when conducting needs assessments and when assessing learning outcomes.

- *Complete an internship in a training department.* **Internships** are opportunities for students to obtain college credit by working in a supervised environment. This allows students to apply what they're learning in the classroom to the workplace. Most colleges and universities have career centers where students can obtain information about internship programs. Many internships are available during summer vacations or throughout the school year. Completing an internship gives you professional work experience that you can place on your resume, and it allows you to begin networking with other training professionals. One of the authors of this book completed summer internships at a Six Flags theme park; for four summers he developed and presented weekly training orientations to new park employees and also developed and presented annual supervisory training programs to new shift supervisors. This internship led to a management position within a training department for an international airline following the author's college graduation.

- *Join a professional training organization.* One of the most prestigious and respected training organizations is the American Society for Training and Development (ASTD).[3] This organization currently serves 70,000 members in 100 countries with 15,000 local chapters. As a member of a professional training organization, you receive professional journals, admission to seminars and workshops, and a comprehensive directory of members. Local chapters conduct monthly meetings, which allow for networking and professional development. Local chapters also encourage students to become involved in ASTD by offering their services at reduced cost. Again, belonging to ASTD allows you the opportunity to network with professionals in the training field, which may lead to your finding mentors, internships, and job opportunities.

- *Focus less on getting your first job in a training department and more on getting a job in an industry, corporation, or organization that excites you.* Sometimes it's more important to get your foot in the door of an exciting industry than it is to wait for the perfect training position. You don't want a training job in an organization that doesn't excite you. When you do get into an industry or organization that is a fit with your interests, you may often have the opportunity to transfer into the training department, which is usually in the department of human resources. For example, at the Walt Disney corporation it's rare for an outsider—someone with no Disney work experience—to be hired for the training department, or what they refer to as "Central Casting." Disney hires from within the organization for many management positions: You must first work on the front line, as a "cast member," before you can put in for a transfer to the training department or human resources when a position becomes available.

- *Develop relationships with continuing education programs.* Community education is growing in popularity, and it has a need for instructors. Volunteer to conduct a training program for your school, religious organization, or community and civic groups. If you have advanced training or are certified in a particular area of study, such as conflict negotiation or leadership, you might consider teaching a course in one of the community education programs that are sprouting up throughout the country. Most of these programs are offered through local colleges, universities, community colleges, and county extension offices. Teaching in a community education program can benefit you in a couple of ways. First, these programs offer an excellent way to meet people who may later hire you. Second, these programs give you an opportunity to try out new training material and content in a venue that may resemble what you would find in more formal training environments.

Training Part-Time

Many professionals do training and consulting on a part-time basis. Some like the additional money; others like the opportunity to travel, visit organizations, and network with a new group. Regardless of what you do on a full-time basis, you may want to consider training and consulting on a part-time basis. Here are suggestions and recommendations for how to make this happen:

- *Become a subject matter expert.* Develop a reputation for being expert in a particular area. For example, if you were an award-winning sales manager, chances are you would have learned a few things about how to sell. To earn extra money, turn that sales expertise into a training program and conduct training as a part-time job.
- *Develop training in your area of expertise.* Using the needs-centered training model, turn your knowledge and expertise into a training program or training modules. Make sure your training content is developed using the training design discussed throughout this book.
- *Develop a Web site to promote your training programs and consulting services.* The box below offers a partial list of potential training and consulting services that today's organizations need. Add the Web site's URL to your e-mail signature so that people are constantly reminded that you provide these additional services.
- *Develop a list of clients.* Once the word gets out that you're the go-to person for a particular type of training, you'll receive calls on a regular basis.
- *Price your training and consulting services appropriately.* Timothy Plax, a professor of communication who does training and development on a part-

A TRAINER'S TOOLBOX

How to Develop Your Training Portfolio

A **training portfolio** is a tool that trainers develop to give employers or potential clients a complete picture of the professional's training experiences, education, accomplishments, and skill sets. Your portfolio showcases your potential. Much more than a cover letter and a resume, your training portfolio is instrumental in interviews to highlight a point, to illustrate the depth of your skills and experience, or to show examples of your work. Professional training portfolios may also contain educational and training courses completed through an institution or company. The items you might want to include in your training portfolio are:

■ *Career summary and goals*. A description of where you have been and where you see your-self going with your career.
■ *Professional philosophy or mission statement*. A concise description of the guiding principles that drive you and give you purpose.
■ *Traditional resume*. A summary of your educa-tion, achievements, and work experience.
■ *Skills, abilities, and marketable qualities*. A detailed examination of your skills and experi-ence. This section should include the name of the skill area; the performance or behavior,

knowledge, or personal traits that contribute to your success in that skill area; your background and specific experiences that demonstrate your application of the skill.
■ *List of accomplishments*. A list that highlights the major accomplishments in your career and whatever awards and special recognition you received.
■ *Samples of your work*. Reports, training plans, and presentations. If you have developed a training program, include it. Also include DVDs, videos, and other media that showcase your work and your platform skills.
■ *Research, publications, and reports*. Published papers and conference proceedings, assess-ment reports, and any consultancy reports you may have completed for a client. Showcase your written communications abilities.
■ *Training courses, workshops, and seminars*. What was the content, and how has it enhanced your skill sets? Describe your professional development.
■ *Certificates*. Copies of any certificates or profes-sional licenses you may have earned in profes-sional development.

time basis, recommends that you price your training and consulting services using your current hourly rate of pay.[4] For example, Plax says that in 2005 the average pay for a faculty member was $65,505, or $1,317.40 per week, or $32.94 per hour; he estimates that a new, one-day training program takes approximately 40 hours to develop and deliver, so a new trainer or consult-ant can ask for $1,500 for one day of training. Regardless of your occupa-tion, multiply your hourly pay rate by the number of hours it took you to develop and deliver a training program in order to calculate your fee.

Becoming an ASTD Certified Trainer

One way to enhance your training credentials is to become a certified trainer. The **American Society of Training and Development** (ASTD) is the world's larg-est association dedicated to workplace learning and performance professionals, those whose job it is to connect learning and performance to measurable results

TRAINING PROGRAMS AND CONSULTING SERVICES IN DEMAND TODAY[5]

Teach or train others

Design training or instructional packages and modules

Evaluate people and systems

Write reports

Define problems

Offer solutions

Interview

Develop and administer surveys

Facilitate group discussions

Conduct focus group research

Analyze quantitative data

Analyze qualitative data

Gather and interpret archival research

Interpret information for others

Write and present speeches

Prepare and give briefings

Offer advice to management

Write research or grant proposals

Conduct human resource audits

Develop instructional and training curricula

Write training manuals

Train the trainers

Develop marketing plans

Design messages (mediated and nonmediated)

for an organization. ASTD has approximately 70,000 members in more than one hundred countries.

By becoming a member of ASTD, you not only join a network of 70,000 professionals who do what you do, but you also gain access to these resources:

- *State of the Industry Report,* which annually analyzes U.S. organizations' training investments and practices.
- *Training + Development magazine*, which keeps readers current on training trends, issues, and best practices.
- *Infoline series*, which provides professionals with how-to advice on a range of training topics.
- *Learning Circuits*, a listserv that offers online news and features about e-learning.
- *Buyer's Guide*, which provides training professionals with a searchable database of products and services.

As a member of ASTD, you will be invited to participate in annual conferences and workshops and to belong to an area chapter, where you can work more closely with the training professionals in your area.

ASTD also provides training certification, which is to not be confused with training certificates. Both certification and certificates are credential enhancers; however, they serve different purposes and have different criteria and goals. **Training certification** is a voluntary process whereby a professional body such as ASTD recognizes or grants a designation to professionals who have met certain qualifications or standards. When ASTD certifies you, their stamp of approval means that you have mastered a body of knowledge and can perform training functions with a high degree of proficiency. A **training certificate** recognizes your having acquired knowledge and skills about training; it is a document that confirms that the professional has completed a course of study. It does not necessarily mean that the professional can perform training functions with a high degree of proficiency—this has not been assessed. A certificate does not assess training performance.

Becoming ASTD-certified is a ten-step process wherein you demonstrate your mastery of the ASTD competency model. This model unifies the training profession, provides a common vocabulary of knowledge and skills, and allows individuals and organizations to align their work with organizational priorities. To be eligible for ASTD certification, a training professional must have two to three years' experience. Contact information for ASTD will be found in the list of resources at the end of this chapter.

HOW TO IDENTIFY TRAINING NEEDS

The needs of employees change and adapt in the same way that the U.S. economy morphs and evolves. To remain current and relevant in today's workplace, training and development professionals must be on the cutting edge of workplace issues and problems and be ready on short notice to step in and help organizations solve their training problems. This section showcases the types of training needed in the twenty-first century, the need for training professionals who can develop and deliver e-training, and the growing need for training professionals who have a wide array of training and development skills.

Types of Training Needed

Although training trends continue to evolve, we are beginning to get a clearer picture of industry's needs as the economy continues to change. Two general types of training needs seem to emerge from the research literature: fundamental soft skills (such as conflict management and leadership) and the more advanced project management skills.

Employers continue to report cases of employees who do not have the soft skills needed to be effective in today's workforce: listening, reading comprehension, speaking to convey information effectively, critical thinking, writing, information technology (software and hardware), mathematics, coordination, monitoring, judgment and decision-making, and active learning.[6] According to one report, one in three working adults lacks the skills needed to succeed at a community college—especially reading, writing, speaking, listening, and critical thinking.[7] The top ten areas of knowledge employers require in their employees are English language, customer and personal service, mathematics, clerical, administration and management, computers and electronics, public safety and security, law and government, education, training, and mechanical.[8]

In addition to these fundamental skills, advanced project management and leadership skills are in demand. The need stems from what Richard Florida refers to as the emerging creative class and Daniel Pink calls the age of "high concept/high tech," both of which have implications for training and development. Florida argues that the economy of the twenty-first century will be one fueled by the **creative class,** or those people who add economic value through their creativity.

Unlike the working and services classes, who are "paid to execute according to plan, members of the creative class are primarily paid to create and have considerably more autonomy and flexibility than the other two classes do."[9] The box below lists fifteen industries where creative talent and the people to manage and train creative talent are needed.

Florida argues that the skills that will be most sought after in this century are those skills that cannot be outsourced to another country. **Outsourcing** is management's decision to save money by contracting with firms in other countries to produce U.S. products and services for a fraction of the cost of producing the same products and services in the United States. Florida argues that many companies have a tendency to outsource most organizational functions, retaining only a small core of executives, marketers, and designers as its own staff. Only those functions that generate intellectual property, creative design, or brand identity remain in house.[10]

Daniel Pink argues that to survive in today's economy, individuals and organizations must examine what they're doing and ask whether someone overseas can do it cheaper or a computer can do it faster.[11] He believes that high-tech skills are no longer enough, that we must be high concept and high touch. High concept involves the ability to create artistic and emotional beauty, to detect patterns and opportunities, to craft a satisfying narrative, and to combine seemingly unrelated ideas into a novel invention. High touch involves the ability to empathize, to understand the subtleties of human interaction, to find joy in one's self and to elicit it in others, and to stretch beyond the quotidian in pursuit of purpose and meaning.[12]

Our analysis of the data suggests that there will be an increased need for nuanced soft skills training for entry-level employees and for middle and upper management positions. Entry-level employees are going to need assistance in developing the fundamental communication skills of reading, writing, speaking, listening, and critical thinking. Middle and upper management people are going to need training in how to lead teams of culturally diverse individuals in working toward common goals. Trainers who are subject matter experts in communication, leadership, and project management will be able to meet both needs. The box on the following page lists and describes many communication, leadership, and project management skills that will be in demand to develop the high-concept, high-touch skills needed to support the evolving creative economies.

CORE INDUSTRIES OF THE CREATIVE ECONOMY (IN DESCENDING ORDER BY MARKET SIZE)[13]

1. Research and Development
2. Publishing
3. Software
4. TV and Radio
5. Design
6. Music
7. Film
8. Toys and Games
9. Advertising
10. Architecture
11. Performing Arts
12. Crafts
13. Video Games
14. Fashion
15. Art

NEEDED PROJECT MANAGEMENT SKILLS[14]

Skill	Definition/Examples
Communication skills	The ability to write, read, speak, and listen at a level that enables one to work in a productive and efficient manner.
Conceptual thinking	The ability to analyze hypothetical situations.
"Change management" skills	The ability to provide accurate information to employees, help employees identify with the organization, develop trust, use humor to reframe, and develop interpersonal skills of openness, responsiveness, and flexibility.
Conflict management	The ability to resolve different points of view constructively.
Customer service	The ability to anticipate, identify, and meet customer needs and expectations.
Decision making	The ability to analyze all aspects of a situation to gain thorough insight to make decisions.
Developing others	The ability to contribute to the growth and development of others.
Diplomacy and tact	The ability to treat others fairly, regardless of personal biases or beliefs.
Empathy	The ability to take perspective and understand the feelings and attitudes of others.
Flexibility	The ability to readily modify, respond to, and integrate change with minimal personal resistance.
Goal achievement	The ability to set, pursue, and attain achievable goals, regardless of obstacles or circumstances.
Influencing others	The ability to personally affect others' actions, decisions, options, or thinking.
Interpersonal skills	The ability to initiate and interact with others in an engaging and interesting manner.
Leading others	The ability to organize, motivate, and inspire people to accomplish goals while creating a sense of order and direction.
Intercultural communication skills.	The ability to recognize cultural differences and adapt verbal and nonverbal messages to enhance communication effectiveness.
Listening and communication skills	The ability to listen to many points of view without bias, asking questions for clarification and paraphrasing content and emotions.
Planning and organizing	The ability to establish a process for activities that lead to implementation of systems, procedures, or outcomes.
Solving problems	The ability to define problems, analyze problems, identify criteria for effective solutions, generate solutions, select the best solution, and implement solutions.
Resiliency	The ability to recover quickly from adversity.
Results oriented	The ability to identify necessary actions to complete tasks and obtain results.
Self-management	The ability to prioritize and complete tasks in order to deliver desired outcomes within allotted time frames.
Self-starting	The ability to initiate and sustain momentum without external simulation.
Teamwork and collaboration skills	The ability to cooperate with others to meet objectives.

Need for E-Training and Blended Learning

Today's workforce requires twenty-first century training. E-training and blended learning, both of which were introduced in Chapter 7, are now essential for a variety of reasons.[15]

- *Global workforce.* Web-based training can deliver custom-made programs tailored to employees anywhere in the world in a minimum amount of time with a maximum flexibility for learning anytime, anywhere, with minimal travel expenses.
- *Flat organizations.* Today's front-line supervisors have multiple jobs and responsibilities, with limited time and support services provided by older and taller organizations. E-learning can allow line managers and supervisors to meet all their responsibilities, including training.
- *Short product cycle development.* Companies that develop new products and services are now able to introduce their wares more quickly into the marketplace. Web-based training helps those organizations' training functions to keep pace with the new speed of conducting business.
- *Contingent labor force.* Today's workforce is increasingly comprised of contingent workers: temporaries, consultants, retirees working part-time, and the self-employed. Web-based training allows organizations to meet the demands of this new type of worker.

It's important to be current with industry needs and demands by knowing how to develop e-training and blended training programs. Chapter 7 should serve as an effective guide for developing e-learning skills. Our research and our conversations at some of the country's leading organizations suggest that the sooner you develop these skills, the sooner you will find employment in a training and development position.[16]

Need for Training Generalists Versus Specialists

Training generalists are practitioners who perform all the jobs and tasks associated with the needs-centered training model. **Training specialists** are practitioners who specialize in only one area of the training and development profession. The titles associated with training specialists include curriculum developer, program designer, trainer, and assessment specialist.

As the training industry continues to morph with the evolving economy, there is a growing need for generalists rather than specialists.[17] The advantages of being a training generalist are the variety it offers and the opportunity to grow professionally. You become knowledgeable and skilled in all training tasks, and that makes you highly marketable when you decide to look for a new training position. One disadvantage is that your job may seem somewhat fractured: One day you're presenting a training program, and the next day you're conducting a needs assessment in order to develop the curriculum for a different training program.

If you work for a small organization, chances are you will to have to be comfortable working as a generalist. However, if you work for a large organization, you may have the opportunity to work as a specialist. Many large training departments are housed in a department of human resources (once called the personnel department) as one of its subdivisions (see the chart in Figure 12.1). Members of

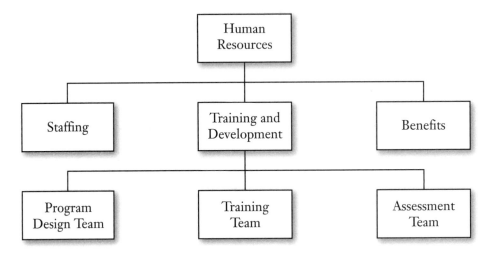

FIGURE 12.1
Human Resources Department: Organizational Chart

the training and development subdivision will be arranged in teams by specialty. All needs and task analysts, in addition to curriculum developers, would be part of the program design team. Presenters, software designers, and media specialists might be part of the training team. Those who focus on training program effectiveness might be part of the assessment team.

Need for Training On-the-Go

There will be times when you may have less than twenty-four hours to prepare a training program. That's training on-the-go. Experienced trainers have learned to accommodate today's constantly changing and unpredictable business environment. At any time an organizational problem may surface where immediate training is needed. For example, an organization experiencing a crisis may urgently need to expand its call center, and you may have only limited time to train people to respond to callers. Or you might be contacted at the last minute to cover for a trainer who is unable to appear or to provide training when someone has failed to schedule a trainer. These are all important opportunities, and you need to be ready to develop, deliver, and assess training on-the-go.

Here are recommendations for how to be ready to train at a moment's notice:

■ *Conduct your needs assessment while you're on the phone accepting the training assignment.* Obtain the following: desired training outcomes or goals, information about the training participants and their prior knowledge, time allotted for your training program, a cell phone or e-mail contact for the person handling tech set-up for your training, and a cell phone contact for your point person once you arrive.

■ *Confirm the terms of your training assignment in a follow-up e-mail.* Confirm the amount of the payment for your services and how and when you will be paid. Confirm how the costs of transportation, food, and lodging will be handled and processed.

- *Develop training materials by modifying what you have done in the past.* You will not have time to develop new materials tailored to the client or the specific needs of the client. Instead, draw on your training inventory or repertoire of training materials. Modify PowerPoint slides and participant's manuals as needed to fit the needs of your new client.
- *Copy all training materials and handouts as a PDF document and forward via e-mail to your client.* Ask the client to copy and collate appropriate numbers of the materials for the training participants. This is especially helpful when you need to fly and you do not want to lug 150 copies of your participant's manual.
- *Forward PowerPoint slides to your tech person via e-mail.* Ask the tech person to test your PowerPoint slides and all embedded videos to make sure they work on the computer or projector at the training location. Always take printed copies of PowerPoint slides in the event of tech snafus.
- *Take your training kit with you.* Many professional trainers have a permanent training supply kit that contains many of the items they need to do their work. These kits often include thumb drives, DVDs, clickers, batteries, computer adapters and power cords, preprinted handouts, games, index cards, sticky notes, flipchart paper and markers, whiteboard markers, erasers, tape, and writing paper.

HOW TO DEVELOP TRAINING PROPOSALS

Regardless of your specific training position, one task that all training practitioners should learn is that of writing and presenting training proposals. A **proposal** is a formal document that sells the training program to the key decision makers in an organization. Key decision makers are the men and women in upper management who decide how the organization's money will be invested. They determine what gets funded and what doesn't. A proposal includes the who, what, where, when, how, and why of a potential training program. In order for most training programs to get off the ground, executive management must endorse and support the program. A training proposal is your way of showing the executive management team why a training program is necessary, how training will be conducted, who will be involved, where and when the program will be conducted, and the return on the investment that training will bring to the organization. Sometimes the executive management team will come to you with a problem and ask the training department or outside consultants for assistance in addressing it. External trainers, or trainers who work for themselves, also typically develop a training proposal before being hired to present a training program.

There are essentially two types of proposals. One is a needs-assessment proposal, and the second is the actual training proposal, which we discuss later in this chapter. The **needs-assessment proposal** explains to the organization's decision makers why some aspect of their organization deserves to be examined more closely. In writing this proposal, your job is to convince the management team that there may be a deficiency within the organization and that training may be the solution to the problem. For example, assume that you manage a telemarketing group and a trainer comes to you to suggest that your telemarketers may be losing too many telephone sales as a result of poor communication skills. A needs-assessment proposal would confirm the problem by identifying, describing, and explaining this problem.

Writing Needs-Assessment Proposals

The needs-assessment proposal must be brief and succinct. Key decision makers tend to overlook lengthy documents. Include only essential information; you can always elaborate on the proposal later when you present your findings. Figure 12.2 shows an outline of what we recommend you include in your needs-assessment proposal, along with approximate page lengths for each section.

The first section of a needs assessment, the introduction, is your opportunity to introduce yourself and to review your credentials, which give you **credibility.** Are you competent, and can management trust you to go snooping around their organization? You get credibility by reporting your **credentials,** your prior training experiences, your education, your research, and whatever recognition you've received for your professional work experience. Your credentials will help shape how others perceive your competence and character. If you're already a member of the organization's training and development team, decision makers may not need an introduction. We recommend that you have one ready in case they do ask.

The second section, the briefing of the problem, is where you describe the problem and explain why it is of concern to the organization. Just describing a problem is not always sufficient. To document its significance, show decision makers how the problem affects the bottom line. For example, you learn in the *Journal of Applied Communication*[18] that telemarketers lose sales as a result of their poor phone and persuasive communication skills. You also learn how sales have been shown to improve with appropriate training. Your job is to be current with communication research and to inform key decision makers of critical research findings that affect their bottom line.

The third section of the proposal, the needs-assessment procedures, includes a brief discussion of the sample, methodology, and data analysis. In the sampling section, you will want to inform decision makers of whom within the organization you

---

Introduction of trainer and credentials (2 pages)

Briefing of problem (4 pages)

Needs assessment procedures (2 pages)

    Sampling

    Methodology

    Data Analysis

FIGURE 12.2
Needs-Assessment Proposal Outline

will include in your needs-assessment study. Using the example above, your sample would include all telemarketers. In the methodology section, you will discuss the methods by which you would conduct your needs assessment, which we discussed in Chapter 3. The final part of the procedures section is your discussion of how you will analyze the data. It's not necessary to go into a lengthy statistical discussion here, but you should assume that some of your key decision makers will have backgrounds in statistics. Not discussing your data analysis could damage your credibility.

Presenting Needs-Assessment Proposals

If key decision makers give you permission to conduct the needs assessment, you will need to present your results when the assessment is completed. We recommend you prepare both a written report and an oral presentation showcasing the results of your assessment.

To prepare the written report of your results, you can simply expand on your needs-assessment proposal, outlined in Figure 12.2. Thus far you have an introduction, a briefing of the problem, and a discussion of the procedures you used to conduct your needs assessment. Now you will need to add two additional sections, results and discussion. Again, a succinct well-written report is more likely to be read than a long, detailed report that lacks clarity. Figure 12.3 outlines what we recommend you include in your needs-assessment results written report, along with approximate page lengths for each section.

In the results section, present your findings in a clear and concise manner. Give your key decision makers a snapshot of what you found in your needs assessment. An easy way to do this is to report your results organized around the questions you asked in your needs-assessment survey. In Figure 12.4, the results for each survey item are organized using the questionnaire format. This figure illustrates how a training and development practitioner in a telemarketing organization presented her results to key decision makers. One part of her needs-assessment survey focused on how effective telemarketers perceived themselves to be.

Briefing of problem (2–4 pages)
Needs assessment procedures (2 pages)
    Sampling
    Methodology
    Data analysis
Results (2–4 pages)
Conclusions (2–4 pages)
    Problem confirmed/disconfirmed
    Possible causes
    Possible solutions

FIGURE 12.3
Needs-Assessment Results Written Report Outline

How effective are you in getting customers to talk to you?

Very Ineffective	Somewhat Ineffective	Average	Somewhat Effective	Very Effective
30%	35%	20%	10%	5%

How effective are you in discussing the advantages of the product?

Very Ineffective	Somewhat Ineffective	Average	Somewhat Effective	Very Effective
2%	2%	19%	47%	30%

How effective are you in answering customers' questions about the product?

Very Ineffective	Somewhat Ineffective	Average	Somewhat Effective	Very Effective
12%	15%	47%	18%	14%

How effective are you in getting a commitment from the customer?

Very Ineffective	Somewhat Ineffective	Average	Somewhat Effective	Very Effective
12%	26%	34%	18%	10%

How effective are you as a telemarketer?

Very Ineffective	Somewhat Ineffective	Average	Somewhat Effective	Very Effective
15%	30%	30%	18%	7%

FIGURE 12.4
Reporting Survey Results Using the Questionnaire Format

When presenting survey results, compute the percentages for each of the response categories. By looking at this snapshot of the data, decision makers can see that there may be a problem among the telemarketers. From this snapshot, it appears that telemarketers consider themselves most ineffective in getting customers to talk to them on the phone and in getting customers to commit to purchasing the product. As a result of these two problem areas, which remain critical to a successful sales call, these telemarketers don't consider themselves to be effective, with 75 percent of them considering themselves to be average to very ineffective in terms of their telemarketing effectiveness.

The final section of the written report, conclusions, confirms (or disconfirms) that there is a problem, in addition to discussing possible causes of and solutions to the problem. If a problem exists, this is where you suggest or hint at a training intervention. You don't sell the training program in this report, you simply offer training as a possible solution. The second type of proposal that we discuss, the training proposal, is where you sell the training program.

To prepare your oral presentation of the needs-assessment results, we recommend the following:

- *Invite key decision makers and opinion leaders to attend your presentation.* Don't waste your time with those who don't have the power to hire you for the job. Invite those who make budgetary decisions because your training program is going to cost money. Ideally, invite other key opinion leaders in the organization. **Opinion leader** is an informal role within an organization that people look to in order to understand how they should interpret certain information. People learn from opinion leaders how to respond to particular issues. Opinion leaders are usually respected persons who have, on average, more education than others in their peer group, are well read and informed, and are articulate.[19] Using the example from above, it would be wise to invite key opinion leaders from the telemarketing group to your presentation. You will need this group on board with you if and when you get the training contract.
- *Be brief.* Don't waste people's time. Present a short briefing summary for each section of the presentation. A **briefing summary** is a succinct statement that includes the who, what, where, when, how, and why of your needs assessment. Provide handouts that include additional information for those who might need it in order to make a training decision. They can refer to this document when time permits.
- *Use visual aids.* Use appropriate visual aids, such as a PowerPoint presentation that includes summary statements, to help your audience interpret more accurately the assessment results. One example of an appropriate visual aid may be the questionnaire items that were used above, along with percentages for each response category. A visual representation of the results will not only help audience members interpret and retain the results but will also help you present and discuss the findings of the needs assessment in a concise manner.
- *Be prepared to answer questions during your presentation.* Your presentation should be interactive. Encourage questions throughout the presentation and anticipate questions. Be prepared to answer the question How do you know this? Be prepared to defend your needs assessment.
- *Request approval for developing a training proposal.* Once you've presented your results and discussed your conclusions, ask key decision makers for their approval to develop a training proposal that will explain how you anticipate addressing the problems or needs of the organization.

Writing Training Proposals

Once key decision makers are interested in what you can do to help them solve their problem, you will prepare a training proposal. The **training proposal** is a formal document that sets forth the training program in detail, including its length, the training content, strategies, materials, an assessment plan, and a training budget.

As the outline of a training proposal in Figure 12.5 shows, most training proposals include eight sections:

1. *Introduction of trainer and credentials.* This section is the same as the one you prepared for the needs-assessment proposal. Remind key decision makers of who you are by reviewing your credentials.

Introduction of trainer and credentials (1 page)

Title and description of training program (1 page)

Target audience (1 page)

Learning objectives (1 page)

Details of training program (5 pages)

> Length of program
>
> Training curriculum
>
> Training methods
>
> Training facility
>
> Training equipment

Assessment of learning objectives (1 page)

Training budget (1 page)

Return on investment report (1 page)

FIGURE 12.5
Training Proposal Outline

2. *Title and description of the training program.* Provide key decision makers with the information they will need to sell the training program to the target audience. Title your training program and write a brief promotional summary describing the training program and the benefits of attending it.

3. *Target audience.* This section is the same as the one you prepared for the needs-assessment proposal. Summarize for key decision makers the audience for the training.

4. *Learning objectives.* This section includes the learning objectives that undergird the training program and that address the needs identified in the needs assessment. Review Chapter 4 for the types of learning objectives and how to describe them. If your training program includes a variety of smaller training sessions or **training modules**, described in Chapter 9, you might want to include learning objectives for not only the entire training program, but also for each of the training modules. For example, you might be doing an entire training session for the telemarketing group on how to increase phone sales; however, the trainees will complete a series of training modules including phone skills, influence and persuasion strategies, and how to close a sale. It is better to write objectives for the entire training program, with specific objectives for each of the training modules.

5. *Details of the training program.* In this section, review not only how long the entire training program will last but also how long each training module will take trainees to complete. Because time is money, you'll want a pretty good estimate of how long you believe the training program will take. Be liberal with your estimates; from our experience, it always takes longer than one expects.

Give decision makers an idea of the training curriculum, the training methods you will use, the number of rooms or space you will need to conduct the training, and the equipment your training will require. If the organization doesn't have the necessary computers, visual presenters, and overhead projectors, you'll need to budget accordingly.

6. *Assessment of learning objectives.* This section states how you will assess the effectiveness of your training program. Include the instruments for assessing cognitive, behavioral, and affective learning objectives in this section of the training proposal.

7. *Training budget.* Training proposals must include a **training budget,** which outlines all the anticipated costs needed to develop, present, and assess the training program. How much money do you need to conduct the training program you're proposing? One way to develop a training budget is by using contact hours. A **contact hour** is the time you spend in the training classroom working with trainees. However, you're paid for more than just your time in the training classroom. Factored into each contact hour are the hours you've invested in conducting the needs assessment, writing and presenting training proposals, writing learning objectives, developing the training curriculum, and assessing learning objectives. Additional costs, such as rental fees for equipment and facilities and travel costs (including hotel, food, and transportation) are either factored into the contact hour pay rate or billed individually to the organization.[20]

Another way to write a training budget, other than using contact hours, is by developing three separate budgets. The first, a preparation budget, includes all costs associated with the needs assessment, the development of the training curriculum, and assessing learning outcomes. The second, a presentation budget, includes all costs associated with presenting the training program, including your training fees and rental fees for audiovisual equipment and training rooms.[21]

The third budget is for a separate "Train the Trainer" program. These programs are useful when there are hundreds or even thousands of employees who need to be trained. Because it's impossible for a single trainer or even a team of trainers to instruct hundreds or thousands of employees, some organizations select key individuals from the front line or rank and file to serve as trainers. Your job is to train the trainers who will eventually train the employees.

8. *Return on investment (ROI) report.* This concept was reviewed in Chapter 11. Key decision makers will be more willing to invest in your training program if they believe they will get a return on their investment. In this section of the training proposal, you're encouraged to prepare a brief report that examines the cost/benefit ratio or the CBR (illustrated in Figure 12.6).

The **cost/benefit ratio** examines the training program's benefits to the organization in relation to how much it will cost. If there are more benefits than costs, decision makers will be more likely to accept your training proposal. However, if the program's costs are greater than the proposed program's benefits, decision makers will probably be less likely to accept your training proposal.

$$CBR = \frac{\text{Program Benefits}}{\text{Program Costs}}$$

FIGURE 12.6
Cost/Benefit Ratio for Determining Return on Investment

Using our continuing example, assume that you will need $4,000 from the organization in order to conduct the training program you're proposing. Let's also assume that you have calculated that the organization is losing approximately $15,000 per year in sales as a result of their telemarketers' deficient telephone and communication skills. If the key decision makers accept your training proposal—and they should with this projected cost/benefit ratio—you will save them approximately $15,000 per year with a one-time cost of only $4,000.[22] This type of CBR will be persuasive to many of the key decision makers who will be reviewing your training proposal.

Although we've described eight sections of a typical training proposal, not every proposal will include all eight sections. To make sure that you meet the needs of whoever will decide whether the proposal is accepted, ask questions to ensure that your proposal includes all the information the key decision makers will need.

Presenting Training Proposals

As you did with the needs-assessment proposal, you will want to present your training proposal to key decision makers and opinion leaders in person. Use your training proposal document as a guide for your presentation. Consider presenting a **job talk,** which is a brief demonstration of one of the shorter training modules. A job talk will give decision makers and opinion leaders an idea of your training style and a preview of the training curriculum you would use. Remember, keep your presentation brief, be prepared to answer questions during your presentation, prepare handouts, use appropriate visual aids, and don't forget to ask for the training job.

That's a most important aspect of the training proposal presentation. You won't get the job unless you ask for it. After reviewing the training budget and the return on investment report, ask the client for the job. And be prepared to negotiate the budgetary concerns that key decision makers might have. Key decision makers may ask for a reduction in some budget items. Know in advance where the wiggle room is—which items are negotiable and which items are nonnegotiable.

Learning how to write and present training proposals is incredibly important for new training practitioners. It's your introduction to most organizations, and it must be impressive. Proposals must be well written and succinct. They must be presented well and to the right audience of men and women who have the power to make budgetary decisions.

SUMMARY AND REVIEW

This chapter covered what it takes to become a training professional, beginning with getting a job in training.

- There are many types of training jobs, particularly for someone who specializes.
- Getting a job in training means getting a college education and developing a network of trainers and higher education professionals.
- Trainers can consider both full-time and part-time training work.
- Becoming certified as an ASTD trainer can enhance your resume.

We discussed the training needs in today's changing workplace.

- Training opportunities have increased especially in fundamental soft skills and project leadership skills.
- E-learning and blended learning courses are in high demand.
- Trainers can decide whether they want to be a generalist or a specialist.
- On-the-go training has gained in popularity as companies meet the rapidly changing needs of their workforce.

Learning to write and present proposals is important for sustaining training jobs.

- Trainers need to develop skills in writing and presenting needs proposals.
- Trainers need to be able to convert those needs into effective training proposals.

RESOURCES FOR THE TRAINING PROFESSIONAL

The following resources are a sampling of helpful guides for the new training practitioner.

Training Guides

S. Albrecht (2006), *Tough Training Topics: A Presenter's Survival Guide* (San Francisco: Pfeiffer).

E. Biech (2010), *The ASTD Handbook for Workplace Learning Professionals* (Alexandria, VA: ASTD Press).

R. C. Clark (2010), *Evidence-Based Training Methods: A Guide for Training Professionals* (Alexandria, VA: ASTD Press).

T.W. Goad (2010), *The First-time Trainer: A Step-by-Step Quick Guide for Managers, Supervisors, and New Training Professionals* (New York: AMACOM).

K. Lawson (2009), *The Trainer's Handbook* (*updated ed.*) (San Francisco: Pfeiffer).

P. P. Philips (2010), *The ASTD Handbook for Measuring and Evaluating Training* (Alexandria, VA: ASTD Press).

R. H. Vaughan (2005), *The Professional Trainer: A Comprehensive Guide to Planning, Deliv-*

ering, and Evaluating Training Programs (San Francisco: Berrett-Koehler).

Web-Based Training Guides

R. C. Clark & R. E. Mayer (2008), *E-Learning and the Science of Instruction: Proven Guidelines for Consumers and Designers of Multimedia Learning* (San Francisco: Pfeiffer).

M. Driscoll & S. Carliner (2005), *Advanced Web-Based Training Strategies* (San Francisco: Pfeiffer).

K. Fee (2009), *Delivering E-Learning: A Complete Strategy for Design, Application, and Assessment* (Philadelphia: Kogan-Page).

W. Horton (2007), *E-Learning by Design* (San Francisco: Pfeiffer).

R. N. Palloff & K. Pratt (2011), *The Excellent Online Instructor: Strategies for Professional Development* (San Francisco: Pfeiffer).

S. S. Smith (2006), *Web-Based Instruction* (Chicago: American Library Association).

Professional Associations

American Society for Training and Development, 1640 King Street, Box 1443, Alexandria, VA

22313. Telephone: 800-628-2783 or 703-683-8100. On the web at www.astd.org. To locate the chapter closest to you, click on www.astd.org and select the "Find a Chapter" menu option.

National Communication Association, 1765 N Street, NW, Washington, DC 20036. Telephone:202-464-4622.Onthewebatwww.natcom.org.

QUESTIONS FOR DISCUSSION AND REVIEW

1. What types of training jobs are available for those looking to become professional trainers?
2. Describe strategies for obtaining a job in training, such as earning a college degree, completing an internship in a training department, and becoming an ASTD certified trainer.
3. Compare and contrast the options of working full-time as a trainer and doing training part-time.
4. Identify and explain the two types of training needed today: fundamental soft skills and project management training.

5. Understand the current need for trainers to adapt technology for developing e-learning and blended learning programs and for developing training on-the-go.
6. What is the difference between training generalists and training specialists? Explain why each is important today.
7. How would you go about training someone to write and present needs-assessment proposals?
8. Develop skills in writing and presenting training proposals.

QUESTIONS FOR APPLICATION AND ANALYSIS

1. Flor is a student in the business department at a large university. Seeing the job market decline, she is looking at careers that match her skills, and she is considering a career in training. What advice would you give Flor to help her obtain a job in the training field?
2. You work in the training department for a large international retailer. The company is regularly adjusting to new policies and procedures, and they have high employee turnover. The training team must travel often to hold seminars and retrain employees. You have set up a meeting with your supervisor to discuss the use of technology in streamlining the training program. Why and how would your organization benefit from e-learning or blended learning training courses?
3. An advertising executive has asked you to train her employees to improve their presentation skills. After conducting a needs assessment, you determine that

many of the agents never had a college course in presentational speaking. Which methods might you use to reach this goal?
4. Raul works for a local call center that takes customer service calls for a cell phone provider. After six months as a team leader, he noticed the new employees struggling to keep up with the call center volume. At the same time, the company raised the prices of phone plans, which resulted in higher numbers of complaint calls. Raul felt that further training in customer service might help. He is meeting with his supervisor to present a proposal to assess the needs of his call agents. What should Raul include in his needs-assessment proposal?
5. Continuing from the previous question, assume that Raul performed the needs assessment and found areas that need improvement, such as conflict management skills. What should he include in his training proposal?

ACTIVITIES FOR APPLYING PRINCIPLES AND SKILLS

1. Review the guidelines for developing an effective training portfolio. Then gather your own work together and determine what you might need to complete your portfolio. Start with your resume and add samples of your work, publications, and awards. Now you have a portfolio ready to help you land that job!

2. Match each of the following training jobs with its appropriate description. Rank the jobs in order of their interest to you.

Training Jobs	Descriptions
1. Task analyst	A. Takes important skills and breaks them down into a step-by-step process.
2. Media specialist	B. Measures the outcomes of the training program.
3. Presenter	C. Identifies what learners do not yet know and need to learn.
4. Web-based training specialist	D. Plans, organizes, staffs, and controls a training and development operation.
5. Assessment specialist	E. Helps to ensure that facilities, equipment, materials, and other components are present.
6. Needs analyst	F. Delivers the training program.
7. Training and development manager	G. Designs, develops, and delivers training via the Web.
8. Program designer	H. Designates audio and visual media to complement the training program.
9. Training and development administrator	I. Translates needs into learning objectives, develops curriculum, and selects training methods.

3. Using the sample needs assessment results below, write a briefing summary to present to key decision makers in an organization.

How effective are you when working in a group or team?

Ineffective	Somewhat	Somewhat effective	Very Effective
20%	ineffective 45%	30%	5%

How favorable do you feel about working in groups or teams?

Not favorable	Tolerable	Somewhat favorable	Very Favorable
0%	25%	30%	45%

How effective is your team when making tough decisions?

Ineffective 5%	Somewhat ineffective 45%	Somewhat effective 45%	Very Effective 5%

How effective is your team at solving problems?

Ineffective	Somewhat	Somewhat effective	Very Effective
5%	ineffective 20%	35%	40%

How effective is your team with being efficient and timely?

Ineffective	Somewhat	Somewhat effective	Very Effective
15%	ineffective 70%	10%	5%

4. Using the same example, work with a partner or a group to develop a training proposal outline, and take turns presenting your arguments to each other.

NOTES

CHAPTER 1

1. See J. L. Winsor, D. B. Curtis, & R. D. Stephens (September 1997), "National Preferences in Business and Communication Education: A Survey Update," *Journal of the Association for Communication Administration,* 3, 174; *The Wall Street Journal* September 9, (2002), 1A.

2. S. A. Beebe (April 2007), "What Do Communication Trainers Do?" *Communication Education,* 56, 249–254.

3. See ASTD 2004 Competency Study, www.mymodel.astd.org. Also see R. H. Vaughn (2005), *The Professional Trainer* (San Francisco: Berrett-Koehler) p. 5. Also see E. Biech (2005), *Training for Dummies* (Indianapolis: Wiley).

4. University of Wisconsin–River Falls, Career Services (June 26, 2010), "What Skills and Attributes Employers Seek When Hiring Students," http://www.uwrf.edu/ccs/skills/htm; C. Luckenbaugh & K. Gray (June 26, 2010), "Employers Describe Perfect Job Candidate," *National Association of Colleges and Employers Survey,* http://www.naceweb.org/pres/display. asp?year=2003&prid+169; R. S. Hansen & K. Handson (June 4 2006), "What Do Employers Really Want? Top Skills and Values Employers Seek from Job-Seekers," http:quintcareers.com/job_skills_values.html.

5. H. Aguinis & K. Kraiger (2009), "Benefits of Training and Development for Individuals and Teams, Organizations, and Society," *The Annual Review of Psychology,* 60, 468.

6. E. E. Scannell & L. Donaldson (2000), *Human Resource Development: The New Trainer's Guide* (Cambridge, MA: Perseus), p. 1.

7. E. T. Klemmer & F. W. Snyder (June 1972), "Measurements of Time Spent Communicating," *Journal of Communication,* 20, 142.

8. P. M. Sirianni & B. A. Frey (2001), "Changing a Culture: Evaluation of a Leadership Development Program at Mellon Financial Services," *International Journal of Training and Development,* 5, 290–301.

9. E. Salas & J. A. Cannon-Bowers (2001), "The Science of Training: A Decade of Progress," *Annual Review of Psychology,* 52, 471–499.

10. See A. Paradise (2007), *State of the Industry: ASTD's Annual Review of Trends in Workplace Learning and Performance* (Alexandria, VA: ASTD).

11. Material for this discussion is adapted from E. Biech (2005), *Training for Dummies* (Indianapolis: Wiley), p. 57.

12. J. A. Kline (April 1983), *Spectra: Newsletter of the Speech Communication Association.*

13. Kline, *Spectra.* Also see S. Beebe, "What Do Communication Trainers Do?"

14. E. Schein (1987), *Process Consultation. Volume II: Lessons for Managers and Consultants* (Reading, MA: Addison-Wesley). For applications to communication consultation see E. E. Rudolph & B. R. Johnson (1983), *Communication Consulting: Another Teaching Option* (Urbana: ERIC Clearinghouse on Reading and Communication Skills).

15. F. E. X. Dance & C. Larson (1972), *Speech Communication: Concepts and Behavior* (New York: Holt, Rinehart and Winston).

16. J. T. Masterson, S. A. Beebe, & N. H. Watson (1989), *Invitation to Effective Speech Communication* (Glenview, IL: Scott, Foresman).

17. D. C. Bryant (December 1953), "Rhetoric: Its Functions and Its Scope," *Quarterly Journal of Speech,* 39, 26.

18. B. Pike (1994). *Creative Training Techniques Handbook* (Minneapolis: Lakewood).

CHAPTER 2

1. Adapted from W. H. Burton (1963), "Basic Principles in Good Teaching–Learning Situations," in L. D. Crow & A. Crow (eds.), *Readings in Human Learning* (New York: McKay), pp. 7–19.

2. E. Thorndike (1928), *Adult Learning* (New York: Macmillan).

3. W. F. Hill (1990), *Learning: A Survey of Psychological Interpretations* (New York: Harper & Row). For additional applications to the training context, refer to E. E. Scannell & L. Donaldson (2000), *Human Resource Development: The New Trainer's Guide* (Cambridge, MA: Perseus).

4. V. P. Richmond (1996), *Nonverbal Communication in the Classroom* (Edina, MN: Burgess); K. Kougl (1997), *Communicating in the Classroom* (Prospect Heights, IL: Waveland Press).

5. Hill, *Learning.* For additional applications to the training context, refer to Scannell & Donaldson, *Human Resource Development.*

6. D. Coyle (2009), *The Talent Code* (New York: Bantam), pp. 74–94.

7. Coyle, *The Talent Code,* p. 79.

8. Coyle, *The Talent Code,* p. 80.

9. Coyle, *The Talent Code,* p. 88.

10. Coyle, *The Talent Code,* p. 92.

11. D. S. Chairburu (2010), "The Social Context of Training: Coworker, Supervisor, or Organizational Support?" *Industrial and Commercial Training,* 42, 53–56.

12. For a discussion of the law of readiness, see G. Mitchell (1998), *The Trainer's Handbook: The AMA Guide to Effective Training* (New York: American Management Association). For a classic discussion of the law of readiness, see E. Thorndike (1928), *Adult Learning* (New York: Macmillan).

13. Hill, *Learning.* For additional applications to the training context, refer to Scannell & Donaldson, *Human Resource Development.*

14. M. Knowles (1990), *The Adult Learner: A Neglected Species* (Houston: Gulf), Also, for andragogical training applications, refer to M. S. Knowles, E. F. Holton, & R. A. Swanson (2001), *The Adult Learner: The Definitive Classic in Adult Education and Human Resource Development* (Woburn, MA: Butterworth-Heinemann); M. Silberman (1990), *Active Training: A Handbook of Techniques, Designs, Case Studies, and Tips*

(San Francisco: Jossey-Bass). R. J. Wlodkowski (1999), *Enhancing Adult Motivation to Learn: A Comprehensive Guide for Teaching All Adults* (San Francisco: Jossey-Bass).

15. For a discussion of the history of adult learning theory, see R. L. Craig (1996), *The ASTD Training and Development Handbook: A Guide to Human Resource Development* (New York: McGraw-Hill), pp. 254–263.

16. P. Hersey & K. Blanchard (1992), *Management of Organizational Behavior: Utilizing Human Resources* (6th ed.) (Englewood Cliffs, NJ: Prentice Hall).

17. R. Zemke & S. Zemke (1984), "Thirty Things We Know for Sure about Adult Learning," *Innovation Abstracts*, 6:8 downloadable at http://www.hcc.hawaii.edu/intranet/committees/FacDevCom/guidebk/teachtip/adults-3.htm.

18. For a summary of research on problem-based learning, see M. Pennell & L. Miles (December 2009), "'It Actually Made Me Think': Problem-Based Learning in the Business Communications Classroom," *Business Communication Quarterly*, 72, 377–394.

19. G. Welty (Spring 2010), *Journal of GXP Compliance*, 14:2, 9.

20. Zemke & Zemke, "Thirty Things."

21. Zemke & Zemke, "Thirty Things."

22. See M. Pennell & L. Miles (December 2009), "'It Actually Made Me Think': Problem-Based Learning in the Business Communications Classroom," *Business Communication Quarterly*, 72, 377–394.

23. H. Gardner (1983), *Frames of Mind: The Theory of Multiple Intelligences* (New York: Basic Books).

24. V. P. Richmond & J. Gorham (1998), *Communication, Learning, and Affect in Instruction* (Acton, MA: Tapestry Press).

25. D. H. Schunk (2000), *Learning Theories: An Educational Perspective* (Upper Saddle River, NJ: Prentice Hall).

26. Zemke & Zemke, "Thirty Things."

27. R. Dunn et al. (January/February 2009), "Impact of Learning-Style Instructional Strategies on Students' Achievement and Attitudes," *Clearing House*, 82:3, 136.

28. L. B. Resnick (1985), "Cognition and Instruction: Recent Theories of Human Competence," in B. L. Hammonds (ed.), *Psychology and Learning: The Master Lecture Series*, vol. 4 (Washington, DC: American Psychological Association), pp. 127–186.

29. G. Welty (Spring 2010), *Journal of GXP Compliance*, 14:2, 9.

30. N. Howe & W. Strauss (2000), *Millennials Rising: The Next Great Generation* (New York: Vintage).

31. Howe & Strauss, *Millennials Rising.*

32. Howe and Strauss, *Millennials Rising.*

33. Howe & Strauss, *Millennials Rising.*

34. H. Karp, C. Fuller, & D. Sirias (2002), *Bridging the Boomer-Xer Gap; Creating Authentic Teams for High Performance at Work* (Palo Alto: Davies-Black).

35. A. Williams & P. Garrett (June 2002), "Communication Evolution Across the Life Span: From Adolescent Storm and Stress to Elder Aches and Pains," *Journal of Language and Social Psychology*, 21, 101–126; also see D. Cai, H. Giles, & K. Noels (1998), "Elderly Perceptions of Communication with Older and Younger Adults in China: Implications for Mental Health," *Journal of Applied Communication Research*, 26, 32–51.

36. J. Montepare, E. Koff, D. Zaitchik, & M. Albert (Summer 1999), "The Use of Body Movements and Gestures as Cues to Emotions in Younger and Older Adults," *Journal of Nonverbal Behavior*, 23, 133–52.

37. D. K. Kolb (1999), *Learning Style Inventory, Version 3* (Boston: Experience Based Learning Systems);

38. S. Joy & K. A. Kolb (2009), "Are There Cultural Differences in Learning Style?" *International Journal of Intercultural Relations*, 33, 60–85.

39. Richmond & Gorham, *Communication, Learning, and Affect in Instruction.*

40. B. McCarthy (1981), *The 4Mat System: Teaching to Learning Styles with Right/Left Mode Techniques* (Oakbrook, IL: EXCEL).

41. Adapted from *Guiding Adult Learning* (Independence, MO: Temple School, 2005).

CHAPTER 3

1. K. H. Lucier (October 2008), "A Consultative Training Program: Collateral Effect of a Needs Assessment," *Communication Education*, 57, 482–489.

2. M. Silberman (1998), *Active Training* (San Francisco: Jossey-Bass/Pfeiffer).

3. H. Aguinis & K. Kraiger (2009), "Benefits of Training and Development for Individuals and Teams, Organizations, and Society," *The Annual Review of Psychology*, 60, 461; also see P. N. Blanchard & J. W. Thacker (2007), *Effective Training: Systems, Strategies, and Practices* (Upper Saddle River, NJ: Pearson Prentice Hall).

4. For more about gap analysis, see R. H. Vaughn (2005), *The Professional Trainer: A Comprehensive Guide to Planning, Delivering, and Evaluating Training Programs* (San Francisco: Berrett-Koehler), p. 50.

5. B. S. Bloom, M. B. Englehart, E. J. Furst, W. H. Hill, & O. R. Krathwohl (1956), *Taxonomy of Educational Objectives: The Classification of Educational Goals. Handbook I: The Cognitive Domain* (New York: Longman).

6. S. Truelove (2006), *Training in Practice* (London: Chartered Institute of Personnel and Development).

7. Truelove, *Training in Practice.*

8. Truelove, *Training in Practice.*

9. K. Lawson (2009), *The Trainer's Handbook* (San Francisco: Pfeiffer/Wiley).

10. Lawson, *The Trainer's Handbook.*

11. G. Mitchell (1998), *The Trainer's Handbook: The AMA Guide to Effective Training* (New York: American Management Association).

12. For additional descriptions and assessment measures used in assessment centers, see Truelove, *Training in Practice*, pp. 39–40.

13. Silberman, *Active Training*, p. 35.

14. Lawson, *The Trainer's Handbook*, p. 17.

CHAPTER 4

1. For a discussion of the differences between goals and learning objectives, see J. E. Brooks-Harris & S. R. Stock-Ward (1999), *Workshops: Designing and Facilitating Experiential Learning* (Thousand Oaks, CA: Sage).

2. A brief but clear discussion of training objectives may be found in E. E. Scannel & L. Donaldson (2000), *Human Resource Development: The New Trainer's Guide* (Cambridge, MA: Perseus).

3. Michael Argyle was the first social psychologist to suggest a model of social skills training. Our skill development model is based on work by M. Argyle (1994), *The Psychology of Interpersonal Behaviour* (London: Penguin); D. A. Romig & L. J. Romig (1985), *Communication and Problem Solving Skills: Trainer Guide* (Austin, TX: Performance Resources); D. A. Romig (2001), *Side by Side Leadership: Achieving Outstanding Results Together* (Austin, TX: Bard Press), p. 146; and R. R. Carkhuff & R. M. Pierce (1975), *The Art of Helping: An Introduction to Life Skills: Teacher Guide* (Amherst, MA: Human Resource Development Press).

4. E. T. Emmer & G. B. Millett (1970), *Improving Teaching Through Experimentation* (Englewood Cliffs, NJ: Prentice Hall).

5. For a review of the role of encouraging and corrective feedback in enhancing communication skill development, see M. L. Hyvarinen, P. Tanskanen, N. Katajavuri, & P. Isotalus (2008), "Feedback in Patient Counseling Training—Pharmacy Students' Opinions," *Patent Education and Counseling*, 70, 363–369.

6. For research supporting the effectiveness of role play in communication skill development, see K. E. Rowan (2008), "Monthly Communication Skill Coaching for Healthcare Staff," *Patient Education and Counseling*, 71, 402–404.

7. S. A. Beebe & S. J. Beebe (2012), *Public Speaking: An Audience-Centered Approach* (Boston: Allyn & Bacon).

8. D. H. Schunk (1987), "Peer Models and Children's Behavioral Change," *Review of Educational Research, 57*, 149–174; B. Sulzer-Azaroff & G. Mayer (1986), *Achieving Educational Excellence Using Behavioral Strategies* (New York: Holt, Rinehart and Winston).

CHAPTER 5

1. V. Montecino (July, 2002), "Criteria to Evaluate the Credibility of WWW Resources," ftp://mason.gmu.edu/~montecin/web-eval-sites.html (Fairfax Country, VA: George Mason University).

2. S.A. Beebe & S. J. Beebe (2012), *Public Speaking; An Audience-Centered Approach* (8th ed.) (Boston: Allyn & Bacon).

3. M. Cipley (July 23, 2010.) "Superheros tangle in copyright battles," *The New York Times*.

4. V. P. Richmond & J. C. McCroskey (1998), *Communication Apprehension Avoidance, and Effectiveness* (5th ed.) (Boston: Allyn & Bacon).

CHAPTER 6

1. M. Silberman (2005), *101 Ways to Make Training Active* (San Francisco: Pfeiffer); M. Silberman (2010), *Unforgettable Experiential Activities: An Active Training Resource* (San Francisco: Pfeiffer).

2. C. Heath & D. Heath (2007), *Made to Stick: Why Some Ideas Survive and Others Die* (New York: Random House).

3. R. W. Preiss & B. M. Gayle (2006), "A Meta-Analysis of the Educational Benefits of Employing Advanced Organizers," in B. M. Gayle, R. W. Preiss, N. Burrell, & M. Allen (eds.), *Classroom Communication and Instructional Processes: Advances Through Meta Analysis* (Mahwah, NJ: Erlbaum).

4. P. L. Witt, L. R. Wheeless, & M. Allen, (2004), "A Meta-Analytical Review of the Relationship Between Instructor Immediacy and Student Learning," *Communication Monographs*, 71, 184–207. See also V. P. Richmond, D. R. Lane, & J. C. McCroskey, (2006), "Teacher Immediacy and the Teacher-Student Relationship," in T. P. Mottet, V. P. Richmond, & J. C. McCroskey (eds.), *Handbook of Instructional Communication: Rhetorical and Relational Perspectives* (Boston: Allyn & Bacon), pp. 167–193.

5. M. Booth-Butterfield & M. B. Wanzer, (2010), "Humor and Communication in Instructional Contexts," in D. L. Fassett & J. T. Warren (eds.), *The Sage Handbook of Communication and Instruction* (Los Angeles: Sage), pp. 221–237. See also J. L. Chesebro & M. B. Wanzer, (2006), "Instructional Message Variables," In T. P. Mottet, V. P. Richmond, & J. C. McCroskey (eds.), *Handbook of Instructional Communication: Rhetorical and Relational Perspectives*. Boston: Allyn and Bacon (pp. 89–116).

6. A. M. Saks & M. Belcourt (2006), "An Investigation of Training Activities and Transfer of Training in Organizations," *Human Resource Management, 54*, 629–648; E. W. Holton, R. A. Bates, & W. E. A. Ruona, (2000), "Development of a Generalized Learning Transfer System Inventory," *Human Resource Development Quarterly*, 11, 333–360.

7. Many of these ideas were adapted from M. Silberman & C. Auerbach, (2006), *Active Training: A Handbook of Techniques, Designs, Case Examples, and Tips* (San Francisco: Jossey-Bass/Pfeiffer).

8. S. J. Carroll, F. T. Paine, & J. J. Ivancevich, (2006), "The Relative Effectiveness of Training Methods: Expert Opinion Research," *Personnel Psychology, 25*, 495–509; J. Gastil, L. Black, & K. Moscovitz (2008), "Ideology, Attitude Change, and Deliberation in Small Face-to-Face Groups," *Political Communication, 25*, 23–46.

9. Adapted from G. E. Myers & M. T. Myers (1976), *Instructor's Manual to Accompany the Dynamics of Human Communication* (New York: McGraw-Hill).

10. B. S. Bloom (1956), *Taxonomy of Educational Objectives: Handbook I: Cognitive Domain* (New York: McKay).

11. Bloom, *Taxonomy of Educational Objectives*.

CHAPTER 7

1. A portion of this chapter was drafted by Tony Longoria, M.A. communication studies, Texas State University-San Marcus and training specialist at CPS Energy, San Antonio, Texas.

2. R. Newton, & N. Doonga, (2007), "Corporate E-Learning: Justification for Implementation and Evaluation of Benefits. A Study Examining the Views of Training Managers and Training Providers," *Education for Information*, 25, 111–130.

3. P. Britt, (2008), "Employers and Educators Embrace E-Learning," *KM World*, 17, 20–21.

4. M. J. Rosenberg, (2006), *Beyond E-Learning: Approaches and Technologies to Enhance Organizational Knowledge, Learning, and Performance* (San Francisco: Pfeiffer).

5. S. Yahya, E. Arniza Ahmad & K. Abd Jalil, (in press), "The Definition and Characteristics of Ubiquitous Learning: A Discussion," *International Journal of Education and Development Using Information and Communication Technology, 6.*

6. M. Weiser, (1991), "The Computer of the 21st Century," *Scientific American*, 265, 66–75.

7. R. Koper, (2007), "Open Source and Open Standards," in J. M. Spector, M. D. Merrill, J. V. Jeroen van Merrienboer, & M. P. Driscoll (eds.), *Handbook on Research on Educational Communication and Technology* (Mahwah, NJ: Erlbaum).

8. L. A. Ho & T. H. Kuo, (2010), "How Can One Amplify the Effect of E-Learning? An Examination of High-tech Employees' Computer Attitude and Flow Experience," *Computers in Human Behavior*, 26, 23–31.

9. J. Adams, (2008), "Rapid Talent Development," *T+D*, 62, 68–73.

10. B. Brandon, (2005), "Exploring the Definition of 'Rapid eLearning,'" Retrieved July 13, 2010, from www.elearning guild.com.

11. R. H. Vaughn, (2005), *The Professional Trainer: A comprehensive Guide to Planning, Delivering, and Evaluating Training Programs* (2nd ed.) (San Francisco: Berrett-Koehler).

12. K. Stephens & T. P. Mottet, (2008), "Interactivity in a Web-Conferencing Learning Environment: Effects on Trainers and Trainees," *Communication Education*, 57, 88–104.

13. M. Bullen & D. P. Janes (2007), *Making the Transition to E-Learning: Strategies and Issues* (Hershey, PA: Information Science).

14. R. H. Lengel & R. L. Daft, (1988), "The Selection of Communication Media as an Executive Skill," *Academy of Management Executive*, 2, 225–232.

15. Adapted from Lengel & Daft, "The Selection of Communication Media."

16. R. Caladine, (2008), *Enhancing E-Learning with Media Rich Content and Interactions* (Hershey, PA: IGI Global).

17. Bullen & Janes, *Making the Transition to E-Learning.*

18. Adapted from K. Fee, (2009), *Delivering E-Learning: A Complete Guide for Design, Application, and Assessment* (Philadelphia: Kogan Page).

19. Caladine, *Enhancing E-Learning.*

20. Caladine, *Enhancing E-Learning.*

21. P. Galagan, (2009), "Twitter as a Learning Tool. Really," *T+D*, 63, 28–31.

22. Many of these ideas were adapted from A. Rosen, (2009), *E-Learning 2.0: Proven Practices and Emerging Technologies to Achieve Results* (New York: American Management Association).

23. C. Heath & D. Heath, (2007), *Made to Stick: Why Some Ideas Survive and Others Die* (New York: Random House). Although Heath and Heath have popularized these ideas, most of the ideas have empirical support. See their endnotes for primary source documentation.

24. Also see W. Horton, (2006), *E-Learning by Design* (New York: Pfeiffer) R. C. Clark & R. E. Mayer, (2007), *E-Learning and the Science of Instruction: Proven Guidelines for Consumers and Designers of Multimedia Learning* (2nd ed.) (New York: Pfeiffer); C. N. Quinn & M. L. Conner, (2005), *Engaging Learning: Designing E-Learning Simulation Games* (New York: Pfeiffer).

25. This figure is a modification of one in A. Rosen, (2009), *E-Learning 2.0: Proven Practices and Emerging Technologies to Achieve Results* (New York: American Management Association), p. 160.

26. This list of references was adapted from a list provided by Susan Boyd, president of Susan Boyd Associates, a computer training firm that specializes in customized application training. Retrieved on August 13, 2010, from http://www.susan-boyd.com/online-training-resources.htm.

27. R. E. DeRouin, B. A. Fritzsche, & E. Salas, (2004), "Optimizing E-Learning: Research-based Guidelines for Learner-Controlled Training," *Human Resource Management*, 43, 147–162.

CHAPTER 8

1. J. G. Saxe (1873). *The poems of John Godfrey Saxe: Complete edition.* Boston: James Osgood and Company.

2. R. Garcia-Retamero & M. Galesic (2010). Who profits from visual aids: Overcoming challenges in people's understanding of risks. *Social Science & Medicine, 70,* 1019–1025.

3. D. Lewalter (2003). Cognitive strategies for learning from static and dynamic visuals. *Learning and Instruction, 13,* 177–189.

4. L. H. Latour & K. McBroom (2009). Listen to what I say so I can see what I need: Visual aids make the difference. *Heart & Lung: The Journal of Acute and Critical Care, 38,* 276–277.

5. T. A. Saleh (2010, May/June). Testing the effectiveness of visual aids in chemical safety training. *Journal of Chemical Health & Safety.* doi: 10.1016/j.jchas.2010.03.012.

6. J. Lanir, K. S. Booth, & K. Hawkey (2010). The benefits of more electronic screen space on students' retention of material in classroom lectures. *Computers & Education, 55,* 892–903.

7. M. J. Tarpley & J. L. Tarpley (2008). The basics of PowerPoint and public speaking in medical education. *Journal of Surgical Education, 65,* 129–132.

8. J. Rotondo & M. Rotondo, Jr. (2002). *Presentation skills for managers.* New York: McGraw-Hill.

9. J. Kupsch & P. R. Graves (1993). *Create high impact business presentations.* Chicago: NTC Learning Works.

10. D. Taylor (2007). Death by PowerPoint. *Developmental Medicine & Child Neurology, 49,* 395.

11. Taylor. Death by PowerPoint.

12. N. Yuviler-Gavish, E. Yechiam, & A. Kallai (2011). Learning in multimodal training: Visual guidance can be both appealing and disadvantageous in spatial tasks. *International Journal of Human-Computer Studies, 69,* 113–122.

13. N. Yuviler-Gavish, E. Yechiam, & A. Kallai (2011). Learning in multimodal training.

14. J. M. Apperson, E. L. Laws, & J. A. Scepansky (2008). An assessment of student preferences for PowerPoint presentation structure in undergraduate courses. *Computers & Education, 50,* 148–153.

15. J. M. Apperson, E. L. Laws, & J. A. Scepansky (2008). An assessment of student preferences for PowerPoint.

16. Kupsch & Graves (1993). *Create high impact business presentations.*

17. C. Wilder & J. Rotondo (2002). *Point, click & wow: A quick guide to brilliant laptop presentations* (2nd ed.). San Francisco: Jossey-Bass/Pfeiffer.

18. J. M. Apperson, E. L. Laws, & J. A. Scepansky (2008). An assessment of student preferences for PowerPoint.

19. J. M. Apperson, E. L. Laws, & J. A. Scepansky (2008). An assessment of student preferences for PowerPoint.

20. Rotondo & Rotondo. *Presentation skills for managers.*

21. Rotondo & Rotondo. *Presentation skills for managers.*

22. S. A. Beebe & S. J. Beebe (2012). *Public Speaking: An Audience-Centered Approach* (8th ed.). Boston, MA: Pearson, p. 276.

23. Beebe & Beebe. *Public Speaking.*

24. Rotondo & Rotondo. *Presentation skills for managers.*

25. Rotondo & Rotondo. *Presentation skills for managers.*

26. M. J. Tarpley & J. L. Tarpley (2008). The basics of PowerPoint and public speaking in medical education.

CHAPTER 9

1. D. C. Berliner (1991), "Educational Psychology and Pedagogical Expertise: New Finds and New Opportunities for Thinking about Training," *Educational Psychologist, 26:2,* 145–155.

2. These lesson plans were developed by Seth Frei, M. A. Texas State University. Used with permission.

3. Adapted from K. Lawson (2009), *The Trainer's Handbook* (San Francisco: Pfeiffer/Wiley).

4. For an excellent review of literature about principles and strategies for informing others, see K. E. Rowan (2003), "Informing and Explaining Skills: Theory and Research on Informative Communication," in J. O. Greene & B. R. Burleson (eds.) *Handbook of Communication and Social Interaction Skills,* (Mahwah, NJ: Erlbaum) pp. 403–438.

CHAPTER 10

1. A. Maslow (1954), *Motivation and Personality* (New York: Harper & Row).

2. Maslow, *Motivation and Personality.*

3. P. Riley (2011), *Attachment Theory and the Teacher-Student Relationship: A Practical Guide for Teachers, Teacher Educators and School Leaders* (New York: Routledge).

4. A. Mehrabian (1971), *Silent Messages* (Belmont, CA: Wadsworth).

5. P. L. Witt, L. R. Wheeless, & M. Allen (2006), "The Relationship Between Teacher Immediacy and Student Learning: A Meta-Analysis," In B. Gayle, R. Preiss, N. Burrell, & M. Allen (eds.), *Classroom Communication and Instructional Processes: Advances Through Meta-Analysis* (Mahwah, NJ: Erlbaum), pp. 149–168.

6. V. P. Richmond, J. Gorham, & J. C. McCroskey (1987), "The Relationship Between Selected Immediacy Behaviors and Cognitive Learning," in M. McLaughlin (ed.), *Communication Yearbook 10* (Beverly Hills, CA: Sage), pp. 574–590. See also J. Gorham (1988), "The Relationship Between Verbal Teacher Immediacy Behaviors and Student Learning," *Communication Education,* 37, 40–53.

7. D. M. Christophel (1990), "The Relationship among Teacher Immediacy Behaviors, Student Motivation, and Learning," *Communication Education,* 39, 323–340; V. P. Richmond (1990), "Communication in the Classroom: Power and Motivation," *Communication Education, 39,* 181–195.

8. J. C. McCroskey, V. P. Richmond, A. Sallinen, J. M. Fayer, & R. A. Barraclough (1995), "A Cross-cultural and Multibehavioral Analysis of the Relationship Between Nonverbal Immediacy and Teacher Evaluation," *Communication Education, 44,* 281–291.

9. M. Allen, P. L. Witt, & L. R. Wheeless (2006), "The Role of Teacher Immediacy as a Motivational Factor in Student Learning: Using a Meta-Analysis to Test a Causal Model," *Communication Education, 55,* 21–31.

10. A. K. Goodboy, K. Weber, & S. Bolkan (2009), "The Effects of Nonverbal and Verbal Immediacy on Recall and Multiple Student Learning Indicators," *Journal of Classroom Interaction,* 44, 4–12.

11. L. L. Pogue & K. Ahyun (2006), "The Effect of Teacher Nonverbal Immediacy and Credibility on Student Motivation and Affective Learning," *Communication Education, 55,* 331–344.

12. A. S. Williams (2010), "Statistics Anxiety and Instructor Immediacy," *Journal of Statistics Education* [Online], 18:2, www.amstat.org/publications/jse/v18n2/williams.pdf.

13 N. R. Faylor, S. A. Beebe, M. L. Houser, & T. P. Mottet (2008). "Perceived Differences in Instructional Communication Behaviors Between Effective and Ineffective Corporate Trainers, *Human Communication,* 11, 145–156.

14. V. P. Richmond & J. C. McCroskey (1999), *Nonverbal Behavior in Interpersonal Relations* (4th ed.) (Boston: Allyn & Bacon).

15. Richmond & McCroskey, *Nonverbal Behavior in Interpersonal Relations.*

16. K. D. Roach (1997), "Effects of Graduate Teaching Assistant Attire on Student Learning, Misbehaviors, and Ratings of Instruction. *Communication Quarterly, 45,* 125–141.

17. S. A. Westmyer & L. M. Flaherty (November 1996). *Student Perceptions of Instructors Based upon Clothing, Credibility, and Context.* Paper presented at the Speech Communication Association Convention, San Diego, CA.

18. J. Lukavsky, S. Butler, & A. J. Harden (1995), "Perceptions of an Instructor: Dress and Students' Characteristics," *Perceptual and Motor Skills, 81,* 231–240.

19. S. Bixler & N. Nix-Rice (1997). *The New Professional Image: From Business Casual to the Ultimate Power Look.* (Holbrook, MA: Adams Media).

20. M. L. Knapp & J. A. Hall (2010), *Nonverbal Communication in Human Interaction* (7th ed.) (Boston, MA: Wadsworth).

21. D. L. Leathers (1997), *Successful Nonverbal Communication: Principles and Applications* (3rd ed.) (Boston: Allyn & Bacon).

22. S. Bixler & L. S. Dugan (2001), *5 Steps to Professional Presence: How to Project Confidence, Competence, and Credibility at Work.* (Holbrook, MA: Adams Media).

23. S. A. Beebe (1974), "Eye Contact: A Nonverbal Determinant of Speaker Credibility," *Speech Teacher, 23,* 21–25.

24. V. P. Richmond (2002), "Teacher Nonverbal Immediacy: Use and Outcomes," In J. Chesebro & J. C. McCroskey (eds.), *Communication for Teachers,* (Boston: Allyn & Bacon), pp. 65–82.

25. Richmond, "Teacher Nonverbal Immediacy," pp. 65–82.

26. D. O'Hair, R. A. Stewart, & H. Rubenstein (2010), *A Speaker's Guidebook: Text and Reference* (4th ed.) (Boston: Bedford/ St. Martin's).

27. Richmond, "Teacher Nonverbal Immediacy"; Adapted from S. A. Beebe & S. J. Beebe (2003), *Public Speaking: An Audience-Centered Approach* (5th ed.) (Boston: Allyn & Bacon).

28. P. Ekman & W. V. Friesen (1969), "The Repertoire of Non-verbal Behavior: Categories, Origins, Usage, and Coding," *Semiotica, 1*, 49–98.

29. E. T. Hall (1966), *The Hidden Dimension,* (Garden City, NY: Doubleday).

30. J. C. McCroskey & L. R. Wheeless (1976), *An Introduction to Human Communication* (Boston: Allyn & Bacon).

31. J. C. McCroskey & V. P. Richmond (1992), "Increasing Teacher Influence Through Immediacy," In J. C. McCroskey & V. P. Richmond (eds.), *Power in the Classroom: Communication, Control, and Concern* (Hillsdale, NJ: Erlbaum), pp. 101–119.

32. T. G. Plax & P. Kearney (1992), "Teacher Power in the Classroom: Defining and Advancing a Program of Research," in McCroskey & Richmond, *Power in the Classroom,* pp. 67–84.

33. P. Kearney & T. G. Plax (1992), "Student Resistance to Control," in McCroskey & Richmond, *Power in the Classroom,* pp. 85–100.

34. See R. A. Bell & J. A. Daly (1984), "The Affinity-Seeking Function of Communication," *Communication Monographs, 51,* 91–115; J. C. McCroskey & L. L. McCroskey (1986), "The Affinity-Seeking of Classroom Teachers," *Communication Research Reports, 3,* 158–167.

35. See A. B. Frymier (1994), "The Use of Affinity-Seeking in Producing Liking and Learning in the Classroom," *Applied Communication Research, 22,* 87–105.

36. Mehrabian, *Silent Messages.*

37. Mehrabian, *Silent Messages.*

38. See P. Kearney, T. G. Plax, V. P. Richmond, & J. C. McCroskey (1984), "Power in the Classroom IV: Alternatives to Discipline," In R. Bostrom (ed.), *Communication yearbook 8* (Beverly Hills, CA: Sage), pp. 724–746.

39. J. J. Teven (2007), "Effects of Supervisor Social Influence, Nonverbal Immediacy, and Biological Sex on Subordinates' Perceptions of Job Satisfaction, Liking, and Supervisor Credibility," *Communication Quarterly, 55,* 155–177.

40. See Richmond, Gorham, & McCroskey, "The Relationship Between Selected Immediacy Behaviors and Cognitive Learning," and J. Gorham (1988), "The Relationship Between Verbal Teacher Immediacy Behaviors and Student Learning," *Communication Education, 37,* 40–53.

41. See, P. Kearny, T. G. Plax, & T. H. Allen (2002), "Understanding Student Reactions to Teachers Who Misbehave," in J. L. Chesebro & J. C. McCroskey (eds.), *Communication for Teachers* (Boston: Allyn & Bacon), pp. 127–140.

42. Kearny, Plax, & Allen, "Understanding Student Reactions to Teachers Who Misbehave."

CHAPTER 11

1. J. J. Phillips (2003), *Return on Investment in Training and Development Programs* (Burlington, MA: Elsevier Science); H. M. Hutchins & L. A. Burke (2007), "Identifying Trainers' Knowledge of Training Transfer Research Findings: Closing the Gap Between Research and Practice," *International Journal of Training and Development,* 11, 236–264.

2. D. I. Prajogo & A. S. Sohal (2006), "The Relationship Between Organization Strategy, Total Quality Management (TQM), and Organization Performance—The Mediating Role of TQM," *European Journal of Operational Research,* 168, 35–50; J. Y. Jung & Y. J. Wang (2006), "Relationship Between Total Quality Management (TQM) and Continuous Improvement of International Project Management (CIIPM)," *Technovation,* 26, 716–722.

3. D. Kirkpatrick (1954), *Evaluating Human Relations Programs for Industrial Foremen and Supervisors* (Kirkpatrick Publishing).

4. L. W. Anderson & D. R. Krathwohl, (eds.) (2001). *A Taxonomy for Learning, Teaching, and Assessing: A Revision of Bloom's Taxonomy of Educational Objectives* (New York: Longman).

5. See D. L. Kirkpatrick (1994), *Evaluating Training Programs: The Four Levels* (San Francisco: Berrett-Koehler); also see D. L. Kirkpatrick (1996), "Evaluation," in R. L. Craig (ed.), *The ASTD Training and Development Handbook: A Guide to Human Resource Development* (4th ed.) (New York: McGraw Hill), (pp. 294–312).

6. N. Faylor, S. A. Beebe, M. L. Houser, & T. P. Mottet, (2008), "Perceived Differences in Instructional Communication Behaviors Between Effective and Ineffective Corporate Trainers," *Human Communication,* 11, 145–156; K. Stephens & T. P. Mottet, (2008), "Interactivity in a Web-Conferencing Learning Environment: Effects on Trainers and Trainees," *Communication Education,* 57, 88–104.

7. B. D. Blume, J. K. Ford, T. T. Baldwin, & J. L. Huang, (2010), "Transfer of Training: A Meta-Analytic Review," *Journal of Management,* 36, 1065–1105.

8. For a review of this measure, see T. P. Mottet & V. P. Richmond (1998), "New is Not Necessarily Better: A Reexamination of Affective Learning Measurement," *Communication Research Reports,* 15, 370–378. Also see R. B. Rubin, P. Palmgreen, & H. E. Sypher (eds.) (1994), *Communication Research Measures: A Sourcebook* (New York: Guilford Press).

9. For a review of this research, see V. P. Richmond & J. C. McCroskey (1992), *Power in the Classroom: Communication, Control, and Concern* (Hillsdale, NJ: Erlbaum).

10. Partially adapted from Nathan Faylor's final class project, submitted on September 15, 1998, in partial fulfillment for Communication Training and Development (COMM 3318D) at Southwest Texas State University.

11. For a complete review of how to construct these exam items, see D. P. Scannell & D. B. Tracy (1975), *Testing and Measurement in the Classroom.* (Boston: Houghton Mifflin).

12. Q. Zhang (2009), "Perceived Teacher Credibility and Student Learning: Development of a Multicultural Model," *Western Journal of Communication,* 73, 326–347; M. E. Comadena, S. K. Hunt, & C. J. Simonds, (2007). "The Effects of Teacher Clarity, Nonverbal Immediacy, and Caring on Student Motivation, Affective and Cognitive Learning," *Communication Research Reports,* 24, 241–248.

13. N. R. Goulden, (1992), "Theory and Vocabulary for Communication Assessments," *Communication Education,* 41, 258–269.

14. For Additional Communication Assessment Instruments, see S. Morreale & P. Backlund (1996), *Large Scale Assessment of Oral Communication: K–12 and Higher Education* (2nd ed.) (Annandale, VA: Speech Communication Association). This resource contains valid and reliable instruments that are adapted to educational environments. With minimal revision, many of these instruments remain appropriate for professional education in the

organizational setting. This resource is available by contacting the National Communication Association at www.natcom.org. Also see W. G. Christ (ed.) (1994), *Assessing Communication Education: A Handbook for Media, Speech, and Theatre Educators* (Hillsdale, NJ: Erlbaum).

15. See Kirkpatrick, "Evaluation."

16. For a Comprehensive Collection of Assessment measures, see R. B. Rubin, A. M. Rubin, E. Graham, E. Perse & D. Seibold (2009), *Communication Research Measures II: A Sourcebook* (New York: Routledge).

17. For a review of the cost/benefit ratio, see J. J. Phillips (1997), *Handbook of Training Evaluation and Measurement Methods* (3rd ed.) (Houston, TX: Gulf Publishing).

CHAPTER 12

1. ASTD Releases State of the Industry Report Press Release (November 12, 2009), retrieved October 27, 2010, from www.astd.org.

2. This partial list of positions was organized after viewing the American Society for Training and Development's online Career Center; retrieved December 16, 2010, from http://www.astd.org/content/careers/

3. To obtain additional information on ASTD, call 1-800-628-2783 or 703-683-8100; write American Society for Training and Development, 1640 King Street, Box 1443, Alexandria, VA 22313-1443; or visit them at www.astd.org. To locate the chapter closest to you, click on www.astd.org and select the "Find a Chapter" menu option.

4. T. G. Plax (2006), "How Much Are We Worth? Estimating Fee for Service," *Communication Education, 55,* 242–246.

5. Plax, "How Much Are We Worth?"

6. Bureau of Labor Statistics, U.S. Department of Labor (2010–2011), *Occupational Outlook Handbook*, retrieved October 24, 2010, from http://www.bls.gov/oco/.

7. A. S. Levin, (March 2010), "Creating a Truly Adequate 21st Century Workforce System Taking No Worker Left Behind National," retrieved October 24, 2010, from http://www.michigan.gov/documents/nwlb/HTML_NWLB_Email_April29_10_319430_7.html

8. Bureau of Labor Statistics, *Occupational Outlook Handbook.*

9. R. Florida (2002), *The Rise of the Creative Class* (New York: Basic Books), p. 8.

10. Florida, *The Rise of The Creative Class.*

11. Pink, *A Whole New Mind,* p. 52.

12. J. Howkins (2001), The Creative Economy: How People Make Money from Ideas (New York), p. 116.

13. D. H. Pink (2006), *A Whole New Mind* (New York: Riverhead Books), p. 51.

14. E. Muzio, E. J. Fisher, E. R. Thomas, & V. Peters (2007), "Soft Skills Quantification (SSQ) for Project Management Competencies," *Project Management Journal,* 38, 30–38; P. Salem (2008), "The Seven Communication Reasons Organizations Do Not Change," *Corporate Communications,* 13, 333–348; D. A. Smith (February 2010), A Leadership Skills Gap," *T & D,* 16–17.

15. D. Boggs (December 23, 2008), "E-learning Benefits and ROI Comparison of e-learning vs. Traditional Training" [White paper], retrieved November 8, 2010, from http://knol.google.com/k/mary-kay-lofurno/e-learning-benefits-and-roi-comparison/nti9bs9a4lxe/16; also see C. D. Dziuban, J. L. Hartman, & P. D. Moskal (March 24, 2004), *Blended learning.* Educause Center for Applied Research: Research Bulletin 7, Boulder, CO.

16. A. Paradise (November 2008), "The 2008 ASTD State of the Industry Report Shows Sustained Support for Corporate Learning," *T & D,* 62, 44–51.

17. S. W. Villachica, A. Marker, & K. Taylor, (2010), "But What Do They Really Expect? Employer Perceptions of the Skills of Entry-level Instructional Designers," *Performance Improvement Quarterly,* 22, 33–51; this trend has also been noted in State of the Industry Reports published by the ASTD.

18. The National Communication Association publishes the *Journal of Applied Communication,* which examines communication problems and solutions in applied or workplace settings. To learn more about this publication, log on to the NCA Web site at www.natcom.org and select the "Publications" menu option.

19. See V. P. Richmond & J. C. McCroskey (2008), *Organizational Communication for Survival: Making Work, Work* (4th ed.) (Boston: Allyn & Bacon).

20. For additional information on how to prepare training budgets, we recommend that you consult professionals in your local chapter of ASTD because rates vary by location. To locate the chapter nearest you, click on www.astd.org and then select the "Find a Chapter" menu option.

21. Another resource for learning how to market and budget your services is W. J. Rothwell, J. Lindholm, & W. G. Wallick (2003), *What CEOs Expect from Corporate Training: Building Workplace Learning and Performance Initiatives That Advance* (Boston: AMACOM).

22. For learning how to compute CBR and ROI, see J. J. Phillips & L. Zuniga (2008), *Cost and ROI: Evaluating at the Ultimate Level* (San Francisco: Pfeiffer).

GLOSSARY

Accommodators Trainees who learn primarily from hands-on field experience and by trial and error. They enjoy carrying out plans and involving themselves in challenging experiences.

Adaptors Nonverbal behaviors or movements that are enacted to satisfy some physical (e.g., scratching an itch) or psychological need (e.g., drumming fingers when nervous).

Affect The degree of liking, appreciation, respect, or value that one has for something or someone.

Affective domain The domain of learning that focuses on changing or reinforcing attitudes, feelings, and motivation.

Affinity Positive attitude one individual has for another.

Affinity-seeking Communicative strategies individuals use to get others to like them.

Ambiguity Occurs when an issue or idea has multiple and conflicting interpretations.

American Society for Training and Development (ASTD) The world's largest association dedicated to workplace learning and training professionals.

Analytic assessment An assessment method that evaluates how well each of the individual behaviors was performed.

Andragogy The science and art of teaching adults. An andragogical approach to teaching and learning is self-directed rather than teacher-directed.

Antisocial BATs Compliance-gaining strategies that are negative and coercive in nature.

Assessment center A room or suite of rooms where employees are given performance tests to identify strengths and weaknesses in their jobs.

Assessment specialist This training job is responsible for measuring the learning outcomes of the training program.

Assimilators Trainees who value sequential thinking and trust expert opinion. They enjoy collecting data and then organizing it or assimilating it into a concise, logical form. Assimilators remain less interested in learning from others' concrete experiences and are more interested in learning from experts.

Asynchronous communication Technology-assisted communication that does not allow for real-time conversations.

Atomistic assessment Assessment method that identifies small, observable behaviors.

Attention span Duration of time that trainees can focus cognitively on a given training activity.

Attitudes Learned predispositions to respond favorably or unfavorably toward something.

Aural learners Those who learn through hearing and speaking. Auditory-oriented learners need opportunities to not only hear what they are to learn but also to articulate what it is they're learning.

Avatar A user's representation of himself or herself online in the form of a name, a picture, or a three-dimensional model.

Behavior alteration messages (BAMs) Words and phrases used to gain compliance from someone.

Behavior alteration techniques (BATs) Communication strategies used to gain compliance from someone.

Behavioral items The behaviors that were taught and developed during the training program.

Blended training When a trainer mixes training methods, technologies, and delivery systems to meet trainees' and organizations' varying needs.

Body The middle of a lecture where trainers organize or chunk content around three our four main points or ideas.

Brainstorming A free flowing of ideas or solutions to problems offered in an evaluation-free environment. This technique encourages creativity among group members.

Bridging An approach to training where trainers instruct trainees using their own training style, but are however willing and able to adapt to a trainee's learning style if there is a learning problem.

Briefing summary A succinct statement that includes the who, what, where, when, how, and why that is included in a needs-assessment proposal or a training proposal.

Bullet points Marks that indicate the beginning of a distinct thought; as used in PowerPoint slides.

Buzz group A small group, usually consisting of five to ten people who discuss a chosen or selected topic.

Case study An experiential activity that includes a narrative or short story about some organizational issue where a problem, the history of the problem, and the characters involved with the problem are described in detail

Channel An avenue of communication (e.g., verbal, vocal, visual, gestural).

Checklists Format for gathering survey data in which a list of skills and knowledge is provided and responders are asked to check those items where they may have little need, some need, or great need to learn information about.

Chronological order Organization of information in a time sequence.

Closed questions Questions that require the recall of specific information. There is a right and wrong answer to the question.

Closure To provide a conclusion to one element of a training lesson and point the learner to the next learning task.

Cognitive domain The domain of learning that focuses on the acquisition of facts, information, theories, principles, and knowledge.

Communication The process of acting on information.

Conflict The disagreement and/or disharmony between individuals as a result of differing goals, objectives, values, beliefs, and attitudes.

Contact hour A method for calculating the cost of a training program. Factored into each contact hour is the numerous hours invested in conducting needs assessments, writing and presenting training proposals, writing learning objectives, developing training curricula, presenting training programs, and assessing learning objectives.

Contingency plan What the trainer will do (a plan B) if presentational aids do not work as planned. A backup plan to use if something goes wrong with the original plan of action.

Convergers A learning approach that seeks utility in ideas, theories, and approaches from a problem-solving perspective; a preference to analyze problems and test theories to find implementable solutions to achieve results.

Cost/benefit ratio A ratio that examines the training program's benefits to the organization in relation to how much the training program costs the organization.

Creative class People who add economic value to an organization through their creativity.

Credentials An individual's prior training experience, education, research, and other forms of recognition that makes one credible or believable to others.

Credibility A perception of believability that is based on perceptions of another's competence or knowledge and character or trustworthiness.

Criteria Standards for an acceptable outcome or decision.

Curriculum The training content organized to achieve the training objectives.

Deep practice The process of mindfully practicing a skill by chunking it up, repeating it, and then feeling how the skill should be performed.

Demonstration When a trainer performs or shows a particular skill.

Descriptive format A narrative that includes subheadings and paragraphs, which describes each element in a training session.

Development Any behavior, strategy, design, restructuring, skill or skill set, strategic plan, or motivational effort that is designed to produce growth or positive change in an individual or organization.

Distractor A set of foils that incorrectly answer the stem of a multiple-choice exam item.

Divergers Learners who prefer observing a situation rather than taking action. Divergers tend to be innovative, imaginative, and concerned with personal relevance. They have a need to know how new information relates to prior experiences before they're receptive to learning new information.

Doctor–patient consulting model Model in which a consultant is hired to both diagnose a problem and recommend an intervention strategy to solve or manage it.

EDIT An acronym that represents a method for processing or unpacking experiential activities; E is engaging in an experiential activity; D is describing the experience; I is making inferences or generalizations beyond the experience; and T is transferring the experience from the training context to other contexts such as the workplace, school, or home.

Education The process of imparting knowledge or information.

Emotions Feeling states that often, but not always, result in behavior change.

Engagement strategy A message that encourages trainees to reflect on or to interact with the information they are receiving.

Essay A type of exam item that challenges trainees to generate the correct answer. Rather than being given a list of possible responses, trainees are challenged to answer the essay question in paragraph form, meaning that the question cannot be answered adequately using a simple response.

Exam A specially designed survey that assesses whether or not trainees learned the training content.

Experiential activity Any training activity that requires trainees to involve themselves physically and/or psychologically in the training content.

Eye depth How deep and personal a trainer's eye contact is with trainees.

Eye scope How much of the room and the audience a trainer sees; the range of eye contact.

Facilitated group discussion Training method that includes three to ten trainees who interact with the assistance of a facilitator who manages the interaction and guides the discussion toward specific learning objectives.

Feedforward message A message that informs others of how to process information.

Focus group A small group of people selected to discuss a particular topic so that others can better gauge how people will respond to a product, topics, or program. May be used to pretest the utility of a training program.

Foils The alternative choices that follow a stem and ultimately answer or complete the stem. There are usually three to five foils per multiple-choice item.

Font A design and size of print type (e.g., Times New Roman 10).

Gap analysis Identifying the gap between what the trainee can do and can't do, the gap between what is expected and what is not yet mastered is the gap in skills that needs to be addressed by the training.

Goal A general statement of what outcomes a trainer would like to accomplish.

Handouts Hard copy materials given to trainees for use in training sessions.

Hard skill Technical skills that typically involve specific right answers or precise procedures to follow.

Highlighting A presentational technique where trainers emphasize certain content by pointing out the importance of a particular piece of information.

Holistic assessment The highest level of behavioral assessment. Rather than assessing discrete or clusters of behaviors, trainers assess the overall quality of the behavioral performance. This form of behavioral assessment focuses on the product rather than the process.

Human communication The process of making sense out of the world and sharing that sense with others and creating meaning through the use of verbal and nonverbal messages.

Immediacy behaviors Behaviors—approach and avoid signals— that indicate a desired level of closeness between individuals.

Immediacy The degree of physical or psychological closeness between individuals.

Impulsive learners The learning approach of learners who work quickly and with less determination; complete accuracy is less important than getting a quick overview of the concept or skill to be learned.

Instructional designer An individual in a training department who develops objectives, curricula, methods, and assessment instruments.

Internal review/preview A message that informs trainees of where they have been and where they are going in a lecture or presentation.

Internships Opportunities for students to obtain college credit toward their degrees for working in a supervised work environment.

Interpersonal conflict Conflict that occurs between individuals.

Intimate zone Interpersonal interaction space, ranging from touching to 18 inches.

Introduction The part of a lecture where trainers capture the interests of trainees by leading off with a story, a visual aid, case study, or question.

Invite The repeated performance of a skill or behavior in an effort to master the behavior.

Job talk A brief demonstration of a training module that gives potential decision makers an idea of one's training style.

Just in time training A training concept whereby trainees receive just the right amount and type of training exactly when it's needed.

Keyed response A foil that correctly answers the stem of a multiple-choice exam item.

Kinesthetic learners Those who learn by touching and doing. Kinesthetically oriented learners remain tactile and prefer to be engaged in movement. They are partial to action and have a tendency to express emotion in physically exuberant ways.

Law of association This general law suggests that every new fact, idea, concept, or behavior is best learned if trainees can relate it to or with something they already know.

Law of effect This general law suggests that trainees learn best under pleasant and rewarding conditions.

Law of frequency This general law suggests that the more often trainees practice a trained behavior, the more likely they are to continue using the desired behavior accurately.

Law of learning A statement that describes the conditions that must be met in order for trainees to learn.

Law of readiness A law of learning that suggests that learning is more likely to occur when what is being taught is something that the learner needs to learn, when the learner is mentally and physically ready to learn.

Learning style The way an individual perceives, organizes, processes, and remembers information.

Learning A change in individuals, due to the interaction of the individuals and their environment, which fills a need and makes them more capable of dealing adequately with their environment.

Lecture An instructional method used to present information efficiently using one-way communication from teacher to student.

Likert scale A five-item scale that seeks to gauge a respondent's attitude toward something with choices of strongly agree, agree, undecided, disagree, and strongly disagree.

Maslow's Hierarchy of Needs A list of basic human needs that must be satisfied in sequence.

Matching Learning approach where trainees are instructed in their own preferred learning styles, which are identified through large-scale surveys or assessments of the trainee.

Maturity The degree of experience rather than age that a trainee brings to the training classroom. Not all young adults are inexperienced or immature, and not all adults are experienced and mature.

Media richness A technology's ability to simulate face-to-face communication.

Media specialist This training job works closely with the program designer in selecting and/or designing audio and visual media to complement and support a training program.

Mnemonic A memory aid or a memory shortcut, as in "TGIF," meaning "Thank God It's Friday."

Modeling Learning by observing others; occurs when people acquire knowledge, attitudes, beliefs, and values and learn how to perform certain behaviors by observing others.

Monotone A vocal characteristic consisting of limited or singular pitch; its lack of variety discourages listening.

Motivation An internal state of readiness to take action or achieve a goal.

Multicolumn format A four-column approach to describing the time, content, methods, and materials needed to present a training session.

Multiple-choice A type of exam item that challenges trainees' to choose among three to five possible answers or foils to a particular question. A multiple-choice item contains a stem, a keyed response foil, and distractor foils.

Needs analyst This training job is responsible for identifying what learners do not yet know or the important or necessary skills that they can't yet perform.

Needs assessment The process of identifying what learners do not yet know or the important or necessary skills that they can't yet perform.

Needs-assessment proposal A formal document that explains to decision makers why their organization or some aspect of their organization deserves to be examined closely because of a possible deficiency.

Needs-centered model A training model anchored in the principle that the primary purpose of any training program is to address the learning needs of the trainee.

Nonverbal communication Communication enacted using unspoken symbols or movements.

Objective A specific, measurable, observable, and attainable training outcome that a trainer is attempting to achieve.

Open (or open-ended) question A question in which no specific structure is offered to frame the respondent's response; may be ambiguous and usually doesn't have correct and incorrect responses.

Opinion leader An informal role within an organization that people look to in order to understand how they should interpret certain information.

Outline format An organized, structured description of all training content and methods presented in traditional outline form.

Outsourcing A management trend among large corporations to contract to have their products manufactured in other countries at a fraction of the cost of production at home.

Part–whole learners Learners who prefer examining the parts rather than the whole or the big picture.

Participant's guide A collection of handouts or a workbook that contains all information, worksheets, activities, and activity instructions that will be presented in the training workshop.

Pedagogy The science and art of teaching children. A pedagogical approach to teaching and learning is teacher-directed rather than self-directed.

Personal zone Interpersonal interaction space, ranging from 18 inches to 4 feet.

Physiological needs Individuals' needs for air, water, shelter, food, and the like, according to Maslow's Need Model.

Pilot test A trial run or test of a training program that can then be used to assess the quality of the training program before it is presented to others.

Plagiarism Use of ideas, words, work from others as if it is yours; not crediting the source as the source.

Plus-one technique Training technique used when training others in how to perform a complicated behavior, skill, or process. The behavior is divided into smaller components, and others are trained one step at a time. After a trainee has mastered a single step or component of the larger process, a new step is added (plus one) and mastered. This process continues until the entire behavioral process has been mastered.

Podcast A radio broadcast or similar program made available on the Internet for downloading to an MP3 player, mobile device, or personal computer.

PRCA   Personal Report of Communication Apprehension; communication apprehension measurement instrument.

Presenter   One who delivers the training program to trainees.

Preview   A message that informs trainees of what is to come next in a lecture or presentation.

Process approach model   Model in which a consultant is hired to work with an individual or organization in all aspects of organizational development, diagnosis, and delivery of intervention strategy.

Program designer   This training job translates needs into learning objectives, develops training curricula, selects appropriate training methods, and develops lesson plans.

Proposal   A formal document that sells a program of training to organizational decision makers.

Prosocial BATs   Compliance-gaining strategies that are positive and relational in nature.

Public zone   Interpersonal interaction space, ranging 12 feet and beyond.

Purchase approach model   Model in which a consultant is hired to provide agreed-upon service, such as training, performed for an individual or organization.

Questionnaire   Another term for survey.

Rank order   Method of assessing needs using a survey asking respondents to rank skills or behaviors in order of importance to them.

Rapid e-learning   A set of software tools that make it possible for subject matter experts to create and publish interactive e-learning quickly.

Reflective learners   Learners who take time to process information. Reflective learners tend to work carefully and with precision.

Reiterating   Restating content using different words, word order, and/or examples.

Repeating   Restating content in the same exact way using the same words and word order.

Retention   How much a trainee can remember after the training session is over. Generally, the more of this, the better.

Return on investment   An investment should yield or produce a return that is greater than the initial investment.

Rhetorical questions   Questions that don't require answers.

Role play   An experiential activity where trainees are encouraged to act out a particular part in a communication transaction. Most simulations include role plays.

Round robin   A facilitation technique where the group leader asks a question and then goes around the group asking each member for his or her response to the question.

RSS feeds   A set of feed formats linked to various sites, used to publish frequently updated content such as blog and wiki entries, news headlines, and podcasts.

Sans serif   A type of print font; sans serif means "without stoke or line"; Arial is a sans serif font.

Scan   An eye contact behavior characterized by one's looking from one side of the room to the other in an attempt to see all of the audience.

Schema   A mental "box" where you can classify and categorize and file concepts. A frame of reference for concepts and experiences one has. A mental system of understanding, interpreting, and storing cognitive or experiential input.

Screencasts   Digital recordings of a user's computer screen output that often contain voice narration and presentational material, such as a software training session.

Semantic differential   A scale that measures attitudes by asking people to choose between two opposite positions.

Serif   A type of print font; serif means "stroke or line"; Times is a serif font.

Set induction   A training technique that helps get trainees ready to learn by gaining their attention and motivating them to learn the information or skill.

Show   To model or demonstrate how a behavior should be performed.

Signpost   An oral or written signal of where you are in a presentation (e.g., at point A, at A1, etc.).

Simulations   Interactive, task-driven exercises that allow trainees to experience a concept or develop skills.

Skill   A desired behavior that can be repeated when needed.

Skill criteria   Descriptions in behavioral terms of what each skill rating reflects.

Skill ratings   The series of numbers or a scale that indicates the level or quality of the performance of a particular behavioral item.

Social bookmarks   Web-based tools that allow users to save in an archive their own copy of any page they have visited on the Web.

Social zone   Interpersonal interaction space, ranging from 4 feet to 12 feet.

Soft skill   Skills that focus on managing people, information, and ideas such as communication, management, and leadership.

Spot grid   An eye contact behavior characterized by one's looking from zone to zone in a room to try to engage the audience visually.

Stimulus prompt   A partial statement or question that requires trainees to complete the statement or answer the question.

Stimulus variation   The training technique of using a variety of methods and strategies to teach skills and information.

Style-flexing   An approach to training where trainers accommodate and challenge their trainees' learning styles. Trainees learn not only the training content but also how to learn in ways that are different from their preferred learning styles.

Subject matter expert (SME)   Person with extensive knowledge of a certain subject.

Survey   A series of written questions or statements designed to illicit information about knowledge, attitudes, or behavior.

Synchronous communication   Technology-assisted communication that occurs in real time and allows the trainer and the trainee to have a conversation.

Task analysis   An outline that describes the step-by-step procedures for performing a specific behavior, skill, or task.

Task analyst   This training job is responsible for taking the skills identified by the needs analyst and breaking them down into step-by-step outlines. Trainers will use this step-by-step outline to teach others in how to perform the skill.

Taxonomy   A way to classify information.

Tell   To present information in a lecture or expository way.

Threaded discussion   A facilitation technique where the group leader asks a question and then integrates carefully all responses and additional follow-up questions into a meaningful and coherent conversation.

360 survey method An approach to seeking information from a broad range of individuals (supervisor, colleagues, self-report) to assess an individual's level of performance.

Training The process of developing skills in order to more effectively perform a specific job or task.

Total quality management A management philosophy, which advocates that doing something right is more important that doing it quickly.

Training and development administrator This training job is responsible for working closely with the manager and insures that the facilities, equipment, materials, participants, and other components of a learning event are present and that training programs run smoothly.

Training and development manager This training job is responsible for planning, organizing, staffing, controlling training and development operations, and bridging the operations of the departments with other units within an organization and to insure that the organization's training and development needs are met.

Training assessment A systematic process of evaluating training programs to ensure that they meet the needs of the trainees and organization.

Training budget A formal document that outlines all of the anticipated costs needed to develop, present, and assess a training program.

Training certificate A document that confirms that a course of study has been completed.

Training certification A voluntary process whereby a professional body such as ASTD grants a designation to someone who has met certain professionals qualifications.

Training generalist Training practitioners who perform all different types of training jobs and tasks including needs assessment, writing learning objectives, developing training curricula, presenting training content, and assessing learning outcomes.

Training methods The procedures and strategies used to present information and help trainees achieve the training objectives.

Training module One session that is part of a larger program of training.

Training objective A concise statement that describes what the trainee should be able to do at the end of a training session.

Training plan A written description of all elements of a training session. It includes the objectives, a description of the training content, training methods, and the audiovisual training resources needed to conduct the training.

Training portfolio A tool that trainers develop that gives employers or potential clients a complete picture of the training professionals accomplishments including a complete review of training experiences, education, accomplishments, and skill sets.

Training proposal A formal document that outlines the training program in detail including length of program, training content, strategies, materials, assessment plan, and training budget.

Training specialist Training practitioners who perform only a limited number of jobs and task related to training and development such as an assessment specialist who focuses only on assessing training effectiveness.

Trigger questions Questions used to simulate group discussion that remain controversial and that deal with claims of value—what is right and wrong, good and bad, and why.

Ubiquitous learning Training that uses wireless telecommunication and other technologies to learn anytime, anywhere.

Visual learners Those who learn by reading and viewing. Visually orientated learners need to see what they are learning.

Vocal cues Volume, articulation, dialect, pitch, inflection, rate, use of pace.

Vodcasts A video broadcast or program made available on the Internet for downloading to a mobile device or personal computer; the video form of podcasting.

Web 2.0 The second generation of the Internet; a more interactive, read-write focused Web.

Web-based training specialist Training professional who designs, develops, & delivers training using the Internet.

Whiteboards White laminated panels used with dry-erase markers to display presentation aid content.

Whole–part learners Learners who prefer having the big picture before moving into the details of the concept or idea.

Wikis Collaborative Web-based sites for sharing text and other resources.

Yes and no responses A direct, closed ended response format in which responders are asked questions for which the responses can either be "yes" or "no".

INDEX

Accommodators, 48–49

Accountability in Web site evaluation, 110

Accuracy in Web site evaluation, 110

Acronyms as mnemonic devices, 128

Adaptors, 239

ADDIE model, 128

Adult learning. *See* Andragogy

Affect, defined, 260

Affective domain of learning, 58, 59, 260–264
  assessment tools for, 261–264
  domains of, 260–261

Affinity seeking
  conflict management and, 245–246
  by trainer, 241–242

Age, learning styles and, 45–47

Aggressive trainees, 243

Aguinis, Herman, 8

Almanacs as training materials, 109

Ambiguity in e-learning, 151

American Society for Training and Development (ASTD), 7, 110–111, 282, 284
  certification by, 286–288

Analogies, 97

Analytic assessment, 269–270

Andersen, Jan, 262

Andragogy, 27–52
  defined, 33
  learning styles and. *See* Learning styles
  pedagogy versus, 32–34
  training applications for, 34–38, 39
  training assumptions for, 33–34, 39

Antisocial behavior alteration techniques, 246, 248

Appearance of trainer, 234–235

Appropriateness of training materials, 114–115

Aristotle, 17

Assessment
  of needs. *See* Needs assessment
  peer, for Web-based training, 163
  self-, for Web-based training, 163
  training. *See* Assessment, training

Assessment centers, 68–69

Assessment specialists, 283

Assessment, training, 21, 255–278
  of affective learning, 260–264
  of behavioral learning, 269–271
  of cognitive learning, 265–269
  interpreting assessment information and, 271–277
  levels of, 259–260
  model of, 257–258
  need for, 258–259
  reporting data and, 275–277

Assimilators, 47–48, 49

Association, law of, 31, 32

ASTD (American Society for Training and Development), 7, 110–111, 282, 284
  certification by, 286–288

Asynchronous communication, 150

Atomistic assessment, 269

Attention span, delivery of training and, 229

Attitudes, 11

Audio aids, 98

Auditory learners, 41–42

Aural learners, 41–42

Baby Boomers, 45, 46

BAMs (behavior alteration messages), 246–247

Bartlett's Familiar Quotations, 109

BATs. *See* Behavior alteration techniques (BATs)

Beckett, Samuel, 93

Behavioral items for training assessment, 270–271

Behavioral learning assessment, 269–271
  domains of behavioral learning and, 269–270
  tools for, 270–271

Behavioral learning objectives, assessment and, 271–274

Behavior alteration messages (BAMs), 246–247

Behavior alteration techniques (BATs), 246
  antisocial, 246, 248
  prosocial, for conflict management, 246–247

Behaviors
  describing, 244–245
  immediacy. *See* Immediacy behaviors

Blackboard (software), 153

Blended learning, 291

Blended training, 153–154

"Blind Men and the Elephant" (Saxe), 174

Bloom, Benjamin, 137

Bloom's taxonomies of learning, 259

Bloom's Taxonomy of Cognitive Learning, 137

Body of lecture, 127

Body posture for presenting lectures, 129

Books as training materials, 108

Bottom-up processors, 44

Brainstorming, 47

Bridging training approach, 50–51

Briefing summaries, 297

Bryant, Donald C., 17

Budgets, training, 299

Bullet points, 177

Buzz groups, 47

Camtasia Studio, 156

Cartoons, 97

Case studies, 133–134

CBR (cost/benefit ratio), 275, 276, 299–300

Certification of trainers, 286–288

Chairburu, Dan, 30

Channels of communication, 15, 234
  for nonverbal communication, 234–237

Checklists
  advantages and disadvantages of, 216
  for needs assessment, 63, 67

Child learning, 32–34

Chronological order for teaching skills, 89

Chunking, 29
  in lectures, 128
  in Web-based training design, 161

Citing of training materials, 115

Clarification, presentation aids for, 175, 176

Closed questions, 137, 138

Closure, 98–100, 165

Clothing of trainer, 234–235

CMS (Course Management System), 153

Coaching trainees through mistakes, 37–38

Cognitive domain of learning, 58, 59, 265–269
  assessment tools for, 265–269
  domains of, 265

Comfortable self, affinity and, 242

Commercial sources of training materials, 111–113

Communication, 15–18
  defined, 15
  nonverbal, 233–234
  process of, 15–16
  training as communication process and, 16–18

Communication skills, tools for assessment of, 273–274

Competent Group Communicator, 273

Competent Speaker Speech Evaluation Form, 273

Complementary model for blended training, 154

Complementing, gestures for, 239

Complexity, teaching simple skills before complex skills and, 89

Conflict
  defined, 242–243
  interpersonal, 243

Conflict management, 242–247
  problem trainee types and, 243
  program outline for, 120–121
  skills for, 243–247

Confucius, 124